# THE COMPLETE
# SOUS VIDE
## COOKBOOK

# THE COMPLETE
# SOUS VIDE
## COOKBOOK

## More Than 175 Recipes with Tips & Techniques

## Chris McDonald

Robert
ROSE

**The Complete Sous Vide Cookbook**
Text copyright © 2016 Chris McDonald
Photographs copyright © 2016 Per Kristiansen
Cover and text design copyright © 2016 Robert Rose Inc.

*For complete cataloguing information, see page 404.*

**Disclaimers**
The recipes in this book have been carefully tested by our kitchen and our tasters. To the best of our knowledge, they are safe and nutritious for ordinary use and users. For those people with food or other allergies, or who have special food requirements or health issues, please read the suggested contents of each recipe carefully and determine whether or not they may create a problem for you. All recipes are used at the risk of the consumer. Consumers should always consult their sous vide manufacturer's manual for recommended procedures and cooking times.

We cannot be responsible for any hazards, loss or damage that may occur as a result of any recipe use.

For those with special needs, allergies, requirements or health problems, in the event of any doubt, please contact your medical adviser prior to the use of any recipe.

Design and production: Kevin Cockburn/PageWave Graphics Inc.
Layout: Alicia McCarthy/PageWave Graphics Inc.
Editors: Tina Anson Mine/Meredith Dees
Recipe editor: Jennifer MacKenzie
Proofreader: Gillian Watts
Indexer: Gillian Watts
Illustrator: Kveta/threeinabox.com
Photographer: Per Kristiansen
Assistant: Mark Luciani
Food stylist: Ian Muggridge
Prop stylist: Lara McGraw

Front cover image: Venison Loin with Savoy Cabbage and Chestnuts (page 56)
Back cover images: Perfect Poached Egg (page 325), Postmodern Dinosaur Bones (page 66), and Barigoule of Artichokes (in sous vide pouch, page 316)

The publisher gratefully acknowledges the financial support of our publishing program by the Government of Canada through the Canada Book Fund.

Canadä

Published by Robert Rose Inc.
120 Eglinton Avenue East, Suite 800, Toronto, Ontario, Canada M4P 1E2
Tel: (416) 322-6552  Fax: (416) 322-6936
www.robertrose.ca

Printed and bound in Canada

2  3  4  5  6  7  8  9  MI  24  23  22  21  20  19  18  17

# Contents

# Preface

In late 2003, when I started experimenting with sous vide at Avalon, my restaurant at the time, I was already a fan of trying out new cooking techniques in order to achieve unique results. Back then the immersion circulators were modified lab equipment and very expensive. We had a chamber vacuum sealer in my restaurant and would play around with improvised hot water baths for cooking. It was very primitive by today's standards, but I could see the potential. It never occurred to me that the technique would enter the home kitchen.

Fast-forward to 2007. At my next restaurant, Cava, I was invited to compete in Gold Medal Plates, a Canadian charity that supports our Olympians. I was responsible for cooking 500 portions for a crowd of black-tie guests at a giant banquet that allowed no open-flame cooking. It seemed like the perfect opportunity to borrow a friend's immersion circulator — which at the time cost $1,600 to purchase — and get cooking. Unfortunately, my elaborate dish based on pork loin was a flop. I hadn't practiced enough with the equipment and the pork wasn't cooked long enough to be delicious.

I bought my first sous vide cookbook around the same time. It was a collaboration between Catalan chefs Salvador Brugués and Joan Roca, of the world-famous El Celler de Can Roca. (I chuckle now when I see it on used-book websites selling for almost as much as the first immersion circulator.) What an eye-opener! The recipes were innovative and fit perfectly into the Spanish idiom that was Cava at the time, even though the book recommended higher temperatures than we now use and required precise timing to achieve three-star results.

Now we mostly set the hot water bath to the temperature we want the food to reach. While it takes longer, the results are worth it. We should be thankful to Douglas Baldwin, a mathematician who worked through all the calculations to make this newer method work and shares it generously on the Internet (www. douglasbaldwin.com/sous-vide.html).

I don't think of sous vide cooking as molecular gastronomy, which to me is about chemistry. Sous vide cooking is about the physics of applying heat to food and how you can achieve better results more simply once you have more control of that heat.

The recipes in this book cover the full range of foods that I know how to cook. They were created or selected to illustrate the possibilities of sous vide cooking and are meant to be templates for your own explorations. In short, these recipes explore how carefully controlled heat alters food to delicious effect. No book of this nature is really complete once it is published — it's just the end of a chapter.

Many of the recipes can be made properly only by using the sous vide method, but a small number show you how you can use your new device to replace other kitchen appliances. In many cases your sous vide device can replace your slow cooker — for example, with Chicken Cholent (page 148). For such recipes sous vide cooking offers little advantage, but I have included them to demonstrate the range and versatility of the equipment. However, the convenience of food that is easy to store, transport and clean up may be sufficient reason enough!

You can go directly to any recipe in this book and start cooking, but I urge you to read the introductory material that covers the basics and food safety. I have written this book as a professional chef speaking to an enthusiastic amateur, including enough additional material and tips to guide those who are new to cooking. You'll also find information on different ingredients, sourcing, substitutions, variations, presentation and scaling up or down — in short, everything you need to make a delicious meal, plus a little extra. Good luck on your sous vide journey!

— *Chris McDonald*

# What Is Sous Vide?

*Sous vide*, translated from the French, means "in a vacuum," which can be a bit misleading. Basically it is the process of cooking food in a sealed container — that's where the vacuum part comes from — in a water bath at a precisely controlled low temperature. It differs from traditional methods in that the food is cooked at the temperature it will be served at. So if you like your steak medium-rare (130°F/54°C), you would cook the meat in a water bath held at that temperature.

What is the value of yet another way of cooking food? There are several good reasons for using the sous vide method, and they relate to both quality and convenience. It's great for entertaining, because you can prepare much of the meal ahead of time. You can even set up your device and let it cook while you are out doing errands or having a nap. The sous vide process also maintains texture better than the usual methods. For instance, in conventional cooking the heat source is much hotter than the desired serving temperature, which increases the risk that the end product will be dry and overcooked. Consider, for instance, that medium-rare steak. To achieve an appropriately cooked center, you run the risk of overcooking the exterior. When you use sous vide, the entire piece of meat is evenly cooked to the desired doneness. Moreover, since it is cooked in a sealed pouch, your steak doesn't dry out. Once you get the hang of it, you will probably leave your device set up on the counter and use it more often than your oven, as I do.

## The History of Sous Vide

Although the basic principles of sous vide have been around for a couple of hundred years, the process wasn't commercialized until the 1960s, when it made its way into industrial settings. The transition to restaurants began in the mid 1970s, when a chef-consultant working at the Restaurant Troisgros, a three-Michelin-star establishment in Roanne, France, developed a method to address the challenges associated with cooking foie gras. With traditional methods, foie gras loses up to 50 percent

## COOKING FOOD SAFELY

Because of the low temperatures used, cooking sous vide raises questions about food safety. Pathogenic bacteria grow rapidly in the "danger zone" — between 40° and 130°F (4° to 54.4°C). Once food reaches temperatures above that range, the bacteria start to perish. The objective is to get food to the safe temperature zone as quickly as possible and for it to remain there throughout the cooking process. With sous vide we now have the opportunity to cook food near this danger zone with confidence. At 130°F (54.4°C), food can actually be pasteurized if it is held at that temperature for long enough (see page 9 for more information).

## PASTEURIZATION

Pasteurization is a process that uses heat to destroy pathogens in food. Louis Pasteur, a French chemist, is credited with its discovery, which was initially used to improve the quality of wine. Previously, food preservation had been associated with salting, pickling, drying or processing at high temperatures over an extended period of time. Pasteur's method, which used lower temperatures, also produced better-quality food. The process is named in his honor.

It's important to know a little bit about pasteurization for meats, poultry, fish and seafood, since not all recipes that employ sous vide techniques result in thorough pasteurization. While most of us can tolerate some pathogens in our food, people with weak immune systems, such as the elderly and young children, cannot. Pregnant women are also vulnerable because their immune system is altered during pregnancy. Any recipe for meat, poultry, fish or seafood that is cooked below 130°F (54.4°C) is unpasteurized and may pose a risk to those with compromised immune systems.

of its weight during cooking, which is expensive wastage for a commercial kitchen. It was found that wrapping the foie gras very tightly in plastic wrap and cooking it slowly in a water bath diminished the amount of waste. At about the same time, a food scientist named Bruno Goussault was developing a similar technology for use in large-scale food-service applications.

Over the years, sous vide gained traction at the chef level and especially with large food-service organizations, where the ability to produce good results by reheating previously cooked food is highly valued. In 2005 Amanda Hesser published an article in the *New York Times* concluding that sous vide "is poised to change the way restaurant chefs cook — and like the Wolf stove and the immersion blender, it will probably trickle down to the home kitchen some day."

Around 2010 that trickle started becoming a surge. Until then, cost had been a barrier because the equipment was very expensive; acquiring just the immersion circulator cost about $1,500. But around that time the manufacturers began to produce cost-effective sous vide equipment. Today you can get your home sous vide equipment up and running for a couple of hundred dollars, outfitted with everything you need to produce delicious food to suit your needs.

## Advantages of Sous Vide

- Sous vide is effectively cooking by numbers. Once you have the time and temperature dialed in, it is hard to make a mistake. You can simply learn the essential applications and then use them again and again.
- Sous vide is a fabulous time-management tool. It frees up your time because you can prepare food in advance and then quickly chill it until you are ready to serve. A quick reheat is all that's required.

- Sous vide can save you money. It works wonders with tougher, less expensive cuts of meat, slowly transforming them into mouth-watering flavor bombs. In addition, it allows you to buy meat in bulk or when it is on sale, then portion and freeze it in sous vide–ready packages to use individually as required. And you can place frozen meals directly into the water bath.
- Sous vide maximizes storage potential. Once food is packaged, it takes up minimal space. You can then cook it or store it until you are ready to use it.
- Sous vide supports your busy lifestyle and is ideal for travelling. The sealed, chilled results can easily be transported to vacation destinations. It truly earns its stripes at rustic destinations, such as campsites, wilderness cabins or even boats, where cookware and utensils may be limited. Your perfectly cooked food just needs to be "finished" wherever you want to eat.
- Sous vide is consistent and predictable. Once you have nailed the time and temperature, you can count on the same results time after time.
- Sous vide is convenient. Set the water bath to the correct temperature and your food will be ready when you are. If dinner is delayed, your food can be kept warm until you need it.
- Using sous vide, you can achieve results that were previously unattainable — for instance, the *onsen* or Japanese hot-spring egg (page 326), which can't be done on the stove. Short ribs (page 64) can be cooked until tender without being cooked to well-done.

# Getting Started

---

## THE ESSENTIALS

If you are about to go out to buy the essentials for getting started with sous vide cooking, I recommend only a few items:

- Sous vide device, which can be either a static bath or an immersion circulator, depending on your needs and budget

- Home sealing unit (many of the recipes in this book require one)

- Instant-read thermometer, mainly for calibration, but once you acquire this piece of equipment you will wonder how you did without it

- One box each of large and small resealable freezer bags

---

## Equipment

The equipment you need for cooking sous vide falls into three basic categories: "hard" (water circulators, baths and sealers), "soft" (bags, pouches and jars), and additional (such as thermometers and torches).

## Hard Equipment

While you could cook food sous vide in a beer cooler full of water heated to a precise temperature, that temperature would be hard to maintain throughout the necessary cooking time. One of the two types of sous vide devices below will provide you with the consistent results you are looking for.

## Self-Contained Static Bath

One of the first sous vide appliances to be developed for the home market was a self-contained water bath that heats the water from the base of the appliance, relying on thermal convection for even heating. In some ways it is like a high-tech slow cooker.

Sous Vide Supreme is an industry leader and its products are well made (I know, because I've used them). Other brands to consider are Burton, an English company, and Oliso, which is based in the United States, and there seem to be new units coming to the market monthly.

### Advantages
- **Noise:** Operation is absolutely silent because there are no moving parts.
- **Evaporation:** almost none — 40 Days and 40 Nights Black Garlic (page 388) would be almost impossible without this device.
- **Beep signal when it comes up to temperature.** (Not all products have this feature, and some might see this as a disadvantage, as it also beeps when it returns to temperature after you put food in.)
- **Maintenance:** no moving parts to break and no impeller to clean.
- **Power use:** Because there is no motor, less power is used.

## Disadvantages

- **Size:** The appliance takes up counter space and you are less likely to put it away after use.
- **Cost:** about 50 percent more than immersion circulators.
- **Cleaning:** While less evaporation and no moving parts means less cleaning, you either have to bail out the water or tip it into the sink to empty and clean it.

## Immersion Circulator

Immersion circulators have an impeller pump that moves water around the container. The container can be a stockpot or a picnic cooler, but most people buy a plastic or polycarbonate storage tub of about 5 gallons (20 L) capacity. I have tried more than half a dozen different units and they all function in a similar fashion. They differ in their construction (whether they are made from plastic or metal), the hardware used to attach them to the container, and their controls. Of the units I have tested, Sansaire, Anova and Nomiku have very good customer support.

## Advantages

- **Flexibility:** You can attach the circulator to any container that is deep enough — about 7 inches (17.5 cm) — and, if necessary, one that is larger than any of the static units.
- **Transportability:** It's easy to take your circulator with you on vacation or to a friend's house.
- **Size:** easier to store.
- **Efficiency:** The set temperature is reached a little more quickly than with a static unit.
- **Cost:** lower price than static units.

## Disadvantages

- **Evaporation:** More water is lost than with a unit that has a tightly fitting lid.
- **Noise:** slightly noisy operation, since the device has moving parts.
- **Maintenance:** The pump can fail, and it requires periodic descaling.

## Additional Uses

Once you have purchased a sous vide device, you can also use it as a bain marie — a hot water bath to hold

---

## HIGH-TECH FEATURES

As sous vide become more popular and the technology develops, the various companies that produce the equipment seem to be trying to outdo each other by adding features such as Bluetooth or Wi-Fi. While I can see some utility for Wi-Fi — it would be useful to be able to preheat the device on your way home from work or have it alert you that your steaks are ready when you are outside gardening — extra features increase the cost and add potential for malfunction. As I write, it appears that apps that will enable you to select a recipe and program the unit to cook to its specifications are on the horizon. However, one iPhone and iPad app that you might find particularly useful is Sous Vide Toolbox. It can accurately predict cooking and reheating times and can even create "what-if" scenarios if you want to change the temperature of the hot water bath by even a degree.

## EQUIPMENT ESSENTIALS

static bath sous vide

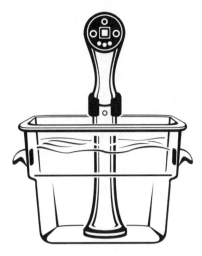

immersion circulator sous vide

home sealing unit

instant-read thermometer

prepared sauces, soups and solid food in pouches at serving temperatures. This can be very handy when cooking for a crowd and when your oven or burners are otherwise in use.

## Commercial Equipment

This equipment list would be incomplete without mentioning a third device that can be used for sous vide cooking: the convection steamer. This is a convection oven that can also inject steam into the oven's cavity to precise humidity levels. While some units are being developed for home use, currently these appliances are available only for commercial use, with prices starting in the five figures.

## Sealers

Aside from cooking in canning jars (more on that later), sealed, watertight pouches or bags from which the air has been expelled are a necessity when cooking sous vide. Since air is a poor conductor of heat and in fact acts as an insulator — think of a goose-down coat trapping air to keep you warm — you want as little as possible between your food and the hot water. Air also causes pouches to float, leading to uneven cooking.

Sealers are relatively inexpensive and they are useful to have in the kitchen, since they can be used for other purposes such as sealing up coffee beans, leftover pieces of cheese, and excess ingredients. As well, they are extremely useful for freezing food properly. Freezer burn occurs when the food is not securely wrapped and comes in contact with air. Tightly packing food destined for the freezer dramatically reduces its incidence and also frees up storage space.

There are two types of home sealing units: edge sealers (the most common) and gasket sealers.

## Edge Sealers

Edge sealers are widely available at affordable prices (about $100). In my experience they stand up to fairly heavy everyday use. They use a specially constructed pouch with micro-grooves that allow air to be sucked out by the unit. This works smoothly unless you have liquid in the pouch, in which case the pump will suck the liquid into the unit, creating problems.

### Advantages
- **Cost:** very affordable.
- **Availability:** Several manufacturers produce these devices, and the pouches are interchangeable among brands.

### Disadvantages
- **Use with liquids:** Edge sealers don't seal food with liquids well.

## Gasket Sealers

There are only a few manufacturers of gasket sealers. These sealers use proprietary pouches that have a zip-type seal and a gasket in one corner, to which a manual or electric pump is attached in order to evacuate the air.

### Advantages
- **Use with liquids:** If you regularly cook sous vide using liquids, you can easily pump air from the pouch while leaving the liquid intact.
- **Storage:** The associated pump is small enough to store in a kitchen drawer.

---

## CHAMBER VACUUM SEALERS

Chamber vacuum sealers are mostly used by professional chefs. I love them! They have much more vacuum power than a traditional sealer and the bags are much cheaper — about three cents each. You can also seal liquids easily, on their own or with solid food. It's a handy tool for doing "cheffy" things such as compressing watermelon and making quick pickles, as well as vacuum-sealing canning jars without heat or a water bath. (I also use my sealer to vacuum-seal spare socks and underwear, so they take up next to no space and stay dry when I go camping or rafting!)

The downsides are that they are very heavy (a small unit weighs about 70 lbs/32 kg) and they occupy a fair bit of space. They are also quite costly, with small semi-commercial units starting at about $500. However, if you can afford it and have the room, I'd give it some thought.

## Disadvantages

- **Cost:** The pouches are quite pricey — often more than $1 each, or about three times the price of sous vide pouches. However, the pouches are very sturdy and are meant to be reused.
- **Maintenance:** Cleaning the pouches is a chore. They need to be turned inside out, washed in hot soapy water, thoroughly dried (a hair dryer works well for this) and then stored in the freezer to prevent bacterial growth.

## Soft Equipment
### Freezer Bags

Resealable freezer bags are not designed for sous vide cooking. That said, they are BPA-free and the manufacturers state that they don't leach toxins when used in sous vide applications. They come in quart and gallon sizes (called small and large in some regions). Because liquids can create problems with most pouches when cooking with liquid, I suggest freezer bags as a preferable option.

When using freezer bags for sous vide cooking, it's important that they have a zipper-type seal, not a slider closing — bags with slider closures won't seal and they are more expensive. It's also important to buy premium bags that are designed for freezing foods. While some people suggest that freezer bag seals may fail at temperatures higher than 175°F (79.4°C), I have routinely used them to cook at temperatures as high as 200°F (93.3°C) without failure. However, as a precaution, I usually hang the zip seal outside the water bath while cooking at high temperatures.

The one potential concern with using a freezer bag is removing the air. Any air left in the bag after sealing will greatly

---

### WATER DISPLACEMENT METHOD FOR SEALING FREEZER BAGS

Combine the food and liquid in a freezer bag. With the opening facing up, immerse the filled bag in warm water as deeply as possible without allowing water to seep in. Then zip the bag shut. If this is done correctly, the air will have been removed from the bag and it should sink. If the bag still floats, then possibly the food itself is buoyant. You will have to resort to either weighing down the bag in the hot water bath (a heavy skillet works well) or open the bag, add some heavy, inert object (I suggest a few stainless-steel spoons) and reseal.

---

### POUCH OR BAG?

In this book I specify the type of container you will need for making each recipe. The term "pouch" refers to the encasement created by a sealer. You will also see the icon "Freezer Bag Friendly," which means that you can use a resealable freezer bag instead of a pouch. Freezer bags are particularly good when a recipe contains liquid. However, when a recipe doesn't contain liquid, I recommend that you use a sealer, if available.

increase the cooking time, because air is a very good insulator. However, since water is heavier than air, you can use the water displacement method (remember Archimedes' principle?) to help remove the air from a freezer bag. It's discussed more thoroughly on page 15.

## Sous Vide Pouches

Sous vide pouches are more expensive than freezer bags but are very sturdy and provide a tighter seal when used correctly. They come in small and large sizes, or you can buy pouch material in rolls and cut them yourself — many edge sealers have cutters built in. Using rolls is much more cost-effective for two reasons: you can cut bags to just the size you need, thus eliminating waste, and there are third-party manufacturers that sell rolls more economically. Look for them at online retailers.

A fairly recent product on the market, made by one of the leading manufacturers of pouches, is known as a "dam bag" or "liquid block bag." These precut pouches in quart (1 L) and gallon (3.8 L) sizes have a special material near the open end that blocks moisture from entering the sealing mechanism and ruining the seal. I find them too expensive, but one of my recipe testers, who doesn't trust his ability to seal freezer bags with the water displacement method, swears by them.

## Canning Jars

Preserving jars are also handy containers for cooking sous vide. They are great if you want to present a food item as a gift (such as Shrimp Escabeche, page 270) or when you want to produce something with a fixed shape, such as Crème Brûlée (page 336). Canning jars come in a variety of sizes and you can use one- or two-piece lids. Even the plastic ones generally used for cold-packed food work well, because sous vide temperatures are not very high.

Leave $\frac{1}{2}$ inch (1 cm) of headspace and make sure the rim of the jar is clean so you get a good seal. Tighten until just finger-tight — the lid will keep out the hot water and, as the jar cools, will form a light seal, similar to when you use these jars for canning. In most cases they can be reused; just use a fresh lid every time, to ensure a good seal. Because glass is denser than water, you don't have to be too concerned about the jar floating, as long as it is filled to about 80 percent of its capacity.

## Additional Equipment

There are a number of other tools that can enhance your experience of cooking sous vide.

## Thermometers

### Instant-Read Thermometer

You will need an instant-read thermometer (my favorite brand is Thermapen, though they are expensive) for calibrating your water bath from time to time and checking the internal temperature of meat. They are available with either a digital or dial face. Most cost less than $20 and last for a long time if the mechanism is kept dry.

### Infrared Noncontact Thermometer

This type of thermometer has a myriad of uses. It is shaped like a pistol that you point to where you want to know the surface temperature. It is perfect for tempering chocolate and taking the temperature of a pot of oil for deep-frying — you don't need to clean it after you use it. You can point it into the refrigerator or oven and get an instant temperature reading. At a restaurant they are handy for checking the heating and cooling systems — just point them at the duct. You can find them on sale for less than $40. (If you are doing any deep-frying and don't want to buy an infrared thermometer, you will need to invest in a candy/deep-fry thermometer.)

### Needle-Probe Thermometer

The early adopters of sous vide cooking approached it like conventional cooking, where the temperature of the ambient cooking medium (in this case water) is higher than the desired final internal temperature of what is being cooked. In sous vide circles this approach has come to be known as "delta T" ($\Delta$T). Think of a roast that you are cooking at 400°F (200°C) to medium-rare — about 130°F (54.4°C). This requires expert timing, usually facilitated by an instant-read thermometer. Needle-probe thermometers, with accompanying water foam tape, were developed to pierce pouches without causing them to lose their seal. They function in the same

## WHAT IS DELTA T?

Delta is a letter in the Greek alphabet that is used in science to denote a change or difference. The T stands for temperature. In thermodynamics and refrigeration, delta T is used to describe a difference in temperature, for example, the ambient temperature of a room compared to the temperature the air conditioning provides. In sous vide cooking the term is used to describe a particular cooking method in which the hot water bath is set to a temperature higher than the final internal temperature of the food. In this book I use this method only for the rabbit recipes, because the desirable results are not achievable otherwise.

way as a traditional meat thermometer. Because most sous vide cooking is now done at the desired final internal temperature, these thermometers are not really necessary, though they're a lot of fun to play with and thus worth a mention.

## Racks

There are stainless-steel wire racks designed for sous vide cooking that stabilize your pouches or bags in the water bath and keep them from coming in contact with one another, and from moving around, if you are using an immersion circulator. Some sous vide units are sold with them. They are almost essential and can be purchased from many outlets that sell sous vide equipment. I highly recommend using racks. Alternatively, you can get creative at a housewares store and look for a dish rack that will fit into your hot water bath.

## Brine Injector

Brine injectors look like super-sized syringes and are very useful for introducing salt brine into corned beef or beef tongue. Brining lean cuts such as pork loin and turkey breast before cooking results in a juicier final product, and injecting the brine speeds up this process. (However, I always follow up with some additional brining to make sure the brine is evenly distributed throughout the meat.) Instructions on how and when to use an injector are included in the relevant recipes in this book. You can find injectors in well-stocked cookware stores or online. Though it's not covered in this book, you can also use an injector to inject fat,

such as olive oil or melted butter, into lean meats to make them juicier.

## Jaccard

I don't advocate buying mechanically tenderized meat, because it is unnecessary with sous vide. The extended cooking time tenderizes the meat, and mechanical tenderization introduces external bacteria into it's interior. However, the Jaccard is a device that can come in handy. Designed to tenderize meat, it has a dozen or more very sharp, needlelike blades that pierce the meat and cut connective tissue. I use it to create small punctures in the meat to facilitate brine penetration, which is almost as effective as using a brine injector and very quick. In fact, when you pierce meat with the Jaccard and then put it in a chamber vacuum sealer with the brine, the brining is done almost instantaneously. Jaccards cost about the same as brine injectors and can be found in the same stores. I particularly like them for rind-on pork belly, which I always brine before cooking. The blades puncture both the rind and the meat, allowing for very thorough brining in less than two days.

## Digital Scale

I highly recommend purchasing a digital scale, even though it is not required for most of the recipes in this book. These scales are inexpensive, and measuring by weight is far more accurate than measuring by volume.

## Torch

Torches are the new kitchen tool for hipster home chefs. We have always used them in professional kitchens to caramelize crème brûlée and for a few other chef tricks that I can't share with you. When cooking sous vide, torches are useful for browning the surface of food, particularly meats. They allow you to create a crisp exterior without further cooking the meat. I am not fond of butane torches because they are expensive, they don't get all that hot, and I find I can taste the butane. I prefer propane or, better still, MAPP gas, a propane-based commercial product that burns at the highest temperature and leaves no residual flavor. These torches are available at hardware stores.

## Safety

As a professional chef writing his first cookbook about a rather technical subject, I feel obliged to be thorough about kitchen safety, food safety and hygiene.

### Kitchen Safety

Kitchen safety is about keeping you and everyone else in your kitchen safe and free from mishap. In this section I am highlighting cautions that I give my cooks and teach to my students.

- Wear closed shoes (not sandals) that don't have slippery soles.
- Don't cook while distracted by TV or talking on the phone. The kitchen is a potentially dangerous place — it requires your full attention.
- Make sure your kitchen is well illuminated and the floor is clean and dry.
- Keep counters clear of nonessential clutter.
- Don't try to catch anything that's falling from the counter or stove — it may be very sharp or very hot. Lunging at it can also cause further disruption.
- Grasp hot pot handles, baking sheets and anything from the oven with dry oven mitts or kitchen towels.

### Food Safety

Food safety is about keeping safe the people who eat your food. "Hygiene" is usually construed as cleanliness. While that is a good start, it really means a whole collection of practices that ensure good health.

- Buy fresh food and cook or process it promptly (for example, brine, package or freeze).
- Wash your hands frequently. Most food-borne illnesses are caused by cross-contamination, not spoilage.
- Damp kitchen towels and sponges can harbor lots of bacteria. Try to keep kitchen towels dry. Use paper towels to mop up spills or wipe down counters and cutting boards. You can sterilize kitchen sponges and

### SANITIZING CUTTING BOARDS

To make a sanitizing spray for use on cutting boards, fill a spray bottle with water (you can use one that previously contained all-purpose cleanser, so long as you wash it thoroughly). Add 1 tsp (5 mL) household bleach. Spray your cutting board with this liquid and wipe it dry with paper towels. Keep the bottle handy for wiping down counters and knives as well as cutting boards.

scrubbies by rinsing them well, then placing them in the microwave oven at High for one minute. If you can't do that, I recommend replacing them every three days.

- Keep food either cold or hot. Bacteria multiply quickly between 40° and 130°F (4.4° to 54.4°C).
- Thaw food thoughtfully. I don't recommend thawing in the microwave, because you may end up with warm and cold spots. The best method is to leave the food in the refrigerator overnight. If you are in a hurry, you may want to thaw it under cold running water. (A benefit of sous vide is that you can cook many things from frozen.)
- Avoid cross-contamination from your cutting board. After cutting raw protein such as meat, poultry or fish, wash the cutting board, then sanitize it (see page 19).
- If you are cooking between the temperatures of 130° and 140°F (54.4° to 60°C), calibrate your sous vide device periodically (see above).
- When you are chilling food in an ice-water bath, make sure that it stays very cold by replacing the ice as it melts.

## The Science of Food Safety

We normally cook food to make it taste good. In some cases we are also making it safe to eat. Usually we don't think about that too much. With sous vide, however, we need to be a little more mindful, because we are sometimes cooking at temperatures on the margin of food safety. We have to remember that eating can be a hazardous business! Here I will talk about pathogens that are sometimes found in food and how we have to approach them from a sous vide cooking perspective.

The pathogenic bacteria we are mainly concerned about are *Salmonella*, *Listeria*, *E. coli* and *Clostridium botulinum*. They are different from spoilage microorganisms and cannot be smelled or tasted. These bacteria can survive in a vacuum pouch and will multiply quickly at temperatures in the danger zone. The application of sufficient heat will cause the bacteria to die, a process called pasteurization. Food can be pasteurized at temperatures as low as 130°F (54.4°C) if held for long enough; it will happen more quickly at higher temperatures.

For many foods it is sufficient to pasteurize just the surface of the meat, where more bacteria are found. A steak that you intend to eat rare is one example. However, when meat and fish have been ground or mechanically tenderized, the surface bacteria have been mixed throughout. These foods should be pasteurized to the core.

Fortunately, there are mathematical models that provide equations for reducing the pathogens in your food. These models outline how long you need to cook food for, and at what temperature, in order to reduce bacteria to a level that is safe to consume. Since there will still be minute amounts of pathogenic bacteria remaining, pasteurized food left at room temperature for a period of time can again become unsafe to eat. I have provided cooking times in the relevant chapters to ensure that the food is pasteurized to its core, taking into account its thickness.

One thing to keep in mind is that the calculations are not linear: a pork chop 2 inches (5 cm) thick needs much more than double the time it takes to cook a pork chop that is 1 inch (2.5 cm) thick. The saving grace is that if you leave your food in longer than necessary, it won't overcook, because the temperature of the food cannot exceed that of the surrounding water bath. Remember that, for safety, the internal temperature of meats (and fish) must reach 130°F (54.4°C) within 6 hours (this is a consideration only for very thick pieces of meat and is covered in the relevant chapters and recipes).

Although not as serious as the pathogens mentioned above, *Campylobacter*, which is responsible for the most bacteriological illnesses, and trichinosis, a parasitic infection that is now largely under control in developed countries, are respectively killed or prevented by pasteurization.

## Sous Vide Basics

The following is a quick guide to getting started if you are cooking sous vide for the first time. The recipe chapters include more detailed information for specific types of food, and the tips that accompany each recipe are intended to answer any specific questions you may have.

### Setup

Sous vide equipment is fairly straightforward and should be set up according to the manufacturer's instructions. If you have purchased a self-contained unit, the process is as simple as plugging in a slow cooker. An immersion circulator, which

## PREVENTING WATER EVAPORATION

Except for the rare recipe that calls for a particularly long cooking time, water evaporation is not a problem with self-contained static units. However, you will experience some evaporation when using an immersion circulator. If you are using a container such as a stockpot, you can usually arrange the lid to loosely cover the top, which mitigates the problem. Some cooks use plastic wrap to improve the seal, but I find this wasteful and somewhat of a nuisance. Bubble wrap left over from packing materials is handy, as it is reusable and insulating.

If you are committed to sous vide cooking and plan to do it regularly, you can purchase the type of container used by most chefs — a rectangular polycarbonate tub. If you are handy, you can buy the lid as well and cut out an opening to accommodate the immersion circulator, so the lid can tightly seal the tub. I am not handy with power tools, so I just pop on the lid and drape a kitchen towel over the uncovered area.

circulates the water while heating it, requires an additional vessel to contain the hot water bath. Stockpots work well. Most immersion circulator units have the capacity to heat 5 to 6 gallons (20 to 24 L) of water. To ensure that you have sufficient water to accommodate evaporation, you need to pay attention to the high- and low-water indicators on the unit. Fill to just below the high-water indicator, and watch to make sure the level does not fall below the low-water indicator while the unit is operating.

## A Trial Run

Once you have set up your equipment, a good first project is preparing an egg in the shell, such as Perfect Poached Egg (page 325). Eggs are the original self-contained sous vide preparation, which means you don't need to get out any bags or pouches yet. Once you get up and running you will soon find that you can cook just about anything sous vide. You may even find that the convenience of sous vide cooking means you buy less prepared food.

## Prepping Food for Sous Vide

Preparing food for sous vide cooking is not that different from getting it ready to cook traditionally. However, a few factors need to be considered.

Bones are problematic. Bones have a tendency to poke through pouches, thus breaking the seal and allowing juices to leak into the hot water bath. Unless you want to retain the bone for aesthetic reasons — for example, in a rib steak — I recommend boning your meat or fish before packaging. If you do want to cook food on the bone, I recommend wrapping it in plastic wrap before sealing. This helps to protect the pouch from punctures.

At the lower temperatures used for sous vide cooking, less fat will render from your meat than when cooking conventionally. Here you have two options. If you plan to remove the meat from the hot water bath and immediately serve or brown it, you may want to trim off any excess fat before cooking. The flavor in fat is water-soluble, so you can

## COOKING MEAT AND FISH FROM FROZEN

Butcher shops and fish stores frequently freeze food in single or double portions, using a chamber vacuum sealer. Food keeps well this way because there is no air trapped inside to cause freezer burn. As long as the food has been packed in one layer, you can cook these packages directly from frozen. You will need to add at least 30 minutes to the cooking time to allow the product to defrost in the hot water bath; if you are using more than single-size portions, add 60 minutes. Remember, it's hard to overcook food at these low temperatures, so I recommend erring on the side of caution and allowing frozen food a little extra time.

add it to broths, for instance. If your recipe recommends a resting time after cooking, such as for pork ribs (page 116) or lamb chops (page 49), you can do some final trimming then. The small amount of fat that renders will bathe your meat in flavor. Once it's cooked and chilled, you can better assess whether the meat needs to be trimmed further. You may not need additional oil for browning.

In some cases I like to peel and prepare vegetables, then seal and cook them with their peelings for added flavor. White Asparagus with Ricotta (page 292) and Fennel with Apple and Dill (page 313) are examples of this approach.

Many of the recipes in this book use spice mixes, which usually contain salt. The question arises whether food should be salted before or after cooking. Generally I like to salt my food as early as possible in its preparation. I feel this helps the salt to integrate better with the inherent flavors of the food. I also think that salting early means you need to use less. Sous vide cooking is no different, with one exception: the protracted cooking time for large cuts of meat means that if they are salted early in the process, they run the risk of acquiring a "hammy" texture — quite dense and a little rubbery. Brining, which can be thought of as "wet salting," is discussed in the relevant chapters and recipes.

### Salting Guidelines

If you are cooking food for 6 hours or less, feel free to salt it (or not) before cooking, to suit your taste. However, if you are cooking a large piece of meat such as a whole leg of lamb, either cook it unsalted or salt very lightly before cooking. This will ensure that the meat does not develop a "cured" quality during the long cooking time.

### Boning Meat

I am a big advocate of doing as much of your own butchery as possible. Not only will you save money, you will also retain all the lovely bones and trimmings, which you can use to make stocks and broths (see pages 399 to 401 for more on broths). If you are new to butchery, a guide such as *The Zwilling J.A. Henckels Complete Book of Knife Skills*, by Jeffrey Elliot and James P. DeWan, is a worthwhile investment.

## Packaging Food for Sous Vide

The technical aspects of packaging and sealing food for sous vide cooking are covered in the equipment section (page 11) and in the relevant recipes. However, there are a few additional points I want to mention that relate to the quality and safety of the product.

- Lightly brushing food, especially meat, with melted butter or oil before sealing helps the pouch adhere to it more closely, which aids in the cooking process.
- Make sure that food is refrigerator temperature when it is being packaged. For instance, if you are browning a steak before cooking it sous vide, place it in the refrigerator for at least one hour after it has been browned, before you package and cook it. For safety reasons, it is best not to expose warm protein to the anaerobic environment of a pouch. Also, you run the risk of squeezing out precious meat juices if you seal it while still supple and warm.
- When packaging, avoid overcrowding the bag or pouch. This will help the food cook evenly and more quickly. With meats and fish, arrange them in one layer before sealing. If you are using freezer bags it can be difficult to package more than one portion per bag, as gravity will cause the pieces to fall on top of each other while you are sealing. So bag your meats and fish individually if necessary.
- Protein is usually quite supple when raw and stiffens as it cooks. Soft fish packaged with solid aromatics such as garlic cloves runs the risk of acquiring an imprint during cooking. In such a case, either make sure that the garlic is off to the side of the pouch or use a freezer bag rather than a home sealer, preferably with some liquid to help ensure a good seal. If your boneless chicken breast is curled when it goes into the hot water bath, for example, it will come out holding that shape. For shrimp to have a nice appearance after cooking, it is best to line them up neatly in the pouch before sealing.

## Cooking

Just as in traditional cooking, sous vide cooking varies with the type of food (the specifics are in the recipe chapters). View your sous vide device as an oven — preheating is required to ensure predictable results.

Meat, fish and poultry are 75 percent water. The muscle tissue is made up of muscle fiber, connective tissue and fat.

## BROWNING: BEFORE OR AFTER?

Much of the flavor in food comes from browning. This process looks like caramelization, but when protein is involved, it is far more complex. Known as the Maillard reaction, it starts when carbohydrates combine with amino acids under heat and results in the formation of hundreds of flavor compounds, as well as the familiar enticing color change. The most common approach to preparing meats and fish sous vide is to lightly season (or brine), package and cook. Once it is cooked, the food is quickly browned in a skillet, on a preheated grill or with a torch. This is the method you are likely to use most of the time. However, there are four situations where browning before cooking is advantageous.

- When you will be finishing your food under uncertain conditions. If you are transporting steaks or burgers to a picnic, for example, and you are not sure if there will be a grill powerful enough to brown them properly, your best bet is to brown the food at home before cooking. You can chill (or freeze) it and use the picnic grill for reheating.

- When you want to build flavor. Browning protein creates many appealing savory flavors (see "The Maillard Reaction," page 34). For some reason, browning before cooking seems to accentuate this process. If you want meaty, savory flavors I recommend browning before cooking. One advantage is that you can then slip the food out of the pouch and directly onto your plate.

- When you want a seared but very rare result. Searing tuna but leaving it extremely rare in the center is difficult (see Rare Seared Tuna, page 242). By placing it in the freezer until it is almost frozen, you can give it a sear while leaving it still cold in the center. You can then cook it very lightly sous vide, just until it is warmed through, ready for serving on warm plates.

- When you want to brown meats thoroughly. Short ribs come to mind here. After cooking the ribs sous vide, they are very hard to brown properly because the meat stiffens up during cooking. Raw short ribs are much more supple and far easier to brown before cooking.

## MORE ABOUT BROWNING BEFORE COOKING

Be aware that when you brown food before cooking it sous vide, you will lose the appealing crust that browning after cooking provides. You can choose to chill previously browned meat, then brown it again just before serving. However, you need to make sure that it is extremely cold before the second browning, to avoid overcooking. Intensely flavored meats such as wild boar and mutton do not lend themselves to being browned twice — you run the risk of creating overly strong flavors.

As the flesh is heated, changes start to occur. The protein molecules begin to coagulate at 120°F (48.9°C), causing the flesh to stiffen up. With a continued rise in temperature, this coagulation squeezes out some of the water and the color begins to change.

Tougher cuts have an abundance of connective tissue, primarily made up of the protein collagen. Collagen begins to break down at 158°F (70°C) and becomes gelatin. This conversion serves two purposes for the cook: it makes the meat less resilient (hence tender) and it lubricates it. This lubrication is the familiar stickiness that you experience when you eat a slow-braised lamb shank, and the gelatin is what makes cooking liquid solidify when it's refrigerated.

Vegetables and fruits require higher temperatures than meat to convert their starch and pectin from raw to cooked, though the temperatures need not be quite as precise. Cooking vegetables in a pouch below the boiling point preserves both nutrients and flavor, because they are not getting washed away into a big pot of water. But when you want to cook vegetables and meat together, such as in a stew, you need a new approach. Cook your vegetables first, either traditionally or sous vide, then add them to the meat or fish and cook at the temperature required for the protein. This lower temperature will not cook your vegetables further, and your dish will be ready when the meat or fish is done.

If you are cooking more than one pouch of food at a time, it is important that the pouches not be pushed together, which would cause uneven cooking. Wire racks (mentioned in the equipment section) are very handy for keeping your bags stable and not touching one another.

## FURTHER INFORMATION

Please refer to the relevant chapters for more detailed information about how to select, prepare, package, cook and finish different types of meat, fish, vegetables, eggs and sweets.

## Finishing

As previously mentioned, when cooking sous vide, you will frequently be browning meat, poultry and fish after cooking rather than before. You can do this in a skillet, under the broiler or on the grill. Keep in mind that thinner cuts will have to be browned at very high temperatures for the shortest time possible to avoid further cooking. If your heat source is not very powerful, the browning will take longer and you may want to start with food straight from the refrigerator.

Propane torches are another effective way to finish food, especially roasts that are difficult to brown using traditional methods. Here's how to get started. Bring the meat or fish to serving temperature, dry it thoroughly with paper towels and lightly brush it with oil or melted butter. Place it on a baking sheet or in a roasting pan, preferably on a wire rack to elevate the meat. Light torch and run it over all sides, until browned, working small areas at a time while keeping the torch moving. The process should take no more than about 1 minute per steak, fish fillet or chicken breast, though it will take longer with roasts, depending on their size. Serve immediately.

## Reheating

Reheating refrigerated food that is in a pouch or bag is easy. If you have leftovers from a traditionally cooked meal such as a stew or casserole, transfer them to a pouch or bag and seal accordingly. You can use any temperature equal to or lower than the temperature used to cook the food in the first place, to avoid cooking the food further. In most cases, food reheated to 140°F (60°C) will be hot enough to be considered at serving temperature, but a little higher — such as 150°F (65.6°C) — gives you a margin of error if, for instance, you are serving a large number of people or you can't preheat your plates. If it fits in a small freezer bag or sous vide pouch, the food will heat through in 30 to 40 minutes. Large bags or pouches should be hot all the way through after 60 minutes.

If you are reheating food that you have previously cooked sous vide, make sure that the water bath temperature is no higher than the temperature you cooked it at in the first place. You don't want to undo all that precision cooking!

## Chilling

Food that is not eaten within 2 hours of cooking sous vide should be chilled rapidly for future consumption, whether it will be served cold or reheated. Putting warm food in the refrigerator is an ineffective way to chill it; it will cool too slowly, while warming up your refrigerator in the process. Since water is a great conductor of heat, an ice-water bath is the best method. To be effective, the bath should be about half ice and half water, not just a few ice cubes in a bowl of water. Most single-serving pouches of food will be cold enough for refrigeration after 30 to 45 minutes, although longer chilling is never detrimental.

## Storing

Once properly chilled, pasteurized food can be stored under refrigeration for 5 days or more. Aim to eat unpasteurized food within 2 days.

Sous vide is a perfect technique for food that can be frozen (as outlined in the respective recipes), since it is already neatly packaged in a pouch or bag with most of the air removed. Air is what causes freezer burn, shortening the storage life of a product. Consult the relevant recipes for further information.

## A FINAL WORD

Learning to cook food sous vide may seem intimidating at first, but with some understanding of the basics, adapting is easy and results come quickly. If you're looking for convenience, precision and quality results, you have come to the right place. It is my hope as well that the recipes in this book will help you expand your repertoire.

# Recipe Assumptions

- Butter is unsalted. In most recipes in this book, you can substitute salted butter and adjust the seasoning in the final dish.
- Olive oil is high-quality supermarket-grade extra virgin olive oil.
- Vegetable oil for deep-frying or browning can be corn, sunflower, peanut or grapeseed oil.
- Meat, fish, seafood and poultry are raw unless otherwise specified.
- Sausage is in its casing unless it is specified that the casing must be removed.
- Garlic has had the germ in the center of the clove removed before chopping (the germ can be bitter and hard to digest). Skip this step if you are roasting or fermenting whole heads of garlic.
- Salt is kosher salt unless otherwise specified. The kosher salt that I use weighs 12 grams per tablespoon, and the imperial measures are based on that amount. Not all kosher salt has the same flake size, and therefore not the same weight per volume.
- All produce is fresh and washed before preparation.
- Produce is of medium size, unless otherwise specified. If size is crucial to the success of the recipe, the weight or volume is specified.
- Inedible parts are removed from produce, unless otherwise specified (for example, bananas are peeled; apples are cored; onions and garlic are peeled; bell peppers are stemmed and seeded).
- When produce is usually peeled but should not be for the recipe, it is specified.
- Wine used in the recipes is dry, unless otherwise specified. Because alcohol is rarely desirable in cooked food, and because sous vide cooking tends to retain the alcohol because of the packaging and cooking temperature, look for wine that is low in alcohol — 11.5 to 12.5 percent is preferred. Avoid oaky red or white wines and aromatic varietals such as Gewürztraminer and Sauvignon Blanc.
- Citrus juices, unless specified, are freshly squeezed rather than bottled.
- Unless otherwise specified, "soy sauce" refers to Chinese light soy sauce. The Pearl River Bridge brand is widely available and quite good.
- Flour is all-purpose white flour, unless otherwise specified.
- Sugar is granulated white sugar, unless otherwise specified.
- Eggs are large and from chickens, unless otherwise specified.
- Milk, unless otherwise specified, means homogenized whole milk with about 3.2 percent butterfat content.
- The amount of oil called for to brown or stir-fry is an approximation that depends on the diameter of the pan. You need an even coating of $\frac{1}{8}$ inch (3 mm) of oil to brown food properly — less is detrimental to the process.
- Where temperatures are mentioned, I have rounded to the nearest tenth of a degree when it applies to sous vide, as most equipment has adjustments to this level of accuracy.
- When oven temperatures are mentioned, I have rounded to the nearest 5°F (3°C). It is worth using an oven thermometer, since few oven controls are that accurate.

# Ingredient Tips

- Keep two kinds of olive oil on hand in your kitchen: your supermarket-grade oil for cooking (see page 29) and a high-quality gourmet extra virgin oil that has a flavor profile you enjoy. Use the latter for drizzling over salads and for finishing dishes.

- If pickling salt or fine salt is called for, choose a version that is not iodized. Occasionally large-flake premium sea salt is called for; Maldon is a good choice.

- If you are not making your own broth, I suggest that you buy "no-salt added" broth in Tetra packs. In most cases you will be adding a few bones and/or vegetables to enhance and freshen it. Because commercial broth tends to be weak, you will allow it to reduce while simmering. If you start with seasoned broth, you may wind up with stock that is too salty. (See the Appendix, page 399, for further information and a recipe on page 401 for Enhanced Broth.)

- Most whole poultry recipes assume an eviscerated, headless bird with feet removed. Should you receive feet, add them to stock for additional body. Remove toenails, if present, and blanch the feet before adding to stock. Pekin ducks frequently come with the head on; it can be added to stocks along with the neck.

- Herbs, especially dried ones, vary greatly in potency. The amounts listed in the recipes are an approximation. Adjust to taste as necessary or desired.

- Tomato paste is best purchased in tubes that resemble toothpaste. That way you can store it in the fridge and none will go to waste when you need just a small amount.

- Fresh chile peppers vary greatly in hotness, and of course hotness is highly subjective. Feel free to adapt recipes to suit your spiciness-enjoyment threshold.

- I consider jalapeño and serrano chiles to be interchangeable in most instances, assuming that you are measuring by quantity, not volume. Serrano chiles are about one-third the size of jalapeños but three times more potent. If you like the vegetal notes of a green pepper, use jalapeños. If you want good clean heat, opt for serrano chiles. In recent decades jalapeño chiles grown in the United States have tended to be less hot than those from Mexico, because most of them are grown for a big Tex-Mex fast-food chain … yes, that one.

- Grana Padano cheese is a good choice for cooking. While many people in North America use Parmigiano-Reggiano in recipes, it's actually considered a table cheese in its native Italy. While it can be used for cooking, the expense is rarely warranted. Grana Padano has flavors that are in a similar vein, and it's less expensive. Another, even less expensive alternative is Sbrinz, from Switzerland. It is widely thought to be the oldest cheese in Europe and happens to be unpasteurized.

- Fresh ginger can be quickly reduced to a paste for marinades by grating it with a Microplane rasp or similar device. If the ginger is unblemished and in good condition, it can be washed, dried and left unpeeled for this process.

# Beef, Veal, Lamb and Venison: The Tender Cuts

# Beef, Veal, Lamb and Venison: The Tender Cuts

The tender cuts of the animals we eat come from muscles that are not heavily used. In quadrupeds these are called the supporting muscles, and they run along the length of the animal between the front and back legs. These cuts account for only 12% to 20% of the meat on a carcass, so they are understandably expensive.

The main advantage in cooking tender cuts sous vide — aside from the repeatable precise results common to all sous vide cooking — is that you can get the doneness that you want from edge to edge of your cut. Another big advantage of using this method is that once you decide on the doneness you like for a particular cut, you can dial in the temperature on the machine, make adjustments for size, and get perfect results every time.

## Red Meat Doneness: Temperatures and Signals

Doneness is when the meat, poultry or fish being cooked reaches a specific temperature range at its coolest point, usually the center of the thickest part. The United States Department of Agriculture (USDA) provides recommendations for red meat doneness temperatures, but they are conservative, to say the least. While I don't see eye-to-eye with the USDA's suggestions, I do agree with (and have used in this book) the temperatures published by Harold McGee in his great reference work *On Food and Cooking*.

Keep in mind that these temperatures are for red meats (beef, lamb, veal and venison). Pork, poultry and fish are different and their doneness is covered in their own chapters. You'll notice that no temperatures are given for medium-well or well-done. That's because nothing advantageous happens to tender cuts when they get to beyond 145°F (62.8°C). The meat continues to shrink, lose juices and stiffens, making it unappealing.

## The Basics

The tender cuts have been grouped together because the procedures for cooking them sous vide are similar. In each recipe I will give you specific guidelines and suggestions for the cut called for in the ingredients list. In the following pages you will find general information on these cuts and some helpful tips on selecting, preparing and cooking them.

### Selecting

Whole tender cuts of red meat, like the ones in this chapter, are considered sterile internally unless they have

| DONENESS | TEMPERATURE |
|---|---|
| Rare | 120°F to 130°F (48.9°C to 54.4°C) |
| Medium-rare | 130°F to 135°F (54.4°C to 57.2°C) |
| Medium | 135°F to 145°F (57.2°C to 62.8°C) |

been mechanically tenderized. Have a conversation with your butcher before buying, to ensure you know what you're getting. Ground meats are not sterile and therefore require different cooking and handling techniques. You'll find them on page 272.

## Prepping

- Beef fat begins to render at 150°F (65.6°C), while lamb fat renders at a slightly higher temperature. This is well above the temperatures you will be using to cook them sous vide, so I advise you to trim excess fat from your tender cuts before cooking. The sous vide technique won't render the fat the way that higher-temperature cooking methods will.
- I like to oil and lightly season many meats and fish before sealing them in their sous vide pouches. The oil helps the pouches seal more tightly around the meat and gives the seasoning something to stick to. I use olive oil because I like the taste, but any neutral-tasting vegetable oil is fine.
- I recommend sealing steaks in individual sous vide pouches to ensure even cooking and cooling.

## Cooking

- Cooking times are based on the thickness and nature of the ingredients

you're using. The introduction to each recipe chapter explains the factors that determine cooking times for specific types of ingredients.

- In this chapter — as with almost all the recipes in this book — the temperature of the hot water bath will be set to the desired final temperature of the food inside the sous vide pouch. Because of this, you can leave the pouch in the bath for up to an hour longer than the time specified, without affecting taste or texture.
- For the recipes in this chapter, no extra cooking time is required to tenderize the meat and convert its collagen to gelatin. These cuts are already tender and contain very little collagen.
- When you're roasting or grilling, you usually let the meat rest when it's done cooking. This allows the difference in temperature between the hotter exterior and the cooler interior to equalize. When you're cooking sous vide, you don't need to rest cooked meat before slicing it. The slow, gradual heating yields meat that's the same temperature from edge to edge.

## Browning

- It's your choice whether to brown tender cuts of beef or venison before or after cooking them in the hot water bath. Browning them right before serving is generally recommended so that they'll arrive at the table sizzling.

- To give delicate veal a more developed flavor, I like to brown it in a skillet before cooking it sous vide. That way I can slip the perfectly finished meat out of the sous vide pouch and onto the plate — and right into my mouth! To avoid overcooking veal, place it in the freezer for 15 to 30 minutes before browning it. Then I chill the browned meat in the freezer for about 10 minutes before packaging it in a sous vide pouch.
- The flavor of lamb can become too pronounced if it's browned before it's cooked sous vide. I recommend that you seal it in a sous vide pouch and cook it in the hot water bath, then brown it afterward, just before serving, for more delicate and delicious results.
- Venison is typically aged less than beef and can be quite wet, so make sure you dry it well before browning. This will ensure that you get a delicious crusty exterior that contrasts with the tender meat inside.
- If you plan to brown and serve the meat right after cooking it sous vide, I recommend opening the pouch and patting the meat dry with paper towels. Then refrigerate it briefly on a plate lined with paper towels to chill it before proceeding. Otherwise you risk overcooking the meat during the browning process.

## THE MAILLARD REACTION

We generally cook tender cuts using dry-heat methods such as pan-frying, roasting or grilling, and we do it at high temperatures to get a nicely browned layer on the outside of the meat. This crust provides a textural contrast to the softer interior. The difference between the two layers is especially pronounced when you cook the meat to less than medium doneness.

Perhaps more important, the crust adds a delicious savory flavor to the meat. Browning is similar to caramelizing, but because it affects proteins as well as sugars, it involves a far more complex sequence of reactions, creating hundreds of flavor compounds. This effect is known as the Maillard reaction, named for the French chemist who discovered it about 100 years ago. It occurs when meat reaches a temperature above the boiling point of water (212°F/100°C), and it can take place only if the surface is dry.

Until recently, it was thought that browning meat helps "lock in" the juices. That's why recipes usually start by browning the meat at a higher temperature, then continuing to cook it at a lower temperature until the center has reached the desired doneness. Luckily for us, this theory has been disproven. When we cook using sous vide techniques, we can choose to brown meats before or after bringing them to the desired doneness level. See "Browning" (page 33) for my advice on when to brown tender cuts of beef, veal, lamb and venison.

# Beef Steak Cooking Times

The times in this chart are minimums and are based on the assumption that you are starting with meat at refrigerator temperature (I recommend this method). Because the meat is cooked to its desired final temperature, it can be left in the hot water bath for up to one hour longer than the cooking time below, without affecting taste or texture.

| STEAK THICKNESS | DONENESS LEVEL | WATER BATH TEMPERATURE | COOKING TIME |
|---|---|---|---|
| 2½ inches (6 cm) | Rare* | 126°F (52.2°C) | 6 hours |
| | Medium-rare | 130°F (54.4°C) | 6 hours |
| | Medium | 136°F (57.8°C) | 6 hours |
| 2 inches (5 cm) | Rare* | 125°F (51.7°C) | 4½ hours |
| | Medium-rare | 130°F (54.4°C) | 4½ hours |
| | Medium | 136°F (57.8°C) | 4½ hours |
| 1½ inches (4 cm) | Rare* | 124°F (51.5°C) | 2½ hours |
| | Medium-rare | 130°F (54.4°C) | 2½ hours |
| | Medium | 136°F (57.8°C) | 2½ hours |
| 1 inch (2.5 cm) | Rare* | 122°F (50°C) | 75 minutes |
| | Medium-rare* | 129°F (53.9°C) | 75 minutes |
| | Medium | 135°F (57.2°C) | 75 minutes |

* Steaks marked with an asterisk are not pasturized internally.

## NOTES

- With the exception of Thin New York Steak Sandwiches (page 38), steaks thinner than those listed above are not well suited to the sous vide approach, because they are likely to overcook.
- Steaks thicker than those listed above are considered roasts and require a different calculation method.
- Avoid cooking tender steaks past medium, because that will make the meat tough and unpalatable.
- Since even a quick browning will result in some additional cooking, the temperatures given for rare become lower as the steaks get thinner.
- Sous vide cooking allows for some juicy cheaper cuts to be cooked to the texture of pricey succulent tenderloin. See "Beef, Veal, Lamb and Venison: The Tough Cuts" (page 57).

## SEAR STEAKS FOR SAFETY

When you cook steaks to rare, the temperature they reach will not be adequate to pasteurize the surface, where bacteria can gather. The good news is that it's easy to remedy this. Simply sear the steak before or after cooking to kill any surface pathogens. Don't serve rare steaks to young children, pregnant women or anyone with a compromised immune system. Please refer to page 20 for more safety information.

## Finding the Sweet Spot for Veal and Lamb

Veal is the meat from young cattle (usually male calves, a byproduct of the dairy industry) and lamb is the meat from young sheep, both less than one year old. The ratio of the various proteins in these meats differs from those found in beef. In order for the proteins to create savory flavors, veal and lamb need to be cooked to a higher temperature.

The sweet spot for lamb doneness is between 133°F (56.1°C) and 150°F (65.6°C). For veal it's a little higher: between 142°F (61.1°C) and 150°F (65.6°C). As you can see, the window of doneness for veal is very small. As cooking students, my colleagues and I would test ourselves to see if we could cook veal to that hard-to-achieve perfect doneness — where the meat is cooked but not dry. Now, with sous vide, it is easy to get proper results without all that testing.

## Doneness for Veal and Lamb: A Matter of Taste

Chefs like me tend to prefer tender meats cooked to minimum doneness so they are as juicy as possible. The final temperatures for the recipes in this book are as low as I can recommend. However, feel free to cook veal or lamb up to 150°F (65.6°C) if you like it more well-done.

Interestingly, the younger the animal is, the more done you will want it, and vice versa. For instance, baby lamb is best cooked all the way up to 145°F to 150°F (62.8°C to 65.6°C), while mutton — from sheep between one and two years old — is tasty cooked medium-rare, or 130°F to 135°F (54.4°C to 57.2°C). The same applies to veal. Fortunately, sous vide cooking allows you this kind of precision.

## Thickness Determines Time

As is always the case with sous vide cooking, the cooking time for veal and lamb is determined by the thickness or diameter of the cut. It takes about 75 minutes for the center of a chop 1 inch (2.5 cm) thick to reach the temperature of the hot water bath; for a 1½-inch (4 cm) chop, it takes about twice as long. Generally, doubling the thickness of a cut more than doubles the cooking time.

For cuts that are thicker than 1½ inches (4 cm), I recommend setting your hot water bath 2°F (1.1°C) higher than your target temperature for the first hour, then lowering it to your target temperature for the remainder of the cooking time. This is the technique I've used in Veal Tenderloin with Exotic Mushroom Sauce (page 46) to ensure that the meat is cooked to the proper doneness.

### PASTEURIZING VEAL AND LAMB

Sous vide cooking is done at much lower temperatures than roasting or grilling, but it will still pasteurize meat if it is left in the hot water bath for a long enough time. If you are concerned about pasteurization, you can add 30 to 90 minutes to your veal or lamb cooking times. This will ensure that bacteria are killed without overcooking the meat. For more information, turn to page 9.

## Venison: Tender and Lean

"Venison" is a broad category of game animals that includes deer, elk and antelope. In this book, however, I use the term to refer to the meat of deer. The meat of domesticated red deer and smaller fallow deer is becoming more popular and increasingly available in specialty butcher shops. Wild white-tailed deer can be delicious, but the quality depends on the animal's age and gender, as well as the manner in which it was killed and butchered.

The venison recipes in this book have been developed and tested using red deer but will work with any species that falls into the category. Antelope and elk are also farmed and have similar cooking characteristics.

## Doneness Temperatures: Venison

Venison is very lean, and tender cuts do not do well when cooked past medium-rare. My recipes direct you to cook venison sous vide to 132°F (55.6°C)

so it comes out medium-rare. This leaves some leeway for the meat to cook a little more during browning without drying out.

If you have a tender cut of venison that is not the exact dimensions called for in the recipes on pages 54 to 56, you can adapt the recipe by using the Beef Steak Cooking Times chart (page 35). Likewise, if you like your venison cooked the way you like your beef, use those temperatures as a guideline.

### PASTEURIZING VENISON

I think venison is most delicious when it's juicy rare or medium-rare, so I cook it at a relatively low temperature. This means the meat will not be pasteurized when it comes out of the sous vide pouch. If you want to pasteurize the meat, you can do so by doubling the cooking time listed in the recipe. For more information, turn to page 9.

# Thin New York Steak Sandwiches

This is a good simple recipe you can use when you see thin New York steaks on special at the supermarket. They are tasty with eggs for brunch or for a relaxed dinner when you get home late. They're also a good alternative to burgers at a picnic.

---

**MAKES
3 SERVINGS**

Freezer Bag Friendly

## Tips

This recipe can be scaled up. Package each steak individually.

Because they are quite thin, the steaks should be well chilled prior to browning.

These steaks are cooked to the temperature for rare meat, but because they are thin, they will wind up closer to medium-rare because of the browning (and reheating, if they are made ahead). If you prefer your steaks more cooked, preheat the hot water bath to 130°F (54.4°C) and proceed with the recipe.

*To make ahead:* Prepare to the end of Step 3. Transfer the pouches to an ice bath and chill for 15 minutes. Refrigerate sealed pouches for up to 5 days or freeze for up to 6 months. To use the frozen steaks, thaw overnight in the refrigerator. See page 39 for reheating instructions.

▷ **Preheat hot water bath to 122°F (50°C)**
▷ **3 sous vide pouches**

| | | |
|---|---|---|
| 3 | New York strip beef steaks, each about ³⁄₄ inch (2 cm) thick | 3 |
| 3 tbsp | olive oil, divided | 45 mL |
| 1 tsp | kosher salt | 5 mL |
| 1 tsp | freshly ground black pepper | 5 mL |
| 1 | baguette (see box, below) | 1 |
| 1½ tbsp | butter, softened | 22 mL |
| 1½ tbsp | Dijon mustard | 22 mL |

1. Brush steaks with 1 tbsp (15 mL) of the oil and sprinkle with salt and pepper. Place steaks on a plate and refrigerate until ready to use, about 10 to 15 minutes (see Tips, at left).

2. Meanwhile, in a medium skillet, heat remaining oil over medium-high heat. Brown steaks, turning once, about 2 minutes per side. Transfer to a clean plate and refrigerate until chilled, about 15 minutes.

3. Place each steak in a separate sous vide pouch and seal. Immerse in preheated hot water bath and cook for 1½ hours. Remove pouches from bath. (To make ahead, see Tips, at left.)

4. Cut baguette crosswise into thirds, then cut each horizontally in half. Heat or toast, if desired. Spread butter and mustard over cut sides of baguette pieces. Remove steaks from pouches, sandwich between baguette pieces, and serve.

---

### Picnic Steaks

If you are serving these sandwiches at a picnic or similar occasion, warm the baguette carefully on a cooler area of the grill while you reheat the cooked steaks on the hotter part, for about 2 to 3 minutes per side.

# New York Steaks with Bordelaise Sauce

This combination is a classic offering at restaurants where the cooks are skilled at sauce making. The sauce requires some advance planning but the results are well worth it. I like my New York steaks medium-rare; if you prefer a different doneness, please refer to Beef Steak Cooking Times (page 35).

## Tip

*To make ahead:* Prepare to the end of Step 2. Transfer pouches to an ice bath and chill for 45 minutes. Refrigerate sealed pouches for up to 1 week or freeze for up to 6 months. To use frozen steaks, thaw overnight in the refrigerator.

▷ **Preheat hot water bath to 130°F (54.4°C)**
▷ **2 sous vide pouches**

| | | |
|---|---|---|
| 2 | New York strip beef steaks, each 1 inch (2.5 cm) thick | 2 |
| 2 tbsp | olive oil, divided | 30 mL |
| | Salt and freshly ground black pepper | |
| 1 | recipe Bordelaise Sauce (page 376) | 1 |

1. Brush steaks with 1 tbsp (15 mL) of the oil and lightly season with salt and pepper.

2. Place each steak in a separate sous vide pouch and seal. Immerse in preheated hot water bath and cook for 3 hours. Remove pouches from bath. (To make ahead, see Tip, at left.)

3. Remove steaks from pouches and pat dry with paper towels. Transfer to a plate and refrigerate for 15 minutes.

4. Brush steaks with remaining oil and season to taste with salt and pepper. Brown steaks using your preferred method (see page 27 for finishing techniques). Arrange on warm plates and serve with sauce.

---

### Reheating Chilled Cooked Steaks

To reheat from refrigerator temperature, preheat the hot water bath to 120°F (48.9°C). Immerse the pouches in preheated bath for 20 minutes (30 minutes for the beef tenderloin, page 40, and ribeye steak, page 41; 45 minutes for rib steak, page 42) before proceeding with the recipe.

# Beef Tenderloin Steaks

Tenderloin is, as the name implies, the most tender cut of beef. Buying steaks that are at least 2 inches (5 cm) thick ensures they won't overcook when you brown them. Because tenderloin is very lean, I like to cook these steaks to rare and brown them well as a finishing touch. If you prefer a different doneness, see Beef Steak Cooking Times (page 35). These steaks pair well with Horseradish Cream (see variation, page 372).

## MAKES 2 SERVINGS

Freezer Bag Friendly

Can Be Scaled Up

## Tips

Beef cooked below 130°F (54.4°C) is not pasteurized and should not be served to pregnant women or people with a compromised immune system (see page 9).

*To make ahead:* Prepare to the end of Step 2. Transfer pouches to an ice bath and chill for 45 minutes. Refrigerate sealed pouches for up to 5 days or freeze for up to 6 months. To use frozen steaks, thaw overnight in the refrigerator. To reheat from refrigerator temperature, preheat hot water bath to 120°F (48.9°C). Immerse pouches in preheated bath for 30 minutes before proceeding with Step 4.

▸ **Preheat hot water bath to 128°F (53.5°C)**
▸ **2 sous vide pouches**

| 2 | beef tenderloin steaks, each 2 inches (5 cm) thick | 2 |
| 2 tbsp | olive oil, divided | 30 mL |
| | Salt and freshly ground black pepper | |

1. Brush steaks with 1 tbsp (15 mL) of the oil and lightly season to taste with salt and pepper.

2. Place each steak in a separate sous vide pouch and seal. Immerse in preheated hot water bath and cook for 4 hours. Remove pouches from bath. (To make ahead, see Tips, at left.)

3. Remove steaks from pouches and pat dry with paper towels. Transfer to a plate lined with paper towels and refrigerate for 20 minutes.

4. Brush steaks with remaining oil and season to taste with salt and pepper. Brown steaks using your preferred method (see page 27 for finishing techniques). If you're using your grill to brown them, make sure to preheat it on the highest setting with the lid closed, then grill the steaks for 2 to 3 minutes per side with the lid open. If you're pan-searing the steaks to brown them, preheat a cast-iron skillet until it's very hot and sear the steaks for 2 minutes per side.

5. Arrange steaks on warm plates. Serve with sauce, if desired.

# Ribeye Steak with Chimichurri Sauce

Steaks cut from the rib section are rich and juicy. Ribeye, a boneless cut, is a perfect introduction to cooking steak sous vide. I like my ribeye medium-rare; if you prefer a different doneness, please refer to Beef Steak Cooking Times (page 35). A steak 1½ inches (4 cm) thick will weigh about 1 pound (500 g). I will let you decide if that is large enough to share! Ribeye is perfect with chimichurri, a pesto-like sauce from Argentina that is typically served with grilled meats.

## MAKES 1 TO 2 SERVINGS

Freezer Bag Friendly

Can Be Scaled Up

## Tip

*To make ahead:* Prepare to the end of Step 2. Transfer pouch to an ice bath and chill for 1 hour. Refrigerate sealed pouch for up to 1 week or freeze for up to 6 months. To use frozen steak, thaw overnight in the refrigerator. Pat dry with paper towels and proceed with Step 4.

▸ **Preheat hot water bath to 130°F (54.4°C)**
▸ **Sous vide pouch**

| | | |
|---|---|---|
| 1 | boneless beef ribeye steak, 1½ inches (4 cm) thick | 1 |
| 3 tbsp | olive oil, divided | 45 mL |
| | Salt and freshly ground black pepper | |
| 1 | recipe Chimichurri Sauce (page 370) | 1 |

1. Brush steak with 1½ tbsp (22 mL) oil and lightly season to taste with salt and pepper.

2. Place steak in sous vide pouch and seal. Immerse in preheated hot water bath and cook for 4 hours. Remove pouch from bath. (To make ahead, see Tip, at left.)

3. Remove steak from pouch and pat dry with paper towels. Transfer to a plate and refrigerate for 20 minutes.

4. Brush steak with remaining oil and season to taste with salt and pepper. Brown steak using your preferred method (see page 27 for finishing techniques).

5. Arrange steak on warm plate(s), slicing if desired. Serve with chimichurri sauce.

---

### Packaging Steaks

When scaling up steak recipes, make sure to package each steak in an individual pouch.

---

# Rib Steak with Green Peppercorn Sauce

Rib steaks, cooked and served on the bone, are as impressive as they are massive — they are also known as "cowboy steaks" because of their size. They are usually about 2½ inches (6 cm) thick, depending on which part of the rib section they are from, and weigh upwards of 2 pounds (1 kg). Here the steak is cooked sous vide to rare or medium-rare, then finished on the barbecue. If you prefer a different doneness, please refer to Beef Steak Cooking Times (page 35).

---

**MAKES
2 PORTIONS**

Freezer Bag Friendly

Can Be Scaled Up

## Tips

The cooking time is lengthy in order to pasteurize the interior of the beef. If you are not concerned about pasteurization, remove steak from hot water bath in Step 2 and proceed to Step 4.

*To make ahead:* Prepare to the end of Step 2. Transfer pouch to an ice bath and chill for 2 hours. Refrigerate sealed pouch for up to 1 week or freeze for up to 6 months. To use frozen steak, thaw overnight in the refrigerator. To reheat from refrigerator temperature, preheat hot water bath to 120°F (48.9°C). Immerse pouch in preheated bath for 45 minutes before proceeding with Step 4.

▸ **Preheat hot water bath to 132°F (55.6°C)**
▸ **Sous vide pouch**

| | | |
|---|---|---|
| 1 | bone-in beef rib steak, 2½ inches (6 cm) thick | 1 |
| 3 tbsp | olive oil, divided | 45 mL |
| | Salt and freshly ground black pepper | |
| 1 | recipe Green Peppercorn Sauce (page 375) | 1 |

1. Brush steak with 1½ tbsp (22 mL) oil and lightly season to taste with salt and pepper.

2. Place steak in sous vide pouch and seal. Immerse in preheated hot water bath and cook for 5 hours. Remove pouch from bath. (To make ahead, see Tips, at left.)

3. Lower heat to 130°F (54.4°C) and continue cooking for an additional 3 to 4 hours.

4. Remove steak from pouch and pat dry with paper towels. Transfer to a plate and refrigerate for 40 minutes.

5. Meanwhile, preheat grill to Medium-High.

6. Brush steak with remaining oil and season to taste with salt and pepper.

7. Place on uncovered grill and cook until nicely browned, about 4 to 5 minutes per side. If you prefer to finish the steak indoors, use the torch method of browning (see page 27 for finishing techniques), as the steak may not fit into skillet.

8. Transfer steak to a cutting board and cut into ½-inch (1 cm) slices. Pass the green peppercorn sauce and fight over the bone!

# Prime Rib Roast

Once you have a few sous vide steak successes under your belt, give this beef roast a try. It's a great way to show off your new skills. The diameter of the roast must be less than 6 inches (15 cm) or it won't fit in a sous vide pouch. The length and weight of the roast can vary.

**MAKES 6 TO 12 SERVINGS**

Freezer Bag Friendly

## Tips

For roast beef, allow at least ½ lb (250 g) per person. For instance, 5 lbs (2.5 kg) will serve 8 to 10 people.

Starting the roast in the hot water bath at 190°F (87.8°C) will pasteurize the surface of the meat quickly and counteract the temperature drop that occurs when a cut of this size is added to the bath.

Larger roasts require longer resting and chilling.

Leftovers are delicious served cold and can be stored in the refrigerator for up to 4 days. If you want to reheat the roast, cut the cooled meat into pieces that weigh about 1½ lbs (750 g) or less. Seal in sous vide pouches or resealable freezer bags and refrigerate for up to 5 days. Preheat hot water bath to 125°F (51.7°C); reheat meat for 30 to 60 minutes, depending on its thickness.

► **Preheat hot water bath to 190°F (87.8°C)**
► **Sous vide pouch**

| 1 | boneless beef ribeye roast, up to 6 inches (15 cm) in diameter, well trimmed | 1 |
| | Olive oil | |
| | Salt and freshly ground black pepper | |
| 1 | recipe Béarnaise Sauce (page 333) or Chimichurri Sauce (page 370) | 1 |

1. Rub oil all over roast and lightly season to taste with salt and pepper.

2. Place in sous vide pouch and seal. Immerse in preheated hot water bath and reduce temperature to 134°F (56.5°C). Cook for 9 hours.

3. Remove pouch from hot water bath and let stand for 20 to 30 minutes. Remove roast from pouch and pat dry with paper towels. Transfer to a plate and season well with salt and pepper. (If desired, use a torch to brown roast and skip steps 4 and 5.)

4. Refrigerate roast for 20 to 30 minutes; the center of the meat should then be about room temperature. Meanwhile, preheat grill to Medium-High.

5. Place roast on well-greased grill and brown, turning, for about 20 minutes or until all sides are well marked.

6. Transfer roast to a cutting board and slice across the grain. Serve with desired sauce on warm plates.

---

### Why Not Rare?

A piece of meat of this size cannot be safely cooked to less than medium-rare — so do not reduce the cooking temperature. If you prefer your roast medium, in Step 2 set the hot water bath to 140°F (60°C) instead of 134°F (56.5°C).

# Beef Tenderloin with Vegetable Pot-au-Feu

This dish was a favorite at my restaurant Avalon, where I could never take it off the menu. It is my take on an Italian dish of poached beef tenderloin, made much simpler by using the sous vide machine. The meat is not browned, so it is cooked to medium-rare. The sauce is an ancient recipe called *pearà* in the Veronese dialect, typically served with *bollito misto*, or boiled meats.

---

| MAKES 4 SERVINGS |
|---|

## Tips

You can easily double this recipe. It is a terrific dish for dinner parties.

Peeled celery root and turnips can be added to (or substituted for) the other vegetables in the pot-au-feu. Celery root cooks fairly quickly, so cut it into slightly larger chunks than the other vegetables.

*To make the vegetables ahead:* Prepare to the end of Step 2. Refrigerate sealed pouches for 24 hours. Proceed with recipe, beginning at Step 6.

▷ **Preheat hot water bath to 190°F (87.8°C)**
▷ **3 sous vide pouches**

VEGETABLE POT-AU-FEU

| | | |
|---|---|---|
| 2 | carrots | 2 |
| 8 | pearl onions | 8 |
| 8 | Brussels sprouts, trimmed | 8 |
| 4 | baby yellow or candy cane beets, peeled and halved | 4 |
| ½ | bulb fennel, trimmed and quartered lengthwise | ½ |
| ¼ cup | butter, melted | 60 mL |
| | Salt and freshly ground black pepper | |
| 1 | beef tenderloin roast (1½ to 2 lbs/ 750 g to 1 kg), about 2½ inches (6 cm) in diameter | 1 |
| 2 tbsp | olive oil | 30 mL |
| | Salt and freshly ground black pepper | |
| 2½ cups | beef consommé (store-bought or homemade) | 625 mL |
| | Fleur de sel | |
| 1 | recipe Veronese Pepper and Breadcrumb Sauce (page 378) | 1 |

1. *Vegetable Pot-au-Feu:* Cut carrots into chunks a little larger than the pearl onions. In a large bowl, combine carrots, onions, Brussels sprouts, beets, fennel and butter. Toss to coat and season to taste with salt and pepper.

## Tips

The hot water bath can be cooled quickly in Step 3 by adding some cold water.

If you are lucky enough to have two sous vide machines, you can save time by setting one at the lower temperature for the meat and the second at the higher temperature for the vegetables. Cook the tenderloin while you prepare the vegetables. Just make sure you time the cooking of the vegetables so they will be ready at the same time as the beef.

I don't usually brown the beef for this dish, but you can if you like. The torch method of browning is best here (see page 27 for finishing techniques).

2. Spoon vegetable mixture into 2 sous vide pouches. Flatten each into a single layer and seal. Immerse in preheated hot water bath and cook for 1 hour. Transfer to an ice bath and chill for 30 minutes. (To make ahead, see Tips, page 44.)

3. Meanwhile, reduce temperature of hot water bath to 134°F (56.5°C). Too cool it quickly, add some cold water.

4. Brush roast with oil and lightly season to taste with salt and pepper.

5. Place roast in sous vide pouch and seal. Immerse in preheated water bath and cook for 3 hours.

6. Immerse vegetable pouches in hot water bath with roast. Cook for 30 minutes more.

7. Meanwhile, in a small saucepan over medium heat, bring consommé to a simmer.

8. Remove roast and vegetable pouches from hot water bath. Cut open pouches and distribute vegetables evenly among 4 large pasta bowls, mounding in the center. Transfer roast to a cutting board and slice into 4 medallions. Pat each dry with paper towels.

9. Place one medallion on top of vegetables in each bowl. Pour consommé around beef and vegetables. Garnish beef to taste with fleur de sel and serve immediately, passing sauce separately.

# Veal Tenderloin with Exotic Mushroom Sauce

Veal tenderloin is a splurge, but well worth it when paired with the nicest mushrooms you can afford. Foraged wild mushrooms are best (make sure you get an expert mycologist to identify them, because mistakes can be extremely dangerous). Store-bought oyster and shiitake mushrooms make a nice base to which you can add wild varieties such as chanterelles, morels or boletes, depending on the season and what's available. Spaetzle is my favorite accompaniment for this dish.

**MAKES 2 SERVINGS**

Freezer Bag Friendly

## Tips

If you prefer your veal more well-done, increase the water bath temperature to a maximum of 150°F (65.6°C). Also, you don't need to reduce the temperature in Step 3.

You can use any homemade meat stock in place of the beef broth (usually with better results). See the Appendix (page 399) for more information.

Unless they are sandy or very dirty, I never wash mushrooms. They are like little sponges, soaking up lots of water, which will keep them from cooking properly. In my kitchen I use a regular paintbrush that is reserved solely for brushing dirt from mushrooms.

▶ **Sous vide pouch**

| | | |
|---|---|---|
| 1 | veal tenderloin (10 to 12 oz/ 300 to 375 g) with uniform diameter of 2 to 2½ inches (5 to 6 cm) | 1 |
| | Salt | |
| 1 tbsp | olive oil | 15 mL |
| | Freshly ground black pepper | |
| 8 oz | mixed exotic mushrooms | 250 g |
| 3 tbsp | butter, divided | 45 mL |
| 1 | shallot, finely chopped | 1 |
| 1 | clove garlic, finely chopped | 1 |
| 1 cup | ready-to-use beef broth (see Tips, at left) | 250 mL |
| 4 | sprigs fresh thyme | 4 |
| 2 tbsp | Madeira (see Tips, at right) | 30 mL |
| 2 tbsp | chopped fresh parsley | 30 mL |
| | Fresh lemon juice, optional | |

1. Pat veal dry with paper towels. Season all sides generously with salt to taste. Place on a plate or wire rack set on a baking sheet or plate. Freeze for 15 to 30 minutes or until surface of veal becomes firm.

2. Preheat hot water bath to 144°F (62.2°C). Heat a large, heavy-bottomed skillet over high heat. Remove veal from freezer and pat dry with paper towels. Rub oil all over meat to coat. Place in skillet and sear, turning frequently, for 3 to 4 minutes or until browned on both sides. Set skillet aside. Transfer veal to a clean plate and freeze for 10 to 15 minutes or until cool.

Madeira adds amazing flavor to this sauce. If you can't find any, substitute red or white vermouth (or a mixture of the two) or port. Fortified wines are best used in small quantities and near the end of cooking, to preserve their delicate aroma and taste.

3. Season cooled veal with pepper to taste. Place in sous vide pouch and seal. Immerse in preheated hot water bath and cook for 30 minutes. Then reduce temperature to 142°F (61.1°C) and cook for 3 hours.

4. Meanwhile, brush any dirt from mushrooms; trim off stems and woody parts (see Tip, page 46). Slice mushrooms. Set aside.

5. In the skillet, over medium-high heat, melt 2 tbsp (30 mL) butter. When foam subsides, add mushrooms and cook until wilted and starting to release their moisture, about 5 minutes. Add shallot and garlic and cook, stirring often, for about 1 minute. Add broth and thyme; increase heat to high. Boil, stirring occasionally, until almost no liquid remains. Remove from heat.

6. Remove pouch from hot water bath. Open pouch and pour any accumulated liquid into mushroom mixture; stir to combine. Transfer veal to a cutting board. Cover with foil and a folded kitchen towel to keep warm.

7. Remove thyme from mushroom mixture. Over medium heat, return to a simmer. Stir in Madeira and simmer for 1 minute. Turn off burner. Stir remaining butter into sauce until it is incorporated and sauce is glossy. Season to taste with salt and pepper. Stir in parsley and add a few drops lemon juice, if desired.

8. Cut veal across the grain into 6 to 8 slices. Arrange on warm plates and serve with mushroom sauce.

# Veal Chops with Onion and Black Olive Sauce

Veal chops are exquisite, expensive and — normally — hard to cook properly. However, the sous vide technique yields perfect results every time. The accompanying sauce is an especially excellent one. It pairs nicely with the veal chops, can be frozen, and is delicious with a number of different meats.

## Tips

This recipe can easily be adapted for the number of guests you have, allowing one chop per person.

You can let the chops sit in the hot water bath for up to 90 minutes after they are cooked. This extra time will also pasteurize the meat.

If you prefer your veal chops more well-done, increase the water bath temperature to a maximum of 150°F (65.6°C).

▶ **2 sous vide pouches**

| | | |
|---|---|---|
| 2 | bone-in veal loin chops, each 1½ inches (4 cm) thick | 2 |
| | Salt | |
| 2 tbsp | olive oil | 30 mL |
| | Freshly ground black pepper | |
| 6 tbsp | Onion and Black Olive Sauce (page 380) | 90 mL |

1. Pat chops dry with paper towels. Oil and season both sides generously with salt to taste. Place on a plate or wire rack set on a baking sheet or plate. Freeze for 15 to 30 minutes or until surface of chops just becomes firm.

2. Meanwhile, preheat hot water bath to 142°F (61.1°C). Then preheat grill to High or heat a heavy-bottomed skillet over high heat.

3. Remove chops from freezer and pat dry with paper towels. Place on grill or in skillet and sear for 1 to 2 minutes per side or just until browned. Place chops on a clean plate and freeze for 10 to 15 minutes or until cool.

4. Season chops to taste with pepper. Place each in a separate sous vide pouch and seal. Immerse in preheated hot water bath and cook for 3 hours.

5. Meanwhile, in a small saucepan, gently warm sauce.

6. Remove pouches from hot water bath. Open pouches and pour any accumulated liquid into sauce; stir to combine.

7. Arrange chops on warm plates. Serve with sauce.

# Grilled Lamb Chops with Pistachio Mint Pesto

Preparing lamb chops sous vide yields perfect results. By cooking them as part of a whole rack first, you can focus on browning them beautifully right before it's time to eat. The pesto is at its most flavorful when you let it come to room temperature before serving.

---

| MAKES |
|:-----:|
| **MAKES 4 SERVINGS** |

Freezer Bag Friendly

## Tips

You can easily halve or double this recipe.

The racks are cooked at a slightly lower temperature than the one I usually recommend, because the chops will cook a bit more while browning. If you like your chops cooked to more than medium-rare, increase the browning time to 3 to 4 minutes per side.

*To make ahead:* Prepare up to the end of Step 3. Refrigerate sealed pouches for up to 1 week or freeze for up to 6 months. Proceed with Step 4.

▶ **Preheat hot water bath to 133°F (56.1°C)**
▶ **2 or 3 sous vide pouches**

| | | |
|---|---|---|
| 2 or 3 | 7- to 8-bone lamb racks | 2 or 3 |
| ¼ cup | olive oil, divided | 60 mL |
| | Salt and freshly ground black pepper | |
| 1 | recipe Pistachio Mint Pesto (page 369) | 1 |

1. Using a sharp knife, trim all but a thin layer of fat from the racks. Rub 2 tbsp (30 mL) oil all over racks to coat.

2. Place each rack in a separate sous vide pouch and seal. Immerse in preheated hot water bath and cook for 2 hours.

3. Remove pouches from hot water bath. Transfer to an ice bath and chill for 1 hour. (To make ahead, see Tips, at left.)

4. Preheat grill to High or heat a heavy-bottomed skillet over high heat.

5. Open pouches and slice racks into chops (each rack should yield 6 or 7 chops). Rub chops all over with remaining oil and season well with salt and pepper.

6. Place chops on grill or in skillet and sear for about 90 seconds per side or until just browned. Arrange chops on warm plates. Serve with pesto on the side.

# Herb-Crusted Lamb Racks

Lamb racks with an herbed breadcrumb crust are always popular and look impressive. Cooking the lamb sous vide takes some of the guesswork out of creating perfect tender, juicy meat. Since you are pulling out all the stops, why not serve Carrots with Orange and Ginger (page 310), Okra with Preserved Lemon (page 308), Saffron Cauliflower with Sultanas (page 309) or Barigoule of Artichokes (page 316) as an accompaniment, depending on the season.

---

**MAKES
4 SERVINGS**

Freezer Bag Friendly

## Tips

You can easily double this recipe, but make sure the lamb racks aren't crowded in the roasting pan. A good trick is to interlock the bones the way you interlock your fingers. This will prop up the racks and they'll take up less space in the pan.

Use a rasp grater for Parmesan cheese. This tool, originally made for woodworking, has been used in restaurant kitchens for about 20 years. It is extremely sharp and fantastic for grating hard cheeses to fluffy, airy goodness. Microplane is a well-known brand.

▸ **Preheat hot water bath to 139°F (59.4°C)**
▸ **2 or 3 sous vide pouches**
▸ **Food processor**

| | | |
|---|---|---|
| 2 or 3 | 7- to 8-bone lamb racks, frenched (see box, at right) | 2 or 3 |
| 2 tbsp | Garlic Oil (page 363) | 30 mL |
| 3 tbsp | Dijon mustard | 45 mL |
| 2 tbsp | liquid honey | 30 mL |
| | Salt and freshly ground black pepper | |

### HERBED CRUMB CRUST

| | | |
|---|---|---|
| 1 cup | fine dry bread crumbs | 250 mL |
| 1 cup | lightly packed grated Parmesan cheese (see Tips, at left) | 250 mL |
| 3 tbsp | finely chopped flat-leaf (Italian) parsley | 45 mL |
| 1 tbsp | finely chopped fresh rosemary | 15 mL |
| 2 tsp | freshly ground black pepper | 10 mL |
| ¼ cup | Garlic Oil | 60 mL |

1. Using a sharp knife, trim all but a thin layer of fat from racks. Rub garlic oil all over racks to coat.

2. Place each rack in a separate sous vide pouch and seal. Immerse in preheated hot water bath and cook for 2 hours.

3. *Herbed Crumb Crust:* Meanwhile, in food processor fitted with the metal blade, combine bread crumbs, cheese, parsley, rosemary and pepper. With motor running, slowly drizzle garlic oil through feed tube to make a sandy paste. Transfer to a bowl and set aside.

*To make ahead:* Prepare to the end of Step 2, then complete Step 5. Refrigerate the sealed pouches for up to 1 week. Proceed with Steps 3 and 4, then complete Steps 6 through 10.

4. In a small bowl, using a fork, mix together mustard and honey until combined. Set aside.

5. Remove pouches from hot water bath. Transfer to an ice bath and chill for 1 hour. (To make ahead, see Tip, at left.)

6. Meanwhile, preheat oven to 275°F (140°C).

7. Remove racks from pouches and pat dry with paper towels. Rub mustard mixture over fat side of racks until well coated. Press handfuls of crumb crust mixture into mustard mixture to adhere. Tap racks lightly to remove any excess.

8. Arrange racks in a roasting pan or on a baking sheet, crust side up and spaced apart. Bake in preheated oven for 40 minutes or until warmed through.

9. Broil lamb for 2 to 4 minutes until crust is browned. (Alternatively, brown with a torch.)

10. Transfer racks to a cutting board and let stand for 3 to 4 minutes. Slice into chops (each rack should yield 6 or 7 chops). Season to taste with salt and pepper and serve on warm plates.

### Frenching

"Frenching" is a butchery term for removing the meat, sinew and fat from the tip of a bone (usually in a rack or a chop) to make it more attractive. This is optional but does make a nice presentation. You can ask your butcher to do it for you or you can do it yourself. For excellent instructions, I recommend that you pick up a copy of *The Zwilling J.A. Henckels Complete Book of Knife Skills*, by Jeffrey Elliot and James P. DeWan.

# Lamb Loin with Merguez

This is a fancy dish that's well suited to entertaining. The lamb loin, located just behind the rack, is equally tender but a bit leaner. Serve with a brown rice pilaf.

## Tips

Have your butcher remove the loins from the saddle.

You can easily double this recipe. The sauce recipe makes enough for 6 servings. To use up a whole batch, I suggest making 1½ times the lamb called for (2¼ lbs/2.125 kg).

▶ **Preheat water bath to 139°F (59.4°C)**
▶ **Sous vide pouch**

| | | |
|---|---|---|
| 1 | recipe Egg and Lemon Sauce (page 334), in sous vide pouch, chilled | 1 |
| 1½ lbs | boneless lamb loin, preferably in 4 pieces | 750 g |
| 1 tbsp | olive oil | 15 mL |
| | Salt and freshly ground black pepper | |
| 4 | large Swiss chard leaves, stems removed | 4 |
| 4 oz | merguez sausage, casings removed | 125 g |

1. Trim lamb to remove all surface fat and sinew. Rub oil all over meat to coat; season to taste with salt and pepper. Place in freezer for about 20 minutes, until surface just starts to stiffen and freeze.

2. In a medium skillet over medium-high heat, sear lamb, turning often, for 2 to 3 minutes or until lightly browned. Transfer to a plate and refrigerate for 20 minutes or until chilled.

3. Meanwhile, in a large pot of boiling salted water, blanch Swiss chard leaves for 1 minute. Transfer to an ice-water bath and let cool.

4. In a small bowl, knead sausage meat until smooth and pliable. Divide into equal portions and press evenly onto one side of each piece of lamb. Season lightly with salt and pepper.

5. Drain Swiss chard and pat dry with paper towels. Wrap around each piece of lamb (if you have 2 pieces of loin, wrap each individually with half of the Swiss chard). Place meat in sous vide pouch in one layer and seal.

If you are lucky enough to have two sous vide machines, you can save time by setting one at the temperature for the lamb and the second at the temperature for the sauce. That way everything will be ready at the same time.

6. Immerse lamb pouch and cook for 1 hour. Add sauce pouch and cook for 30 minutes more (see Tip, at left).

7. Remove pouches from hot water bath. Remove lamb from pouch and cut into 1-inch (2.5 cm) slices. Arrange slices on warm plates and serve with sauce.

### Merguez Sausage

Merguez is a spicy North African lamb sausage. If you can't get any, substitute hot Italian sausage for a slightly different effect.

# Venison Loin Steaks with Juniper Butter and Wilted Kale

Venison loin steaks are also known as venison strip loin or New York steaks. Have your butcher trim them so there is no fat or membrane covering them. Juniper is a terrific seasoning for game meats that complements their big, rich flavor. The kale allows you to capture the goodness of the juices that accumulate in the venison pouches. I like to serve these steaks with a somewhat sweet side dish such as spiced pears or roasted winter squash.

---

| MAKES 2 SERVINGS |
|---|

Freezer Bag Friendly

## Tips

This recipe can easily be adapted to the number of guests you have, allowing one steak per person.

Almost any green can be substituted for the kale. I also like to use mizuna in this recipe. If using mizuna or baby kale, reduce the wilting time to 1½ to 2 minutes.

▶ **Preheat hot water bath to 132°F (55.6°C)**
▶ **2 sous vide pouches**

| | | |
|---|---|---|
| 2 | venison loin steaks, each 1 to 1½ inches (2.5 to 4 cm) thick | 2 |
| 2 tbsp | olive oil, divided | 30 mL |
| | Salt and freshly ground black pepper | |
| 1 tsp | finely chopped garlic | 5 mL |
| 4 cups | stemmed, chopped kale | 1 L |
| 1 tsp | soy sauce | 5 mL |
| ¼ cup | Juniper Butter (page 366) | 60 mL |

1. Trim steaks, removing all sinews. Pat dry with paper towels. Brush with 1 tbsp (15 mL) oil and season lightly with salt and pepper.

2. Place steaks in separate sous vide pouches and seal. Immerse in preheated hot water bath and cook for 1½ hours.

3. Remove pouches from hot water bath. Reserving liquid, remove steaks from pouches and place on a warm plate. Set aside until ready to use. If using a grill, preheat to High.

4. Pour liquid from pouches into a medium skillet. Place skillet over medium heat, add garlic and bring to a simmer (there won't be much liquid, so watch carefully to keep the garlic from burning). Add kale and raise heat to medium-high. Cook, stirring and adding a little water if necessary to prevent sticking, for 2 to 3 minutes or until kale starts to wilt. Stir in soy sauce. Season to taste with pepper.

## Tips

If you prefer your venison more well-done, adjust the temperature of the hot water bath to correspond with your preferred doneness for steak, using the Beef Steak Cooking Times chart on page 35. Ignore the cooking time in the steak chart, however, and use the time specified in this recipe.

You can also use a torch to brown the steaks, if you prefer. If you do, you will not need to brush them with the remaining olive oil.

**5.** If using, heat a heavy-bottomed skillet over high heat. Pat steaks dry with paper towels and brush on remaining oil. Place steaks on preheated grill or in skillet; sear for 1 to 2 minutes per side or just until browned (see Tips, at left). Season to taste with salt and pepper.

**6.** Arrange steaks on warm plates. Serve with kale and top with juniper butter.

---

### Denuding

"Denuding" is a butchery term for trimming meat of all fat and gristle and any surface membrane. Commercial venison frequently comes that way. If yours doesn't, ask your butcher to do this step for you.

---

### Timing the Venison

You can leave the steaks in the hot water bath for up to 90 minutes after they are cooked. This extra time will also pasteurize the meat.

# Venison Loin with Savoy Cabbage and Chestnuts

I consider the loin the best cut of venison, and my preference is for red deer because they are larger and more flavorful than fallow deer. Although cabbage may sound like a pedestrian side dish, trust me — with the chestnuts, the whole is much greater than the sum of its parts. You will need to manage your time and sous vide resources carefully to make these two dishes for the same meal.

**MAKES
4 SERVINGS**

Freezer Bag Friendly

## Tips

You can easily halve or double this recipe. If you double the recipe, make a double batch of the cabbage too.

If you prefer your venison more well-done, brown for longer in Step 4 or adjust the temperature to correspond with your preferred doneness for steak. (Use the Beef Steak Cooking Times chart on page 35). Ignore the cooking time in the steak chart, however, and use the time specified in this recipe.

You can let the roast sit in the hot water bath for up to 2 hours after it is cooked. This extra time will also pasteurize it.

You can also use a torch to brown the venison, if you prefer. Do not brush with the remaining oil.

▶ **Preheat hot water bath to 130°F (54.4°C)**
▶ **Sous vide pouch**

| | | |
|---|---|---|
| 1 | recipe Savoy Cabbage with Chestnuts (page 296) | 1 |
| 1 | whole denuded boneless venison loin roast (1 to 1¼ lbs/ 500 to 625 g; see box, page 55) | 1 |
| 3 tbsp | olive oil, divided | 45 mL |
| | Salt and freshly ground black pepper | |

1. Pat roast dry with paper towels. Brush 1½ tbsp (22 mL) oil over meat to coat; season lightly with salt and pepper.

2. Place meat in sous vide pouch and seal. Immerse pouch in hot water bath and cook for 2 hours.

3. Remove pouch from water bath. Remove roast from pouch and transfer to a warm plate. Let stand for 20 to 30 minutes.

4. To finish venison, preheat grill to High or heat a heavy-bottomed skillet over high heat. Pat roast dry with paper towels and brush with remaining oil. Place on grill or in skillet and sear for 1 to 2 minutes per side or just until browned. Season lightly with salt and pepper.

5. Slice roast crosswise into ½-inch (1 cm) slices and serve with Savoy Cabbage and Chestnuts.

# Beef, Veal, Lamb and Venison: The Tough Cuts

# Beef, Veal, Lamb and Venison: The Tough Cuts

The tougher cuts from the quadrupeds that we eat are the hardworking muscles. They tend to be at the extremities or closer to the ground: necks, shoulders, shanks and legs. The toughness comes from the muscle fibers and the connective tissue surrounding them. We tend to braise or stew these cuts. Cooking these muscles slowly over long periods of time tenderizes the meat while simultaneously allowing the surrounding connective tissues to dissolve into gelatin. The gelatin adds body texture to the cooking liquid. These methods are considered "moist heat" as opposed to the "dry heat" techniques of grilling, pan-frying or even deep-frying.

The temperature of moist-heat methods cannot go above the boiling point of the surrounding liquid, which is roughly the same as the boiling point of water. Any chef will tell you that the best results are achieved at a temperature somewhat below a boil. Using sous vide, we can control this temperature precisely and keep it in the optimal range for these cuts.

## Cooler Is Better

A simmer, which happens just below the boiling point, is classically the temperature at which one braises or stews. It is an effective method to tenderize tougher cuts. However, lower temperatures, like the ones we can employ in a sous vide machine, yield better results. You can cook these meats for extended periods and don't need to go as high as you would in a traditional stew or braise.

As the cooking temperature rises and the internal temperature of a cut increases, juices within the meat are squeezed out of the muscle fibers. The higher the temperature, the more juice is squeezed out. Cooking tough cuts sous vide delivers maximum tenderness and juiciness, which traditional methods don't often deliver. In fact, boiled beef (a favorite of mine) should never really boil; it should simmer slowly to preserve those juices. An even smarter strategy is to make a flavorful broth (using conventional methods) from the bones, meat trimmings and vegetables (see page 401) while cooking the meat sous vide. Once they are both cooked and seasoned, they can be united just before serving.

## Cooking Temperatures for Tough Cuts

Shoulders and shanks consist of lots of small muscles and are full of connective tissue. This tissue binds one muscle to another and attaches them to the bones. Retail cuts from the shoulder, such as blade or chuck steaks and roasts, are frequently composed of more than one muscle. The collagen in their connective tissues requires a temperature of at least 158°F (70°C) before it turns into gelatin. This conversion serves two purposes: it makes the texture less resilient and it lubricates the surrounding meat. This lubrication is the familiar stickiness that you experience when you eat a braised lamb shank. The meat will become crumbly and shreddable at higher temperatures; though it can be useful for tacos and some other preparations, this result is not generally desirable.

Tough cuts without connective tissue, such as beef flank, become tender at temperatures as low as 130°F (54.4°C), so you can enjoy them rare to medium-rare. The hind of beef is made up of large muscles that are butchered and sold individually, such as eye of round and the inside and outside round. These can, therefore, be treated much the same as beef flank.

Lamb and veal need at least 140°F (60°C) for a savory result. The harder-working muscles of the shoulders and shanks need temperatures as high as 158°C (70°C) to dissolve the collagen. The same applies to venison shoulders and shanks, though the legs, of farmed venison in particular, can be cooked to rare, like beef steaks.

## The Basics

The tough cuts have been grouped together because the procedures for cooking them sous vide are similar. In each recipe I give you specific guidelines and suggestions for the cut called for in the ingredient list. Accompanying the recipes are pieces of general information on these cuts and some helpful tips on selecting, preparing and cooking them.

## Selecting

As a chef, I like to make the most of inexpensive cuts, and sous vide helps make that possible. These cuts frequently come from shoulders, shanks and necks, and cooking the meat low and slow means you don't have to worry about it drying out. The fat can be left on the meat, basting it in its pouch as it cooks. Remember, the flavor in fat is water-soluble, so I don't throw it out.

Many of the cuts in this chapter are available frozen. This is generally fine, but select those that have been professionally frozen and sealed in tight-fitting plastic pouches. Defrost in the refrigerator overnight (larger cuts can take even longer) and then proceed with the recipe (see "Reheating Frozen Meat," page 61).

Cuts of beef, veal and lamb are considered sterile internally unless mechanically tenderized. Since the meat in this chapter is cooked for lengthy periods of time, both pasteurizing the meat and making it tender, it does not need to be pierced, since that would encourage the loss of valuable juices. So it's best to avoid mechanically tenderized cuts for sous vide cooking.

## Prepping: Salting and Browning

I generally like to salt meats early in the cooking process. However, because of the extended times used in sous vide cooking, this can create a cured quality if the meat is cooked for more than about 18 hours. Unless you want this characteristic (in corned beef, for example), I suggest that you salt after the sous vide stage or only very minimally before.

As mentioned in the previous chapter (see "The Maillard Reaction," page 34), browned meat tastes good. If you're planning to brown the meat, you have a choice of whether to brown it before, after or both. Browning before cooking sous vide has two advantages: (1) raw meat is more supple and therefore easier to brown properly than precooked meat, and (2) browning early leads to a more pronounced flavor in the final dish. If you are making a beef stew such as Beef Cheek Goulash (page 105), you will need to brown the cheeks before cooking. Browning first also streamlines portioning and serving at mealtime.

Occasionally you may want to build additional flavor by browning both before and after cooking, such as in Blade Steak with Ancho Chile and Orange (page 76).

## Sealing

If your recipe has liquid in it, its probably easier to use resealable freezer bags rather than a home sealer. If you have a chamber vacuum sealer, you will likely be using it for all your sous vide cooking. If you are cooking meat sous vide without liquid, consider coating it with olive oil or vegetable oil before sealing. This will help with heat transfer from the hot water bath and help the bag or pouch stick to the meat.

## Cooking

In sous vide cookbooks, the tough-cut recipes are often where you will see the greatest variance in cooking times and temperatures between authors. As with any other type of cooking, you can achieve good (though different) results using different methods. I have tried hundreds of combinations of times and temperatures, and the ones you'll see in this chapter work well and result in the textures that I prefer.

I have found extended cooking times for very bony cuts, such as oxtail, result in off flavors. I don't recommend cooking for more than 36 hours, so adjust the temperature accordingly. I incorporate a higher temperature in these recipes to get the meat cooked within this time.

With sous vide, you can cook meat from frozen. It is a little tricky to determine the cooking time, but adding one hour to the original time is a good general rule. Freezing cooked meat and using the sous vide equipment to reheat it is a better option, as there is less moisture in cooked meat to turn to ice crystals and damage it.

---

### REHEATING FROZEN MEAT

Your sous vide device is a great tool for reheating frozen meats that you have already cooked in airtight pouches using the sous vide technique. To prep, preheat your hot water bath to 130°F (54.4°C) or a temperature that does not exceed the original cooking temperature of the meat. Immerse the frozen meat and allow 60 to 70 minutes per inch (2.5 cm) of thickness to come to serving temperature.

---

## Resting

As the cooking temperature rises and the internal temperature of these tough cuts increases, juices within the meat are squeezed out of the muscle fibers. The higher the temperature, the more juice is released and the drier the meat will be. Luckily, the highest temperature that you will need to set your sous vide machine to is 172°F (77.8°C). This temperature will soften the cuts that are full of connective tissue and break down meats that you want to serve shredded. (This is still 40°F/22.2°C below boiling, which is where traditional braises and stews cook.) Some of the liquid expelled by the meat will reabsorb if given a chance. It is best to allow meats cooked at these higher temperatures to cool in their pouches at room temperature for 30 to 60 minutes before chilling. If serving immediately, let the meat rest for at least 20 to 30 minutes in a warm place, such as beside the stove, on top of your sous vide device or in a warm turned-off oven, while you prepare the rest of the meal.

## CHECK THE JUICES

You can tell quite a bit about the nature of what you've cooked by looking at the juices in the pouch. Remember that they used to be in the meat, so this is juice you've lost. Some loss is inevitable and expected, but if there is quite a bit and your meat seems dry, try lowering the cooking temperature next time. If the liquid in the pouch is firm after you've chilled it in the fridge, this means that the juices are gelatinous and that connective tissue turned to gelatin during cooking, which is good. If the liquid feels soft and looks watery, then there was no gelatin, which means you don't have to use a temperature high enough to convert collagen.

# Beef Ribs: S, M, L and XL

Beef ribs are sold in a variety of sizes. They come from several primal cuts of the steer and are butchered in different ways. Cooks who own sous vide equipment adore short ribs, and rightly so — they turn out perfectly with long, slow cooking.

There is quite a bit of controversy in sous vide circles regarding the best times and temperatures for cooking short ribs. Some recipes call for temperatures as low as 130°F (54.4°C). The meat itself may be tender but the collagen will still be intact, and you also run the risk of off odors due to extended cooking times. (The collagen contained in short ribs won't all dissolve and turn into gelatin below about 158°F/70°C, which is important, because that gives the ribs a sticky texture.) Since short ribs are very forgiving, you can raise the temperature to 185°F (85°C). Your ribs will cook in half the time and still be juicier than if you had cooked them in the oven.

One thing to keep in mind is that, as short ribs cook, the meat shrinks and pulls away from the bone. This makes browning them in a skillet difficult after cooking them sous vide. If you plan to serve the ribs with a sauce in a traditional braise-like fashion, brown them before you cook them sous vide. If you want to reheat the cooked ribs under a broiler or on a grill, brush them with a little bit of a strongly flavored glaze or barbecue sauce before they hit the heat, and again partway through this finishing step.

# Miami Ribs

Miami ribs, also known by their Korean name *kalbi* (or *galbi*), are short ribs that are sliced thinly across the bones and then marinated and grilled. The marinade is supposed to tenderize the meat (and it likely would if left to stand long enough). Here I've suggested a shortcut. We'll cook the ribs in the marinade, which both saves time and guarantees that the ribs will be wonderfully tender.

## Tips

You can easily double or triple this recipe.

*To make ahead:* Prepare through Step 3. Refrigerate sealed bag for up to 7 days or freeze for up to 6 months (if transferred to a well-sealed pouch). To use frozen ribs, thaw overnight in the refrigerator. To reheat from refrigerator temperature, proceed with Step 4, adding 1 minute to each side during browning.

A torch is an effective tool for browning the ribs very quickly without overcooking them. Make sure the ribs are at room temperature if you're using this method (see page 27 for finishing techniques).

▶ **Preheat hot water bath to 158°F (70°C)**
▶ **Large resealable freezer bag**

| | | |
|---|---|---|
| ¼ cup | soy sauce | 60 mL |
| ¼ cup | light (fancy) molasses | 60 mL |
| ¼ cup | sake or dry sherry | 60 mL |
| 1½ tbsp | unseasoned rice vinegar | 22 mL |
| 1 tbsp | finely chopped garlic | 15 mL |
| 1 tbsp | grated fresh gingerroot | 15 mL |
| 1 tsp | freshly ground black pepper | 5 mL |
| 1½ lbs | ⅜-inch (9 mm) butterflied beef short ribs | 675 g |
| 1 tsp | sesame oil | 5 mL |

1. In a heatproof glass measuring cup, stir together soy sauce, molasses, sake and vinegar. Microwave on High for about 1½ minutes or until boiling. Stir in garlic, ginger and pepper. Let cool completely.

2. Place ribs in a large bowl, add soy sauce mixture and toss to coat. Place ribs and liquid in freezer bag. Line up ribs as much as possible so that no more than two are overlapping and none are folded over themselves. (This ensures even cooking and makes the cooked ribs easier to flatten.) Seal bag. Immerse in preheated water bath and cook for 8 to 10 hours.

3. Remove bag from hot water bath and let stand at room temperature for 30 minutes. Open bag and place ribs in a colander, discarding liquid in bag (or, if desired, reserve it to brush on a batch of barbecued short ribs). Pat ribs dry with paper towels and return to bag. Seal bag, transfer to an ice bath and chill for 30 minutes.

4. Preheat grill to High or preheat broiler. Place ribs on grill or on a baking sheet under broiler. Grill or broil, turning once, until heated through and lightly browned, about 2 minutes per side. Serve on warm plates.

# Short Ribs Bourguignon

Purchasing precut "stewing beef" for beef bourguignon can often lead to unreliable results because you don't know the exact cut of meat that you're buying. I much prefer to prepare it myself so I know what's going into my meal. This recipe is perfect for cold weather — I like to serve it with roasted root vegetables or mashed potatoes, which soak up the rich wine-based sauce.

---

**MAKES
4 SERVINGS**

Freezer Bag Friendly

## Tips

You can easily halve or double this recipe.

Ask your butcher for brisket short ribs. They are more evenly shaped than those from the chuck.

If you increase the temperature of your hot water bath to 185°F (85°C), your ribs will be finished in half the time but will be a little drier.

You can skip the browning in Step 1 and begin at Step 2 if you prefer. Your ribs will taste a little more like boiled beef, which I like.

▶ **Preheat hot water bath to 158°F (70°C)**
▶ **2 sous vide pouches**
▶ **Large resealable freezer bag**

| | | |
|---|---|---|
| 3 tbsp | vegetable or olive oil | 45 mL |
| 4 | pieces beef short ribs (about 3 lbs/1.35 kg total) | 4 |
| 1 | recipe Base Sauce for Coq au Vin, Beef Bourguignon, Lamb Shanks and Short Ribs (page 364), chilled | 1 |
| | Salt and freshly ground black pepper | |

1. In a large skillet, heat oil over medium-high heat. Meanwhile, pat ribs dry with paper towels. Brown well, in batches if necessary, about 8 to 10 minutes per batch. As completed, transfer to a plate lined with paper towels and let cool.

2. Place 2 rib pieces in each sous vide pouch. Seal pouches. Immerse in preheated hot water bath and cook for 20 to 24 hours.

3. Remove pouches from water bath and let stand at room temperature for 30 minutes. (To make ahead, see Tips, at right.)

4. Meanwhile, reduce temperature of hot water bath to 130°F (54.4°C; see Tips, at right). Open pouches and transfer contents, with sauce, to freezer bag. Seal, immerse and reheat for 30 to 40 minutes.

5. Open bag and transfer ribs to warm plates. Season sauce to taste with salt and pepper, if necessary. Pour over ribs.

## Tips

The hot water bath can be cooled quickly in Step 4 by adding some cold water.

*To make ahead:* Prepare through Step 3. Transfer to an ice bath and chill for 20 minutes. Refrigerate sealed pouches for up to 7 days or freeze for up to 6 months. To use frozen ribs, thaw overnight in the refrigerator. To reheat from refrigerator temperature, proceed with Step 4.

## Variation

**BBQ Short Ribs:** Omit the Base Sauce and cook ribs as directed in Steps 2 and 3. Preheat grill to Medium or preheat broiler. Open pouches and pat cooked ribs dry with paper towels. Brush with your favorite barbecue sauce or leftover cooking liquid from Miami Ribs (page 63) or Drunken Oxtail (page 107). Place on preheated grill or on a baking sheet under broiler. Grill or broil, brushing with more sauce as necessary, for 10 to 15 minutes or until glazed and lightly browned.

### Weeknight Ribs

If you don't want to make the sauce, season the ribs well and serve them with prepared horseradish, mashed potatoes and a salad. Start one day ahead and you'll have a delicious, easy weeknight meal.

# Postmodern Dinosaur Bones

In this recipe we'll extract the ribeye from a whole beef rib roast, then "glue" the rib cap to the bones, using an enzyme. The newly assembled meat is cooked sous vide until tender and then glazed with barbecue sauce, either in the oven or on the grill. You'll end up with beef ribs that have four times more collagen-rich meat than usual, a marvel for your taste buds. Serve with coleslaw and beer.

---

**MAKES 4 TO 6 LARGE SERVINGS**

Advanced

## Tips

This recipe is infinitely variable in quantity. The only constraint is the capacity of your hot water bath.

Select a full 7-bone rib roast that has a large cap. An obliging butcher might be willing to do the roast prep that's outlined in Step 1, or even buy back the more valuable ribeye portion of the roast. If not, however, you'll have 7 nice ribeye steaks or a boneless roast to cook another time.

▶ **Preheat hot water bath to 158°F (70°C)**
▶ **1 or 2 sous vide pouches**
▶ **Small fine-mesh sieve**

| | | |
|---|---|---|
| 1 | 7-bone beef prime rib roast (see Tips, at left) | 1 |
| 2 tbsp | Activa RM (see box, at right) | 30 mL |
| 1 cup | barbecue sauce (approx.; see Tips, at right) | 250 mL |

1. Using a sharp, firm slicing or carving knife, remove cap of roast in one piece. Set aside. Making short strokes and cutting down the length of the bones, cut off entire ribeye portion of roast in one piece; set aside for another use (see Tips, at left). You will end up with the cap and a set of 7 bones that resembles a giant rack of spareribs.

2. Place bones on a cutting board, cut side up. Position cap, cut side down, on the rack (it will probably extend across 4 bones). Line up cap over the meatiest bones. Cut away remaining bones and reserve for another use (or cook them alongside this recipe).

3. Spoon Activa RM into fine-mesh sieve. Lift cap from bones to expose both cut sides. Using about 1 tbsp (15 mL) Activa for each, sprinkle evenly over cut sides of cap and bones where the two surfaces will adhere. Replace cap on bones and press surfaces together. Wrap tightly in plastic wrap and refrigerate overnight or for up to 24 hours. (If you have a vacuum chamber sealer, seal wrapped roast in a pouch to squeeze the two pieces together more firmly. Then proceed to Step 5.)

## Tips

For this recipe I prefer tonkatsu sauce, a Japanese barbecue sauce that is typically used for fried pork cutlets. It is fruity and acidic and not as sweet as American-style barbecue sauces. Bull-Dog is a very good and widely available brand. If you like, a quick Internet search will find you a number of homemade versions that you can make without too many ingredients.

*To make ahead:* Prepare through Step 6. The beef will keep for up to 10 days in the refrigerator or in the freezer for up to 6 months in well-sealed pouches. To use frozen roast, thaw overnight in the refrigerator. To reheat from refrigerator temperature, proceed with Step 7.

A convection oven is ideal for glazing the ribs with barbecue sauce. Reduce the oven temperature by 50°F (28°C) and watch carefully, as the circulating hot air cooks food a bit more quickly.

4. Remove meat from refrigerator and check to see if it will fit in a single sous vide pouch and the hot water bath. If it is too large, slice through the plastic wrap between the middle bones to create two 2-bone roasts. Place in sous vide pouch(es) and seal.

5. Immerse pouch(es) in preheated hot water bath and cook for 24 hours.

6. Remove pouch(es) and transfer to an ice bath. Chill for 1 hour. (To make ahead, see Tips, at left.)

7. Open pouch(es) and remove roast(s). Rinse under warm water to remove rendered fat and gelatinized juices. Pat dry with paper towels. Slice between ribs, creating four 1-bone portions. Preheat oven to 400°F (200°C) or grill to Medium (see Tips, at left). Brush ribs liberally with barbecue sauce.

8. Place ribs on a baking sheet and roast (or grill on preheated barbecue), turning and brushing occasionally with additional barbecue sauce, for 15 to 20 minutes or until glazed and lightly caramelized. Transfer to warm plates. Serve immediately.

### Activa RM

A few of the recipes in this book call for transglutaminase, an enzyme that binds proteins together. The culinary vanguard has been using it for about 20 years. It goes by the brand name Activa RM, though restaurant kitchens usually call it "meat glue." It is available online at Modernist Pantry (www.modernistpantry.com). There are several versions designed for specific uses, but RM is commonly available and the most versatile. Read the instructions before use and try to avoid inhaling the powder as you sprinkle it. Buy Activa RM in small quantities. Seal any leftover powder in the original packaging inside a sous vide pouch and store in the freezer. Use opened packages within 2 months to ensure that the powder is at its peak effectiveness.

# Beef Flank, Skirt and Hanger Steaks

Beef flank steak has great flavor and is very lean. Since it is less than 1 inch (2.5 cm) thick, it is not what most people think of as steak. There isn't a large amount of it on a steer but it is usually easy to find and the price is moderate, considering that it has a 100% yield. When cooked traditionally, it has to be carefully sliced across the grain; otherwise it is quite tough. With sous vide, you can tenderize flank with a low temperature for a fairly long time. Because of its long, flat shape, cultures all over the world have taken to stuffing flank steak — a good way to make the meat go a long way. Here I have included a favorite of mine from Argentina.

Skirt and hanger steaks are part of the cow's diaphragm muscle. They can be treated like flank, even though they are about half as thick. Popular in Mexican cuisine and in the southwestern United States (think arracheras or fajitas), these cuts have a finer flavor and are about the same price, but they can be difficult to find. Call your butcher to confirm availability.

# Matambre

Matambre is an Argentinean favorite commonly made with flank steak, but I use skirt steak instead. The name is a combination of the Spanish words *mata* ("kill") and *hambre* ("hunger"). In this recipe the ingredients are rolled up inside the meat like a jelly roll, creating a scrumptious and unique dish. Serve hot or cold.

---

| MAKES |
| 6 APPETIZER |
| SERVINGS |

**Freezer Bag Friendly**

## Tip

Flank steak makes a good substitute for the skirt steak in this recipe. However, if it is thicker than ½ inch (1 cm), it will have to be butterflied so that it is thin enough to roll well. You can ask your butcher to do this for you.

▶ **3 sous vide pouches**
▶ **Food processor**
▶ **Butcher's twine**

| | | |
|---|---|---|
| 1 | bunch Swiss chard | 1 |
| 1½ cups | fresh bread crumbs (page 385) | 375 mL |
| 1 tsp | Worcestershire sauce | 5 mL |
| | Salt and freshly ground black pepper | |
| 1 | beef skirt steak (1½ lbs/675 g; see Tips, at left) | 1 |
| 3 | hard-boiled eggs (page 327), quartered lengthwise (see Tips, at right) | 3 |
| 9 | anchovy fillets | 9 |
| 2 tbsp | olive oil | 30 mL |
| 3 | cloves garlic, finely chopped | 3 |
| | Chimichurri Sauce (page 370) | |

## Tips

If you don't want to prepare the hard-boiled eggs sous vide, you can cook them in a saucepan on the stove.

*To make ahead:* Prepare through Step 6, but do not cook. Refrigerate uncooked rolls in sealed pouches for up to 2 days before proceeding with the recipe. Or prepare through Step 8 — the refrigerated cooked rolls will keep in sealed pouches for up to 5 days (do not freeze).

1. Remove and discard stems from Swiss chard. Wash leaves in cold water. Drain well.

2. In a large saucepan of boiling salted water, blanch Swiss chard for 3 minutes. Drain and chill in cold water. Transfer to a large tea towel and squeeze dry. Set aside.

3. In food processor fitted with the metal blade, pulse Swiss chard until finely chopped. Add bread crumbs a little at a time, stopping the motor for each addition, and pulse until a fairly smooth paste forms. (You may not need all the bread crumbs. Look for a moist paste that holds together but doesn't exude juice.) Add Worcestershire sauce and season to taste with salt and pepper. Set aside.

4. Cut steak across the grain into 3 equal pieces. If steak is more that $\frac{1}{2}$ inch (1 cm) thick, place between two sheets of waxed paper. Using the bottom of a saucepan or the flat side of a meat mallet, pound to $\frac{1}{2}$-inch (1 cm) thickness.

5. Preheat hot water bath to 140°F (60°C).

6. One at a time, lay a steak piece on work surface with the grain perpendicular to you. Spread one-third of Swiss chard mixture over steak, right to edges, pressing to make a layer slightly thinner than the meat. Lay 4 hard-boiled egg quarters across short edge closest to you. Crisscross 3 anchovy fillets over eggs, making sure they reach both edges. Starting at short edge closest to you, roll up steak around fillings. Tie each end of roll with butcher's twine and then in the center. Repeat with remaining steak pieces, Swiss chard mixture, eggs and anchovies.

7. Place each roll in a separate sous vide pouch and seal. Immerse in preheated hot water bath and cook for $1\frac{1}{2}$ hours.

8. Remove pouches from hot water bath. Transfer to an ice bath and chill for 40 minutes. (To make ahead, see Tips, at left.)

9. Serve cold or hot. To serve cold, open pouches and remove rolls. Cut into slices $\frac{1}{2}$ inch (1 cm) thick. To serve hot, preheat water bath to 130°F (54.4°C). Immerse sealed pouches in preheated bath and cook for 30 minutes. Open pouches, remove rolls and slice as directed. Serve either with chimichurri sauce.

# Warm Flank Steak Salad with Potatoes and Artichokes

Cooking flank steak sous vide gives the meat big, beefy flavor and a tenderness that is difficult to match with another cooking method. This is the perfect fancy brunch dish. Everything can be prepared days in advance, allowing for stress-free entertaining. Add a poached egg on top for a luxurious touch.

<table>
<tr><td>MAKES<br>4 SERVINGS</td></tr>
</table>

## Tips

New potatoes are small and can be difficult to scrub, but you need to do that thoroughly to prevent them from tasting like the dirt clinging to them. If your potatoes are on the larger side, cut them in half.

If you are lucky enough to have two sous vide machines, you can save time by setting one at the lower temperature for the meat and the second at the higher temperature for the vegetables.

▶ **Preheat hot water bath to 130°F (54.4°C)**
▶ **2 sous vide pouches**
▶ **Large resealable freezer bag**
▶ **Fine-mesh sieve**

| | | |
|---|---|---|
| 1 | beef flank steak (about 18 oz/500 g) | 1 |
| 1 tbsp | olive oil | 15 mL |
| | Salt and freshly ground black pepper | |
| 2 tbsp | coarsely chopped fresh parsley | 30 mL |

### POTATOES

| | | |
|---|---|---|
| 12 oz | small white-skinned new potatoes, scrubbed (see Tips, at left) | 340 g |
| 1 tbsp | olive oil | 15 mL |
| | Salt and freshly ground black pepper | |

### ARTICHOKES

| | | |
|---|---|---|
| 3 tbsp | freshly squeezed lemon juice, divided | 45 mL |
| 1 lb | baby artichokes | 450 g |
| ¼ cup | olive oil | 60 mL |
| ¼ cup | ready-to-use chicken broth | 60 mL |
| 2½ tsp | kosher salt | 12 mL |
| ½ tsp | freshly ground black pepper | 2 mL |
| 1 | bay leaf | 1 |

### VINAIGRETTE

| | | |
|---|---|---|
| 1 tbsp | Dijon mustard | 15 mL |
| 1 tbsp | red wine vinegar | 15 mL |
| | Salt | |

## Tips

*To make the steak ahead:* Prepare through Step 2. Refrigerate sealed pouch for up to 5 days or freeze for up to 6 months. To use frozen steak, thaw pouch in cold water for 1 hour before proceeding with Step 9.

*To make the potatoes and artichokes ahead:* Prepare through Step 6. Immerse in an ice bath and chill for 20 minutes. Refrigerate sealed pouches for up to 4 days. Reheat in a bowl of hot water for 20 minutes before proceeding with Step 7.

1. Brush steak with oil. Place in a sous vide pouch and seal. Immerse in preheated hot water bath and cook for 24 hours.

2. Remove pouch from hot water bath, transfer to an ice bath and chill for 30 minutes. (To make the steak ahead, see Tips, at left.)

3. Meanwhile, increase hot water bath temperature to 194°F (90°C).

4. *Potatoes:* In a medium bowl, toss potatoes with oil to coat. Season to taste with salt and pepper. Place in a sous vide pouch and seal, arranging in a single layer.

5. *Artichokes:* Prepare artichokes according to instructions on page 398, using 2 tbsp (30 mL) of the lemon juice. Drain and transfer to resealable freezer bag. Add remaining 1 tbsp (15 mL) lemon juice, oil, broth, salt, pepper and bay leaf. Seal bag, arranging in a single layer.

6. Immerse potato and artichoke pouches in preheated hot water bath and cook for 45 minutes. Remove from hot water bath. (To make the potatoes and artichokes ahead, see Tips, at left.)

7. Cut open potato pouch to cool. Open artichoke bag and drain in fine-mesh sieve set over a large bowl to catch cooking liquid. Discard bay leaf. Set aside potatoes and drained artichokes in a warm bowl.

8. *Vinaigrette:* Whisk mustard and vinegar into reserved artichoke cooking liquid. Season to taste with salt.

9. Preheat grill to High or heat a heavy-bottomed skillet over high heat. Season steak to taste with salt and pepper. Place on grill or in skillet and sear for 30 seconds per side, or just until browned. (Remember that flank steak is quite thin and can easily overcook while browning.)

10. Spoon potato and artichoke mixture onto warm plates. Cut steak across the grain into slices ¼ inch (0.5 cm) thick. Add to bowl with vinaigrette and toss to coat. Arrange over potatoes and artichokes; drizzle remaining vinaigrette overtop. Garnish with parsley and serve immediately.

# Franken Flanken

Flank steak has great flavor but it's quite thin and can be difficult to cook perfectly. And, if you don't slice it thinly across the grain, your guests might find it a bit tough. Wouldn't it be nice if flank steak came in the same convenient form as a New York steak? Well, now it can be — Activa RM (the brand name for transglutaminase, or "meat glue") can make this happen. Once you have reshaped the meat, cooked it and cut it into steaks, you can finish them using your preferred method.

**MAKES
4 STEAKS**

Advanced

## Tips

A whole beef flank steak is usually about the size you need for this recipe. If your steak is larger or smaller that the weight called for, that's fine. Just make sure you use enough Activa RM to ensure that the meat will bond well.

*To make ahead:* Prepare through Step 6. The meat will keep for up to 5 days in the refrigerator or in the freezer for up to 6 months in well-sealed pouches. To use frozen steak, thaw overnight in the refrigerator. To reheat from refrigerator temperature, proceed with Step 7.

▸ **Sous vide pouch**
▸ **Small fine-mesh sieve**

| | | |
|---|---|---|
| 1 | beef flank steak (2 lbs/ 900 g) | 1 |
| 2 tbsp | Activa RM (see box, page 67) | 30 mL |
| | Salt and pepper | |

1. Place steak on a cutting board and trim off any connective tissue. Cut meat crosswise into 3 equal pieces (so they will stack perfectly).

2. Lay one piece on cutting board with thin edge to the left. Spoon Activa RM into fine-mesh sieve. Sprinkle about one-quarter on surface of first piece of steak. Sprinkle both sides of thickest piece of steak and press it on top of the first one. Sprinkle remaining Activa on third piece of steak and stack on top of the others, with the thin edge to the right. Stack as neatly and evenly as possible, creating a piece of meat 3 times as thick as original steak. Press to adhere surfaces together.

3. Place meat stack in pouch and seal using vacuum sealer (or wrap meat tightly in plastic wrap, then place in sous vide pouch and seal). Refrigerate for 8 to 12 hours.

4. Preheat hot water bath to 145°F (62.8°C).

5. Immerse pouch in preheated water bath and immediately reduce temperature to 130°F (54.4°C). Cook for 24 to 26 hours.

The finished steaks will be quite rare. Because they are chilled, you can give them a good browning as a finishing touch. If you're using your grill to brown them, make sure to preheat it on the highest setting with the lid closed. Oil and season steaks with salt and pepper, then grill for 2 to 3 minutes per side with the lid open. If you're pan-searing the steaks to brown them, preheat a cast-iron skillet until it's very hot. Sear oiled and seasoned steaks for 2 minutes per side.

**6.** Remove pouch from hot water bath. Let cool at room temperature for 30 minutes so meat reabsorbs some of its juices. Transfer to an ice bath and chill for another 30 minutes. (To make ahead, see Tips, page 72.)

**7.** Open pouch, remove meat and pat dry with paper towels. Slice crosswise into 4 equal steaks. Season and brown steaks, using your preferred method (see Tip, at left).

### Safer Steaks

Remember, meat's surface can harbor bacteria from the packing house or butcher shop. By starting the steak at a higher temperature and then lowering the heat as soon as it enters the hot water bath, you will help reduce the risk of bacterial danger. Another option is to blanch the entire flank steak in boiling water for 15 seconds and then chill it rapidly before cutting and assembling the stack. This will result in stripes in your steaks, however.

# The Chuck

The primal cut of beef from the shoulder is called the chuck. It comprises between 26% and 30% of the weight of the carcass, and it's all hard-working muscles. Before sous vide, you really had to know how to cook this cut to make a tasty dish. In North America this means that lots of it ends up as ground beef. With sous vide, here's your chance to turn a sow's ear into a silk purse!

If you see beef labeled with the words *chuck, blade, flatiron* or *cross rib* in your supermarket, you know you are dealing with the shoulder, which has a reputation for being economical and having great flavor. Braising is the typical cooking method associated with these cuts. Also, the best stewing beef comes from this part of the cow. There is plenty of fat and connective tissue in most of these cuts, which results in a juicy dish if prepared correctly.

## BOILED BEEF: A MISUNDERSTOOD DELICACY

As a professional chef, it hurts my feelings that North Americans have little appreciation for boiled beef. Every country in Europe has its signature version. The best I've ever had was served at an Austrian restaurant in New York called Danube (sadly, it's now gone). In Austria this dish is called *Tafelspitz*, but Danube, being a very fancy restaurant, took it up a rung or two and called it "Kavalierspitz." After lunch I went into the kitchen and spoke with the chef, Mario Lohninger, who told me he used a flatiron roast to make the dish. I have used this cut ever since for any boiled beef recipe I cook, from *bollito misto* to *pot-au-feu*. The moral of the story: don't ignore boiled beef next time you're in Austria — and make sure you have the apple horseradish sauce and creamed spinach that will be offered along with it.

# Beef Flatiron for Boiled Beef

With the escalation of beef prices over the past decade, flatiron steaks are often on offer as a substitute for more premium cuts. To make them, butchers remove the thick layer of connective tissue from the muscle, producing steaks that are rather thin. These flatiron steaks are best cooked like a flank steak — just to rare — and then thinly sliced across the grain. Instead of using ready-cut steaks, this recipe calls for a chunk of the whole roast. The sous vide technique melts the connective tissue into luscious gelatin that bathes the meat.

## MAKES 4 TO 5 SERVINGS

Freezer Bag Friendly

## Tips

A whole flatiron roast weighs about 5 lbs (2.25 kg). You can easily halve this recipe for a 2-serving portion of 1 lb (450 g). Adjust the cooking time to 16 to 18 hours.

Suitable alternative cuts are brisket (trimmed of exterior fat) or a piece of sirloin, preferably one that includes some of the tri-tip portion.

*To make ahead:* Prepare through Step 2. Transfer to an ice bath and chill for 30 minutes. Refrigerate sealed pouch for up to 10 days or freeze for up to 6 months. To use frozen roast, thaw overnight in the refrigerator. To reheat from refrigerator temperature, preheat hot water bath to 125°F (51.7°C); immerse pouch for 1½ to 2 hours before proceeding with Step 3.

▸ **Preheat hot water bath to 170°F (76.7°C)**
▸ **Sous vide pouch**

| 1 | beef flatiron roast (2 lbs/900 g; see Tips, at left) | 1 |
| | Salt and freshly ground black pepper | |

1. Place roast in sous vide pouch and seal. Immerse in preheated hot water bath and cook for 20 to 24 hours.

2. Remove pouch from hot water bath. Let stand at room temperature for 15 to 20 minutes, so meat reabsorbs some of its juices. (To make ahead, see Tips, at left.)

3. Open pouch and cut meat crosswise into slices ½ inch (1 cm) thick. Season to taste with salt and pepper and serve immediately.

### Temperature Precision

It took many trials to get the temperature right for this roast, because of the thickness of the tissue that runs through the center. Resist the temptation to lower the water-bath temperature, and be sure to let the meat rest in its pouch to help it regain some of its juices.

# Blade Steak with Ancho Chile and Orange

This is actually three recipes in one: a blade "skillet steak" to serve two that can also be shredded and served in tacos for three or four people. Or, if you buy a blade roast, you can prepare a "pot roast" to serve six (see Variations, page 77).

Freezer Bag Friendly

## Tips

This recipe makes more sauce than you will likely need for 2 servings of steak. Save the remaining sauce for another dish or reserve it for making tacos with any leftover meat.

You can use a boneless steak if desired. If your steak does have a bone, cut it out when serving or, if it is well-centered, leave it attached to one of the portions.

▶ **Preheat hot water bath to 158°F (70°C)**
▶ **Large resealable freezer bag**
▶ **Blender**

| | | |
|---|---|---|
| 1 tbsp | lard, rendered bacon fat or butter | 15 mL |
| ½ cup | finely sliced onion | 125 mL |
| ½ cup | finely sliced carrot | 125 mL |
| ½ cup | diced red bell pepper | 125 mL |
| 1 | large or 2 medium cloves garlic, sliced | 1 |
| 1½ cups | lager beer | 375 mL |
| 1 | bone-in blade steak (1¼ lbs/ 565 g; see Tips, at left) | 1 |
| 2 tbsp | vegetable oil, divided | 30 mL |
| 1 | large or 2 medium ancho chiles | 1 |
| 1 tsp | tomato paste | 5 mL |
| 1 tsp | red wine vinegar | 5 mL |
| ¼ tsp | dried thyme | 1 mL |
| ½ tsp | ground cumin | 2 mL |
| 2 tsp | light (fancy) molasses | 10 mL |
| 2 tsp | salt (approx.), divided | 10 mL |
| ¼ tsp | freshly ground black pepper | 1 mL |
| 1 | orange | 1 |

1. Preheat oven to 300°F (150°C).

2. In a medium skillet, heat lard over medium heat. Cook onion, carrot, bell pepper and garlic, stirring often, until softened, about 15 minutes. Lower heat and add beer. Cover with lid and simmer until carrots are tender, about 15 minutes.

3. Meanwhile, dry steak with paper towels and salt lightly. In a heavy skillet or cast-iron frying pan, heat half the vegetable oil over medium-high heat. Add meat and brown well on both sides, about 15 minutes. Remove from heat and set aside to cool.

*To make ahead:* Prepare through Step 7. If well chilled (about 30 minutes for steak and between 60 and 90 minutes for a pot roast) in an ice-water bath after Step 7, the meat will keep for up to 7 days refrigerated or for up to 6 months in the freezer. Defrost in the refrigerator overnight, if needed. Reheat steak (or roast: see variation, below) in a hot water bath preheated to 125°F (51.7°C) for 20 or 40 minutes, respectively, and then proceed with Step 8.

**4.** Place chile on a baking sheet. Transfer to preheated oven and warm for 3 to 4 minutes, until softened. Remove from oven and let cool slightly. While still warm, remove stem and seeds and discard. Chop chile into 1-inch (2.5 cm) pieces.

**5.** Add chile, tomato paste, red wine vinegar, thyme, cumin, molasses, 1 tsp (5 mL) salt and black pepper to vegetable skillet. Stir briefly to moisten, about 2 or 3 minutes. Set aside to cool.

**6.** Pour vegetable mixture into freezer bag. Add steak and seal. Immerse bag in preheated hot water bath and cook for 20 to 22 hours.

**7.** Remove bag from water bath and let stand at room temperature for 1 hour to reabsorb juices. (To make ahead, see Tip, at left.)

**8.** Meanwhile, grate 1 tbsp (15 mL) orange zest. Juice orange.

**9.** Remove steak from bag, scraping off any vegetables clinging to meat, and place on paper towels. Transfer vegetables and liquid from bag into blender. Add orange zest, orange juice and 1 tsp (5 mL) salt. Blend until smooth. Add more salt if necessary. Warm in a small saucepan over low heat while finishing steak.

**10.** Heat remaining oil in a heavy skillet over medium-high heat. Wipe steak dry and cook, turning once, until well browned, 10 to 12 minutes. Cut steak in half. Serve on warm plates, accompanied by sauce.

## Variations

**Tacos:** Increase the water temperature to 167°F (75°C). After Step 7, transfer steak to a cutting board and shred into 1-inch (2.5 cm) pieces, discarding bone if present. Continue with Step 10. When meat is browned, add contents of bag and simmer briefly, stirring continuously, until sauce is reduced slightly and meat is well coated. (Be careful not to burn the sauce.) Serve on warm tortillas, topped with fresh cilantro sprigs. Accompany with lime wedges.

**Pot Roast:** Tripling the amount of meat in this recipe, you can use a whole 3 to 4 lb (1.35 to 1.8 kg) boneless chuck, blade or cross rib roast. Double the amounts of the remaining ingredients. The dish then becomes a pot roast, albeit with big, spicy flavor. Increase the cooking time to 24 to 26 hours.

# Beef Brisket

Brisket of beef is called breast when it comes from lamb or veal. It represents about 3.5% of a steer's carcass weight and is wedged between the foreleg and the shoulder. There's not a lot of it, but it is all usable. Brisket has big, beefy flavor but always needs to cook for a long time at a low temperature. Commercially, most of it ends up as corned beef or pastrami. However, restaurants that pride themselves on their burgers will frequently grind this cut.

## BEEF BRISKET: WHICH END TO CHOOSE?

Beef brisket has a wonderfully rich flavor and is sold boneless as a whole or half. The two halves, called the point and the plate, are slightly different — the point is quite a bit fattier and, for me, a better choice for corned beef. The plate is slightly leaner, so it works well in pot roast–style recipes. Briskets are quite economical. If you grind a whole one, it makes terrific hamburger meat, with the ideal fat content for juicy burgers.

# Beef Brisket "Pot Roast"

As a kid I would often go to my friend's house for dinner on the Jewish Sabbath and enjoy this cut of beef. His mom rubbed the brisket with powdered onion soup mix, wrapped it in foil and baked it. It was one of my favorite dishes at the time. This very simple meaty brisket almost begs for a sauce made from canned mushroom soup, retro-style, but English mustard or horseradish also works well.

## MAKES
## 4 SERVINGS

**Freezer Bag Friendly**

## Tips

Use brisket from the plate portion of the cut. The point will be too fatty for most people.

Use this recipe to prepare briskets of various sizes, from 1 lb (450 g) to the largest piece that will fit in your hot water bath. Cook smaller briskets of 1 to 2 lbs (450 to 900 g) for 20 hours; increase to 24 to 25 hours for larger ones.

*To make ahead:*
Prepare through Step 3. Remove pouch from hot water bath, transfer to an ice bath and chill for 20 minutes. The sealed pouch will keep refrigerated for up to 7 days or frozen for up to 6 months. To use frozen brisket, thaw overnight in the refrigerator. To reheat from refrigerator temperature, preheat hot water bath to 130°F (54.4°C); immerse for 1 hour and proceed with Step 4.

▶ **Preheat hot water bath to 158°F (70°C)**
▶ **Sous vide pouch**

| | | |
|---|---|---|
| 1 | piece beef brisket (see Tips, at left), 1½ to 2 lbs (675 to 900 g) | 1 |
| | Salt and freshly ground black pepper | |
| 3 tbsp | vegetable oil | 45 mL |

1. Pat brisket dry with paper towels and season very lightly to taste with salt and pepper.

2. In a skillet large enough to hold brisket, heat oil over high heat. Add meat and cook, turning once, for 10 to 12 minutes or until browned on both sides. Transfer to a platter and let cool enough to handle.

3. Place brisket and any accumulated juices in sous vide pouch and seal. Immerse in preheated hot water bath and cook for 20 to 24 hours. (To make ahead, see Tips, at left.)

4. Remove pouch from hot water bath. Let stand at room temperature for 15 to 20 minutes so the meat reabsorbs some of its juices.

5. Open pouch and transfer brisket to a cutting board. Season to taste with additional salt. Cut across the grain into slices ½ inch (1 cm) thick and serve on warm plates.

# Corned Beef

Corned beef is great with cabbage and potatoes as a boiled dinner, sliced for Reuben sandwiches, or chopped and made into corned beef hash. This recipe creates a corned beef that is so much tastier than grocery-store versions. It yields a good amount of meat and it's hardly worth making less, because it keeps very well. The curing takes time, so keep in mind that you'll need to start the recipe at least a week before you plan to serve it. The number of servings you get will depend on how you use the beef.

**MAKES 4 TO 6 SERVINGS**

Freezer Bag Friendly

## Tips

You can use a brisket that's up to 50% larger with the same quantity of brine. If you want to use an even larger piece, adjust the brine amount accordingly. Brine for the same length of time but increase the cooking time to 30 to 36 hours.

A large, airtight plastic container is ideal for brining the beef. Just keep in mind that it has to fit in your refrigerator. I use leftover containers that I've salvaged from restaurants, such as those that are used to hold bocconcini or shucked scallops. Make sure to wash and sanitize your brining container very well, before and after each use.

▷ Sous vide pouch
▷ Large non-reactive container (see Tips, at left)
▷ Fine-mesh sieve
▷ Brine injector (see box, page 81)

| | | |
|---|---|---|
| 8 cups | water, divided | 2 L |
| 1 cup | kosher salt | 250 mL |
| ¼ cup | granulated sugar | 60 mL |
| 2 tbsp | pickling spice | 30 mL |
| ½ oz | curing salt (about 2 ¾ tsp/13 mL; see box, at right) | 15 g |
| 2 | large cloves garlic | 2 |
| 2 | small dried red chiles | 2 |
| 1 | beef brisket, preferably the point half (see box, page 78), about 2½ lbs (1.125 kg) | 1 |

1. In a large saucepan, bring 4 cups (1 L) water to a simmer over medium-high heat. Add kosher salt, sugar, pickling spice, curing salt, garlic and chiles; stir until salt and sugar are dissolved. Pour into non-reactive container, add remaining water and let cool. (You can speed up the cooling process by substituting ice for the remaining water. Add ice cubes until the ice and hot brine mixture equals 8 cups/2 L.)

2. Strain brine mixture through fine-mesh sieve. Discard garlic and chiles. Place brisket in container. Fill injector with about 1 cup (250 mL) strained brine. Holding brisket in container with one hand, inject brine into meat (much of it will leak into container, but that is fine). Cover brisket completely with brine. Cover container and refrigerate for 6 to 7 days.

## Tips

If you want to give your brisket a slightly smoky flavor, add 1 tsp (5 mL) liquid smoke to the pouch in Step 5.

If you have leftover sliced corned beef (not in the sealed pouch), cover and refrigerate it for up to 6 days.

**3.** Preheat hot water bath to 158°F (70°C).

**4.** Remove brisket from brine. Discard brine. Rinse brisket under cold running water for 5 minutes.

**5.** Drain brisket, place in sous vide pouch and seal. Immerse in preheated hot water bath and cook for 24 to 28 hours.

**6.** Remove pouch from hot water bath and let stand at room temperature for 20 to 30 minutes. Chill in an ice-water bath for 20 minutes. Refrigerate sealed pouch until ready to use or for up to 3 weeks.

**7.** To serve cold, open pouch and remove corned beef. Slice and serve as desired. To serve hot, preheat water bath to 122°F (50°C). Immerse sealed pouch in preheated bath for 1 hour. Open pouch, slice meat across the grain and serve (see Tips, at left).

### Curing Salt

Curing salt is available online at Modernist Pantry (www.modernistpantry.com). You can replace the curing salt with kosher salt if it is unavailable or not desired.

### Brine Injectors

A brine injector is a huge syringe used for injecting marinades or brines into meats. Look for one at a well-stocked cookware store or online. You can substitute a large surgical syringe, but they are far smaller. Another option is a Jaccard tenderizer (see page 18 for more details).

# Beef Hind

Beef hind contains about 25% of the weight of meat on a steer carcass. The inside round, outside round and eye of round are some of the recognizable cuts. Since the hind legs are working muscles, the meat is quite tough. With almost no marbling, I find that it is too lean to be juicy when cooked. (Marbling in meat refers to the flecks of fat found in the muscle tissue. The more marbled a cut of meat, the juicer it will be.) The eye of round is included here because its shape is so convenient.

Legs of veal and lamb are also quite lean, but the younger age of the animals makes them quite tender. Farmed venison is slaughtered at a relatively young age, so if cooked close to rare, it can be as tender as lamb legs. Wild venison comes from a harder-working and sometimes older animal, so I like to use it in ground meat preparations instead.

## EYE OF ROUND

The eye of round is the leanest cut of beef and has no connective tissue. I feel that it's overpriced for its merits, but it does offer a couple of benefits for the home cook: a convenient shape with no waste. A whole eye of round weighs on average about 5 lbs (2.25 kg), although this cut can weigh up to 8 lbs (3.6 kg), and thick roasts are 4 to 5 inches (10 to 12.5 cm) in diameter. When it's cooked at more than the lowest possible temperature, this meat ends up dry, but cooking at a low temperature over a long period of time leaves the meat perfectly medium rare.

I've included two methods to cook eye of round sous vide. The first recipe uses a large-diameter cut that is browned before cooking and eaten as hot or cold roast beef. The second recipe is for cut steaks that require browning after cooking. The cooking temperatures are the same and the extended times vary only slightly according to their diameter. Because sous vide times are determined by the thickness of the meat, you can use any length and weight of eye of round for either of these recipes. Using your sous vide device makes its price seem a bargain!

# "Roast" Eye of Round

This is probably the best use for this tough cut of beef. Because of its shape, eye of round is easy to slice thinly for roast beef sandwiches. Browning the meat before cooking it sous vide means better flavor and color as a result.

## Tips

This recipe works best when a thick eye of round is used. You get a nice large eye to slice.

Each pound (450 g) will serve 2 generously for dinner or make about 4 sandwiches.

This temperature yields a medium-rare roast. For safety reasons you can't cook below this temperature, because it would be too low to kill the internal bacteria.

*To make ahead:* Prepare through Step 3. Remove pouch from bath. If chilled in an ice-water bath for 30 minutes after cooking, the roast will keep refrigerated for 7 days in a well-sealed pouch. (Freezing tends to make the meat dry out.) To reheat from refrigerator temperature, preheat hot water bath to 125°F (51.7°C), then immerse pouch for 50 to 60 minutes. Proceed with Step 4.

▸ **Preheat hot water bath to 130°F (54.4°C)**
▸ **Sous vide pouch**

| 1 | whole (8 lbs/3.6kg) or half (4 lbs/ 1.8 kg) beef eye of round roast (see Tips, at left) | 1 |
| 3 tbsp | vegetable or olive oil (approx.) | 45 mL |
| | Salt and freshly ground black pepper | |

1. Pat roast dry with paper towels. Refrigerate, uncovered, until ready to use, about 1 to 4 hours, so that meat is well chilled.

2. In a skillet large enough to hold roast, over high heat, heat enough oil to cover bottom of skillet. Add roast and cook, turning often, for about 10 minutes or until browned all over. Transfer to a platter and allow to cool enough to handle, about 10 minutes.

3. Place roast in sous vide pouch and seal. Immerse in preheated hot water bath and cook for 36 to 40 hours. (To make ahead, see Tips, at left.)

4. Remove pouch from hot water bath. To serve hot, remove beef from pouch and season to taste with salt and pepper. Slice thinly across the grain and serve as desired. To serve cold, transfer sealed pouch to an ice bath and chill for 30 minutes. Remove beef from pouch and season to taste with salt and pepper. Slice thinly across the grain and serve as desired.

# Eye of Round Faux Filet Mignon

In this recipe, eye of round is cooked whole and then sliced and browned as small steaks. These are great topped with a fried egg for brunch or in steak sandwiches, where true filet mignon would seem extravagant. You can make three or four servings with this recipe when it's masquerading as filet mignon. It will serve four for steak sandwiches or as steak and eggs.

---

**MAKES 3 TO
4 SERVINGS**

Freezer Bag Friendly

## Tips

This recipe works best with a roast cut from a small eye, 3 to 4 inches (7.5 to 10 cm) in diameter.

You can double or triple this recipe easily by using a 2- or 3-lb (900 g or 1.35 kg) roast. If you are cooking all the steaks, use a larger skillet or brown them in batches, adding oil if necessary.

*To make ahead:* Prepare through Step 2. Increase chilling time in ice bath to 30 minutes. Refrigerate sealed pouch for up to 6 days. (I don't recommend freezing the roast, because the meat has a tendency to dry out.) To reheat from refrigerator temperature, proceed with Step 3.

You can also use a torch to brown the steaks (see page 27 for finishing techniques). Just make sure not to chill the meat in Step 2.

▶ **Preheat hot water bath to 130°F (54.4°C)**
▶ **Sous vide pouch**

| 1 | piece beef eye of round roast (1 lb/450 g; see Tips, at left) | 1 |
|---|---|---|
| 3 tbsp | vegetable oil, divided | 45 mL |
| | Salt and freshly ground black pepper | |

1. Place roast in sous vide pouch and seal. Immerse in preheated hot water bath and cook for 36 hours.

2. Remove pouch from hot water bath. Transfer to an ice bath and chill for 20 to 30 minutes, so beef is well chilled prior to browning. (To make ahead, see Tips, at left.)

3. Open pouch, remove roast and pat dry with paper towels. Cut crosswise into 3 or 4 steaks. Lightly brush steaks with some of the oil and season to taste with salt and pepper.

4. In a medium skillet, heat remaining oil over high heat. Add steaks and sear, turning once, for 1½ minutes per side, until lightly browned (see Tips, at left). Serve on warm plates.

---

# Vitello Tonnato

An unusual northern Italian veal dish, vitello tonnato is served cold in a mayonnaise-style sauce containing tuna. It is traditionally made with a cut from the leg, so the eye of round is perfect here.

## Tips

You can easily double this recipe.

If you are concerned about the raw egg yolk in the sauce, feel free to pasteurize it using the method described on page 324.

For the most delicious results, I recommend using homemade "Canned" Tuna (page 238), but commercial canned tuna works fine if you don't have time to make it from scratch.

For a richer taste, use the olive oil you drained from your homemade "Canned" Tuna. If you don't have any, regular olive oil is fine.

*To make ahead:* Prepare through Step 2. Refrigerate sealed pouch for up to 6 days. (I don't recommend freezing the roast because the meat has a tendency to dry out.) Proceed with Step 3.

▸ **Preheat hot water bath to 135°F (57.2°C)**
▸ **Sous vide pouch**
▸ **Mini food processor or immersion blender**

| | | |
|---|---|---|
| 12 oz | veal eye of round | 340 g |
| 2 oz | drained "Canned" Tuna (page 238) or commercial canned tuna | 55 g |
| 1 tbsp | drained capers | 15 mL |
| 1 | egg yolk | 1 |
| 1 tsp | brandy | 5 mL |
| 1 tsp | freshly squeezed lemon juice | 5 mL |
| 1 tsp | Dijon mustard | 5 mL |
| ¼ tsp | freshly ground black pepper | 1 mL |
| 5 | drops hot pepper sauce | 5 |
| ⅔ cup | olive oil (see Tips, at left) | 150 mL |
| | Salt (optional) | |
| 2 tbsp | finely chopped flat-leaf (Italian) parsley | 30 mL |

1. Place veal in sous vide pouch and seal. Immerse in preheated hot water bath and cook for 7 hours.

2. Remove pouch from hot water bath. Transfer to an ice bath and chill for 30 minutes. (To make ahead, see Tips, at left.)

3. Meanwhile, in food processor fitted with the metal blade or in a tall cup using immersion blender, combine tuna, capers and egg yolk. Pulse until incorporated. Add brandy, lemon juice, mustard, pepper and hot pepper sauce. With the motor running, drizzle in oil through the feed tube, processing until emulsified. Season to taste with salt, if necessary. Pour into a small bowl, cover and refrigerate until ready to use, or for up 6 days.

4. Remove veal from pouch and pat dry with paper towels. If desired, stir cooking liquid in the pouch into sauce to thin to desired consistency.

5. Slice veal thinly across the grain and arrange on cold plates. Pour sauce evenly over veal, ensuring that it is well covered. Garnish with parsley and serve.

# Cold Veal in Herbed Mayonnaise

This dish is inspired by Vitello Tonnato (page 85), but its herbal components add a different dimension. It's delicious as a cold main dish and it's also excellent as a filling for sandwiches.

**MAKES
4 APPETIZER
SERVINGS**

Freezer Bag Friendly

## Tips

You'll notice that I've increased the hot water bath temperature for this recipe to 136°F (57.8°C), instead of the 135°F (57.2°C) I used to cook the veal for Vitello Tonnato (page 85). I like the veal for the latter to be very soft, whereas I like it firmer in this dish. Feel free to adjust the temperature to suit your taste.

*To make ahead:*
Prepare through Step 3. Refrigerate sealed pouch for up to 6 days. (I don't recommend freezing the roast because the meat has a tendency to dry out.) Proceed with Step 4.

▸ **Preheat hot water bath to 136°F (57.8°C)**
▸ **Sous vide pouch**

| 12 oz | veal eye of round | 340 g |
| 2 tbsp | Dijon mustard | 30 mL |
| ¾ cup | mixed chopped parsley, tarragon and chives | 175 mL |
| ½ cup | mayonnaise | 125 mL |

1. Pat veal dry with paper towels. Using a spatula, spread mustard evenly over meat.

2. Spread parsley, tarragon and chives on a small platter or baking sheet. Roll roast in herbs, pressing to adhere as much as possible. Wrap tightly in plastic wrap. Place in sous vide pouch and seal. Immerse in preheated hot water bath and cook for 7 hours.

3. Remove pouch from hot water bath. Transfer to an ice bath and chill for 30 minutes. (To make ahead, see Tips, at left.)

4. Place mayonnaise in a small bowl. Open pouch and, with a spatula, scrape herbs into mayonnaise. Pat veal dry with paper towels. Stir in enough of the cooking liquid from pouch to create desired consistency. Slice veal thinly across the grain and arrange on cold plates. Spoon sauce evenly over veal, ensuring that it is well covered. (Or use the veal and sauce in sandwiches.)

# Shanks and Shoulders

Lamb and veal, by definition, come from animals that are less than one year old, so most cuts are quite tender. The shanks, neck and cheeks are the exceptions to this rule. Shoulders fall somewhere on the spectrum between those tougher cuts and the tender leg, so they benefit from either slow roasting or spending some extra time in the sous vide bath.

Lamb hind shanks weigh about 1 lb (450 g) each. Fore shanks weigh a bit less, but both are usually served whole. Veal shanks weigh about 4 to 5 lbs (1.8 to 2.25 kg) and are usually cut crosswise by the butcher (with a bandsaw) into individual portions. The meat is rich and savory, even though the pieces are about half bone, and they can often be found on restaurant menus. The large amount of collagen embedded in the connective tissue makes lamb and veal shanks quite forgiving to cook. Long, slow cooking is the key to making them tender and delicious, so sous vide is an ideal cooking technique.

Shoulders are tasty and some of the best-value cuts. However, keep in mind that lamb shoulders can be very tricky to bone. I suggest having your butcher do it for you, or buy boneless shoulder. Packaged boneless shoulders are commonly available, fresh or frozen, from Australia and New Zealand. Veal shoulders are large and are generally merchandised like beef shoulders. If you're looking for an economical option, shoulder steaks and chops are always less expensive than shanks, and they taste just as good.

Venison shanks, when you can get them, can be treated like lamb shanks and are about the same size. On the other hand, the shoulders can be quite tough. I suggest that you treat them like lamb shoulders for brochettes (see variation, page 93) or grind them. You can use ground venison wherever ground beef or lamb is used, either blended with another meat or by itself. Meat sauces, meatballs, spinach pies and old-fashioned (real) mincemeat with suet come to mind.

# Veal Shoulder Chops with Leeks

The delicate flavor of leeks matches perfectly with veal. While I don't usually use cream in beef preparations — except for Beef Stroganoff — adding cream to this dish gives it an extra layer of decadence (see variation, page 89). Shoulder chops are relatively inexpensive and frequently on special, probably because they contain three or four different muscles of varying degrees of tenderness. Sous vide to the rescue!

---

| MAKES |
|:---:|
| **2 SERVINGS** |

Freezer Bag Friendly

## Tips

You can easily halve or double this recipe. Make sure to seal chops individually.

Leeks can be tricky to clean. See page 400 for more information.

▸ **Preheat hot water bath to 158°F (70°C)**
▸ **2 small resealable freezer bags**

| | | |
|---|---|---|
| 2 tbsp | vegetable oil | 30 mL |
| 2 | bone-in veal shoulder chops (each 12 oz to 1 lb/340 to 450 g) | 2 |
| | Salt and freshly ground black pepper | |
| 2 tbsp | butter | 30 mL |
| 2 cups | finely chopped leeks (white and light green parts only; see Tips, at left) | 500 mL |
| 6 tbsp | dry white wine | 90 mL |
| 2 tsp | Dijon mustard | 10 mL |

1. In a large skillet, heat oil over medium-high heat. Brown veal chops on both sides, about 4 minutes per side. Set aside on a plate. Lightly season with salt and pepper.

2. Drain fat from skillet, reduce heat to medium and melt butter. Add leeks and cook, stirring occasionally, until softened, about 4 minutes. Pour in wine, gently stirring and scraping up any browned bits from bottom of pan. Add any veal juices accumulated on plate. Remove from heat and allow to cool slightly, about 10 minutes.

3. Place chops in separate freezer bags. Add half of the leek mixture to each bag. Seal bags. Immerse bags in preheated hot water bath and cook for 8 hours. (To make ahead, see Tip, at right.)

## Tip

*To make ahead:* Prepare through Step 3. Remove from hot water bath and pat dry. Transfer to an ice bath and chill for 20 minutes. Refrigerate sealed bags for up to 6 days or freeze for up to 6 months. To use frozen chops, thaw overnight in the refrigerator. To reheat from refrigerator temperature, preheat hot water bath to 130°F (54.4°C); immerse pouch for 30 to 40 minutes before proceeding with Step 4.

**4.** Remove bags from hot water bath and open. Scrape any leeks clinging to chops into a small skillet. Transfer chops to warm plates; cover with foil and a folded kitchen towel to keep warm. Add cooking liquid to skillet, plus any leeks remaining in bags. Bring to a simmer over medium-low heat. Remove from heat and stir in mustard. Pour over chops and serve immediately.

## Variation

**Veal Shoulder Chops with Creamy Leeks:** You can make this dish more luxurious by adding 2 tbsp (30 mL) heavy or whipping (35%) cream to each bag before sealing it. In Step 4, simmer the liquid for about 10 minutes or until thickened and sauce-like.

# Osso Bucco

This is a classic osso buco recipe, and cooking the shank pieces sous vide yields predictable results, which makes it ideal for a nice dinner or for company. There is plenty of concentrated flavor in the small quantity of cooking liquid inside the pouch — you can reduce and drizzle it over the finished shanks, or stir it into orzo or risotto to serve alongside. Be sure to have your butcher give you veal shanks that are open at both ends so that the delicious marrow is accessible. And don't forget to set the table with long, narrow spoons to scoop it out.

---

## Tips

You can easily double or triple this recipe. Just make sure you bag each pair of shanks separately.

Veal short ribs (often called simply veal ribs) are delicious prepared this way. If using them in this recipe, start with Step 2.

▸ **Preheat hot water bath to 158°F (70°C)**
▸ **Small resealable freezer bag**

| | | |
|---|---|---|
| 2 | cross-cut pieces veal shank (about 12 oz/340 g each) | 2 |
| | Salt and freshly ground black pepper | |
| 1/3 cup | all-purpose flour | 75 mL |
| 2 tbsp | vegetable or olive oil | 30 mL |
| 3/4 cup | finely chopped onion | 175 mL |
| 1/2 cup | finely chopped carrot | 125 mL |
| 1/4 cup | finely chopped celery | 60 mL |
| 2 | cloves garlic, peeled and sliced | 2 |
| 1 tbsp | tomato paste | 15 mL |
| 1/2 | bay leaf | 1/2 |
| 1/2 cup | dry white wine | 125 mL |

1. Using a sharp knife, make 5 vertical slices through the connective tissue on the outside of each shank to help prevent curling. Place in a bowl of cold water and let stand for 15 to 20 minutes to clean up the marrow.

2. Drain shanks and pat dry with paper towels. Season liberally with salt and pepper, then dredge shanks in flour, shaking off and discarding excess. In a medium skillet, heat oil over medium-high heat. Add shanks and brown, turning once, for about 3 minutes per side. Using a slotted spoon, transfer to a plate and let cool.

## Tips

*To make ahead:* Prepare through Step 6. Transfer to an ice bath and chill for 30 minutes. Refrigerate sealed bag for up to 6 days or freeze for up to 6 months. To use frozen shanks, thaw overnight in the refrigerator. To reheat from refrigerator temperature, preheat hot water bath to 130°F (54.4°C); immerse pouch for 40 to 50 minutes before proceeding with Step 7.

You can stir the cooking liquid and vegetables into risotto or orzo in Step 7 to serve alongside the veal, if you prefer.

**3.** Meanwhile, reduce heat to medium and cook liquid in pan until juices are evaporated and skillet stops hissing — at this point the only liquid left in the pan will be the fat from the shanks. Drain off half the fat and discard. Add onion and carrot to pan and cook, stirring occasionally, for 5 minutes or until softened and lightly browned.

**4.** Add celery, garlic, tomato paste and bay leaf to pan; cook, stirring occasionally, for 2 minutes. Add wine and bring to a simmer, scraping bits from bottom of pan. Remove from heat and let cool.

**5.** Place cooled shanks and vegetable mixture in freezer bag and seal. Immerse in preheated hot water bath and cook for 12 hours.

**6.** Remove bag from hot water bath. Let stand at room temperature for 20 minutes so that the meat can reabsorb some of its juices. (To make ahead, see Tips, at left.)

**7.** Open bag and scrape any vegetables clinging to the meat back into the bag. Remove veal from bag and place on warm plates. Cover with foil and a folded kitchen towel to keep warm. Transfer vegetables and liquid in bag to a small skillet and cook over medium-low heat, stirring occasionally, until slightly thickened. Strain liquid over meat, discarding vegetables, and serve immediately (see Tips, at left).

# "Braised" Lamb Shanks

Classically a braise is done by browning a whole cut of meat on the stovetop and then cooking it in a covered pan with a small amount of liquid, which produces a concentrated sauce. Here the sous vide pouch takes care of creating that warm, moist cooking environment. Lamb shanks are so flavorful that you can skip browning them. However, browning before cooking sous vide will give you even bigger flavor, so do it if you feel so inclined.

---

**MAKES
4 SERVINGS**

Freezer Bag Friendly

## Tips

You can cook as many shanks as you like. Package them in pairs as directed, or singly if you prefer.

If you are in a hurry, set the hot water bath to 185°F (85°C). The shanks will be done in 7 hours, but they will not be as moist.

*To make ahead:* Prepare through Step 2. Let stand at room temperature for 15 minutes longer. Immerse pouch in an ice-water bath for 20 to 30 minutes. Refrigerate sealed pouch for up to 7 days or freeze for up to 6 months. To use frozen shanks, thaw pouch overnight in the refrigerator. To reheat from refrigerator temperature, proceed with Step 3.

▸ **Preheat hot water bath to 158°F (70°C)**
▸ **2 sous vide pouches**
▸ **Large resealable freezer bag**

| | | |
|---|---|---|
| 4 | lamb shanks, about 13 to 16 oz (370 to 450 g) | 4 |
| 1 | recipe Fermented Black Bean Sauce (page 382) or Base Sauce for Coq au Vin, Beef Bourguignon, Lamb Shanks and Short Ribs (page 364) | 1 |
| | Salt | |

1. Place 2 shanks in a sous vide pouch, facing in opposite directions so that the shank end of one is next to the meatier end of the other. Repeat with remaining lamb shanks in a separate sous vide pouch. Seal pouches. Immerse in preheated hot water bath and cook for 20 to 24 hours.

2. Remove pouches from hot water bath. Let stand at room temperature for 15 minutes so meat reabsorbs some of the juices. (To make ahead, see Tips, at left.)

3. Reduce hot water bath temperature to 130°F (54.4°C). Open pouches and remove shanks. Transfer shanks and cooking liquid to resealable freezer bag. Add sauce.

4. Immerse bag in hot water bath and cook for 40 minutes. Open bag, season to taste with salt, if necessary, and serve on warm plates.

---

## Variation

**Barbecued Lamb Shanks:** After Step 2, mix the liquid from the pouches with ½ cup (125 mL) boldly seasoned barbecue sauce (omit Steps 3 and 4). Preheat grill to Medium. Brush shanks with mixture. Grill for about 15 minutes, occasionally brushing with additional mixture, until starting to get crispy.

# Lamb Shoulder for Skewers

Shoulder is the most economical cut of lamb for grilling on skewers. The good news: this cut contains a little intramuscular fat that will keep kebabs juicy. The bad news: some of the muscles in this cut can be a bit tough. Unless you like your lamb rare, cooking it sous vide before grilling takes care of that.

## MAKES 4 TO 5 SKEWERS

**Freezer Bag Friendly**

## Tips

This recipe can be scaled up or down to suit your needs. Seal in pouches weighing no more than 1 lb (450 g) each.

Chimichurri Sauce (page 370) is a great accompaniment to grilled lamb or venison.

If you are using wooden or bamboo skewers, soak them in water for at least 30 minutes or overnight, to prevent burning.

I like to add 2 tbsp (30 mL) dill pickle or caper brine to the pouch to lightly season the lamb and add a bit of umami (a savory note).

*To make ahead:* Prepare through Step 2. Refrigerate sealed pouch for up to 5 days or freeze for up to 6 months. To use frozen lamb, thaw overnight in the refrigerator. To reheat from refrigerator temperature, proceed with Step 3.

▸ **Preheat hot water bath to 142°F (61.1°C)**
▸ **Sous vide pouch**
▸ **Four or five 8-inch (20 cm) metal or soaked wooden skewers (see Tips, at left)**

| | | |
|---|---|---|
| 1 lb | boneless lamb shoulder | 450 g |
| 2 tbsp | olive oil | 30 mL |
| | Salt and freshly ground black pepper | |

1. Cut lamb into 1-inch (2.5 cm) cubes, trimming off any cartilage and connective tissue. Place cubes in sous vide pouch, spreading out to form a single layer, and seal. Immerse in preheated hot water bath and cook for 10 to 12 hours.

2. Remove pouch from hot water bath and let stand at room temperature for 30 minutes. Transfer to an ice bath and chill for 30 minutes. (To make ahead, see Tips, at left.)

3. Preheat grill to Medium-High or preheat broiler.

4. Open pouch and pat meat dry with paper towels. Thread lamb onto skewers. Brush oil all over skewers and season to taste with salt and pepper.

5. Place skewers on preheated grill or on a baking sheet under preheated boiler. Grill or broil for about 5 minutes, turning occasionally, until lamb starts to brown. Serve on warm plates.

## Variation

**Venison Shoulder Skewers:** Farmed venison shoulder works well in this recipe. Reduce the hot water bath temperature to 130°F (54.4°C) and increase the cooking time to 16 to 18 hours.

# Spinach and Sourdough–Stuffed Lamb Shoulder

Unless you are going to shred the meat for tacos or a similar dish, lamb shoulders are much easier to work with and cook if they are boneless. Here we fill the spaces left by the bones with a savory spinach stuffing. Fresh sourdough bread crumbs are important to this recipe, as they lend a tangy flavor, but in a pinch you can use fresh crumbs made from a neutral white bread instead.

## Tips

Bunched spinach can be gritty, so be sure to wash it thoroughly before you use it.

Here's a quick and easy way to squeeze the water out of blanched spinach: place a small handful at a time on a clean, lint-free tea towel and twist to squeeze out the liquid.

▸ **Preheat hot water bath to 142°F (61.1°C)**
▸ **Sous vide pouch**
▸ **Food processor**
▸ **Rimmed baking sheet or roasting pan with rack**

| | | |
|---|---|---|
| 1 | bunch spinach, preferably the crinkly variety, trimmed (see Tips, at left) | 1 |
| 5 tbsp | olive oil, divided | 75 mL |
| ¼ cup | finely chopped shallots | 60 mL |
| 1 tbsp | finely chopped garlic | 15 mL |
| | Salt | |
| 2 cups | fresh sourdough bread crumbs (page 385) | 500 mL |
| 1½ tbsp | drained capers | 22 mL |
| 2 tsp | Worcestershire sauce | 10 mL |
| | Freshly ground black pepper | |
| 1 | boneless lamb shoulder (about 3½ lbs/1.5 kg) | 1 |

1. In a large pot of boiling salted water, blanch spinach for 1½ minutes. Drain, transfer to a bowl of ice water and chill for 4 to 5 minutes. One handful at a time, squeeze water out of spinach (see Tips, at left). You should be left with about ¾ cup (175 mL). Set aside.

2. In a medium skillet, heat 3 tbsp (45 mL) oil over medium heat. Add shallots, garlic and ½ tsp (2 mL) salt. Cook, stirring often, for 5 minutes or until softened. Remove from heat.

## Tips

You may not need all of the filling, or some may squeeze out during cooking. Don't worry — any left over makes a tasty omelet filling.

*To make ahead:* Prepare through Step 5. Refrigerate sealed pouch for up to 5 days or freeze for up to 6 months. To use frozen lamb, thaw overnight in the refrigerator. To reheat from refrigerator temperature, proceed with Step 6.

If your oven doesn't have a convection setting, increase the temperature to 425°F (220°C).

3. Place bread crumbs in food processor fitted with the metal blade. Scatter spinach overtop. Add shallot mixture, capers, Worcestershire sauce and ½ tsp (2 mL) pepper. Process until a paste forms, periodically scraping down sides of bowl.

4. Place lamb, fat side down, on work surface. Using a small, sharp knife, trim off any cartilage and connective tissue. Spread spinach mixture over lamb, pushing it into the gaps. Starting at one long edge, tightly roll lamb lengthwise around filling. Tie at 1½-inch (4 cm) intervals with kitchen string, or wrap roll tightly in plastic wrap. Place roll in sous vide pouch and seal. Immerse in preheated hot water bath and cook for 12 to 14 hours.

5. Remove pouch from hot water bath and let stand at room temperature for 30 minutes. Transfer to an ice bath and chill for 30 minutes. (To make ahead, see Tips, at left.)

6. Preheat oven (preferably a convection oven; see Tips, at left) to 400°F (200°C). If meat is wrapped in plastic wrap, remove. Open pouch and carefully rinse lamb under cold tap water. Pat dry with paper towels and coat with remaining 2 tbsp (30 mL) olive oil. Season to taste with additional salt and pepper.

7. Place lamb on baking sheet or on rack in roasting pan. Roast for 30 to 40 minutes or until exterior starts to brown and center is heated through to about 130°F (54.4°C).

8. Remove lamb from oven. Cut crosswise into slices ¾ inch (2 cm) thick. Serve on warm plates.

# Lamb Neck Tagine with Seven Vegetables

A tagine is a Moroccan stew, and this one is a terrific excuse to try out your sous vide vegetable-cooking skills. Lamb neck has a rich flavor, is relatively inexpensive and adds a savory base note to this stew, which contains a delicious assortment of vegetables.

---

**MAKES 8 SERVINGS**

## Tips

You can halve this recipe, but that means you will be preparing quite small quantities of each vegetable. Feel free to leave one out if you like, but I recommend keeping all the root vegetables.

You can substitute another tough lamb cut, such as shoulder, for the neck. Lamb necks contain bones, so the amount called for in this recipe will yield about 1 lb (450 g) cooked meat. If you substitute boneless shoulder, use 1 lb (450 g) and halve the cooking time. Feel free to add more lamb if you want a meatier dish.

▶ **Preheat hot water bath to 158°F (70°C)**
▶ **Sous vide pouch**
▶ **Large resealable freezer bag**

| | | |
|---|---|---|
| 2 to 2½ lbs | bone-in lamb neck (whole or in pieces) | 900 g to 1.25 kg |
| 1 | recipe Carrots with Orange and Ginger (page 310), in sealed pouch | 1 |
| 1 | recipe Turnips with Honey and Lemongrass (page 312), in sealed pouch | 1 |
| ½ | recipe Saffron Cauliflower with Sultanas (page 309), in sealed pouch | ½ |
| ½ | recipe Balsamic Pearl Onions (page 314), in sealed pouch | ½ |
| 1 | recipe Fennel with Apple and Dill (page 313), in sealed pouch | 1 |
| 1 | recipe Okra with Preserved Lemon (page 308), in sealed pouch | 1 |
| 1 cup | rinsed, drained canned chickpeas | 250 mL |
| ½ cup | sun-dried tomatoes, coarsely chopped and drained (if oil-packed) | 125 mL |
| 3 tbsp | olive oil | 45 mL |
| 8 | cloves 40 Days and 40 Nights Black Garlic (page 388) | 8 |
| 1 tsp | chopped fresh garlic | 5 mL |
| 1 tsp | Saffron Salt (page 351) | 5 mL |
| 1 tsp | kosher salt | 5 mL |
| ¾ tsp | ground white pepper | 3 mL |
| ¾ tsp | ground ginger | 3 mL |
| ½ tsp | ground turmeric | 2 mL |
| ¼ tsp | ground cinnamon | 1 mL |
| | Chopped fresh herbs, such as parsley, mint or cilantro (optional) | |

*To make ahead:*
Prepare through Step 8. Transfer freezer bag to an ice bath and chill for 40 minutes. Refrigerate sealed bag for up to 4 days. To reheat from refrigerator temperature, proceed with Step 9.

1. Place lamb neck in sous vide pouch and seal. Immerse in preheated hot water bath and cook for 20 to 24 hours.

2. Remove pouch from hot water bath and let cool enough to handle. Remove lamb from pouch and pour cooking liquid into a medium bowl. Using your hands, pull meat away from neck bones. Remove and discard any layers of fat and thick sinew (save the bones for enriching stock — they still have lots of flavor). Tear lamb into large shreds and add to cooking liquid in bowl. Refrigerate until ready to use.

3. Reduce temperature of hot water bath to 130°F (54.4°C). Immerse carrot pouch in preheated bath and cook for 15 minutes or until butter sauce is liquefied.

4. Meanwhile, open turnip pouch and pour contents into a large bowl. Remove lemongrass pieces and discard. Open cauliflower and onion pouches. Add cauliflower and onions to turnips, reserving onion cooking juices separately for another use.

5. Open fennel pouch and drain off cooking liquid or reserve for another use. Cut fennel crosswise into 1/2-inch (1 cm) pieces. Add to vegetable mixture.

6. Remove carrot pouch from hot water bath. Open pouch and pour carrots and cooking liquid into vegetable mixture.

7. Open okra pouch and add preserved lemon and any cooking liquid to vegetable mixture. Cut okra crosswise into rounds 1/2 inch (1 cm) thick; add to vegetable mixture.

8. Add lamb, chickpeas, sun-dried tomatoes, oil, black garlic, chopped garlic, saffron salt, kosher salt, pepper, ginger, turmeric and cinnamon to vegetables. Stir gently to combine. Transfer mixture to freezer bag and seal. (To make ahead, see Tip, at left.)

9. Preheat hot water bath to 140°F (60°C). Immerse bag and reheat for 40 minutes if starting from warm, or 90 minutes if starting with refrigerated tagine. Pour mixture into a warm serving bowl. Garnish with herbs (if using) and serve.

# Grilled Lamb Leg with Pipian Verde

Pipian verde is a Mexican green sauce made with chiles and herbs. It tastes wonderful with lamb. Ask your butcher to butterfly the lamb for you — that will save you time and effort in the kitchen. Sweet potatoes or corn on the cob is a good side to serve with this zesty lamb.

---

**MAKES ABOUT 8 SERVINGS**

Freezer Bag Friendly

## Tips

Mexican oregano has a particular flavor that's nice in this recipe. If you can't find any, substitute half regular (Greek) oregano and half rubbed marjoram.

This recipe is also delicious made with baby goat instead of lamb. Use an equivalent weight, likely 2 legs.

▸ **Sous vide pouch**
▸ **Spice grinder or mortar and pestle**
▸ **Food processor**

### PIPIAN VERDE

| | | |
|---|---|---|
| ½ cup | raw green pumpkin seeds (pepitas) | 125 mL |
| ⅓ cup | sesame seeds | 75 mL |
| 1 tbsp | whole black peppercorns | 15 mL |
| 2 tsp | fennel seeds | 10 mL |
| 2 tsp | Mexican oregano (see Tips, at left) | 10 mL |
| 2 | bay leaves | 2 |
| 2 tsp | kosher salt | 10 mL |
| 4 | jalapeño peppers, roasted (see box, page 131), peeled and seeded | 4 |
| 1 | bunch fresh cilantro (leaves and tender stems) | 1 |
| 1 | head garlic, roasted (see box, page 104) and peeled | 1 |
| 1 tsp | cider vinegar | 5 mL |
| 1 | butterflied boneless lamb leg (about 5 lbs/2.25 kg) | 1 |

### FINISHING SAUCE

| | | |
|---|---|---|
| 4 oz | feta cheese | 115 g |
| 1 | clove garlic, finely chopped | 1 |
| 2 tbsp | olive oil | 30 mL |

1. *Pipian Verde:* In a dry medium skillet over high heat, toast pumpkin seeds, stirring constantly, for 2 to 3 minutes or until starting to pop. Continue to cook for 2 to 3 minutes more, until popping stops. Transfer to a small bowl and let cool.

---

## Tips

*To make ahead:* In Step 8, chill pouch in ice-water bath, then refrigerate for up to 6 days or freeze for up to 6 months. If frozen, defrost in refrigerator overnight. Preheat hot water bath to 125°F (51.7°C). To reheat from refrigerator temperature, immerse pouch in bath for 1 hour. Proceed with Step 9.

If you end up with extra spice paste, reserve it for another use. It's great for seasoning lamb stews or stirred into rice to serve with grilled lamb chops.

2. Return skillet to heat. Add sesame seeds and toast, stirring constantly, for 4 to 5 minutes or until light golden. Add to bowl with pumpkin seeds. Stir in peppercorns and fennel seeds. Let cool.

3. Transfer seed mixture to spice grinder. Add oregano, bay leaves and salt. Grind to a powder.

4. In food processor fitted with the metal blade, combine jalapeños, cilantro, garlic, vinegar and spice powder. Process until a paste forms.

5. Place lamb on a large sheet of plastic wrap. Spread pipian verde evenly over both sides. Wrap lamb loosely in plastic wrap, place in sous vide pouch and seal. Refrigerate overnight or for up to 36 hours.

6. Preheat hot water bath to 140°F (60°C).

7. Immerse pouch in preheated hot water bath and cook for 12 hours.

8. Remove pouch from hot water bath. Chill in ice-water bath for 30 minutes. Let stand on counter until cool enough to handle, about 15 to 20 minutes. (To make ahead, see Tips, at left.)

9. Preheat grill to Medium. Scrape spice paste from pouch and reserve (see Tips, at left). Set lamb aside on a platter or baking sheet while preparing the sauce.

10. *Finishing Sauce:* Pour 1 cup (250 mL) reserved spice paste into food processor (discard any remaining paste or reserve for another use). Add feta, garlic and oil and process until smooth. Spread all over lamb.

11. Place lamb on preheated grill and cook, turning occasionally, for 12 to 15 minutes or until starting to brown. Cut crosswise into slices and serve on warm plates.

# Beef Shank Pho

Pho is a very popular Vietnamese noodle and meat dish served in a copious amount of savory broth. It's the go-to late-night meal of many a chef, and I hear that it's also perfect food for a hangover. Beef shank is inexpensive and flavorful, making it a perfect meat choice for do-it-yourself pho.

---

**MAKES
4 SERVINGS**

Freezer Bag Friendly

## Tips

You can halve or double this recipe easily.

For even more delicious results, use homemade beef stock in place of the beef broth.

Ceylon cinnamon, also known as true cinnamon, is a little different from the product that's usually marketed as cinnamon, which is cassia, a relative. True cinnamon has a gentler and more complex flavor than cassia. Look for it in Latin American or Asian grocery stores.

The saw-leaf plant, also known as culantro, tastes like a pungent version of cilantro, which can be used as a substitute. Look for it in Latin American or Asian grocery stores.

---

▶ **Preheat hot water bath to 161.6°F (72°C)**
▶ **4 sous vide pouches**
▶ **Fine-mesh sieve**

| | | |
|---|---|---|
| 4 | cross-cut pieces beef shank (about 12 oz/340 g each) | 4 |
| 4 tsp | fish sauce | 20 mL |
| **BROTH** | | |
| 1 | onion (unpeeled) | 1 |
| 1 | piece fresh gingerroot (about 3 inches/7.5 cm long) | 1 |
| 6 cups | ready-to-use reduced-sodium beef broth (see Tips, at left) | 1.5 L |
| 1 | star anise pod | 1 |
| 1 | whole clove | 1 |
| 1 | small piece Ceylon cinnamon (about 2 inches/5 cm; see Tips, at left) | 1 |
| 2 tbsp | fish sauce | 30 mL |
| 1 tbsp | granulated sugar | 15 mL |
| 8 oz | dried flat rice noodles (¼ inch/ 0.5 cm wide) | 225 g |

**GARNISHES**

Fresh Thai basil leaves, torn or coarsely chopped

Fresh saw leaf (see Tips, at left) or cilantro leaves, torn or coarsely chopped

Lime wedges

Sliced green or red onion

Hot pepper sauce, such as Sriracha

1. Rinse beef shanks under cold running water and pat dry with paper towels. Place each in a separate sous vide pouch. Add 1 tsp (5 mL) fish sauce to each pouch and seal. Immerse in preheated hot water bath and cook for 24 hours.

---

## Tip

*To make the beef ahead:* Prepare through Step 4. Transfer pouches to an ice bath and chill for 20 minutes. Refrigerate sealed pouches for up to 7 days or freeze for up to 6 months. Defrost shanks in their pouches in the refrigerator overnight. The broth will keep for 3 days when chilled and refrigerated, but it does not freeze well. To reheat from refrigerator temperature, preheat hot water bath to 140°F (60°C), immerse pouches and heat for 30 to 45 minutes. It is best to make the broth the day or the day before you need it. The noodles should be prepared on the day of serving. When the broth is made, proceed with Step 5.

2. *Broth:* Cut onion and ginger in half lengthwise. Place a dry medium skillet over high heat, preheat grill to High or preheat broiler. Place onion and ginger, cut sides down, in pan, on grill or under broiler. Cook for about 15 to 20 minutes or until charred.

3. In a medium saucepan, combine charred onion and ginger, broth, star anise, clove, cinnamon, fish sauce and sugar. Bring to a simmer over medium heat. Reduce heat to medium-low and simmer until aromatic, about 30 to 40 minutes. Strain through fine-mesh sieve into a bowl, discarding solids. Return broth to saucepan and keep warm.

4. Remove pouches from hot water bath. Let stand at room temperature for 15 minutes or until slightly cooled. (To make the beef ahead, see Tip, at left.)

5. Meanwhile, soak rice noodles according to package directions. Drain and set aside.

6. Bring broth to a simmer. Add noodles and stir until softened and heated through.

7. Distribute noodles and broth among warm bowls. Open pouches and place contents of each on top of one noodle bowl. Pass garnishes at the table.

# Venison Sauerbraten

Sauerbraten is essentially a pot roast made from a tough cut of red meat (usually beef) that's been tenderized, in part, by long marinating. This is my version of that classic, made with venison. Serve it with dumplings, spaetzle or simple boiled potatoes.

---

**MAKES 4 TO 6 SERVINGS**

Freezer Bag Friendly

## Tips

You can easily halve or double this recipe.

Farm-raised and wild venison both work well in this recipe. You can also substitute a cut of beef from the leg, such as eye of round, inside round or sirloin tip, if you like.

This recipe turns out a fairly rare venison, which I prefer. If you like your meat more well-done, I recommend substituting beef for the venison, as it will be a little less dry. Choose the temperature you prefer for your beef.

▶ **Sous vide pouch**
▶ **Large resealable freezer bag or non-reactive bowl**
▶ **Fine-mesh sieve**
▶ **Blender or immersion blender with tall cup**
▶ **Instant-read thermometer**

### MARINADE

| | | |
|---|---|---|
| 1 tbsp | vegetable oil | 15 mL |
| 1 | small onion, chopped | 1 |
| 1 | small carrot, chopped | 1 |
| 1 cup | water | 250 mL |
| 1 tsp | kosher salt | 5 mL |
| 1 tsp | pickling spice | 5 mL |
| ½ tsp | whole black peppercorns | 2 mL |
| 1 | bay leaf | 1 |
| 1 cup | dry red wine | 250 mL |
| 2¼ lbs | boneless venison hind or shoulder roast (see Tips, at left) | 1 kg |
| ½ cup | red wine vinegar | 125 mL |

### SAUCE

| | | |
|---|---|---|
| 1 | onion | 1 |
| 1 tbsp | granulated sugar | 15 mL |
| 1 tbsp | butter | 15 mL |
| 2 tbsp | sultana raisins | 30 mL |
| | Hot water | |
| ¼ cup | rendered beef, pork or duck fat, divided | 60 mL |
| 2 tbsp | browned flour (preferably rye) | 30 mL |
| ½ oz | gingersnap cookies (about 2) | 15 g |
| | Salt and freshly ground black pepper | |
| 1 tbsp | vegetable oil | 15 mL |
| | Chopped fresh parsley, optional | |

1. *Marinade:* In a medium skillet, heat oil over medium heat. Add onion and carrot and cook, stirring often, for 5 minutes or until softened. Increase heat to high and add water, salt, pickling spice, peppercorns and bay leaf. Bring to a boil. Stir in wine and return to a boil. Remove from heat and let cool completely.

2. In freezer bag, combine venison and marinade; seal bag. Refrigerate for 3 days, turning and shaking bag daily to make sure marinade penetrates the meat evenly.

3. Preheat hot water bath to 130°F (54.4°C).

4. Remove venison from bag, scraping off solids and reserving marinade. Place meat in sous vide pouch and seal. Immerse in preheated hot water bath and cook for 8 hours.

5. Meanwhile, in a small saucepan, bring reserved marinade to a boil over medium heat. Strain through fine-mesh sieve into a bowl, discarding solids. Wipe out pan. Return marinade to pan. Stir in vinegar and bring to a simmer over medium-low heat. Simmer, stirring occasionally, until reduced to 1¼ cups (300 mL). Set aside.

6. *Sauce:* Halve onion and remove and discard root. Slice onion thinly lengthwise. Heat a small, heavy-bottomed skillet over medium-low heat. Add onion, sugar and butter and cook, stirring occasionally, until deep brown, about 1 hour. Transfer onion mixture to a plate and set aside.

7. Place sultanas in a small bowl. Pour enough hot water overtop to cover. Let stand for 15 minutes or until plumped. Drain and set aside.

8. Meanwhile, in a medium skillet, heat half the rendered fat over medium heat. Add flour and cook, stirring constantly, for about 2 minutes. Slowly, while whisking, add reserved marinade mixture to skillet and bring to a boil. Remove from heat and let cool slightly.

9. Pour marinade mixture into blender or immersion blender cup. Add sultanas and gingersnaps; blend until smooth. Season to taste with salt, if necessary. Transfer contents of blender to a bowl and stir in onion mixture; set aside.

*continued on next page*

**10.** Remove pouch from hot water bath and pat venison dry with paper towels. Transfer to an ice bath and chill for 30 minutes. (To make ahead, see Tip, page 103.)

**11.** Open pouch and pat venison dry with paper towels. Rub oil all over meat and season to taste with additional salt and pepper.

**12.** In a skillet large enough to hold venison, heat remaining rendered fat over medium-high heat. Add meat to pan and cook, turning often, for 10 to 12 minutes or until browned all over. Use a thermometer to check if the internal temperature is warm (120° to 130°F/49° to 54°C). If the center is not yet heated through, continue to brown in skillet. Alternatively, preheat oven to 275°F (135°C), transfer venison to oven and cook until heated through.

**13.** Meanwhile, pour sauce into a small saucepan and bring to a simmer over medium heat.

**14.** Cut venison across the grain into $\frac{1}{2}$-inch (1 cm) slices. Transfer to warm plates and spoon enough sauce over each serving to partially cover. Garnish with parsley, if desired.

### Roasted Garlic

Roast garlic has a mild, sweet flavor all its own. It keeps for at least a week, covered and refrigerated, so I usually make more than I need. Once I have it on hand, I find all kinds of uses for it, such as in vinaigrettes, pasta and rubs.

There are quite a few methods to make roasted garlic. Here's the one that I like: Choose large heads of garlic with large cloves (I prefer the hardneck varieties). Break up heads into cloves but do not peel them. In a skillet with a lid, arrange cloves in one layer. Turn heat to medium-low and cover. Shake skillet every 2 to 3 minutes so that the cloves cook evenly.

Start checking the garlic after 10 minutes — you want the cloves to be exuding juice and collapsing. You should be able to squash one quite easily with the back of a fork. The total cooking time is about 20 minutes. Allow to cool and peel what you need (store extra cloves unpeeled). The cooking garlic is quite aromatic, so you may want to use your exhaust fan during the process.

# Beef Cheek Goulash

Goulash is a gutsy dish. Beef cheeks, with their big flavor, are a perfect cut to use here. Serve the goulash with dumplings, noodles, boiled potatoes or polenta.

### MAKES 4 TO 5 SERVINGS

Freezer Bag Friendly

## Tips

You can easily double this recipe. Use 2 bags so that the beef cooks evenly.

If beef cheeks are unavailable, beef brisket makes a good substitute. Choose a lean piece and cook at 158°F (70°C) for 20 hours.

▶ Preheat hot water bath to 172°F (77.8°C)
▶ Large resealable freezer bag
▶ Fine-mesh sieve

| | | |
|---|---|---|
| 1 oz | cured pork fatback or fatty pancetta, finely chopped | 30 g |
| 1 | onion, finely chopped | 1 |
| 1 | carrot, finely chopped | 1 |
| 1 | red bell pepper, finely chopped | 1 |
| 1 tbsp | minced garlic | 15 mL |
| 1 tbsp | sweet Hungarian paprika | 15 mL |
| 2 tsp | tomato paste | 10 mL |
| ¼ tsp | caraway seeds | 1 mL |
| 1¾ lbs | beef cheek meat, cut into ¾-inch (2 cm) cubes (see Tips, at left) | 790 g |
| 2 tbsp | all-purpose flour | 30 mL |
| 2 tsp | kosher salt (approx.) | 10 mL |
| 1 tsp | freshly ground black pepper | 5 mL |
| 2 to 3 tbsp | vegetable oil | 30 to 45 mL |
| 1½ cups | enhanced beef broth (page 401) | 375 mL |
| | Freshly chopped parsley, optional | |

*continued on next page*

## Tip

*To make ahead:* Prepare through Step 4. Transfer to an ice bath and chill for 30 minutes. Refrigerate sealed bag for up to 6 days or freeze for up to 6 months. To use frozen goulash, thaw overnight in the refrigerator. To reheat from refrigerator temperature, preheat hot water bath to 130°F (54.4°C). Immerse pouch for 1 hour before proceeding with Step 5.

1. In a small skillet, cook fatback over medium heat, stirring, until fat is rendered but not browned, about 6 minutes. Add onion and carrot and cook, stirring, for 5 minutes. Add bell pepper, garlic, paprika, tomato paste and caraway seeds. Reduce heat to medium-low and cook, stirring occasionally, until thick, about 10 minutes. Remove from heat and let cool.

2. Meanwhile, pat beef dry with paper towels. In a medium bowl, toss together beef, flour, 2 tsp (10 mL) salt and the pepper, until well coated. In a large skillet, heat 2 tbsp (30 mL) oil over high heat. Brown beef in batches, stirring, for 12 to 15 minutes per batch. As completed, transfer each batch to a platter in a single layer, and let cool. Adjust heat to avoid burning and add more oil between batches, as necessary.

3. When vegetable mixture and beef are cool enough to handle, place in freezer bag and seal. Immerse in preheated hot water bath and cook for 12 hours.

4. Remove bag from water bath and let cool at room temperature for 30 minutes. (To make ahead, see Tip, at left.)

5. Open bag and transfer beef to a warm serving dish. Cover with foil and a folded kitchen towel to keep warm. Strain cooking liquid through fine-mesh sieve into a small saucepan. Bring to a simmer over medium heat, stirring occasionally, until liquid is thickened, about 10 minutes. Season to taste with additional salt, if necessary. Pour over beef. Garnish with parsley, if desired, and serve.

# Drunken Oxtail

My assistant, Mandom, gave me this idea as a twist on Chinese drunken chicken. Oxtail, when properly prepared, is a most seductive meat. When I was in cooking school in the early 1980s, they often gave us oxtails to work with because they cost less than a dollar per pound (450 g). Sadly, that's no longer the case — it seems people now realize how delicious they are. This recipe makes two dinner-size servings or three or four good-sized snacks. You'll probably want to make a double or triple batch, because oxtails are about 50% bone. And once you start eating them, you won't want to stop! Have plenty of wet napkins or finger bowls handy.

**MAKES 2
MAIN-COURSE
SERVINGS**

Freezer Bag Friendly

## Tips

You can easily double or triple this recipe. One large oxtail will make about a double batch. Use 1 bag per tail.

Oxtails are frequently only available frozen. They freeze well, so don't let that keep you from using them. Thaw oxtail overnight in the refrigerator before using it in the recipe.

▶ **Preheat hot water bath to 172°F (77.8°C)**
▶ **Cheesecloth and butcher's twine**
▶ **Large resealable freezer bag**
▶ **Fine-mesh sieve**

| | | |
|---|---|---|
| 6 | cloves garlic | 6 |
| 5 | whole cloves | 5 |
| 3 | sprigs fresh thyme | 3 |
| 2 tsp | whole black peppercorns | 10 mL |
| 1½ cups | dry red wine | 375 mL |
| 2 tbsp | soy sauce | 30 mL |
| 1 tbsp | packed brown sugar | 15 mL |
| 1 tsp | fish sauce (or ¼ tsp/1 mL salt) | 5 mL |
| 2 | bay leaves | 2 |
| 1¼ lbs | fresh or thawed frozen oxtail, cut into pieces at the joints | 565 g |
| 2 tbsp | water | 30 mL |
| 1 tbsp | cornstarch | 15 mL |

1. Cut garlic cloves in half. Remove and discard the germ (the sprout in the center). Lay a small square of cheesecloth on work surface and place garlic, cloves, thyme and peppercorns on top. Tie with butcher's twine to make a bundle.

2. In a small saucepan, bring wine to a boil. Remove from heat. Stir in soy sauce, brown sugar, fish sauce, bay leaves and spice-and-herb bundle. Let cool slightly, about 15 minutes.

*continued on next page*

## Tips

*To make ahead:* Prepare through Step 4. Transfer to an ice bath and chill for 30 minutes. Refrigerate sealed bag for up to 5 days or freeze for up to 6 months. To use frozen oxtail, thaw overnight in the refrigerator. Preheat hot water bath to 130°F (54.4°C). Immerse bag in water bath for 30 minutes before proceeding with Step 5.

Oxtails are delicious served over mashed potatoes or soft polenta. But they're equally good eaten as is, standing over the stove — the way I do!

Don't throw out the leftover sauce. Dilute it slightly and use it as a braising liquid for beef short ribs or lamb shanks.

**3.** Place oxtail in freezer bag and add wine mixture. Seal bag. Immerse in preheated hot water bath and cook for 30 to 34 hours.

**4.** Remove bag from hot water bath and let stand at room temperature for 30 minutes. (To make ahead, see Tips, at left.)

**5.** Open bag and strain cooking liquid through fine-mesh sieve into a medium saucepan. Discard solids. Set oxtail aside and keep warm while you prepare the sauce.

**6.** Drag paper towels across the surface of the cooking liquid to remove excess fat (it is not essential that you get every last bit). Bring liquid to a simmer over medium heat, stirring occasionally, and simmer until reduced by about one-quarter to one-third. Skim off any film that develops on the surface. (The sauce will be strongly seasoned and quite salty.)

**7.** In a small bowl, whisk water with cornstarch until blended. Increase heat to medium-high and bring sauce to a boil. Whisk in cornstarch mixture and cook, whisking, for 2 minutes, until thickened and glossy.

**8.** Remove sauce from heat and add oxtail, stirring to coat and reheat slightly. Using a slotted spoon, transfer oxtail to a warm plate. Save sauce for another use (see Tips, at left).

# Pork

# Pork

Today's commercial pork doesn't offer the savory flavor that our parents and grandparents expected from this meat. Pork is bred to be lean these days, so you will need new tricks and techniques to keep it moist and make it delicious. Sous vide is one of them.

Of all the domesticated meats, pork is the one that most clearly reflects how the animal was raised — nurture, it turns out, is more important than nature. What a pig is fed and where it lives are two of the most significant factors that determine the taste and texture of the meat it yields. The difference between commodity and ethically raised pork is pronounced.

But nature does help start the process off right. Specialty and heritage breeds are excellent, and since many of them don't take well to feedlot confinement, those breeds in themselves give the pork a kind of guaranteed-quality badge of honor. Most heritage breeds put on weight slowly, so they are older at slaughter time and therefore more flavorful. Their meat is likely to be somewhat marbled with fat, which contributes to flavor and juiciness. Strike up a conversation with the pork vendor at your local farmers' market or with a butcher at a specialty meat shop. You will likely be able to preorder the cuts you desire.

## The Basics

Pork in North America has suffered from a bit of an identity crisis over the past 60 years or so. In the 1950s pork started to fall out of favor with home cooks, who now had access to cheaper chickens.

By 1973 the per capita consumption of poultry had surpassed pork and has been climbing ever since, while pork consumption has remained constant. "Pork. The Other White Meat" was an advertising slogan of the U.S. National Pork Board that pitched pork as an alternative to turkey or chicken, but this only contributed to the confusion and gave producers license to produce leaner pigs (the slogan was replaced by "Pork. Be Inspired" in 2011). Chefs love pork, and so do consumers around the globe: it is the most commonly eaten meat in the world. So put on your chef's hat and give pork a chance!

## TRICHINOSIS

Trichinosis is a parasitic infection found in game and pork. It was a concern in pigs a few generations ago, but it is now effectively nonexistent because of good animal husbandry. As well, the pork in all the recipes in this chapter is pasteurized, and therefore safe to eat.

## Selecting

- The ethically raised pork that I cook with always has a rosier color than the pale pink flesh of commodity-raised pork. This is largely because of the age of the animal, the fact that it gets more exercise, and its outdoor diet. When selecting pork, look for a darker color, which will give you more developed flavor.

## WHY BRINING IS A GOOD IDEA

Brining pork — especially commercial pork — frequently leads to better results. Brine helps to season the meat evenly at the outset and leaves it with more moisture after cooking. The small amount of sugar in a brine helps counteract the hardening effect encouraged by the salt.

Some of the recipes in this chapter require brine for optimal results. If brining is called for, I've made sure to mention it specifically. Where it isn't, you can still brine your pork for a day or two (but not more than three days, unless directed) for even juicier results.

Unused brine can be kept refrigerated for 5 to 7 days before use, but be sure to discard it after using.

- While pork freezes well (I always keep some bacon in my freezer), all frozen meat or fish will lose some of its moisture when defrosted. Commodity-raised pork, like chicken, has a tendency to be dry anyway, so aim to use fresh, ethically raised pork.
- Pork chops can come from the rib or the loin. The meat tastes roughly the same but rib chops include the bone, which is good for presentation, and they have a little more fat near the outside of the cut. Loin chops may have little or no bone and less fat near the outer edges; they also tend to be a little less expensive. Whichever you choose, select chops that are more than ½ inch (1 cm) thick. Thinner chops are at their best breaded and pan-fried.
- Pork for stews can technically come from any part of the pig. However, leg meat can be too lean and therefore dry, even when cooked with this moist-heat method, and loin, tenderloin and rib cuts are more expensive than you need. If I am making a stew that requires small pieces on the fattier side, I usually use trimmings from juicy belly and rib cuts (I save them up in the freezer until I need them). If I am buying a large quantity, then I buy shoulder and cut it to the size I need.
- Pork side ribs are a little fattier than back ribs, with more connective tissue and little pieces of crunchy cartilage that are great to chew on, and they are also less expensive than back ribs. I prefer them for all these reasons. Whichever you choose, count on buying about 1 lb (450 g) per person for a good-size serving.

## Prepping

- When packaging pork chops and ribs for sous vide cooking, keep in mind that the bones can be quite sharp. It is best to wrap chops and ribs in plastic wrap first, to keep the bones from puncturing the pouch or bag when you seal it.
- Seasoning ribs overnight helps add flavor. If I am not brining them, I either pack them with a favorite barbecue sauce or season them with a salted spice mix like the one on page 350.
- Pork tenderloins are very "user-friendly." You just need to remove the silverskin from the outside to

ensure tenderness. Fold the tail back over the rest of the tenderloin to create a uniform diameter for even cooking.

## Cooking

- Pork chops and tenderloin are relatively inexpensive, and their size and availability make them perfect for informal meals. I tend to cook these tender cuts at 140°F (60°C), which is also the internal temperature that I cook pork to when I'm not using the sous vide technique. This leaves them ever-so-slightly pink in the center. If you prefer your pork more well-done, feel free to raise the temperature of the hot water bath up to 150°F (65.6°C).

- The size of the eye (the central meaty part) may vary a bit, but a boneless pork loin or rib chop that is about ¾ inch (2 cm) thick makes a nice portion. It will cook through in 3 to 4 hours at 140°F (60°C). Cooking time always depends on the thickness rather than the length of a piece of meat, so pork tenderloin (whether it's a portion or a whole one) will cook through in about the same length of time as chops.

- Ribs are everyone's favorite. They have enough fat to stay juicy and contain lots of connective tissue, which, when properly cooked, gives them great texture. I like a little chew when it comes to ribs, so I cook them at 144°F (62.2°C), but you can increase the temperature of the hot water bath to a maximum of 158°F (70°C) if you like meat that falls off the bone. Keep in mind that the higher you raise the temperature, the more fat renders and the more juices are lost. If you choose to cook ribs at a higher temperature, make sure they are bathed in a liquid such as one of the moist seasoning mixes on page 117 or even store-bought barbecue sauce, and let them stand at room temperature for 30 to 40 minutes before chilling to help them reabsorb some of the lost liquid.

## Browning

- Whether you brown pork before or after cooking is largely up to you. Raw meat browns more easily than cooked, in part because the meat is more supple and makes better contact with the skillet or barbecue surface.

- If I am not going to barbecue the pork after cooking it sous vide, I usually brown it, let it cool slightly, seal it in a sous vide pouch, and then immerse it in the hot water bath. That way I can just cut open the pouch and slide the ready-to-eat meat onto warm plates.

- If I am going to brown the meat on the barbecue after cooking it sous vide, I slip the raw meat directly into the sous vide pouch, seal it and immerse it in the hot water bath. When it's finished, I chill it well to ensure that it doesn't overcook on the barbecue. Then I quickly brown the finished meat on the preheated grill and serve it piping hot.

# Pork Chops with Onion and Apple

This simple but utterly delicious pork preparation can be made using boneless or bone-in cuts. Because we are cooking at a low temperature, the apple retains its texture. Mashed potatoes are the classic accompaniment.

<table>
<tr><td>MAKES<br>2 SERVINGS</td></tr>
</table>

Freezer Bag Friendly

## Tips

You can halve or double this recipe. If doubling, use 2 pouches and divide the apple mixture equally.

Cooking at the temperature specified in this recipe will leave your pork slightly pink and juicy. If you want your meat more well-done, increase the temperature of the hot water bath to a maximum of 150°F (65.6°C). I find that 143°F (61.7°C) makes a good compromise.

*To make ahead:* Prepare through Step 5. Remove from hot water bath, transfer to an ice bath and chill for 30 minutes. Refrigerate sealed pouch for up to 5 days or freeze for up to 6 months. To use frozen chops, thaw overnight in the refrigerator. To reheat from refrigerator temperature, preheat hot water bath to 130°F (54.4°C); immerse pouch for 30 minutes before proceeding with Step 6.

▶ **Sous vide pouch**

| | | |
|---|---|---|
| 2 | pork loin or rib chops (each 6 to 7 oz/170 to 200 g) | 2 |
| | Salt and freshly ground black pepper | |
| 1 tbsp | vegetable oil | 15 mL |
| 2 tbsp | butter, divided | 30 mL |
| 1 | onion, sliced | 1 |
| 1 | green apple, peeled, halved and cored | 1 |
| 2 | sprigs fresh thyme | 2 |

1. Place chops on a plate and season with salt and pepper. Let stand at room temperature for 30 minutes.

2. Meanwhile, preheat hot water bath to 140°F (60°C).

3. Pat chops dry with paper towels. In a medium skillet, heat oil over medium-high heat. Add chops and cook, turning once, for 5 minutes or until browned on both sides. Transfer to a plate and set aside.

4. Reduce heat to medium and melt 1 tbsp (15 mL) butter in pan. Add onion and cook, stirring occasionally, for 15 minutes or until lightly browned. Cut apple vertically into 10 half-moon slices. Add to pan and cook, stirring occasionally, for 4 to 5 minutes or until slightly softened. Remove from heat and let cool.

5. Place chops, apple mixture, thyme and remaining butter in sous vide pouch. Arrange chops in a single layer, then seal. Immerse pouch in preheated hot water bath and cook for 2½ to 3½ hours.

6. Open pouch, remove thyme and discard. Place chops on warm plates. Garnish with onion and apple slices and cooking juices from pouch.

-------------------------------------------------------------

## Variation

**Pork Tenderloin with Onion and Apple:** Substitute 10 oz (280 g) trimmed pork tenderloin for the pork chops. Slice across the grain before serving.

# Basic Pork Chops

This is an excellent base recipe that works equally well with boneless or bone-in cuts and that you can enhance with a variety of sauces. It also works with pork tenderloin (see variation, page 115). I've suggested three of my favorite sauces, but this pork is also succulent and delicious served with a simple squeeze of fresh lemon juice or Dijon mustard.

---

| MAKES |
| --- |
| 2 SERVINGS |

**Freezer Bag Friendly**

## Tips

You can easily halve or double this recipe. If you double the recipe, use 2 pouches.

Cooking at the temperature specified in this recipe will give you juicy pork that's slightly pink in the center. If you want your meat more well-done, increase the temperature of the hot water bath to a maximum of 150°F (65.6°C). I find that 143°F (61.7°C) is a good compromise that yields more doneness without sacrificing taste.

▶ **Sous vide pouch**

| | | |
| --- | --- | --- |
| 2 | pork loin or rib chops (each 6 to 7 oz/170 to 200 g) | 2 |
| 1 | recipe Pork Brine (page 353), optional | 1 |
| | Salt and freshly ground black pepper, optional | |
| 1 tbsp | vegetable oil | 15 mL |
| 1 tbsp | butter | 15 mL |
| | Sauce Robert (page 372), Lingonberry Cream Sauce (page 373) or Morel Mushroom Cream Sauce (page 374), optional | |

1. If desired, in a large bowl or resealable plastic freezer bag, immerse chops in brine. Cover or seal tightly and refrigerate overnight or for up to 48 hours. Remove chops from brine and discard brine.

2. If not brining, place chops on a plate and season to taste with salt and pepper (if using). Refrigerate for 30 to 60 minutes.

3. Meanwhile, preheat hot water bath to 140°F (60°C).

4. Pat chops dry with paper towels. In a medium skillet, heat oil over medium-high heat. Add chops and cook, turning once, until browned on both sides, about 5 minutes. Transfer to a plate and set aside until cool enough to handle, about 5 minutes.

5. Transfer chops and accumulated juices to sous vide pouch. Make sure chops are arranged in a single layer, then seal. Immerse in preheated hot water bath and cook for 2½ to 3½ hours. (To make ahead, see Tips, at right.)

6. Open pouch and transfer chops to warm plates. Serve with sauce, if desired.

---

## Tips

*To make ahead:* Prepare through Step 5. Remove pouch from hot water bath, transfer to an ice-water bath and chill for 30 minutes. Refrigerate sealed pouch for up to 6 days or freeze for up to 6 months. To use frozen chops, thaw overnight in the refrigerator. To reheat from refrigerator temperature, preheat hot water bath to 130°F (54.4°C); immerse pouch for 30 minutes before proceeding with Step 6.

Another good way to reheat chops is by browning them a second time on a grill or grill pan. Open the refrigerated pouch and pat chops dry. Preheat grill or grill pan to Medium-High. Reheat chops by cooking for 2 to 3 minutes on each side. Season with salt and pepper, if desired, and serve.

## Variation

**Basic Pork Tenderloin:** Substitute 10 oz (280 g) trimmed pork tenderloin for the pork chops. Slice across the grain before serving.

### Speed It Up

I am well aware that 3 hours of cooking time can be hard to manage on a school night. Here is what I suggest to make this meal become a reality when you are in a hurry: Brine the pork the night before or skip that step. Preheat the hot water bath to 149°F (65°C). Cook as directed, but for only 1 hour. Brown the pork on a grill or in a grill pan before or after cooking, as desired, about 2 to 3 minutes per side. Prepare your sauce while the meat is cooking and you'll have everything on the table in a timely fashion.

# Pork Ribs

This is the master recipe for pork back or side (spare) ribs. At their most essential, the ribs are sprinkled with a seasoned salt (Barbecue Pork Rib Rub) and cooked sous vide, then finished under the broiler or on a grill, with or without your favorite barbecue sauce. The variations that follow use wet seasoning pastes, so the ribs almost braise while cooking sous vide, ensuring a juicy result. All these recipes benefit from seasoning overnight before cooking.

---

**MAKES
2 SERVINGS**

Freezer Bag Friendly

## Tips

You can easily halve or double this recipe to suit your needs. If you double the recipe, use 2 pouches.

The flavor of these ribs is vastly improved if they are allowed to spend at least 8 hours in contact with the rub. If you are in a hurry, you may cook them right after seasoning and sealing in Step 2.

▶ **Sous vide pouch (see Tips, at left)**

| | | |
|---|---|---|
| 2 lbs | pork back or side ribs, cut into two 1-lb (450 g) pieces | 900 g |
| 2 to 4 tbsp | Barbecue Pork Rib Rub (page 359) | 30 to 60 mL |
| | Barbecue sauce, optional | |

1. Rinse ribs under cold running water. Pat dry with paper towels and arrange on a baking sheet. Coat both sides of ribs evenly with Barbecue Pork Rib Rub. Use 2 tbsp (30 mL) if you are planning to use the optional barbecue sauce, or 4 tbsp (60 mL) if you are not planning to use barbecue sauce.

2. Tear off a piece of plastic wrap large enough to completely envelop the ribs when stacked one on top of the other. Place plastic wrap on work surface. Arrange one rack of ribs in center of wrap, meaty side up. Nestle second rack on top, also meaty side up. Bring plastic wrap up around ribs and wrap tightly. Place package in sous vide pouch and seal (see Tips, at left). Refrigerate for 8 to 10 hours or for up to 24 hours.

3. Preheat hot water bath to 144°F (62.2°C). Immerse pouch and cook for 10 to 12 hours.

4. Remove pouch from hot water bath, transfer to an ice bath and chill for 30 minutes. (To make ahead, see Tips, at right.)

5. Open pouch and remove plastic wrap from ribs, discarding any liquid from pouch. Pat ribs dry with paper towels. Preheat barbecue to Medium-High or preheat broiler.

## Tips

If you prefer your ribs falling off the bone, increase the hot water bath temperature to a maximum of 158°F (70°C).

*To make ahead:* Prepare through Step 4. Refrigerate sealed pouch for up to 1 week or freeze for up to 6 months. To use frozen ribs, thaw in refrigerator overnight. Proceed with Step 5.

**6.** Brush ribs with barbecue sauce (if using). Place ribs on grill or on a baking sheet under broiler. Grill or broil, brushing halfway through with more barbecue sauce (if using), for 10 to 15 minutes or until heated through and lightly caramelized.

## Variations

**East-Inspired Ribs:** In Step 1, replace the Barbecue Pork Rib Rub and barbecue sauce with Chinese Black Bean Pork Seasoning (page 360), Thai Pork Barbecue Seasoning (page 361), or Super-Simple Korean Rib Marinade (below).

**Latin–American Inspired Ribs:** In Step 1, replace Barbecue Pork Rib Rub and barbecue sauce with Tamarind-Chipotle Seasoning Paste (page 362).

These variations give your ribs a wide variety of flavors. The moisture in the sauces ensures that the meat will turn out extra-juicy.

### Super-Simple Korean Rib Marinade

Kimchi makes a fiery and delicious single-ingredient seasoning for ribs or pork belly. It's so easy: Measure 1½ cups (375 mL) napa cabbage kimchi with its liquid. Drain kimchi, reserving liquid. Coarsely chop cabbage and stir into reserved liquid. Use immediately or transfer to a bowl, cover and refrigerate for up to 7 days. This makes enough for 2 lbs (900 g) of pork back or side ribs or 1 to 1½ lbs (450 to 675 g) of pork belly (rind on or off).

# Essential Char Siu–Style Pork Belly

Char siu was originally a Cantonese preparation of roast pork. It was adapted by the Japanese, who call it *chashu* and eat it mostly as a topping for steaming bowls of ramen. This recipe is designed for the same use and also as a base for two delicious variations on the theme: Filipino Pork Belly Adobo (page 120) and Babi Kecap (page 121). The number of servings varies depending on the application.

---

**MAKES 6 TO 8 SERVINGS**

Freezer Bag Friendly

## Tips

You can easily halve or double this recipe to suit your needs. If you double the recipe, use 2 bags.

*To make ahead:* Prepare through Step 5. Refrigerate for up to 1 week or freeze for up to 6 months. To use frozen pork belly, thaw in the refrigerator overnight. Proceed with Step 6.

▶ **Preheat hot water bath to 155°F (68.3°C)**
▶ **Large resealable freezer bag**

| 2 lbs | fresh pork belly (rind on or off) | 900 g |
|---|---|---|
| 6 tbsp | soy sauce | 90 mL |
| 6 tbsp | sake | 90 mL |
| 1 tbsp | liquid honey | 15 mL |
| 2 | green onions, thinly sliced | 2 |
| 1 tbsp | finely chopped gingerroot | 15 mL |

1. If the pork belly has the rind attached, use a sharp paring knife to score it at 1-inch (2.5 cm) intervals across the belly. Repeat in the opposite direction, scoring at a 90-degree angle to the first set of slashes.

2. In a heatproof glass measuring cup or small saucepan, stir together soy sauce, sake and honey. To cook off some of the alcohol in the sake, microwave on High for 2 minutes or bring to a boil on the stove over medium heat for about 2 minutes. Remove from heat and stir in green onions and ginger. Refrigerate for 10 minutes or until chilled.

3. Transfer pork belly and soy sauce mixture to freezer bag.

4. Seal bag and immerse in preheated hot water bath. Cook for 10 to 12 hours.

5. Remove bag from hot water bath, transfer to an ice bath and chill for 30 minutes. (To make ahead, see Tips, at left.)

6. Remove pork belly from bag, reserving cooking liquid (see Tip, at right). Pat dry with paper towels and remove skin, if desired.

## Tip

The reserved cooking liquid is required to make Filipino Pork Belly Adobo (page 120) and Babi Kecap (page 121). You can also use it to season ramen broth. In all three cases, strain the liquid through a fine-mesh sieve before using. It will keep for at least 7 days in the refrigerator or frozen for 12 months.

**7.** Preheat broiler. Place pork belly on a baking sheet and broil for 10 minutes, turning once, or until heated through and lightly browned. Slice and serve on warm plates.

## Variation

**Char Siu–Style Pork Shoulder:** Boneless pork shoulder also works well in this recipe. Choose a piece that is about the same weight and shaped like a brick (remember, sous vide cooking times are determined by the shape and thickness of the food). Reduce the hot water bath temperature to 150°F (65.6°C). Cook for a full 12 hours to ensure tenderness.

### A Bit about Pork Belly

Pork belly has become trendy in North America only in the past 15 years. It has, however, been popular in Asia for a lot longer. Depending on the piece, it is roughly 50% fat. The meat is particularly savory, mostly because it self-bastes with its fat as it cooks.

Pork belly frequently comes rind-on. The times and temperatures in the recipes on pages 118 to 121 will leave the rind with a slightly chewy texture. The rind contains lots of collagen, which lends the juices an unctuous texture — that's why I suggest you leave it on during cooking. Just remove it before serving if you and your guests don't want to eat it.

You'll need about 6 oz (170 g) raw pork belly per person if it's being served as a main course. You can reduce that amount to half if the belly is part of a meal with several other dishes.

### More Twists on Pork Belly

To make a European-style preparation such as pork belly with lentils, or to tuck pork belly into *choucroute garnie*, use this recipe for Essential Char Siu–Style Pork Belly. After Step 1, brine the pork for 1 to 2 days, using my recipe for Pork Brine (page 353). Omit Steps 2 and 3 and proceed with the recipe, omitting Step 7 if desired.

# Filipino Pork Belly Adobo

This luscious sweet-and-sour pork belly is considered the national dish of the Philippines. And Filipinos are right to love it so much: it's hearty, filling and incredibly satisfying. Serve with steamed rice and a simple vegetable such as green beans or Okra with Preserved Lemon (page 308).

**MAKES 6 TO 8 SERVINGS**

## Tips

You can easily halve or double this recipe.

It is best to make this recipe the same day that you plan to eat it. Prepare the pork belly in advance.

Adding 1 or 2 ground small dried chiles will add a nice spicy heat, if desired.

In this recipe the pork becomes tender and almost ready to fall apart just as the liquid is reduced to a slightly sticky, quite dark glaze on the meat. If the pork is ready before the sauce, transfer it to a plate and cover while continuing to reduce the sauce. If the sauce is ready but the pork needs further cooking, add water to the skillet, a little at a time, to keep the sauce from over-reducing.

You can also make this dish with the leaner variation, Char Siu–Style Pork Shoulder (page 119).

| | | |
|---|---|---|
| 1 | batch Essential Char Siu–Style Pork Belly (page 118), prepared through Step 4 | 1 |
| ¼ cup | cider vinegar | 60 mL |
| 2 tbsp | finely chopped garlic | 30 mL |
| 1 | onion, halved and thinly sliced | 1 |
| 2 tbsp | grated piloncillo sugar (see box, below) | 30 mL |
| 1½ tsp | freshly ground black pepper | 7 mL |
| 4 | bay leaves | 4 |

1. Cut prepared pork belly into 1-inch (2.5 cm) chunks, leaving rind on (if present). Set aside.

2. In a large, heavy-bottomed skillet, combine pork belly, vinegar, garlic, onion, sugar, pepper and bay leaves. Bring to a boil over medium heat and boil for 5 minutes.

3. Reduce heat to medium and simmer, adjusting heat as necessary to maintain a slow simmer and stirring occasionally, for 20 to 25 minutes, until juices are reduced to a sticky caramelized glaze and pork is very tender but not falling apart. (The cooking time will depend on the diameter of your skillet; go larger if you are unsure.) To prevent burning, check the mixture constantly as the juices reduce.

4. Serve pork on warm plates.

### Piloncillo

Piloncillo is a Latin American unrefined sugar made by boiling down sugarcane juice. Palm sugar is more appropriate for Filipino cuisine, but it can be difficult to find the right kind. Piloncillo comes in cones, which are easily grated with a box grater. Just grate the amount you need for the recipe and store the rest in a cool, dark place in an airtight container. Piloncillo has nice caramel and molasses notes; you can substitute turbinado or muscovado sugar in a pinch.

# Babi Kecap

The key flavoring in this Indonesian pork dish is a sweet soy sauce called kecap (or ketjap) manis, which is sweetened with palm sugar. There is a similar Vietnamese dish called *thit kho*, which has the unmistakable flavor of umami-rich fish sauce. These dishes are often prepared when meat is scarce, so you can eat small amounts with lots of rice.

## MAKES 8 SERVINGS

## Tips

You can easily halve or double this recipe.

It is best to make this recipe the same day that you plan to eat it. Prepare the pork belly in advance.

Do not substitute Char Siu–Style Pork Shoulder (variation, page 119) for the pork belly. This dish requires the richness of the belly.

Kecap (ketjap) manis is often found in Dutch grocery stores. Conimex, a Dutch company, makes a very good version.

Like the Filipino adobo, the idea here is that the pork becomes tender and almost ready to fall apart just as the liquid is reduced (see Tips, page 120).

| | | |
|---|---|---|
| 1 | batch Essential Char Siu–Style Pork Belly (page 118), prepared through Step 4 | 1 |
| 1 cup | sliced shallots | 250 mL |
| ¼ cup | finely chopped garlic | 60 mL |
| ¼ cup | prepared tamarind paste (see box, page 135) | 60 mL |
| ¼ cup | kecap manis (Indonesian sweet soy sauce) | 60 mL |
| 2 tbsp | chopped hot red chile peppers (or 3 tbsp/45 mL sambal oelek) | 30 mL |
| 1½ tbsp | finely chopped gingerroot | 22 mL |
| ½ tsp | ground white pepper | 2 mL |
| 1 | small star anise pod | 1 |
| 1 cup | coarsely chopped fresh cilantro | 250 mL |

1. Cut prepared pork belly into 1-inch (2.5 cm) chunks, leaving rind on (if present).

2. In a large, heavy-bottomed skillet, combine pork belly, shallots, garlic, tamarind paste, kecap manis, chiles, ginger, white pepper and star anise. Bring to a boil over medium heat and boil for 5 minutes.

3. Reduce heat to medium-low and simmer, adjusting heat as necessary to maintain a slow simmer and stirring occasionally, until juices are reduced to a sticky caramelized glaze and pork is very tender but not falling apart, about 20 to 25 minutes. (The total cooking time will depend on the diameter of your skillet; go larger rather than smaller if you are unsure.) To prevent burning, check the mixture constantly as the juices reduce (see Tips, page 120).

4. Spoon pork onto warm plates, discarding star anise. Garnish with cilantro and serve.

# Georgian Pork Shoulder Roast with Pomegranate Glaze

On a recent wine trip to the country of Georgia, I became enchanted with its culture. The food is unique; it is an herb-based cuisine, so there are surprising blends of flavors. The autumn farmers' markets look as though they have been plucked from the Garden of Eden. In Georgia this dish might be accompanied by plain simmered red beans, which complement its exotic flavors.

---

**MAKES 6 SERVINGS**

**Freezer Bag Friendly**

## Tips

You can easily double this recipe. If you are cooking a piece that's twice the size, increase the cooking time to 10 to 12 hours. In this case I recommend that you buy a piece of pork with the rind on and reheat it very carefully, so the rind is evenly crisp.

Your butcher can roll the pork for you. This involves tying up the meat after the bones have been removed.

*To make ahead:* Prepare through Step 4. Refrigerate sealed bag for up to 7 days or freeze for up to 6 months. To use frozen pork, thaw in refrigerator overnight and proceed with Step 5.

▷ **Sous vide pouch**
▷ **Instant-read thermometer**

### SPICE BLEND

| | | |
|---|---|---|
| ½ tsp | fenugreek seeds | 2 mL |
| ½ tsp | cumin seeds | 2 mL |
| 1½ tsp | coriander seeds | 7 mL |
| ½ tsp | kosher salt | 2 mL |
| 1½ tbsp | sweet Hungarian paprika | 22 mL |
| ½ tsp | cayenne pepper | 2 mL |
| | Water | |
| 1 tbsp | finely chopped garlic | 15 mL |

### ROAST

| | | |
|---|---|---|
| 2½ to 3 lbs | boneless rolled pork shoulder roast (rind on or off) | 1.125 to 1.35 kg |
| 2 cups | fresh or unsweetened bottled pomegranate juice | 500 mL |
| 2 tsp | finely chopped garlic | 10 mL |
| ½ tsp | hot pepper sauce, such as Tabasco sauce | 2 mL |
| | Salt | |
| 1 | pomegranate, peeled and arils separated | 1 |
| 1½ cups | coarsely chopped fresh cilantro | 375 mL |

1. *Spice Blend:* In a spice grinder, combine fenugreek, cumin and coriander seeds and salt. Grind to a fine powder. Transfer to a small bowl and stir in paprika and cayenne. Add water a little at a time, stirring constantly, until a thick paste forms. Stir in garlic.

2. *Roast:* Pat pork dry with paper towels. Rub spice blend all over meat. Wrap in plastic wrap, place in sous vide pouch and seal. Refrigerate overnight or for up to 24 hours.

## Tips

Fruit juices are difficult to reduce significantly without their sugars caramelizing. Reducing them in the microwave can be a nuisance, because you have to be vigilant about boil-overs and you need to open the door every 2 minutes or so to evacuate the steam. However, using a microwave yields a reduced juice with greater purity of flavor.

If you have a rotisserie attachment for your grill, you can also use that to reheat the pork instead of browning on the barbecue.

3. Preheat hot water bath to 145°F (62.8°C). Immerse pouch in preheated bath and cook for 6 to 7 hours.

4. Remove pouch from hot water bath. Transfer to an ice bath and chill for 45 minutes, replenishing ice as necessary. (To make ahead, see Tips, page 122.)

5. Meanwhile, in a small saucepan or small bowl, combine pomegranate juice, garlic and hot pepper sauce. Heat saucepan over medium-low heat or microwave bowl on High (see Tips, at left) until juice mixture is reduced and starts to thicken (you should end up with no more than one-third of the liquid that you started with). Set aside.

6. Preheat barbecue to Medium-High or preheat broiler. Open pouch and scrape spices off pork; discard spices. Strain cooking liquid in pouch into reduced juice mixture. Place pork on grill or on a baking sheet under broiler. Watching carefully to prevent burning, grill or broil, turning occasionally, for 15 minutes or until browned and heated through — about 130°F (54.4°C) on instant-read thermometer. If desired, brush some of the juice mixture over pork during last 5 minutes (again, watch carefully, as this sauce can burn quickly).

7. Cut pork into slices 1/2 inch (1 cm) thick. Arrange on a warm platter or distribute among warm plates. Drizzle with reduced juice mixture and season to taste with salt. Garnish with pomegranate arils and cilantro.

### Pork Shoulder: Big and Versatile

Pork shoulders are large and sold as blades, Boston butts (the upper part) or picnic shoulders (the part that includes the foreleg). The blade may be a little more expensive, but it's easier to work with and has some advantages. The "capicollo" portion, located in the blade, is an extension of the loin muscle as it heads toward the neck. It is well marbled, evenly shaped and a perfect candidate for pulled pork or any other well-cooked barbecue-style preparation. Incidentally, a whole blade has the ideal ratio of meat to fat for making sausages.

The picnic shoulder lies below the blade. It includes the hock, which can also be bought separately at a very reasonable price. The rest of the picnic shoulder has only a leg bone and is therefore very easy to bone. This cut is typically used to make what we call picnic hams. The meat is marginally tougher than the cuts above it, but sous vide cooking takes care of that beautifully; it will work for any recipe that calls for shoulder.

# Maiale al Latte

Pork cooked in milk — *maiale al latte* in Italian — is a relatively obscure recipe that has become popular in the past few decades. It was first published by Pellegrino Artusi more than 100 years ago. My variation employs lambda carrageenan, a seaweed-derived product used in food processing, to keep the milk from separating during cooking. I like to serve this dish with slow-cooked Swiss chard and soft polenta. Any leftover pork is great cold in sandwiches.

## Tips

You can easily double this recipe. If you are cooking a single piece of pork leg that is double the size called for in the ingredient list, increase the brining time to 3 days and the cooking time to 12 hours. In this case I recommend that you use a piece that has the rind on. Broil it very carefully so the rind is evenly crisp.

You can substitute pork shoulder for the leg, cooking it for the same amount of time at the same temperature. To ensure that the dish isn't overly greasy, choose a lean shoulder cut and remove any excess surface fat. Boneless pork loin can also stand in for the leg if you prefer; reduce the hot water bath temperature to 141.8°F (61°C) and cook for 4 to 5 hours.

- Large resealable freezer bag
- Large non-reactive bowl
- Instant-read thermometer
- Immersion blender
- Cheesecloth and butcher's twine

| | | |
|---|---|---|
| 1 | piece boneless pork leg, preferably rind-on (2 lbs/900 g; see Tips, at left) | 1 |
| 1½ | recipes Pork Brine (page 353) | 1½ |
| 2½ cups | whole milk | 625 mL |
| ¼ tsp | lambda carrageenan | 1 mL |
| 2 | small sprigs fresh rosemary | 2 |
| 6 | juniper berries, crushed | 6 |
| 2 | bay leaves | 2 |
| 2 | green onions, coarsely chopped | 2 |
| 1 | clove garlic, halved lengthwise | 1 |
| 1 | small piece lemon zest (about ½ by 2 inches/1 by 5 cm) | 1 |
| 1 tsp | cornstarch | 5 mL |
| 2 tsp | water | 10 mL |
| | Ground white pepper | |
| | Vegetable oil, optional | |
| | Chopped fresh parsley | |

1. If pork leg has the rind on, use a small, sharp knife to score the rind at ½-inch (1 cm) intervals in one direction. Repeat in opposite direction, scoring at a 90-degree angle to first set of cuts. Place leg in non-reactive bowl and pour brine overtop. Cover and refrigerate for 2 days.

2. Preheat hot water bath to 145°F (62.8°C).

3. Lift pork out of brine; discard brine. Rinse meat under cold water and pat dry with paper towels. Set aside.

## Tips

*To make ahead:* Prepare through Step 5. Remove from hot water bath, transfer to an ice bath and chill for 45 minutes. Refrigerate sealed pouch for up to 5 days (do not freeze, as the milk will separate). To reheat from refrigerator temperature, preheat hot water bath to 125°F (51.7°C); immerse pouch for 45 minutes before proceeding with Step 6.

If the milk in the pouch separates into curds and whey, let it cool slightly. Pour it into a blender and purée until smooth. Proceed with Step 7, monitoring the temperature with the instant-read thermometer. When it reaches 175°F (79.4°C), add another ¼ tsp (1 mL) lambda carrageenan the same way as in Step 4, then continue with the recipe. Carrageenan is used in this recipe to stabilize the milk emulsion (see box, at right). The amount used here equals about 0.1% of the weight of the milk.

4. In a small saucepan, heat milk over low heat until thermometer reads 175°F (79.4°C). Remove from heat. Blending constantly with immersion blender, gradually sprinkle in carrageenan; blend well.

5. Place rosemary, juniper berries, bay leaves, green onions, garlic and lemon zest on a small square of cheesecloth. Tie with butcher's twine to make a bundle. Place pork, milk mixture and seasoning bundle in freezer bag and seal. Immerse bag in preheated hot water bath and cook for 6 to 7 hours.

6. Remove bag from hot water bath, open bag and transfer pork to a plate. Pour milk mixture into a medium saucepan, squeezing seasoning bundle to remove as much liquid as possible.

7. Cook milk mixture over medium heat, stirring often, until reduced to desired level of saltiness (the pork has been brined, so don't over-reduce the liquid or it will be too salty). In a small bowl, stir cornstarch with water until smooth. Bring sauce to a boil and slowly stir in enough cornstarch mixture to thicken sauce (discard any remaining cornstarch mixture). Season to taste with white pepper. Set aside and keep warm.

8. If pork has its rind, preheat broiler. Broil pork, skin side up, for 8 to 10 minutes or until browned. Be mindful not to place meat too close to broiler element, or it will burn. If pork does not have its rind, in a large, heavy-bottomed skillet, heat ¼ inch (0.5 cm) oil over medium-high heat. Cook meat, turning, for 8 to 10 minutes or until browned all over.

9. Slice pork and transfer to warm plates. Top with reduced sauce and garnish with parsley.

---

### Lambda Carrageenan

Lambda carrageenan belongs to a family of products derived from Irish moss. It has been used for more than 2,000 years to thicken puddings in parts of the British Isles and is widely used today in dairy products, such as yogurt and ice cream, as a thickener and emulsifying stabilizer. You'll also notice it in raw vegan diets, where it's used to thicken soups, smoothies and nut milks. Lambda carrageenan is available at Modernist Pantry (www.modernistpantry.com).

# Bigos (Polish Hunter's Stew)

This rich stew is one of the national dishes of Poland. It was originally made with game, hence the English translation of its name. Now this dish is more commonly made with several types of pork, and sometimes duck as well. It is best prepared a day ahead and reheated. The stew is delicious on its own or accompanied by boiled potatoes.

**MAKES
6 SERVINGS**

Freezer Bag Friendly

## Tip

This recipe can be doubled. Just divide the stew between 2 freezer bags.

▶ **Preheat hot water bath to 149°F (65°C)**
▶ **Large resealable freezer bag**
▶ **Large skillet with lid**
▶ **Cheesecloth and butcher's twine**

| | | |
|---|---|---|
| 5 tbsp | rendered pork, duck or chicken fat, divided | 75 mL |
| 1 cup | finely chopped onion | 250 mL |
| 4 cups | shredded green cabbage | 1 L |
| 1 cup | canned tomatoes, with juice | 250 mL |
| 2 tbsp | Madeira | 30 mL |
| 1 | carrot, chopped | 1 |
| ½ oz | dried porcini mushrooms (cèpes) | 15 g |
| | Hot water | |
| 1 lb | boneless stewing pork (leg or shoulder), cut into 1-inch (2.5 cm) pieces | 450 g |
| 10 | black peppercorns, cracked | 10 |
| 6 | juniper berries, crushed | 6 |
| ½ tsp | caraway seeds | 2 mL |
| 1 | bay leaf | 1 |
| 8 oz | Polish sausage (kielbasa), cut into ½-inch (1 cm) pieces | 225 g |
| 8 oz | double-smoked slab bacon, rind removed, cut into ½-inch (1 cm) pieces | 225 g |
| 2 lbs | prepared sauerkraut, rinsed and drained | 900 g |
| 1 | green apple, peeled and grated (optional) | 1 |
| | Salt and freshly ground black pepper | |

1. In large skillet with lid, melt 3 tbsp (45 mL) fat over medium heat. Add onion and cook, stirring often, until softened but not browned, about 10 minutes. Add cabbage, tomatoes, Madeira and carrot. Reduce

## Tip

*To make ahead:*
Prepare through Step 6.
Refrigerate sealed bag
for up to 1 week or freeze
for up to 6 months. To
use frozen stew, thaw in
refrigerator overnight.
Proceed with Step 7.

heat, cover and simmer for about 30 minutes or until
cabbage is thoroughly wilted. Uncover, remove from
heat and set aside.

**2.** Place dried mushrooms in a small bowl. Pour in
enough hot water to cover and let soak for about
15 minutes or until softened. Lift mushrooms out of
soaking liquid without disturbing any grit at bottom of
bowl. Chop coarsely. Carefully pour soaking liquid into
another small bowl, leaving grit behind.

**3.** In another large skillet, melt remaining fat over
medium-high heat. Add pork and cook, stirring
often, for 15 minutes or until well browned. Using a
slotted spoon, transfer pork to a plate and set aside.
Pour reserved mushroom-soaking liquid into pan and
reduce heat to medium; bring to a boil, scraping up any
browned bits from bottom of pan. Boil, stirring, until
reduced to about $\frac{1}{4}$ cup (60 mL). Remove from heat
and set aside.

**4.** Place peppercorns, juniper berries, caraway seeds and
bay leaf on a small square of cheesecloth. Tie with
butcher's twine to make a bundle.

**5.** Place pork, any accumulated juices, cabbage mixture,
mushrooms, spice bundle, sausage, bacon, sauerkraut
and apple (if using) in freezer bag and seal. Immerse in
preheated hot water bath and cook for 8 hours.

**6.** Remove bag from hot water bath. Transfer to an ice
bath and chill for 40 minutes, replenishing ice if
necessary. Remove bag from ice bath, pat dry with
paper towels and refrigerate overnight. (To make ahead,
see Tip, at left.)

**7.** Preheat hot water bath to 130°F (54.4°C). Immerse bag
in preheated hot water bath and reheat for 1 hour.

**8.** Open pouch and discard spice bag. Pour stew into a
warm serving bowl. Mix well and season to taste with
salt and pepper, if necessary. Serve on warm plates.

## Variation

**Duck Bigos:** If you want an even meatier dish, Duck
Confit (page 176) is the perfect addition. Reheat the
duck in a skillet, making sure to brown the skin.
Separate the legs into thighs and drumsticks and serve
on top of the stew.

# Pulled Pork

Pulled pork makes sloppy, addictively tasty sandwiches. It's also great tucked into tortillas and served taco-style. If you're using pulled pork in tacos, serve them with plenty of shredded romaine lettuce and perhaps a little shredded Cheddar cheese.

---

**MAKES 8 SERVINGS**

Freezer Bag Friendly

## Tips

You can easily halve or double this recipe. If you're doubling it, divide the shoulder in half and seal each piece in a separate sous vide pouch.

*To make ahead:* Prepare through Step 3. Transfer pouch to an ice bath and chill for 45 minutes, replacing ice as necessary. Refrigerate sealed pouch for up to 1 week or freeze for up to 6 months. To use frozen pork, thaw in refrigerator overnight. To reheat from refrigerator temperature, preheat hot water bath to 125°F (51.7°C); immerse pouch for 40 minutes before proceeding with Step 4.

This dish can be a base for more than just sandwiches and tacos. Try tossing it with the macaroni before baking macaroni and cheese, fill omelets with it, or squeeze it dry and use as a ravioli filling.

▶ **Sous vide pouch**

| | | |
|---|---|---|
| 1 | boneless pork shoulder roast (3 lbs/1.35 kg) | 1 |
| 3 tbsp | Barbecue Pork Rib Rub (page 359) | 45 mL |
| 2 tbsp | vegetable oil | 30 mL |
| ½ cup | barbecue sauce | 125 mL |
| 2 | green onions, thinly sliced | 2 |
| | Toasted buns or corn or flour tortillas | |

1. Pat shoulder dry with paper towels and coat all over with rub. Place in sous vide pouch and seal. Refrigerate overnight or for up to 24 hours (no longer than that).

2. Preheat hot water bath to 158°F (70°C). Immerse pouch in preheated bath and cook for 24 hours.

3. Remove pouch from hot water bath. Let stand at room temperature for 20 minutes. (To make ahead, see Tips, at left.)

4. Open pouch and transfer pork and cooking juices to a large bowl. Using hands or 2 forks, shred meat. Place a sieve over another large bowl. Drain pork in sieve (without pressing) and reserve juices.

5. Add oil to pork and toss to coat. Heat a large, heavy-bottomed skillet over medium-high heat. Add pork and brown, turning occasionally, for about 15 minutes or until edges just begin to crisp but pork is still juicy. Return cooking juices to pork and stir to combine.

6. In a small saucepan over medium heat, bring barbecue sauce to a simmer. Add to pork, along with green onions. Stir to coat. Serve warm on buns or tortillas.

# Pork Hocks

Pork hocks are inexpensive and have a robust flavor. This recipe makes hocks with a pure but slightly "hammy" quality, thanks to the brine. The hocks can be sliced or diced and served cold in salads or added to soups, but they are most at home as part of a platter of *choucroute garnie* or added to a pot of baked beans.

---

### MAKES ABOUT 2 LBS (900 G)

Freezer Bag Friendly

## Tips

You can easily halve or double this recipe.

If you plan to use the hock cold, you may want to remove the rind after cooking. If you plan on cooking the meat further in another dish, leave the rind on to add extra richness.

If you want to make the rind tender enough to use in another dish, remove it from the hock after cooking. Preheat hot water bath to 158°F (70°C). Seal the rind in a fresh sous vide pouch, immerse in the preheated bath and cook for 6 hours.

The hock can be frozen for up to 6 months. Defrost overnight in the refrigerator before use.

▶ **Sous vide pouch**
▶ **Non-reactive bowl or large resealable freezer bag**
▶ **Marinade or brine injector**

| | | |
|---|---|---|
| 1 | pork hock (rind on or off), about 2 lbs (900 g) | 1 |
| 1½ | recipes Pork Brine (page 353), strained | 1½ |

1. Place hock in non-reactive bowl. Fill injector with brine. Holding hock in bowl with one hand, inject brine into meaty parts, refilling injector as necessary and using about ½ cup (125 mL) brine in total (much of it will leak into the bowl, which is fine). Pour remaining brine over hock. Cover and refrigerate for 5 days.

2. Preheat hot water bath to 158°F (70°C).

3. Lift hock out of brine (discard brine). Rinse hock under cold running water and drain well.

4. Transfer hock to sous vide pouch and seal. Immerse in preheated hot water bath and cook for 18 to 20 hours.

5. Remove pouch from hot water bath and let stand at room temperature for 20 to 30 minutes. Transfer to an ice bath and chill for 30 minutes. Serve immediately or store in the refrigerator for up to 2 weeks.

# Pozole Verde

Pozole (or posole), the famous Mexican pork stew, comes in red, white and green versions, which represent the colors of the country's flag. The color choice is partly a regional preference, and you can get all three types in the capital city. The green (*verde*) version is the one I like best. Pozole is traditionally eaten for lunch on Thursdays, preferably followed by a nap.

## Tips

You can easily double this recipe, dividing the ingredients equally between 2 bags. It isn't worth the trouble to make less than a single batch, however.

Mexican oregano has a particular flavor that's nice in this recipe. If you can't find it, substitute 1 tsp (5 mL) common (Greek) oregano and 1 tsp (5 mL) rubbed marjoram.

The pork you use for this stew should be on the fattier side. I like trimmings from belly pieces and ribs, or pork shoulder.

▶ **Preheat hot water bath to 158°F (70°C)**
▶ **Large resealable freezer bag**
▶ **Spice grinder or coffee grinder**
▶ **Food processor**

| | | |
|---|---|---|
| ¼ cup | raw pumpkin seeds (pepitas) | 60 mL |
| 2 tbsp | sesame seeds | 30 mL |
| 2 tsp | black peppercorns | 10 mL |
| 1 tsp | fennel seeds | 5 mL |
| 1 tbsp | kosher salt (approx.) | 15 mL |
| 2 tsp | dried Mexican oregano (see Tips, at left) | 10 mL |
| 1 | bay leaf | 1 |
| 2 | jalapeño peppers, roasted (see box, page 131), seeded and peeled | 2 |
| 1 | poblano pepper, roasted, seeded and peeled | 1 |
| 1 | small bunch fresh cilantro (leaves and stems) | 1 |
| 1 | head garlic, roasted (see box, page 104) and peeled | 1 |
| 1 tsp | freshly squeezed lime juice | 5 mL |
| 1 | can (28 oz/796 mL) whole tomatillos, drained | 1 |
| 1 lb | boneless pork (see Tips, at left), cut in ½-inch (1 cm) cubes | 450 g |
| 1 | can (29 oz/822 g) white hominy, drained and rinsed | 1 |
| 2 cups | ready-to-use chicken or beef broth (approx.) or homemade pork stock | 500 mL |
| | Minced red onion | |
| | Dried Mexican oregano, optional | |
| | Diced avocado | |
| | Lime wedges | |
| | Sliced radish | |
| | Coarsely chopped cilantro | |

## Tips

Diced boneless, skinless chicken thighs can replace all or part of the pork, if desired. Cook thighs for 3 to 4 hours.

*To make ahead:* Prepare through Step 5. Remove from hot water bath, transfer to an ice bath and chill for 30 minutes. Refrigerate sealed pouch for up to 5 days. To reheat from refrigerator temperature, preheat hot water bath to 130°F (54.4°C); immerse pouch for 45 minutes before proceeding with Step 6.

1. In a dry medium skillet over high heat, toast pumpkin seeds, stirring constantly, for 2 to 3 minutes or until starting to pop. Continue to cook, stirring constantly, for 2 to 3 minutes more or until popping stops. Transfer to a small bowl and let cool.

2. Return skillet to heat. Add sesame seeds and toast, stirring often, for 5 minutes or until light golden. Add to bowl with pumpkin seeds. Stir in peppercorns and fennel seeds. Let cool.

3. Transfer cooled seed mixture to spice grinder. Add 1 tbsp (15 mL) salt, oregano and bay leaf. Grind to a powder.

4. In food processor fitted with the metal blade, combine jalapeño peppers, poblano pepper, cilantro, garlic, lime juice and spice powder. Process until a paste forms. Pour into a small bowl and set aside. Without cleaning work bowl, add tomatillos to food processor. Pulse until slightly chunky.

5. Place tomatillos, pepper mixture, pork and hominy in freezer bag and seal. Immerse in preheated hot water bath and cook for 12 hours. (To make ahead, see Tips, at left.)

6. Just before serving, in a medium saucepan, bring broth to a boil over high heat.

7. Remove pouch from hot water bath. Open and pour pozole into a large warm bowl. Stir in enough broth to create the desired soupy consistency (save any remaining broth for another use). Season with additional salt, if necessary. Pass garnishes at the table.

### Roasted Jalapeño and Poblano Peppers

Poblano peppers have thin flesh and their skin is rather tough. I find this distracting, so I always roast them. Jalapeños take on a less vegetal taste when roasted. They are softer in texture and can be peeled afterwards, if you prefer. Prepare both in the same manner as roasted bell peppers: on a grill, under a broiler or over a gas flame. If you plan to peel them, place them in a covered container while cooling, so they can steam a bit. I make these as I need them, since they keep only a few days in the refrigerator. Note that roasted jalapeños taste hotter than their raw counterpart.

# Mexican-Style Pickled Pig's Trotters

My love for pickled pig's trotters originated during the time I spent cooking in Mexico. These are served chilled as a snack or with other *antojitos* (little cravings). They are frequently offered before a bowl of Pozole Verde (page 130), with plenty of ice-cold beer.

**MAKES 4 TO 6 APPETIZER SERVINGS**

Freezer Bag Friendly

## Tips

You can easily double or triple this recipe. Use 2 or 3 pouches accordingly.

You'll need to ask your butcher to cut the trotters into pieces of the correct size. Whole ones are too difficult to cut using regular kitchen tools.

▶ **Preheat hot water bath to 160°F (71.1°C)**
▶ **Sous vide pouch**
▶ **Large non-reactive bowl**

| | | |
|---|---|---|
| 6 | pig's trotters, cut into 1½-inch (4 cm) chunks (see Tips, at left) | 6 |
| 1 | recipe Pork Brine (page 353), optional | 1 |
| | Salt, optional | |

**PICKLING LIQUID**

| | | |
|---|---|---|
| 4 | pickled jalapeño peppers (see Tips, at right), drained and sliced | 4 |
| 1 | large white onion, sliced | 1 |
| 1 | carrot, thinly sliced | 1 |
| 1 tbsp | olive oil | 15 mL |
| 1½ cups | water | 375 mL |
| ½ cup | liquid from jar of pickled jalapeños | 125 mL |
| ¼ cup | cider vinegar | 60 mL |
| 4 | cloves garlic, halved lengthwise | 4 |
| 2 tsp | dried Mexican oregano (see Tips, at right) | 10 mL |
| 1½ tsp | kosher salt | 7 mL |
| 1 tsp | whole black peppercorns | 5 mL |
| 1 tsp | dried thyme | 5 mL |
| ½ tsp | cumin seeds | 2 mL |
| 2 | bay leaves | 2 |

**1.** If desired, place trotters in a non-reactive bowl and pour brine overtop. Cover and refrigerate overnight or for up to 18 hours. Drain trotters, discarding brine. If you don't want to brine them, rinse trotters under cold running water for 10 to 15 minutes. Season unbrined trotters liberally with salt.

You can increase or decrease the number of jalapeños to suit your heat tolerance. The number that I've called for yield a dish that is spicy, but not excessively so.

Dried Mexican oregano has a particular flavor that's nice in this recipe. If you can't find any, substitute 1 tsp (5 mL) common (Greek) oregano and 1 tsp (5 mL) rubbed marjoram.

**2.** Transfer trotters to sous vide pouch and seal. Immerse in preheated hot water bath and cook for 36 hours.

**3.** *Pickling Liquid:* Meanwhile, in non-reactive bowl, combine pickled jalapeños, onion, carrot and oil. Set aside. In a medium saucepan, combine water, jalapeño liquid, vinegar, garlic, oregano, salt, peppercorns, thyme, cumin seeds and bay leaves. Bring to a boil. Pour boiling liquid over vegetables. Let cool. Refrigerate, covered, until trotters are cooked.

**4.** Remove pouch from hot water bath. Open pouch and add trotters and cooking liquid to pickling liquid. Cover and refrigerate overnight or for up to 10 days.

**5.** Serve trotters cold with a little of the pickling liquid, accompanied by some of the vegetables.

-----------------------------------------------------------------

## Variation

**Mexican-Style Pickled Pig Tails:** Pig tails can also be pickled this way. Substitute the same weight of whole or halved pig tails for the trotters. Increase the hot water bath temperature to 172°F (77.8°C) and cook for 12 hours. Proceed with the recipe.

# Sri Lankan Black Pork Curry

This unusual curry is so dark that it's nearly black. It is traditionally made with Sri Lankan roasted curry powder, but that can be hard to find outside the country. Here we toast some of the spices and supplement with regular store-bought curry powder to approximate that taste. Tamarind is one of the key flavors in cola drinks, and it lends a nice tang to this curry. Serve with any type of plain rice.

---

**MAKES 4 SERVINGS**

Freezer Bag Friendly

## Tips

You can easily double this recipe.

The pork you use for this stew should be on the fattier side. I like trimmings from belly pieces and ribs, or pork shoulder.

I have used jalapeño peppers in this recipe because they are relatively mild and readily available. The chiles that you find in Sri Lanka are more like what we often call Thai green chiles. Use them if you like, but don't seed them; just remove their stems and chop. Be careful, as they are quite hot.

Cardamom is frequently sold in beige or greenish pods. Open them with your thumbnail to extract the seeds.

▶ Preheat hot water bath to 144°F (62.2°C)
▶ Large resealable freezer bag
▶ Spice grinder or coffee grinder

| | | |
|---|---|---|
| 2 tbsp | vegetable oil, divided | 30 mL |
| 1 lb | pork (see Tips, at left), cut in ½-inch (1 cm) cubes | 450 g |
| ¾ cup | finely chopped onion | 175 mL |
| 2 tbsp | finely chopped gingerroot | 30 mL |
| 1 tbsp | finely chopped garlic | 15 mL |
| 3 tbsp | prepared tamarind paste (see box, page 135) | 45 mL |
| 2 | jalapeño peppers, seeded and chopped (see Tips, at left) | 2 |
| 1 tbsp | brown sugar | 15 mL |
| 3 tbsp | chopped fresh cilantro | 45 mL |

CURRY SPICE BLEND

| | | |
|---|---|---|
| 1 | stalk lemongrass (thick root-end only), trimmed and finely chopped | 1 |
| 1 | piece (2 inches/5 cm) Ceylon cinnamon stick (see Tips, at right) | 1 |
| 1 | whole clove | 1 |
| 2 tbsp | black peppercorns | 30 mL |
| 1 tsp | cardamom seeds (see Tips, at left) | 5 mL |
| 1 tsp | mustard seeds | 5 mL |
| 1 tsp | salt | 5 mL |
| 2 | bay leaves | 2 |
| 2 tsp | curry powder | 10 mL |

## Tips

Ceylon cinnamon, also known as true cinnamon, is a little different from the product that's usually marketed as cinnamon, which is cassia, a relative. True cinnamon has a gentler and more complex flavor, and it's softer and easier to grind. Look for it in Latin American and Asian grocery stores.

*To make ahead:* Prepare through Step 3. Remove from hot water bath, transfer to an ice bath and chill for 30 minutes. Refrigerate sealed pouch for up to 6 days or freeze for up to 6 months. To use frozen curry, thaw overnight in the refrigerator. To reheat from refrigerator temperature, preheat hot water bath to 130°F (54.4°C); immerse pouch for 30 minutes before proceeding with Step 4.

1. In a large skillet, heat 1 tbsp (15 mL) oil over high heat. Add pork and cook, stirring often, for 7 to 8 minutes or until browned all over. Transfer pork to a plate. Reduce heat to medium and add remaining oil to pan. Add onion and cook, stirring often, for about 10 minutes or until soft but not browned. Add ginger and garlic and cook, stirring, for 3 to 4 minutes or until fragrant. Stir in tamarind paste, jalapeños and sugar. Remove from heat and let cool.

2. *Curry Spice Blend:* Meanwhile, in a small, dry skillet over medium heat, combine lemongrass, cinnamon stick, clove, peppercorns, cardamom seeds, mustard seeds and salt. Toast, stirring constantly, for 5 minutes or until fragrant and mustard seeds start to pop. Remove from heat and let cool. Transfer spice mixture to grinder and grind to a powder. Pour into a small bowl and add bay leaves and curry powder.

3. Place pork with juices, onion mixture and spice blend in freezer bag and seal. Immerse in preheated hot water bath and cook for 8 hours. (To make ahead, see Tips, at left.)

4. Open bag and remove bay leaves. Spoon curry into warmed deep plates. Garnish with cilantro and serve.

---

### Tamarind Paste

Tamarind is a tropical souring agent widely used in Southeast Asian and Latin American cuisine. Look for 8 oz (227 g) packages in stores that cater to people from those areas. To prepare tamarind paste, unwrap the block and place in a small heatproof bowl. Cover with boiling water (about 1 cup/250 mL) and leave to cool. Using your fingers, squish the paste into the water and then press it through a fine-mesh sieve, discarding the solids. The result should be the consistency of mashed potatoes. Once prepared, you can store tamarind paste in the refrigerator for up to 4 days or freeze it for up to 12 months. Check the ingredient list on the package — sometimes salt is added, which means you should reduce the salt in the recipe to compensate.

# Pork and Peanut Curry

I created this souped-up variation of Sri Lankan Black Pork Curry because I wanted a richer, saucier option. It is reminiscent of West African cuisine because ground peanuts are used as a thickener. I like to serve it with Indian-style flatbread to mop up the tasty sauce.

## Tips

You can easily double this recipe.

Scotch bonnet peppers are common in West African cuisine. When you're making the base curry for this recipe, you can substitute jalapeños for the Scotch bonnets that are called for, if you prefer. The curry will be a little less spicy as a result.

▶ **Blender or food processor**

| | | |
|---|---|---|
| 1½ tbsp | vegetable oil | 22 mL |
| 1 cup | each chopped onion, celery, green bell pepper, and tomato | 250 mL |
| 1 | Scotch bonnet pepper, finely chopped (see Tips, at left), optional | 1 |
| 1½ tsp | finely chopped gingerroot | 7 mL |
| 1 cup | ready-to-use chicken or beef broth | 250 mL |
| ¾ cup | unsalted roasted peanuts | 175 mL |
| 1 | recipe Sri Lankan Black Pork Curry (page 134) | 1 |
| | Salt, optional | |
| | Chopped fresh cilantro | |

1. In a large skillet, heat oil over medium heat. Add onion and cook, stirring often, for 10 minutes or until softened. Increase heat to medium-high and add celery, bell pepper, tomato, Scotch bonnet pepper (if using) and ginger. Cook, stirring often, for 10 minutes or until vegetables are softened and liquid is slightly reduced. Remove from heat and let cool.

2. In blender, combine vegetable mixture, broth and peanuts. Purée until smooth. Pour into a medium saucepan and add curry. Bring to a simmer over medium heat and cook, stirring often, for about 5 minutes.

3. Season curry to taste with salt, if necessary. Ladle into warmed deep plates and garnish to taste with cilantro.

---

### Get Inventive

You can use my recipes for Sri Lankan Black Pork Curry (page 134) and Pork and Peanut Curry (above) as bases to create your own inventions. The first is quite unusual and will make a fairly dry curry. The second is a saucier variation on the first.

# Poultry and Rabbit

# Poultry and Rabbit

## The Basics

If you are new to sous vide cooking, chicken is a good place to start, because it's relatively inexpensive and you see the results quickly. These results are significant, because we are accustomed to cooking chicken to well done.

However, cooking poultry sous vide does present some particular challenges. First, you have to be careful to pasteurize the meat to kill any salmonella bacteria, which can cause illness. Second, poultry skin cooked sous vide can be difficult to get nice and crisp — though I have a couple of foolproof methods for solving this problem (see box, page 142). And third, poultry breasts and legs have different protein structures and fat content, so it is best to cook them separately. The good news is that there are straightforward solutions to all these challenges.

Sous vide is especially good for preparing chicken and turkey for soups, sandwiches and salads. You can cook it to a firmer texture for dicing or to falling apart for shredding and adding to dishes such as tacos. If you purchase poultry with the skin on, you can leave it on for extra flavor during cooking and simply remove it before serving.

Duck is not in the repertoire of many home cooks, though I'm hoping to change that. In this chapter I'll give you a number of tasty recipes that can act as a jumping-off point for your own creations.

Rabbit presents its own challenges in the kitchen. The recipes here make the best use of the various parts, including how to deal with the bony bits.

I've included information throughout the chapter on these different types of meat, and some helpful tips on selecting, preparing and cooking them.

## Selecting

Just as for pork and beef in the previous chapters, you have choices when it comes to the quality of the poultry and rabbit that you buy. As usual, quality comes at a price and the tastiest meat comes from animals that have been raised more slowly and with a more varied diet. It seems that "you are what you eat" applies to the animals we eat as well. Today's chicken is a miracle of genetics as well as husbandry. It takes a mere six weeks to bring a chicken to market, making it among the least expensive meats that you can buy. Poultry has never been as cheap as it is now, and it has never been consumed in such high quantities around the world.

When it comes to chicken, I look for larger birds with plump breasts, which tend to be a little bit older — I find that I get more flavor than I would with a younger bird. Almost all the chickens available on the market are Cornish Cross hybrids. If you can find standard breeds such as Barred Rock or Hampshire, give them a try. They will likely have more flavor, although the legs will require a little extra cooking for tenderness and the breasts will be somewhat smaller than what you are used to.

Like chicken, commercial turkey in North America comes from one breed: the Broad Breasted White. There are, however, 13 recognized heritage turkey breeds; you may find one at your farmers' market or specialty butcher shop around Thanksgiving and Christmas. The flavor will be better, but expect to pay two to three times more than for commodity-raised turkey.

Whichever you choose, try to buy poultry fresh. Chickens and turkeys are quite lean, so you want to keep as much moisture in the meat as possible. If you must freeze meat, you will lose less moisture if you freeze cooked meat rather than raw. Defrost it in the refrigerator overnight and either brown it lightly to reheat or slip a sous vide pouch into a hot water bath between 130°F (54.4°C) and the original cooking temperature from the recipe.

## Prepping

Sous vide cooking allows very precise temperature control, so brining poultry isn't required to keep the meat from drying out. However, marinating poultry in a seasoned brine (such as Spiced Brine, Variation, page 350) will assist in adding flavor to the meat. It's especially helpful when you're cooking supermarket poultry, particularly turkey. Check the package to be sure that the meat hasn't been brined at the factory during processing; there should be no additional ingredients other than the poultry itself.

I recommend sealing breasts or legs in individual sous vide pouches to ensure even cooking and cooling.

## Cooking

The breast muscles of chicken and turkey are very lean, so they don't require as high a cooking temperature as the legs. Breasts come out juicy if they are cooked sous vide at anywhere between 136.5°F (58°C) and 145°F (62.8°C). Chefs like me tend to like their meat on the underdone side so that it's as juicy as possible, although you may find poultry cooked at the lowest temperature in that range too soft for your liking. No problem, though — a good starting point for firmer, more well-done chicken or turkey is 140°F (60°C). Just don't turn up the hot water bath to more than 149°F (65°C), or those breasts will emerge dry.

## WHAT ABOUT THE BONES?

While a few recipes in this chapter require the bones to be left in for optimal results, I generally advocate for cooking poultry boneless. There are three reasons for taking this approach:

1. bones generally add to the thickness of the meat, thereby increasing the cooking time;

2. their sharp edges have a tendency to poke through pouches, which will ruin the seal; and

3. if you bone the birds yourself, the bones can be used to make stock or to enrich ready-made broth for sauces or soup. See page 399 for further instructions.

Chicken and turkey legs are best cooked sous vide at a temperature between 141°F (60.5°C) and 149°F (65°C). This will yield tender legs with a texture that's similar to roasted. If you like, you can cook the legs further until they shred easily; the meat will still be savory and delicious. To make legs that can be shredded for use in tacos and casseroles (turkey Tetrazzini comes to mind), you will need to raise the hot water bath temperature to 167°F (75°C). You can cook the two parts together if you like. Half-chickens — split up the centre into two pieces that each contain breast and leg meat — are tasty cooked sous vide and finished on the barbecue. Setting your sous vide machine to between 141°F (60.5°C) and 143.6°F (62°C) will give you nicely cooked light and dark meat.

## Pasteurizing Poultry

Poultry (including chicken, turkey and quail) and rabbit can harbor pathogens such as salmonella. For this reason they must be pasteurized to ensure that any harmful bacteria are killed. The sous vide cooking times in this chapter have been calculated to ensure pasteurization unless otherwise noted. Because of the precise temperatures achievable with sous vide techniques, you can cook poultry for an extended time at a much lower temperature than you could previously, resulting in juicier birds. Please see page 9 for a complete discussion of pasteurization.

## Browning

With poultry you have the additional benefit of creating a nice crispy skin. Unfortunately, skin that is browned before cooking sous vide loses its crispness. I suggest that you brown lightly for color and complexity before cooking sous vide. If you want a crisp skin, cook it separately and garnish your dish with it (see "Crisping Poultry Skin," page 142).

Your choice whether to brown the meat before or after cooking will depend largely on logistics. If you want to have chicken cooked and ready for a backyard barbecue, then cook it without browning first. If you want something quick and easy, brown (or don't brown) it first; then slip it out of the pouch and onto the plate with the rest of your meal.

# Poultry Cooking Times: Ensuring Pasteurization

The times in this chart are minimums and are based on the assumption that you are starting with poultry, with or without bones, that is at refrigerator temperature. Poultry that has been cooked sous vide can be left in the hot water bath for at least 1 hour longer than the recommended cooking time with no ill effects. Times in excess of this may affect texture adversely, leaving the poultry mushy.

| THICKNESS AT THICKEST PART | MINIMUM TIME | MINIMUM TEMPERATURE |
|---|---|---|
| ½ inch (1 cm) | 1 hour and 50 minutes | 136.5°F (58°C) |
| ¾ inch (2 cm) | 2 hours | 136.5°F (58°C) |
| 1 inch (2.5 cm) | 2 hours and 20 minutes | 136.5°F (58°C) |
| 1½ inches (4 cm) | 3 hours and 20 minutes | 136.5°F (58°C) |
| 2 inches (5 cm) | 4 hours and 15 minutes | 136.5°F (58°C) |
| 2½ inches (6 cm) | 5 hours | 138°F (58.9°C) |
| 3 inches (7.5 cm) | 6 hours | 140°F (60°C) |
| 3½ inches (9 cm) | 6 hours | 146°F (63.3°C) |
| 4 inches (10 cm) | 6 hours | 156°F (68.9°C) |

## NOTES

- These temperatures are general guidelines for pasteurizing poultry and can be used as a guide for cooking breasts. For best results, please consult individual recipes that use similar poultry.
- Leg meat is generally cooked at temperatures from 140°F to 170°F (60°C to 76.7°C). If consulting the thickness chart for cooking legs, use 140°F (60°C) or the temperature that you prefer.

- If you are following a recipe from this chapter and have leg or breast meat that is thicker than specified, measure the thickness and cook according to the time and temperature specified in this chart.

## CRISPING POULTRY SKIN

Crisping poultry skin that has been subjected to sous vide cooking is extremely difficult. While leaving the skin on poultry will help keep it moist during its time in the hot water bath, the skin becomes waterlogged and loses some of its structure because of melting of the collagen. If you want really crispy skin, your best bet is to remove it from the chicken, duck or turkey before cooking the poultry, and crisp it separately. Here is how to crisp chicken skin (duck and turkey skin will likely take about 30 minutes longer):

1. Preheat oven to 350°F (180°C), with rack in lower third of oven.

2. Spread out skin on a cutting board. With the edge of a spoon, scrape off any fat deposits.

3. Place a sheet of parchment paper over a flat baking sheet. Arrange skin on parchment in one layer and salt lightly. Cover with another sheet of parchment and place another baking sheet or similar on top — the idea is to keep the skin from curling.

4. Bake in lower third of oven for 20 to 30 minutes or until skin is dark golden brown. Place skin on a plate lined with paper towels to drain and cool (the skin will crisp up as it cools).

5. Store in a covered container at room temperature for no more than 3 days. The skin can be gently reheated at 200°F (100°C) for 4 to 5 minutes, if desired.

# Basic Chicken Breasts

This simple recipe is a good introduction to sous vide cooking. Here I pan-sear the breasts at the last minute to add flavor, but you can just as easily grill them or serve them straight from the pouch.

## Tips

You can easily adapt this recipe to the number of guests you have. Plan on serving one breast per person.

Packaging the breasts individually ensures precise cooking and quick cooling. You can, however, cook a pair of chicken breasts in the same pouch, as long as they do not overlap.

*To make ahead:* Prepare through Step 1. Remove pouches from hot water bath, transfer to an ice bath and chill for 30 minutes. Refrigerate sealed pouches for up to 6 days or freeze for up to 6 months. To reheat, preheat hot water bath to 140°F (60°C). Immerse pouches in preheated water bath for 20 minutes for refrigerated breasts or 40 minutes for frozen breasts. Proceed with Step 2.

If you want to enjoy extra-crispy chicken skin, see box, page 142.

▶ **Preheat hot water bath to 140°F (60°C)**
▶ **2 sous vide pouches**

| | | |
|---|---|---|
| 2 | boneless chicken breasts (skin-on or skinless), each about 5 to 6 oz (140 to 170 g) | 2 |
| | Salt and freshly ground black pepper | |
| 2 tbsp | vegetable oil | 30 mL |

1. If chicken has skin, remove or leave it on as desired. Season breasts to taste with salt and pepper. Place each breast in a separate sous vide pouch and seal. Immerse in preheated hot water bath and cook for 2 to 2½ hours. (To make ahead, see Tips, at left.)

2. Remove pouches from hot water bath, open and remove chicken breasts. Discard cooking juices. Pat meat dry with paper towels.

3. In a medium skillet, heat oil over high heat until almost smoking. Add chicken and sear, turning once, for about 30 seconds per side. Season lightly to taste with additional salt and pepper. Serve, skin side up, on warm plates.

---

### Using Frozen Chicken Breasts

This recipe can also be prepared using frozen chicken breasts. Seal them, unseasoned, in separate sous vide pouches, immerse in preheated hot water bath, and increase cooking time to 3 hours. Season to taste after completing Step 3.

---

# Chicken Breasts in Mayonnaise

This is a simple variation on Basic Chicken Breasts (page 143). Cooking the breasts with mayonnaise makes them extra juicy, and if you use homemade mayonnaise (which I always do), the heat will pasteurize the egg yolks in it as well. The pouches come out of the water bath containing a delicious sauce along with the meat. Drizzle the sauce over a chicken sandwich or use it as a dressing for chicken salad.

**MAKES
4 CHICKEN
BREASTS**

Freezer Bag Friendly

## Tips

You can easily multiply this recipe to make as many chicken breasts as you want.

You can cook a pair of chicken breasts in the same pouch, as long as they do not overlap.

If you use homemade mayonnaise, make sure it is well emulsified, so it doesn't separate during cooking.

If you find the texture of this chicken too soft for your taste, you can increase the temperature of the hot water bath to a maximum of 145°F (62.8°C) for a firmer but still juicy result.

Cooked breasts will keep in their pouches for up to 6 days if refrigerated after Step 2.

▷ **Preheat water bath to 136.5°F (58°C)**
▷ **4 sous vide pouches**

| 4 | boneless, skinless chicken breasts (each about 5 to 6 oz/ 140 to 170 g) | 4 |
| | Salt and freshly ground black pepper | |
| ¼ cup | mayonnaise (see Tips, at left) | 60 mL |

1. Season chicken breasts to taste with salt and pepper. Place each breast in a separate sous vide pouch. Add 1 tbsp (15 mL) mayonnaise to each pouch. Seal pouches and immerse in preheated hot water bath. Cook for 2 to 2½ hours. (To make ahead, see Tips, at left.)

2. Remove pouches from hot water bath, transfer to an ice bath and chill for 30 minutes. Pat sealed pouches dry with paper towels.

3. Press pouches to squish around mayonnaise to incorporate cooking juices. Remove chicken breasts from pouches, reserving mayonnaise mixture. Serve chicken cold, with or without mayonnaise mixture, as desired.

--------------------------------------------------------------

## Variation

**Crispy Fried Chicken Breasts in Mayonnaise:** Lightly coat cooked chicken breasts with mayonnaise from the pouch, then roll them in panko or dry bread crumbs. In a medium skillet, heat about ½ inch (1 cm) vegetable oil over medium heat. Fry chicken, turning occasionally, until crisp and golden, about 5 minutes.

Ribeye Steak with Chimichurri Sauce (page 41)

Veal Tenderloin with Exotic Mushroom Sauce (page 46)

Postmodern Dinosaur Bones (page 66)

Matambre (page 68)

Corned Beef (page 80)

Spinach and Sourdough–Stuffed Lamb Shoulder (page 94)

Filipino Pork Belly Adobo (page 120)

Pozole Verde (page 130)

# Basic Chicken Thighs

This is my go-to starter recipe for cooking chicken thighs sous vide. You can serve them cold if you wish (see Variations, below), but I like to sear them as directed and serve them as a hot main course.

Freezer Bag Friendly

## Tips

You can easily double or triple this recipe. Seal pairs of thighs in separate pouches for cooking.

*To make ahead:* Prepare through Step 1. Remove pouches from hot water bath, transfer to an ice bath and chill for 30 minutes. Refrigerate sealed pouches for up to 6 days or freeze for up to 6 months. To reheat, preheat hot water bath to 140°F (60°C). Immerse pouches in preheated water bath for 20 minutes for refrigerated thighs or 40 minutes for frozen thighs. Proceed with Step 2.

If you want to enjoy extra-crispy chicken skin, see box, page 142.

▸ **Preheat hot water bath to 149°F (65°C)**
▸ **1 or 2 sous vide pouches**

| 4 | boneless chicken thighs (skin-on or skinless), each about 3½ oz (100 g) | 4 |
| | Salt and freshly ground black pepper | |
| 2 tbsp | vegetable oil | 30 mL |

1. If chicken has skin, remove or leave it on as desired (see Tips, at left). Lay thighs on work surface and season lightly with salt and pepper. Arrange in one layer in a sous vide pouch (use 2 pouches if necessary) and seal. Immerse in preheated hot water bath and cook for 2 hours. (To make ahead, see Tips, at left.)

2. Remove pouches from hot water bath, open and remove chicken thighs. Discard cooking juices. Pat chicken dry with paper towels.

3. In a medium skillet, heat oil over high heat until almost smoking. Add chicken and sear, turning once, for about 30 seconds per side. Season lightly to taste with additional salt and pepper. Serve, skin side up (if skin is present), on warm plates.

## Variations

**Shredded Chicken Thighs:** For making preparations such as tacos, increase the temperature of the hot water bath to 165°F (73.9°C). Prepare through Step 1. Remove pouches from hot water bath and let stand at room temperature until cool enough to handle but still warm. Open pouches and remove thighs. Remove skin if present. Using your hands, shred meat to desired size and add to your favorite recipe.

**Diced Cold Chicken Thighs for Salads, Casseroles or Soups:** Prepare through Step 1. Remove pouches from hot water bath, transfer to an ice bath and chill for 1 hour. Open pouches and remove thighs. Remove skin if present. Dice to desired size and add to your favorite recipe.

# Curried Chicken Thighs

This is my preferred recipe when I want curry flavors on a weeknight. It is inexpensive and much healthier than takeout butter chicken. I serve the thighs with simple minted cucumbers and plain white rice.

## Tips

This recipe can be scaled up to serve as many people as you like. Use a separate bag for each 12 oz (340 g) of chicken thighs.

These chicken thighs will be tastier and more tender if you let them marinate overnight. If you are in a hurry, refrigerate them for at least 4 hours before cooking.

Curry powders vary wildly in flavor and spiciness. Find one you like and don't store it for longer than about 9 months for optimal flavor.

*To make ahead:* Prepare through Step 3. Remove from hot water bath, transfer to an ice bath and chill for 1 hour. Refrigerate sealed bag for up to 6 days. To reheat from refrigerator temperature, preheat hot water bath to 136°F (57.8°C). Immerse pouches for 20 minutes for refrigerated thighs or 40 minutes for frozen thighs. Proceed with Step 4.

▶ **Small resealable freezer bag**

| | | |
|---|---|---|
| 1 cup | plain full-fat yogurt | 250 mL |
| 1 to 2 tbsp | curry powder (see Tips, at left) | 15 to 30 mL |
| 1 tbsp | soy sauce | 15 mL |
| ½ tsp | hot pepper sauce, such as Tabasco | 2 mL |
| 4 | boneless chicken thighs (skin-on or skinless), each about 3½ oz (100 g) | 4 |
| | Salt | |
| | Freshly ground pepper | |

1. In a medium bowl, stir together yogurt, curry powder, soy sauce and hot pepper sauce. Trim any stray cartilage off chicken thighs, if necessary. Add to yogurt mixture and stir to coat completely.

2. Transfer chicken thighs and yogurt mixture to freezer bag. Arrange in one layer and seal. Refrigerate overnight or for up to 24 hours (see Tips, at left).

3. Preheat hot water bath to 149°F (65°C). Immerse bag in preheated water bath and cook for 2 hours. (To make ahead, see Tips, at left.)

4. Remove bag from hot water bath. Open bag and transfer chicken thighs and sauce to warm plates. Season lightly with salt and pepper. Serve immediately.

------

## Variation

**Broiled Curried Chicken Thighs:** I also like to broil these thighs after they have been cooked ahead and chilled (see Tips, at left). Prepare desired garnishes (such as raita) and preheat broiler. Remove sealed bag from refrigerator, remove thighs and scrape off excess sauce. Place thighs, skin side up (if skin is present), on a baking sheet. Broil for about 10 minutes or until browned. Serve on warm plates.

# Jerked Chicken

Here is a simple recipe that's delicious as a snack on movie night with friends or as part of a big barbecue menu for a crowd. A mixture of drumsticks and wings is good, but you can use all of one or the other if you prefer.

**MAKES**
**1 LB (450 G)**

**SERVES 1 AS A MAIN, 2 TO 3 AS AN APPETIZER**

Freezer Bag Friendly

## Tips

This recipe can be scaled up or down to make whatever quantity you need. Just make sure each bag contains no more than 1 lb (450 g) chicken.

Prepared jerk seasoning paste can usually be found in supermarkets. If you have a favorite homemade version, by all means use it in this recipe.

*To make ahead:*
Prepare through Step 3. Refrigerate for up to 6 days or freeze for up to 6 months. Defrost overnight in refrigerator, if necessary. Proceed with Step 4.

▶ **Large resealable freezer bag**

| | | |
|---|---|---|
| 1 lb | chicken wings and drumsticks (or all of one or the other) | 450 g |
| 1 cup | jerk seasoning paste (see Tips, at left) | 250 mL |

1. In a large bowl, toss chicken pieces with seasoning paste to coat. Place chicken in freezer bag and seal. Refrigerate overnight or for up to 24 hours.

2. Preheat hot water bath to 156°F (68.9°C). Remove bag from refrigerator. Press chicken flat inside bag to ensure that it's in a single layer and reseal if necessary. Immerse bag in preheated water bath and cook for 2 to 3 hours.

3. Remove bag from bath and transfer to an ice-water bath for 30 minutes. (To make ahead, see Tips, at left.)

4. Preheat grill to High or preheat broiler. Open bag and remove chicken; discard liquid. Pat chicken dry with paper towels. Place on grill or on a baking sheet under preheated broiler. Grill or broil, turning once, for 4 to 5 minutes or until starting to get crispy. Serve on warm plates.

## Variations

**Buffalo-Style Wings and Drumsticks:** Substitute ½ cup (125 mL) prepared Buffalo wing sauce (such as Frank's RedHot or Durkee's) for the jerk seasoning paste. Toss to coat, then seal in freezer bag as directed. Refrigerate for up to 4 hours before proceeding with Step 2 (do not marinate overnight).

**Decadent Buttery Wings and Drumsticks:** Prepare through Step 2. Remove bag from bath, then remove chicken from bag and set aside. Drain cooking liquid in bag into a small saucepan. Bring to a boil over medium heat and cook, stirring occasionally, until liquid is reduced by half. Reduce heat to very low and whisk in 3 tbsp (45 mL) butter. Remove from heat. Toss chicken with butter mixture before broiling, or brush it on during grilling. The butter is delicious on toast with eggs.

# Chicken Cholent

This recipe is an excellent example of how your sous vide equipment can function like a slow cooker. Cholent is a traditional Jewish stew that is simmered overnight on the eve of the Sabbath so it can be served for lunch the next day, when cooking and other work are forbidden. This one features the flavors of Sephardic Jewish cooking, which is influenced by the cuisines of Spain, North Africa and the Middle East.

---

**MAKES
4 SERVINGS**

Freezer Bag Friendly

## Tip

You can easily halve or double this recipe. If you're doubling the recipe, use 2 bags.

▶ **Large resealable freezer bag**

| | | |
|---|---|---|
| 2 cups | cold water | 500 mL |
| ¾ cup | wheat berries, rinsed well and drained | 175 mL |
| 2 lbs | bone-in, skin-on chicken thighs | 900 g |
| | Salt and freshly ground black pepper | |
| 3 tbsp | olive oil | 45 mL |
| 2 | onions, minced | 2 |
| 4 | cloves garlic, minced | 4 |
| 1 | can (28 oz/796 mL) whole tomatoes, with juice | 1 |
| 1 | can (14 oz/398 mL) chickpeas, drained and rinsed | 1 |
| ¾ cup | Moroccan oil-cured black olives (see Tip, at right) | 175 mL |
| ½ | preserved lemon (page 386), pulp discarded, skin rinsed and chopped, optional | ½ |
| 2 tbsp | turbinado sugar or liquid honey | 30 mL |
| 2 tsp | kosher salt | 10 mL |
| 1 tsp | freshly ground black pepper | 5 mL |
| ½ tsp | ground ginger | 2 mL |
| ½ tsp | saffron threads, crumbled | 2 mL |
| ½ tsp | ground cinnamon | 2 mL |
| ¼ tsp | ground cumin | 1 mL |
| 1 | bay leaf | 1 |
| 4 | whole, shell-on eggs, optional | 4 |

**1.** In a small saucepan, combine cold water and wheat berries and bring to a boil over high heat. Cover, reduce heat to low and simmer until tender, about 1 hour, adding more water to keep wheat submerged, if necessary.

Moroccan oil-cured olives are unique. They are fruity and almost sweet, and they plump up nicely in this recipe. If they are unavailable or you don't care for them, you can omit them or substitute brined green olives such as Picholines.

2. Meanwhile, pat chicken thighs dry with paper towels. Season liberally to taste with salt and pepper. In a large skillet, heat oil over medium-high heat. Brown thighs, in batches if necessary, turning once, for 5 to 6 minutes per batch. As completed, transfer each batch to a plate lined with paper towels and let cool. Set aside.

3. Reduce heat to medium. Add onions to pan. Cook, stirring often, for 6 minutes or until softened and starting to color. Add garlic and reduce heat to medium-low. Cook, stirring often, for 3 to 4 minutes. Stir in tomatoes, with juice. Increase heat to medium, bring to a simmer and cook, occasionally breaking up tomatoes with a fork or whisk, for 15 minutes.

4. Stir in chickpeas, olives, preserved lemon, sugar, salt, pepper, ginger, saffron, cinnamon, cumin and bay leaf. Remove from heat and set aside.

5. Preheat hot water bath to 149°F (65°C). Bring a small saucepan of water to a boil. Add eggs (if using) and cook for 90 seconds. Using tongs, transfer eggs to preheated hot water bath.

6. Drain wheat berries, discarding cooking liquid. Place wheat berries, chicken thighs and tomato mixture in freezer bag and seal. Immerse in preheated hot water bath and cook for 14 to 20 hours.

7. Remove bag and eggs from hot water bath. Open bag and spoon cholent onto warm plates. Serve eggs on the side, peeled or unpeeled, according to family custom.

## Variations

This recipe is very adaptable. Try leaving out the olives and adding Carrots with Orange and Ginger (page 310) or Balsamic Pearl Onions (page 314) to the tomato mixture in Step 4. Cubed boneless lamb shoulder works instead of the chicken and can be cooked at the same temperature for the same amount time. White beans can replace the chickpeas, and mushrooms, quartered and sautéed, add a nice earthy flavor. The possibilities are really endless here!

# Chicken with Vietnamese Flavors

Marinating a whole chicken for an entire day and then cooking it sous vide in the marinade really helps the flavors penetrate the meat. This is a wonderful dish to make ahead of time if you are going to a picnic or a place where the heat source for cooking is uncertain. The fully cooked meat needs only a brief broil or grill before it's ready to serve.

**MAKES 2 TO 4 SERVINGS**

Freezer Bag Friendly

## Tips

You can easily halve this recipe.

Dark soy sauce is aged a bit longer than light soy sauce, has a deeper flavor and usually has some molasses added to it. It is used in dishes where you want to impart color. Mushroom soy sauce is a variety of dark soy sauce. If you come across it, you can use it here.

▶ **2 large resealable freezer bags**

| | | |
|---|---|---|
| 1 | whole chicken (2½ to 3 lbs/ 1.125 to 1.35 kg) | 1 |
| 4 | stalks lemongrass | 4 |
| ¼ cup | freshly squeezed lime juice | 60 mL |
| ¼ cup | fish sauce | 60 mL |
| 3 tbsp | chopped gingerroot | 45 mL |
| 2 tbsp | dark soy sauce (see Tips, at left) | 30 mL |
| 4 tsp | granulated sugar | 20 mL |
| 1 tsp | ground white pepper | 5 mL |
| 5 | cloves garlic, chopped | 5 |
| 1 | bunch fresh cilantro, coarsely chopped | 1 |
| 2 | small dried red chile peppers, crushed (see Tips, page 160) | 2 |

1. Place chicken on a cutting board. Using a sharp chef's knife or kitchen shears, cut along both sides of the backbone and remove. Cut through the breastbone to make 2 halves. Cut out wishbone. (Or ask your butcher to cut the chicken in half for you.) Freeze bones for making stock, if desired. Set aside.

2. Trim off woody ends of lemongrass. Cut off and discard tops, leaving 7-inch (18 cm) stalks. Chop stalks and transfer to a medium bowl. Stir in lime juice, fish sauce, ginger, soy sauce, sugar, white pepper, garlic, cilantro and chiles.

3. Place each half-chicken in a separate freezer bag. Divide seasoning mixture equally between bags and seal. Refrigerate overnight or for up to 24 hours.

**4.** Preheat hot water bath to 141°F (60.5°C). Immerse bags in preheated bath and cook for $3\frac{1}{2}$ to $4\frac{1}{2}$ hours.

**5.** Remove bags from hot water bath, transfer to an ice bath and chill for 30 minutes. (To make ahead, see Tip, at left.)

**6.** Preheat barbecue to Medium or preheat broiler. Open bags and remove chicken; discard liquid. Pat dry with paper towels, wiping off any clinging seasoning mixture. Place chicken, skin side up, on grill or on a baking sheet under preheated broiler. Grill or broil for about 3 minutes. Turn over and cook for 10 to 15 minutes or until skin is crisp and chicken is heated through. Serve on warm plates.

# Buttermilk Fried Chicken

This is an ideal method for creating fried chicken that's simultaneously juicy and crisp. Cooking the chicken sous vide yields precisely cooked meat. That way, when you're frying it, you can focus on achieving a perfectly golden, crispy crust. Coleslaw and corn on the cob are my must-have classic accompaniments for this meal.

---

> **MAKES
> 4 SERVINGS**

Freezer Bag Friendly

## Tips

This recipe can be doubled or halved. If you're doubling it, preheat the oven to 200°F (100°C). As you finish frying the chicken pieces, transfer them to a baking sheet lined with paper towels and place in preheated oven to keep warm. Make sure to fry the breast pieces last, as they can dry out more easily in the oven.

If you prefer, you can make this recipe using all chicken legs or all breasts, for a total of 2½ lbs (1.125 kg) of meat. Refer to the chart on page 141 for cooking times and temperatures for leg or breast meat and add to the hot water bath in Step 3. Omit Step 4.

Your butcher can carry out Step 1 for you, if desired.

▶ **Preheat hot water bath to 141°F (60.5°C)**
▶ **2 sous vide pouches**
▶ **Large, deep, heavy-bottomed saucepan or Dutch oven**
▶ **Candy/deep-fry or infrared thermometer**

| | | |
|---|---|---|
| 1 | whole chicken (2½ to 3 lbs/ 1.125 to 1.35 kg; see Tips, at left) | 1 |
| | Salt and freshly ground black pepper | |
| 3 cups | all-purpose flour (see Tips, at right) | 750 mL |
| 2 tbsp | garlic powder | 30 mL |
| 2 tbsp | onion powder | 30 mL |
| 2 tbsp | sweet Hungarian paprika | 30 mL |
| 1 tbsp | kosher salt | 15 mL |
| 1 tsp | cayenne pepper | 5 mL |
| 1 tsp | freshly ground black pepper | 5 mL |
| 2 cups | buttermilk or plain kefir | 500 mL |
| | Vegetable oil for frying | |

1. Place chicken on a cutting board. Using a sharp chef's knife or kitchen shears, cut along both sides of the backbone and remove. Cut off tips and flat sections of the wings, leaving just the first joint attached to the breast. Turn over chicken and cut in half through the breastbone. Cut out breastbone and wishbone. Cut off leg portions, keeping skin intact as much as possible. Cut each breast crosswise into 2 pieces of equal weight, leaving a small, thick piece attached to each wing. Separate thighs from drumsticks at the joint. Save bones and trimmings for stock, if desired.

## Tips

To make your fried chicken gluten-free, substitute your favorite all-purpose gluten-free flour blend. Alternatively, in Step 6, whisk together 1 cup (250 mL) each cornstarch, white rice flour and water chestnut flour (available in Asian grocery stores), transfer the mixture to a food processor fitted with the metal blade, and process to break down water chestnut flour.

*To make ahead:* Prepare through Step 5. Refrigerate sealed pouches for up to 6 days or freeze for up to 6 months. To use frozen chicken, thaw overnight in the refrigerator before proceeding with Step 6.

Great care must be exercised when frying in a pot with this amount of oil. If you have a deep-fryer, I suggest that you use it for this recipe. In a pot, a thermometer with a digital timer and a remote probe is handy and adds an element of safety. Set the temperature alert to the temperature specified in the recipe. That way, the alarm will ring when the temperature is reached.

**2.** Pat chicken pieces dry with paper towels. Season liberally to taste with salt and pepper. Place thighs and drumsticks in one sous vide pouch. Place breast pieces in other sous vide pouch. Spread out pieces so they are not overlapping; seal pouches.

**3.** Refrigerate breast pouch. Immerse thigh-and-drumstick pouch in preheated hot water bath and cook for 1 to 2 hours.

**4.** Lower hot water bath temperature to 138°F (58.9°C) and immediately add breast pouch. Continue to cook for 3 hours more.

**5.** Remove chicken pouches from hot water bath, transfer to an ice bath and chill for 30 minutes. (To make ahead, see Tips, at left.)

**6.** Meanwhile, in a large bowl, whisk together flour, garlic powder, onion powder, paprika, salt, cayenne and black pepper. Pour buttermilk into a medium bowl.

**7.** Open pouches and pat chicken dry with paper towels. One piece at a time, dredge chicken in seasoned flour, shaking off excess. Dip into buttermilk, rolling to coat completely and letting excess drip back into bowl. Dredge chicken again in seasoned flour mixture, turning to coat completely. Place coated chicken on a baking sheet or platter and set aside. When all pieces are completed, refrigerate baking sheet, uncovered, until ready to use, for at least 1 hour and up to 2 hours (this will help keep the chicken from overcooking). Discard any excess flour mixture and buttermilk.

**8.** Pour enough of the oil into heavy, deep saucepan to come 1 inch (2.5 cm) up the side, being sure to leave enough space to more than accommodate the amount of oil that will be displaced when the chicken is added. Heat oil until thermometer reads 370°F (188°C). Starting with legs and drumsticks, add chicken to oil, in batches to prevent crowding, and cook, turning often, for 6 minutes or until golden brown and crisp. As completed, transfer pieces to a plate lined with paper towels. Cover with foil and a folded kitchen towel to keep warm. Serve on warm plates.

# Coq au Vin

The French name of this dish translates as "rooster with wine." Few of us have access to roosters these days, so they are no longer the typical choice for making this dish. Sous vide techniques update this traditional recipe. Potatoes, either mashed or boiled, are an ideal accompaniment.

---

**MAKES
4 SERVINGS**

Freezer Bag Friendly

## Tips

You can easily double this recipe. Just make sure to use 4 sous vide pouches.

If you prefer, you can make this recipe using all chicken legs or all breasts, for a total of 2½ lbs (1.125 kg) of meat. Refer to the chart on page 141 for cooking times and temperatures for leg or breast meat and add to the hot water bath in Step 5. Omit Step 6.

Your butcher can carry out Step 1 for you, if desired.

▶ **2 sous vide pouches**

| | | |
|---|---|---:|
| 1 | whole chicken (2½ to 3 lbs/ 1.125 to 1.35 kg; see Tips, at left) | 1 |
| | Salt and freshly ground black pepper | |
| 2 tbsp | olive oil | 30 mL |
| 1 cup | dry red wine | 250 mL |
| 1 | chunk pancetta or salt pork (5 oz/140 g) | 1 |
| 1 tbsp | butter | 15 mL |
| 12 | button mushrooms, trimmed | 12 |
| 2 tsp | chopped garlic | 10 mL |
| 1½ cups | enriched chicken broth (page 401) | 375 mL |
| 12 | pearl onions, peeled and parboiled, or Buttery Pearl Onions (variation, page 315) | 12 |
| 3 tbsp | cold water | 45 mL |
| 1 tbsp | cornstarch | 15 mL |
| 2 tbsp | chopped fresh parsley | 30 mL |

1. Place chicken on a cutting board. Using a sharp chef's knife or kitchen shears, cut along both sides of the backbone and remove. Cut off tips and flat sections of the wings, leaving just the first joint attached to the breast. Turn over chicken and cut in half through the breastbone. Cut out breastbone and wishbone. (Or ask your butcher to cut the chicken in half for you.) Cut off leg portions, keeping skin intact as much as possible. Cut each breast crosswise into 2 pieces of equal weight, leaving a small, thick piece attached to each wing. Separate thighs from drumsticks at the joint. Save bones and trimmings for making stock, if desired (see page 399).

2. Pat chicken pieces dry with paper towels and season with salt and pepper. Place on a large plate or tray and refrigerate for up to 1 hour.

3. Meanwhile, preheat hot water bath to 141°F (60.5°C).

## Tips

Reducing wine in the microwave is a splendid method because it minimizes oxidation. If you reduce the liquid in a heatproof glass measuring cup, it's also very easy to keep track of how much it has reduced. If you don't have a microwave, you can do this on the stove instead. Place the wine in a small saucepan over medium-low heat and simmer until reduced by half.

The finished stew (without garnish) can be made ahead and refrigerated for 4 to 5 days or frozen for up to 6 months. Transfer to a freezer bag, seal and refrigerate or freeze. Defrost in the refrigerator overnight. Remove from pouch and reheat gently in a saucepan over medium heat, or reheat bag for about 40 minutes in a hot water bath preheated to 130°F (54.4°C). Serve on warm plates garnished with parsley.

**4.** In a large skillet, heat oil over medium-high heat. Brown chicken in batches, turning once, for 4 to 5 minutes per batch. Using a slotted spoon, transfer chicken to a plate lined with paper towels and let drain. Refrigerate until chilled, about 30 minutes.

**5.** Place thighs and drumsticks in one sous vide pouch and breast pieces in the other. Spread out so pieces are not overlapping; seal pouches. Refrigerate breast pouch. Immerse thigh-and-drumstick pouch in preheated hot water bath and cook for 1 to 2 hours.

**6.** Lower hot water bath temperature to 138°F (58.9°C) and immediately add breast pouch. Continue to cook for 3 hours more.

**7.** Meanwhile, place wine in a 2-cup (500 mL) heatproof glass measuring cup and microwave on High for 2 minutes at a time, until reduced by half (see Tips, at left). Set aside.

**8.** Cut pancetta into ½-inch (1 cm) cubes. In a small saucepan of boiling water, blanch for 1 minute. Drain and chill in cold water. Set aside.

**9.** In a small skillet, melt butter over medium heat. When butter stops foaming, add mushrooms and stir for 2 minutes. Add garlic and stir for 2 to 3 minutes. Season to taste with salt and pepper. Set aside.

**10.** Remove chicken pouches from hot water bath. Let stand at room temperature while preparing the sauce.

**11.** Pour broth into a medium saucepan. Stir in reduced wine. Bring to a simmer over medium heat. Open chicken pouches and pour all the cooking liquid into pan. Stir in mushroom mixture, pearl onions and pancetta. Increase heat and bring to a boil.

**12.** In a small bowl, stir cold water into cornstarch until smooth. Gradually whisk cornstarch mixture into boiling sauce mixture and cook, stirring, for about 1 minute, until thickened to consistency of heavy cream. (You may not need all the cornstarch mixture; discard any leftovers.) Season to taste with additional salt, if necessary.

**13.** Place chicken in a large skillet over medium heat. Pour sauce over chicken (there will not be enough to completely cover the meat). Cover and cook for 5 minutes or until heated through. Serve on warm plates. Garnish with parsley.

# Cold Turkey Breast for Sandwiches

This turkey breast is much better than anything at the supermarket. The key to its tenderness and rich flavor is the spiced brine, which lightly seasons the meat and keeps it moist while it cooks. My favorite club sandwich always includes this turkey, dressed up with avocado and spicy mayonnaise.

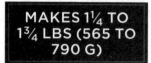

**MAKES 1¼ TO 1¾ LBS (565 TO 790 G)**

Freezer Bag Friendly

## Tips

This recipe can easily be doubled. One half (or side) of a full turkey breast generally weighs between 1½ and 2 lbs (675 to 900 g). If you want to cook both sides of a turkey breast, split it down the middle and use 1½ batches of Spiced Brine. You can brine both halves together, but cook them in individual sous vide pouches.

*To make ahead:*
Prepare through Step 3. Refrigerate for up to 5 days or freeze for up to 6 months. To use frozen turkey, thaw overnight in the refrigerator.

To serve the turkey warm, prepare through Step 2 and serve immediately. If you've made the turkey ahead and it's at refrigerator temperature, preheat hot water bath to 140°F (60°C). Immerse sealed pouch for 45 minutes.

▶ **Sous vide pouch**

| 1 | boneless turkey breast (skin-on or skinless), 1½ to 2 lbs (675 to 900 g; see Tips, at left) | 1 |
| 1 | recipe Spiced Brine (variation, page 350), well chilled | 1 |

1. Place turkey in a large, deep dish that will allow the breast to lie flat with a little space around the edges. Pour enough brine over turkey to cover (discard any remaining brine or save for another use). Cover and refrigerate for least 24 hours, and no longer than 3 days.

2. Preheat hot water bath to 141°F (60.5°C). Remove turkey from brine and pat dry with paper towels. Discard brine. Place turkey in sous vide pouch and seal. Immerse in preheated hot water bath and cook for 3 to 4 hours.

3. Remove pouch from hot water bath. Transfer to an ice-water bath and chill for 45 minutes. (To make ahead, see Tips, at left.)

4. Remove turkey from pouch, discarding any cooking liquid. Remove and discard skin. Slice across the grain.

---

### Ensure That Turkey Is Pasteurized

A boneless turkey breast can be quite thick, sometimes up to 3 or 4 inches (7.5 to 10 cm). Make sure you measure the thickness of the breast to ensure that it will pasteurize during the cooking process. If the breast is thicker than 2½ inches, refer to the chart on page 141 and cook accordingly.

---

# Turkey Breast with Stuffing and Gravy

This is an inventive way to get your turkey-dinner fix any time of the year. Served with homemade cranberry sauce, this dish is great for a small Thanksgiving get-together or a turkey TV dinner gone to heaven.

## MAKES 6 SERVINGS

## Tips

Turkeys vary greatly in size. This recipe works well with either a single large breast or a double breast from a smaller bird. If you are working with a large breast or want to use both breasts from a single bird, you can double the entire recipe and make 2 cylinders, cooking them in separate sous vide pouches. You will then have enough to serve 12 to 14 people.

For extra-delicious results, brine the turkey breast in Spiced Brine (variation, page 350) for 2 days after prepping it in Step 1. Store turkey bones and trimmings separately in an airtight container, covered, in the refrigerator. Rinse breast and pat dry with paper towels. Proceed with recipe, omitting the rest of the salt.

▸ **Sous vide pouch**
▸ **Fine-mesh sieve**

| | | |
|---|---|---|
| 1 | bone-in, skin-on turkey breast (1½ to 2 lbs/675 to 900 g) | 1 |
| 5 | mushrooms (any variety) | 5 |

**STUFFING**

| | | |
|---|---|---|
| 2 tbsp | butter | 30 mL |
| 1 cup | finely chopped onion | 250 mL |
| ½ cup | finely chopped celery | 125 mL |
| 2 tsp | finely chopped garlic | 10 mL |
| ½ tsp | kosher salt | 2 mL |
| 3 cups | diced crustless white bread (½-inch/1 cm cubes) | 750 mL |
| 1 tsp | rubbed dried sage | 5 mL |
| 1 tsp | freshly ground black pepper | 5 mL |
| | Milk | |

**GRAVY**

| | | |
|---|---|---|
| 1 tbsp | poultry fat (chicken, turkey or duck) or butter | 15 mL |
| ½ | onion, coarsely chopped | ½ |
| 1 tbsp | all-purpose flour | 15 mL |
| 1½ cups | ready-to-use unsalted chicken broth | 375 mL |
| 1 | small bay leaf | 1 |
| | Salt | |
| 1 cup | Cranberry Sauce (page 381), optional | 250 mL |

*continued on next page*

## Tips

Butterflying is a butchering technique that evens out the thickness of a piece of meat or fish. Holding a sharp knife parallel to the work surface, make a horizontal cut most of the way through the thicker part of the piece, leaving about ½ inch (1 cm) intact. Then open it up like a book.

The turkey roll needs to remain a nice tight cylinder as it cooks. This recipe works best if you use a chamber vacuum sealer.

1. Using a sharp chef's knife, remove bones, skin and cartilage from turkey breast. Coarsely chop bones, skin and cartilage. Set aside breast meat and trimmings separately. Remove and chop stems from mushrooms and reserve. Finely chop mushroom caps and set aside for stuffing.

2. *Stuffing:* In a medium skillet, melt butter over medium heat. Add finely chopped onion, chopped mushroom caps, celery and salt. Cook, stirring, for 4 to 5 minutes, until mushrooms have released their liquid. Add garlic and cook, stirring, for 1 minute. Transfer mushroom mixture to a large bowl. Add bread, sage and pepper; stir until well combined. Add just enough milk to moisten and make the mixture sticky (about 3 to 5 tbsp/45 to 75 mL — the amount will depend on how dry the bread is). Cover and refrigerate until ready to use.

3. Using a sharp boning or slicing knife, butterfly thicker side of turkey breast to create one large piece roughly even in thickness (see Tips, at left). Place between 2 sheets of plastic wrap. Using the flat side of a cleaver or a meat mallet, pound lightly to an even ½-inch (1 cm) thickness. Remove plastic and fold in any shaggy bits at the edges.

4. Salt both sides of turkey lightly. Place on the work surface a clean piece of plastic wrap large enough to wrap around the meat. Place turkey, skinned side down, on plastic wrap with one long edge close to you. About one-third of the way from long edge, mound stuffing in a ridge. Rotate turkey 180 degrees so uncovered side is closest to you. Using plastic wrap and starting at uncovered long edge, roll meat around stuffing, tucking in any that spills out as you roll. Continue rolling to create a fat cylinder. Pull plastic wrap tightly around roll to help seal it.

5. Preheat hot water bath to 145°F (62.8°C). Slide wrapped cylinder into sous vide pouch and seal. Immerse pouch in preheated water bath and cook for 3 to 4 hours. (To make ahead, see Tip, at right.)

## Tip

*To make ahead:* Prepare through Step 5. Remove pouch from hot water bath, transfer to an ice bath and chill for 1 hour, replenishing ice as necessary. Refrigerate sealed pouch for up to 6 days. Proceed with Steps 6 through 8. Transfer gravy to a small resealable freezer bag and refrigerate for up to 6 days. To reheat from refrigerator temperature, preheat hot water bath to 130°F (54°C). Immerse sealed turkey pouch and gravy bag in preheated bath for 1 hour. Proceed with Step 9.

6. *Gravy:* In a medium saucepan over medium heat, melt poultry fat. Add reserved turkey bones, skin and cartilage, mushroom stems and coarsely chopped onion. Cook, stirring occasionally, for 15 minutes or until onion is lightly browned. Reduce heat and sprinkle flour overtop. Cook, stirring often, for 4 to 5 minutes.

7. Gradually whisk in broth and bring to a simmer, stirring. Reduce heat to medium-low. Add bay leaf and simmer, stirring occasionally, for 45 minutes or until thickened and slightly reduced. If gravy is too thick, add water, a little at a time, to thin to desired consistency. Remove from heat and set aside.

8. Right before turkey is finished cooking, return gravy to a simmer over medium heat. Strain through fine-mesh sieve into a small clean saucepan. Cover and keep warm over low heat.

9. Remove pouch from hot water bath. Open pouch and slide turkey roll onto a cutting board. Pour any cooking liquid in pouch into gravy, whisk to combine and salt to taste.

10. Remove plastic wrap. Cut turkey roll crosswise into slices $\frac{1}{2}$ inch (1 cm) thick. Serve on warm plates with gravy and cranberry sauce (if using).

# Turkey Thigh Chili

Turkey thighs make a light, inexpensive main course and add richness to this chili. Choose a not-too-sweet barbecue sauce for this recipe; a smoky one will give the chili a subtle but more complex flavor. You can also substitute homemade turkey stock for the chicken broth if you have it. I like to top bowls of this chili with sour cream and serve it with garlic bread, but shredded cheese, chopped fresh cilantro and tortilla strips make nice garnishes too.

## Tips

You can easily double or triple this recipe. Put no more than 1 lb (450 g) in each bag.

Mexican oregano has a unique flavor, with notes of camphor. Do not substitute common (Greek) oregano for it in this recipe; a better option is dried marjoram. Because dried marjoram is often pungent and very finely crumbled, reduce the amount to ½ tsp (2 mL).

You can make this chili as spicy as you like. Dried red chile peppers are easy to find in Asian or Latin American markets; I like *chiles de árbol* for this dish. If you don't have any on hand, you can substitute a big pinch of cayenne pepper, but it offers only heat, not flavor.

▶ **Large resealable freezer bag**
▶ **Spice grinder or mortar and pestle**

| | | |
|---|---|---|
| ½ | recipe Spiced Brine (variation, page 350) | ½ |
| 8 oz | boneless, skinless turkey thighs | 225 g |
| ¼ cup | barbecue sauce | 60 mL |
| 1 tsp | dried Mexican oregano (see Tips, at left) | 5 mL |
| ½ tsp | black peppercorns | 2 mL |
| ½ tsp | cumin seeds | 2 mL |
| 2 | small dried red chile peppers (see Tips, at left) | 2 |
| 1½ tbsp | rendered poultry fat or vegetable oil (see Tips, at right) | 22 mL |
| 1 | onion, minced | 1 |
| 2 or 3 | cloves garlic, minced | 2 or 3 |
| 1 cup | canned diced tomatoes, with juice | 250 mL |
| 2 cups | cooked white kidney or pinto beans, drained and rinsed | 500 mL |
| 1 cup | ready-to-use chicken broth | 250 mL |
| 1 | bay leaf | 1 |
| | Salt | |

1. Pour brine into freezer bag and add turkey. Seal bag and refrigerate for least 24 hours, and no longer than 3 days.

2. Preheat hot water bath to 161.6°F (72°C).

3. Remove turkey from brine; rinse and pat dry with paper towels. Discard brine and rinse bag. Place barbecue sauce in bag. Add turkey and seal. Immerse in preheated water bath and cook for 10 to 12 hours.

## Tips

Melted chicken or duck fat gives this chili more flavor than vegetable oil. Don't use fat rendered from a roasted bird, because it can taste burnt.

*To make ahead:* Prepare through Step 4. Refrigerate sealed bag for up to 5 days or freeze for up to 6 months. To use frozen turkey, preheat hot water bath to 140°F (60°C); immerse bag in bath for 10 minutes or until thawed and sauce is liquefied. Proceed with Step 5.

Like most stews, this chili tastes better after a day or two in the fridge. The best way to reheat it is to pack the finished chili into resealable plastic freezer bags. Preheat hot water bath to 140°F (60°C); then reheat bags for 40 to 60 minutes or until hot. Never boil the chili when you reheat it, or you will negate all the careful work you did cooking the turkey sous vide.

**4.** Remove bag from hot water bath, transfer to an ice bath and chill for 40 minutes. (To make ahead, see Tips, at left.)

**5.** Meanwhile, in a small, dry skillet over medium heat, toast oregano, peppercorns, cumin seeds and chiles, stirring constantly, for 2 to 3 minutes or until fragrant. Let cool. Transfer to spice grinder and grind to a powder.

**6.** In a large saucepan, heat poultry fat over medium heat. Add onion and cook, stirring often, for 10 minutes or until softened and golden. Add garlic and spice mixture; cook, stirring, for 2 to 3 minutes or until fragrant but garlic is not darkened. Stir in tomatoes with juice, reduce heat and simmer, stirring occasionally, for 20 minutes or until mixture is thickened and sauce-like.

**7.** Open bag and transfer turkey to a cutting board. Pour cooking liquid from bag into tomato mixture; stir in beans, broth and bay leaf. Simmer for 15 minutes. Season to taste with salt.

**8.** Remove and discard skin, bone and cartilage from turkey. Chop into bite-size pieces and add to bean mixture. Remove from heat, cover and let stand for 10 minutes. Discard bay leaf. Ladle chili into warm bowls.

# Tasty Turkey Thighs

This recipe results in really tasty dark meat. The turkey takes on a different textures, depending on the time and cooking temperature that you choose. Cook it at the higher temperature and you get meat that you can shred for tacos or casseroles. Cook it low and slow and you have something more like duck confit. It can be crisped up and served whole or carefully taken off the bone and cut into chunks to add to your favorite recipes, such as stews and cassoulet.

---

**MAKES 2 LBS (900 G)**

Freezer Bag Friendly

## Tips

This recipe can be halved, doubled or tripled. Use as many pouches as necessary, making sure the turkey legs or thighs don't overlap.

If the thighs or legs are large, divide them between 2 sous vide pouches. Divide the fat equally between the pouches before sealing.

Cooked thighs, sealed in their pouch, will keep refrigerated for up to 1 month or frozen for up to 6 months. Defrost overnight in the refrigerator before using.

▶ **Sous vide pouch**

| | | |
|---|---|---|
| 2 tbsp | Spiced Salt (page 350) | 30 mL |
| 2 | cloves garlic, chopped | 2 |
| 2¼ lbs | bone-in, skin-on turkey thighs or legs (1 to 3 pieces) | 1 kg |
| 3 tbsp | rendered duck, chicken or pork fat (see box, below) | 45 mL |

1. In a large bowl, stir together spiced salt and garlic. Add turkey thighs, tossing to coat and rubbing salt mixture into skin. Cover bowl or transfer to a resealable freezer bag. Refrigerate overnight or for up to 24 hours.

2. Preheat hot water bath to desired temperature: 167°F (75°C) for shreddable meat or 150°F (65.6°C) for firmer, confit-like meat.

3. Remove turkey from salt mixture and rinse under cold running water. Pat dry with paper towels. Transfer turkey to sous vide pouch. Add fat to pouch. Arrange thighs so they are in one layer and seal. Immerse in preheated hot water bath and cook for 12 hours for shreddable meat, or for 18 to 20 hours for firmer, confit-like meat.

4. Remove pouch from hot water bath. Let stand for 20 to 30 minutes. Transfer to an ice bath and chill for 30 minutes. Refrigerate sealed pouch until ready to use.

---

### Making Poultry Glaze and Fat

The cooking liquid in the pouch is delicious, so don't discard it. Warm it up to liquefy the fat and pour it into a small jar to chill. The rendered fat will rise to the top, leaving a small layer of salty "poultry glaze" underneath. Separate the two and use the glaze to enhance soups or sauces (use it within 5 days or freeze it for later). The fat should be melted and brought to a boil to pasteurize it. Once you've done that, let it cool, cover tightly and refrigerate. Rendered poultry fat keeps for about 8 weeks, refrigerated. Use it for roasting potatoes or to make poultry confit.

---

# Duck

Duck can take on a variety of tastes and textures, depending on the temperature you choose to cook it at and how long it spends in the hot water bath. There are three primary species you are likely to come across, each with its own unique qualities: Pekin, Muscovy and Moulard. Although I've specified which type of duck is best for each recipe, you can substitute one for another as long as their sizes are the same. This will ensure that the duck is cooked to its optimal temperature.

- **Pekin ducks:** These white birds, also known as Long Island ducks, are the most readily available. The dressed weight of a Pekin is 4 to 5 lbs (1.8 to 2.25 kg), and it will serve two to four people, depending on the recipe. These ducks tolerate conventional farming techniques quite well and are slaughtered at 7 to 8 weeks of age. Their meat is quite tender and their legs can be cooked relatively quickly. Pekin ducks can be quite fatty, so I like to cook them at a temperature that will render some of the fat. Because you are not likely to know the conditions under which they were raised, I recommend that you treat them like chicken, cooking the meat long enough to ensure pasteurization (see box, page 167).
- **Muscovy ducks:** Muscovy ducks are about twice the size of Pekins and are slaughtered at about 14 to 16 weeks of age. Their meat is leaner and can be a little tough, so cooking them sous vide is ideal. The taste is best described as beefy, and while they have less fat, their skin gives them that iconic duck flavor. Legs of Muscovy and Moulard ducks work equally well for Duck Confit (page 176) and similar preparations.
- **Moulard ducks:** Moulard ducks are a sterile cross between the Muscovy and Pekin that was developed for production of foie gras. They physically resemble a Muscovy but have quite a bit more fat. Their meat is more tender than Muscovy meat, but to me it's not quite as delicious. The term *magret* refers to the breast of this breed and is traditionally served rare or medium-rare, as steak often is. Muscovy duck breasts can be served similarly, but I suggest that you age them for 5 to 6 days in a sealed sous vide pouch to tenderize them before cooking.

# Duck Fat

Depending on what type of duck you choose, you may wind up with some extra fat. Pekin ducks are usually sold whole, and you may find some fat deposits in the cavity or excess skin on the carcass. Pull or cut them off and set them aside. Muscovy and Moulard ducks may have more fat on the legs and breasts than you want. Working with a well-chilled duck and a sharp knife, carefully shave down the excess on the breast to about ¼ inch (0.5 cm). Cut around the leg meat so that the fat protrudes about ¼ inch (0.5 cm) beyond the meat (the fat will shrink a little during cooking).

The fat can be chopped and then rendered by simmering it in a saucepan with some water and then straining it. Store, covered, in the refrigerator for up to 8 weeks or freeze for up to 12 months. There are several recipes in this book that call for duck fat, so it will come in handy!

## GOOSE

Domestic goose is a special treat when you can find it. The flavor is deeper and richer than duck and the birds have more fat. Aging the breasts as for Muscovy duck is recommended, since they can be a little tough. Warm Duck Breast Salad with Walnuts and Apples (page 172), Duck Confit (page 176) and Potted Duck (page 178) can all be made with goose.

# Drunken Duck Ramen with Sous Vide Egg

Duck and sherry are an unbeatable combination, and sherry adds a delicious dimension to broths. Here's a recipe in which a single duck can feed six people. Feel free to substitute noodles of your choice for the ramen.

Freezer Bag Friendly

## Tips

You can halve this recipe. Doubling it is tricky because of the quantity of noodles. If you choose to do so, use 2 pots to cook the noodles or cook them in 2 batches. You'll also need an extra freezer bag as well.

If you prefer boneless duck pieces in your soup, prepare the duck through Step 1 but do not cut the breast into pieces after dividing it in half. Proceed with Steps 2 to 5, placing each half in a separate freezer bag and dividing sherry mixture between 2 bags. When duck is cooked, remove skin and bones and begin Step 6, adding cooked skin and bones to saucepan. Cut duck meat into spoon-size pieces and place in a resealable plastic freezer bag. Place bag in hot water bath as directed in Step 8. Proceed with recipe.

- ▶ **Large resealable freezer bag**
- ▶ **Spice grinder or mortar and pestle**
- ▶ **Fine-mesh sieve**

| | | |
|---|---|---|
| 1 | whole Pekin duck, about 4 to 5 lbs (1.8 to 2.25 kg; see box, page 163) | 1 |
| 1 cup | dry or medium-dry amontillado sherry | 250 mL |
| 1 tbsp | black peppercorns | 15 mL |
| | Salt | |
| 8 cups | ready-to-use unsalted chicken broth | 2 L |
| 1 | sheet nori (about 8 inches/20 cm square) | 1 |
| 8 oz | enoki mushrooms | 225 g |
| 6 | whole shell-on eggs (see Tips, page 166) | 6 |
| 4 | packages (each 3 oz/85 g) dried ramen noodles | 4 |
| 4 | green onions, chopped | 4 |
| | Shichimi togarashi, optional (see Tips, page 166) | |

1. Place duck on a cutting board. Using a sharp chef's knife or kitchen shears, cut along both sides of backbone and remove. Cut off tips and flat portions of wings, leaving just the first joint attached to the breast. Cut off feet, neck and head, if attached. Rinse backbone, neck, head, feet and wingtips under cold running water. Drain and place in a medium bowl. Turn over duck and cut in half through breastbone. Cut thighs off drumsticks and cut each thigh in half crosswise, through the bone. Cut each breast into 3 equal pieces, leaving bones in and first wing joint attached. You will now have 12 bone-in duck pieces. Cover and refrigerate overnight (see Tips, page 166).

*continued on next page*

## Tips

Your butcher can carry
out Step 1 for you,
if desired.

You can use duck eggs
instead of chicken
eggs, if desired (though
I find them too large
for my taste). If you do
use them, increase the
cooking time in the hot
water bath to 12 minutes.

Shichimi togarashi is a
Japanese seasoning
powder made primarily
of ground dried chiles.
Substitute chile flakes if
you don't have it, or omit
if desired.

**2.** Pour sherry into a glass measuring cup. To burn off
some of the alcohol, microwave on High for 2 minutes,
or bring to a boil in a small saucepan over medium
heat for 2 minutes. Set aside to cool.

**3.** Meanwhile, in a small, dry skillet over medium heat,
lightly toast peppercorns with 1 tbsp (15 mL) salt,
for 3 to 4 minutes or until fragrant. Remove from
heat and let cool slightly. Transfer to spice grinder
and grind to a powder. Stir into sherry until salt is
dissolved. Let cool.

**4.** Place duck and sherry mixture in freezer bag and seal.
Refrigerate overnight or for up to 24 hours.

**5.** Preheat hot water bath to 167°F (75°C). Immerse bag
in preheated bath and cook for 4 hours. (To make the
duck ahead, see Tips, at right.)

**6.** Meanwhile, in a medium saucepan, combine reserved
duck bones, feet, neck, head and wingtips with
broth. Bring to a simmer over medium heat. Simmer,
skimming occasionally, for 2 hours, adding water as
necessary to keep the bones submerged.

**7.** Strain broth mixture through fine-mesh sieve into
a large, heatproof glass measuring cup. Skim fat off
surface. If amount is less than 8 cups (2 L), top up
with water as necessary. Season to taste with salt, if
necessary. Return to pan, cover and keep at a simmer.
(To make the broth ahead, see Tips, at right.)

**8.** Remove bag from hot water bath (do not turn off sous
vide machine). Open bag. Without removing duck
from bag, pour cooking liquid into broth mixture.
Reseal bag and return to hot water bath to keep warm
(bag may float).

**9.** Cut nori into strips 1 inch (2.5 cm) wide, then cut
strips into finest julienne possible. Trim bottoms off
enoki mushrooms to separate into individual stems.
Set aside.

**10.** Bring a large pot of water to a boil over high heat.
Meanwhile, set eggs on work surface to bring to room
temperature. Place eggs in a sieve or colander and
immerse in boiling water for 90 seconds. (The sieve
makes it easier to remove and peel them later.)

## Tips

*To make the duck ahead:* Prepare through Step 5. Remove bag from hot water bath, transfer to an ice bath and chill for 30 minutes. Refrigerate sealed bag for up to 7 days or freeze for up to 6 months. Preheat hot water bath to 160°F (71.1°C) and reheat bag for 40 minutes. Proceed with Step 8.

*To make the broth ahead:* Prepare through Step 7. Strain broth into an airtight container and refrigerate for up to 4 days. Just before serving, return to saucepan and reheat over medium heat until simmering.

**11.** Immediately transfer eggs, still in sieve, to hot water bath. Cook for 10 minutes. Remove from hot water bath and transfer to an ice bath for 1 minute. Peel off shells.

**12.** Meanwhile, cook noodles according to package directions (reserve seasoning packets for another use), stirring occasionally with a fork to break them up.

**13.** *Assembly:* Warm 6 deep soup bowls and place 2 pieces of duck in each. Drain noodles and divide evenly between bowls. Place 1 peeled egg in each bowl. Divide enoki mushrooms and scatter over each bowl. Divide simmering broth among bowls. Garnish with nori and green onions. Serve immediately, passing shichimi togarashi (if using) at the table.

### Pasteurizing Duck

Both Muscovy and Moulard ducks are typically raised in a less intensive way and processed in smaller quantities than Pekin ducks, which come from large producers and processors. This makes the risk of pathogens in the meat much smaller, so they don't generally require pasteurization. Searing is sufficient to kill any pathogens on the surface. The legs require plenty of cooking time to become tender, so they will be pasteurized anyway when they emerge from the hot water bath. Pekin ducks are usually commercially raised; for safety they should be pasteurized to the core.

# Korean Duck Tacos

For these tasty tacos I took inspiration from the Korean-Mexican food trucks that have become popular on the West Coast of the United States over the past few years. Once the duck is cooked, the tacos come together quickly. Save the bones to enhance some store-bought chicken broth.

<table>
<tr><td>

**MAKES 12 TACOS**

</td></tr>
</table>

## Tips

You can easily double this recipe. In Step 5, distribute the duck pieces between 2 pouches.

Your butcher can carry out Step 2 for you, if desired.

▸ **Sous vide pouch**
▸ **Spice grinder or mortar and pestle**

| | | |
|---|---|---:|
| 2 tbsp | whole Szechuan peppercorns | 30 mL |
| 2 tbsp | kosher salt | 30 mL |
| 1 | whole Pekin duck, about 4 to 5 lbs (1.8 to 2.25 kg; see box, page 163) | 1 |
| 2 tbsp | vegetable oil | 30 mL |
| 1½ cups | napa cabbage kimchi, drained and coarsely chopped | 375 mL |
| 12 | sprigs fresh cilantro, coarsely chopped | 12 |
| 12 | small (6 inches/15 cm) corn tortillas (see Tips, at right) | 12 |
| 6 | green onions, chopped | 6 |

1. In a small, dry skillet over medium heat, lightly toast peppercorns, stirring constantly, for about 3 minutes or until fragrant. Transfer to spice grinder and add salt. Grind to a powder.

2. Place duck on a cutting board. Using a sharp chef's knife or kitchen shears, cut along both sides of backbone and remove. Cut off tips and flat portions of wings, leaving just the first joint attached to the breast. Cut off feet, neck and head, if attached. Rinse backbone, neck, head, feet and wingtips under cold running water. Drain and place in a medium bowl (save trimmings for stock, if desired, or discard). Turn over duck and cut in half through the breastbone. Remove legs from carcass and cut thighs off drumsticks. Cut each thigh in half crosswise, through the bone. Cut each breast into 3 equal pieces, leaving bones in and first wing joint attached. You will now have 12 bone-in duck pieces (see Tips, at left). Set aside.

3. Rub pepper mixture all over duck. Transfer to a plate and cover loosely with plastic wrap. Refrigerate overnight or for up to 24 hours.

## Tips

*To make ahead:* Prepare through Step 5. Remove from hot water bath, transfer to an ice bath and chill for 30 minutes. Refrigerate sealed pouch for up to 1 week. To reheat from refrigerator temperature, immerse sealed pouch in a bowl of hot water for about 15 minutes. Proceed with Step 6.

If you like, you can double up the tortillas, as they often do on the taco trucks. Stack 2 tortillas before topping with duck mixture and garnishes.

**4.** Preheat hot water bath to 180°F (82.2°C).

**5.** Pat duck dry with paper towels. Arrange pieces in sous vide pouch and seal. Immerse in preheated water bath and cook for 6 hours. (To make ahead, see Tips, at left.)

**6.** Remove pouch from hot water bath. Let cool enough to handle. Open pouch and transfer duck to cutting board. Remove skin, in 1 or 2 pieces if possible, and cut it into ¼-inch (0.5 cm) strips. Using your hands, pull the duck meat into shreds to make about 1½ cups (375 mL).

**7.** In a small skillet, heat oil over medium heat. Add duck skin and cook, stirring often, until crisp, about 10 minutes. Using a slotted spoon, transfer to a plate lined with paper towels and let drain. Add duck meat to pan; cook, stirring often, for 5 minutes or until heated through. Stir in kimchi and cilantro. Remove from heat.

**8.** Wrap 6 tortillas in a damp tea towel and microwave on High for 1 minute or until warm and supple (or briefly pass each one over a gas flame or grill to heat and soften). Repeat with 6 more tortillas. Divide duck mixture evenly among tortillas. Garnish each with green onions and crispy duck skin. Serve immediately.

### Pekin Ducks

Korean Duck Tacos, Simmered Soy Duck (page 170) and Drunken Duck Ramen with Sous Vide Egg (page 165) call for Pekin ducks, the most common domestic breed in North America. They are a handy size and readily available. I have taken inspiration from the cuisines of Asia for these recipes, but feel free to adapt the techniques on these pages to make your favorite duck dishes from other parts of the world.

# Simmered Soy Duck

This is another of my favorite Asian-inspired duck dishes, one that's closer to Japanese in style. To make a light meal, serve it with steamed white rice and pickled vegetables. For a more substantial meal, add some grilled or fried squid.

## Tips

You can easily halve or double this recipe. If you're doubling the recipe, use 2 bags.

Your butcher can carry out Step 1 for you, if desired.

If you like, substitute ½ cup (125 mL) mirin (sweet Japanese cooking wine) for the sugar and water and skip Step 2.

Dark soy sauce is aged a bit longer than light soy sauce, has a deeper flavor and usually has some molasses added to it. It is used in dishes where you want to impart color. Mushroom soy sauce is a variety of dark soy sauce. If you come across it, you can use it here.

▸ **Large resealable freezer bag**
▸ **Fine-mesh sieve**

| | | |
|---|---|---|
| 1 | whole Pekin duck, about 4 to 5 lbs (1.8 to 2.25 kg; see box, page 163) | 1 |
| ½ cup | water | 125 mL |
| 2 tbsp | granulated sugar (see Tips, at left) | 30 mL |
| 6 tbsp | light soy sauce | 90 mL |
| 6 tbsp | dark soy sauce (see Tips, at left) | 90 mL |
| 1 | piece (12 inches/30 cm) daikon radish (unpeeled), cut into ¾-inch (2 cm) cubes | 1 |
| 8 | dried shiitake mushrooms | 8 |
| | Hot water | |
| 4 cups | ready-to-use unsalted chicken broth | 1 L |
| 4 cups | broccoli florets | 1 L |
| 2 | green onions, chopped | 2 |

1. Place duck on a cutting board. Using a sharp chef's knife or kitchen shears, cut along both sides of backbone and remove. Cut off tips and flat portions of wings, leaving just the first joint attached to the breast. Cut off feet, neck and head, if attached. Rinse backbone, neck, head, feet and wingtips under cold running water. Drain, place in a medium bowl, and set aside. Turn over duck and cut in half through breastbone. Remove legs from carcass and cut thighs off drumsticks. Cut each thigh in half crosswise, through the bone. Cut each breast into 3 equal pieces, leaving bones in and first wing joint attached. You will now have 12 bone-in duck pieces (see Tips, at left). Set aside.

2. In a small saucepan over medium heat, combine water and sugar. Bring to a simmer and stir until dissolved, about 6 to 7 minutes. Let cool.

3. Place duck pieces in freezer bag. Add sugar mixture and light and dark soy sauces. Seal bag and refrigerate overnight or for up to 24 hours.

## Tips

*To make duck and daikon mixture ahead:* Prepare through Step 5. Remove bag from hot water bath, transfer to an ice bath and chill for 30 minutes. Refrigerate sealed bag for up to 1 week. To reheat, preheat hot water bath to 140°F (60°C). Immerse bag and heat for 40 minutes. Proceed with Step 9.

*To make broth mixture ahead:* Prepare through Step 7. Chill broth, transfer to an airtight container and refrigerate for up to 4 days. Proceed with Step 8.

**4.** Preheat hot water bath to 167°F (75°C).

**5.** Add daikon to bag with duck and reseal. Immerse in preheated water bath and cook for 4 hours. (To make duck and daikon mixture ahead, see Tips, at left.)

**6.** Place mushrooms in a small bowl and pour in enough hot water to cover (weigh them down with a small plate or bowl to keep submerged). Let stand until softened, about 15 minutes. Drain mushrooms, reserving soaking liquid. Cut stems off mushrooms and reserve. Cut each mushroom cap into 6 pieces. Set aside.

**7.** Meanwhile, in a medium saucepan, combine duck bones, head, feet and broth. Bring to a simmer over medium heat. Add reserved mushroom liquid and stems. Reduce heat and simmer, skimming occasionally, for 2 hours, adding water as necessary to keep bones submerged. Strain broth through fine-mesh sieve. (To make broth ahead, see Tips, at left.)

**8.** Skim fat from surface of broth and discard or save for another use, if desired. Pour broth into a large measuring cup. If amount is less than 4 cups (1 L), top up with water as necessary. Set aside.

**9.** Remove bag from hot water bath. Open bag and set aside duck and daikon mixture. Strain cooking liquid through fine-mesh sieve into a small, heatproof glass measuring cup. Add ⅔ cup (150 mL) of the cooking liquid to broth (save remainder for another use, if desired). Set aside.

**10.** In a saucepan of boiling salted water, blanch broccoli for 2 minutes. Drain and set aside.

**11.** Pour broth mixture into a medium saucepan. Add mushroom caps and bring to a simmer over medium-low heat. Add duck and daikon mixture and broccoli. Stir to combine. Ladle into warm bowls, garnish with green onions and serve immediately.

# Warm Duck Breast Salad with Walnuts and Apples

Duck breast is rich and satisfying — the perfect complement to assertive greens such as the ones used here. This blend of apples, walnuts, watercress, frisée and potatoes is wonderful with the duck and makes a satisfying lunch or light dinner in autumn or winter. In smaller portions, it can also be a delicious starter as part of a larger menu.

**MAKES 4 MAIN-COURSE SERVINGS OR 6 APPETIZER SERVINGS**

Freezer Bag Friendly

## Tips

You can easily halve or double this recipe. If doubling, use 2 bags.

The duck in this recipe is not pasteurized. While the risk is very low, do not serve this to young children, the elderly, pregnant women or people with a compromised immune system. See page 9 for more details.

If you have access to fresh goose breast, you can use it here. Goose breasts are usually larger than duck, so you may not need 2 whole breasts.

Extra virgin olive oil can be substituted for the walnut oil if desired.

> ► **Preheat oven to 350°F (180°C)**
> ► **Sous vide pouch**
> ► **Small resealable freezer bag**
> ► **2 rimmed baking sheets, 1 lined with parchment paper**

| | | |
|---|---|---|
| 2 | boneless skin-on Muscovy or Moulard duck breasts (each 12 to 14 oz/340 to 400 g; see Tips, at left) | 2 |
| | Spiced Salt (page 350), or salt and freshly ground black pepper | |
| ¾ cup | walnut pieces | 175 mL |
| 3 tbsp | vegetable oil | 45 mL |
| 12 oz | small white-skinned new potatoes, cooked (see Tips, at right) | 340 g |
| 1 | bunch watercress, stemmed | 1 |
| 1 | head frisée, separated into leaves | 1 |
| 1 | tart green apple, diced | 1 |

### VINAIGRETTE

| | | |
|---|---|---|
| ¼ cup | walnut oil | 60 mL |
| 2 tbsp | red wine vinegar | 30 mL |
| 1 tsp | chopped garlic | 5 mL |
| ½ tsp | Dijon mustard | 2 mL |
| | Salt and freshly ground black pepper | |

1. Using your hands and a small knife to help, remove skin and fat from each duck breast in 1 piece. Place skin and fat between 2 pieces of parchment paper or plastic wrap. Using the flat side of a meat mallet or a rolling pin, pound gently to a scant ¼-inch (0.5 cm) thickness.

You can also use
Buttery New Potatoes
(page 297), which are
cooked sous vide, or
simple boiled potatoes
for this salad.

If you have any leftover
rendered duck fat, save
it for other uses. Let it
cool, then cover and
refrigerate for up to
8 weeks or freeze for
up to 6 months.

**2.** Arrange skin in a single layer on prepared baking sheet. Season very lightly to taste with spiced salt. Cover with a second sheet of parchment paper and weigh down with second baking sheet to keep skin from buckling. Spread walnuts over top baking sheet. Place trays in oven and bake until walnuts are lightly toasted and fragrant, about 15 minutes.

**3.** Remove trays and transfer nuts to a clean, dry tea towel. Have a look at the duck skin — it should be rendering its fat and starting to brown. Return baking sheets to oven for another 5 to 10 minutes, until skin is mahogany brown, like that of roast duck.

**4.** Drain skin on a plate lined with paper towels. Transfer rendered fat to a small glass measuring cup. Set aside for vinaigrette. With the aid of the tea towel, rub as much skin as possible from walnuts. Remove nuts from towel and set aside.

**5.** Place duck breasts on a plate and season to taste with additional spiced salt. Refrigerate for 30 minutes or until well chilled.

**6.** In a medium skillet, heat oil over high heat. Add duck breasts and sear, turning once, for 1 minute per side. Transfer to a clean plate and refrigerate until chilled, about 10 minutes.

**7.** Preheat hot water bath to 122°F (50°C). Place duck breasts in pouch, ensuring that they do not overlap, and seal. Immerse in preheated water bath and cook for 2 to 3 hours.

**8.** *Vinaigrette:* Meanwhile, in a medium bowl set over a medium saucepan of simmering water, combine walnut oil, $\frac{1}{4}$ cup (60 mL) reserved duck fat, vinegar, garlic and mustard. Whisk until blended and warm. Season to taste with salt and pepper.

**9.** Place potatoes in freezer bag, add vinaigrette and seal. Immerse bag in preheated hot water bath with duck during last 30 minutes to 1 hour of cooking.

**10.** Remove duck pouch from hot water bath. Open bag and transfer duck to a cutting board. Slice thinly crosswise. Cut reserved duck skin into $\frac{1}{2}$-inch (1 cm) pieces.

**11.** *Assembly:* Divide watercress and frisée among plates. Add duck skin, walnuts and apple. Place duck slices on top. Remove potatoes from bath and spoon onto salads. Drizzle with the warm vinaigrette and serve.

# Porkducken

Generally speaking, I find that Moulard and Muscovy duck breasts cook better using more conventional methods. However, I wanted to include more than just one breast recipe in this book, and this one is well suited to the sous vide method. Admittedly, this duck-and-pork mash-up is a bit crazy, but it makes a little duck go a long way with the addition of less expensive pork tenderloin. And it's incredibly delicious. Buttered new potatoes and sauerkraut cooked with smoky bacon are terrific side dishes to serve with the meat.

**MAKES
4 SERVINGS**

Advanced

## Tips

This recipe can be doubled or tripled. Seal each roll in a separate sous vide pouch.

For extra-delicious results, brine the trimmed tenderloin for up to 2 days, using a half-batch of Spiced Brine (variation, page 350). Rinse the meat and pat dry with paper towels before proceeding with Step 3. Omit seasoning with salt and pepper in Step 4.

▷ **Sous vide pouch**
▷ **Small fine-mesh sieve**

| | | |
|---|---|---|
| 1 | pork tenderloin (12 oz/340 g) | 1 |
| 6 to 8 oz | boneless, skin-on Muscovy or Moulard duck breast | 170 to 225 g |
| | Salt and freshly ground black pepper | |
| 2 tsp | Activa RM (approx.; see Tips, at right) | 10 mL |
| 2 tbsp | vegetable oil | 30 mL |

1. Trim any excess fat and silverskin off the pork tenderloin. Set aside. Using a sharp chef's knife, cut duck breast lengthwise into slices, as thinly as possible. Arrange slices on a sheet of plastic wrap, leaving room between them, and top with another sheet of plastic wrap. Gently pound the slices to an even ⅛-inch (3 mm) thickness. Remove top sheet of plastic.

2. Place top sheet of plastic wrap on a work surface. Arrange duck slices, overlapping and with skin edges down, lengthwise in a row on plastic, forming a rectangle 10 to 12 inches (25 to 30 cm) long. (The skin edges of the slices will create a striped pattern on the other side.)

3. Now you need to make a trial run. Fold in the tail of the tenderloin so that its length matches that of the lined-up duck slices. Using the plastic wrap as an aid, wrap the duck around the pork to see if the rectangle is large enough to go all the way around. If it isn't, you'll need to pound the slices a little more until the duck can wrap right around the tenderloin — set aside pork, place another sheet of plastic on top of duck, and lightly pound the arranged slices.

4. Season tenderloin well with salt and pepper to taste.

## Tips

Activa is a brand name for transglutaminase. This enzyme is also called "meat glue" because it binds proteins together. The bonds are strongest after at least 5 hours in the refrigerator. RM is the most common and versatile type of Activa and the only one that you are likely to need. It is available online at Modernist Pantry (modernistpantry.com) and in cooking stores that cater to professionals. For more information, see box, page 67).

*To make ahead:* Prepare through Step 7. Chill in an ice bath for 20 minutes. Refrigerate sealed pouch for up to 5 days. To reheat from refrigerator temperature, preheat hot water bath to 100°F (37.8°C). Immerse pouch for 20 minutes, then proceed with Step 8, reducing cooling time to 10 minutes.

5. Spoon Activa RM into fine-mesh sieve. Remove top sheet of plastic from duck (if present) and sprinkle half the Activa over slices. Sprinkle the rest evenly over tenderloin (use a little more if necessary). Fold in tail of tenderloin as before. Line up long edge with bottom long edge of sliced-duck rectangle.

6. Using plastic wrap as an aid and starting at bottom edge, roll duck tightly around tenderloin. Wrap roll tightly in plastic wrap. Pierce wrap with a pin over the length and circumference of cylinder to release any trapped air. Place roll in sous vide pouch and seal. Refrigerate for 4 hours or overnight to allow meat to adhere (see Tips, at left).

7. Preheat hot water bath to 131°F (55°C). Immerse pouch in preheated bath and cook for 4 hours. Remove pouch from bath. (To make ahead, see Tips, at left.)

8. Remove roll from pouch and remove plastic wrap. Pat meat dry with paper towels. Season to taste with additional salt and pepper, place on a clean plate and let cool for about 20 minutes.

9. In a nonstick skillet or well-seasoned cast-iron frying pan, large enough to accommodate length of roll, heat oil over medium-high heat. Add roll and sear quickly, turning often, until lightly browned, about 5 to 6 minutes.

10. Transfer roll to a cutting board and cut crosswise into ¾-inch (2 cm) slices. Serve immediately on warm plates.

### Moulard and Muscovy Ducks

The recipes on pages 172 through 179 call for Moulard or Muscovy ducks, both of which are less readily available than Pekin duck but more interesting in flavor. Because these birds are much larger than the commoner Pekin ducks, the recipes separate the legs from the breasts, which optimizes their attributes. For more on these breeds, see page 163.

# Duck Confit

I can't think of any meat lover who doesn't like duck confit. It's rich, meltingly tender and incredibly savory. I like to add confit to *choucroute garnie* and cassoulet, but it's also delicious on its own, accompanied by Savoy Cabbage with Chestnuts (page 296).

---

| MAKES |
|:---:|
| **4 PIECES** |

**Freezer Bag Friendly**

## Tips

This recipe can be halved, doubled or tripled. Seal pairs of legs in separate pouches for cooking.

This recipe can also be made with Pekin duck legs. Reduce the amount of spiced salt and garlic by half, and refrigerate for 8 to 12 hours in Step 2. Reduce the cooking time to 12 to 18 hours.

▶ **2 sous vide pouches**

| | | |
|---|---|---|
| 4 | Muscovy or Moulard duck legs (each 12 to 14 oz/340 to 400 g; see Tips, at left) | 4 |
| ¼ cup | Spiced Salt (page 350) | 60 mL |
| 2 | cloves garlic, chopped | 2 |
| ½ cup | rendered duck fat (see box, at right) | 125 mL |

1. Pull any lumps of fat off inside of each duck leg. Place legs, skin side down, on a cutting board. Trim off excess fat, leaving ¼ inch (0.5 cm) of skin and fat beyond edge of meat. Reserve trimmed skin and fat for rendering.

2. In a large bowl, stir together spiced salt and garlic. Add duck legs and toss to coat, rubbing mixture into each piece. Cover bowl or transfer to a resealable freezer bag and refrigerate overnight, or for up to 24 hours.

3. Preheat hot water bath to 149°F (65°C).

4. Rinse duck legs under cold running water. Pat dry with paper towels. Arrange 2 legs in each sous vide pouch, without overlapping. Divide rendered fat between pouches and seal. Immerse in preheated hot water bath and cook for 18 to 24 hours.

5. Remove pouches from hot water bath, transfer to an ice bath and chill for 30 minutes. Refrigerate sealed pouches until ready to use, or for up to 8 weeks (see box, at right).

## Tips

If you have access to goose legs, you can substitute them here. Increase the curing time from 24 to 36 hours in Step 2. Cook for 24 hours in Step 4.

The cooking liquid in the pouch is delicious, so don't discard it. Heat the liquid, pour into a small jar and chill. The fat will rise to the top, leaving a small layer of salty "poultry glaze" underneath. Separate the two and use the glaze to enhance soups or sauces (use within 5 days or freeze it for later). The fat should be melted and brought to a boil to pasteurize it. Once you've done that, let it cool. Transfer to an airtight container, cover tightly and refrigerate for up to 8 weeks or freeze for up to 6 months. Use it for roasting potatoes or to make more confit.

### Rendering Duck and Pork Fat

In a small saucepan, combine duck skin and fat (to make rendered pork fat, use diced fresh pork fat). Cover with cold water and bring to a simmer over medium heat. Reduce heat slightly and simmer for 30 to 60 minutes or until all of the water has evaporated. Strain through a fine-mesh sieve into a bowl. Discard solids (or salt and snack on them, the way cooks do). Let cool. Transfer to an airtight container and refrigerate for up to 8 weeks or freeze for up to 12 months.

If you need more duck fat than you can make yourself, a good online source for rendered duck fat in the United States is D'Artagnan (http://www.dartagnan.com/).

### Optimal Aging

I find that aging the confit duck legs in the refrigerator improves their flavor tremendously. For me, 3 weeks is the optimal length of time for giving the duck a smoother and better flavor. If you are short on time, the duck can be used right away.

# Potted Duck

Also known as duck rillettes, potted duck makes a great appetizer. Serve it with crusty bread, mustard and your favorite pickled vegetables. The jars of duck also make fantastic gifts, especially around the holidays.

---

| | MAKES ABOUT 2 CUPS (500 ML) |
|---|---|

Freezer Bag Friendly

## Tips

This recipe can easily be doubled or tripled. Seal pairs of legs in separate pouches for cooking and have additional jars on hand.

This recipe can also be made with a similar weight of Pekin duck legs. Refrigerate for 8 to 12 hours in Step 2. Reduce the cooking time to 12 to 18 hours in Step 4.

▶ Sous vide pouch
▶ Four 4 oz (125 mL) or two 8 oz (250 mL) straight-sided canning jars, with lids

| 2 | Muscovy or Moulard duck legs (each 12 to 14 oz/340 to 400 g; see Tips, at left and right) | 2 |
|---|---|---|
| 2 tbsp | Spiced Salt (page 350) | 30 mL |
| 2 | cloves garlic, chopped | 2 |
| 3 tbsp | rendered pork or duck fat (see box, page 177, and Tips, at right) | 45 mL |
| 1 tbsp | port or oloroso sherry, optional | 15 mL |

1. With your hands and using a paring knife if necessary, remove skin and surface fat from duck legs. Using paring knife, separate thighs from drumsticks.

2. In a large bowl, stir together spiced salt and garlic. Add duck legs and toss to coat, rubbing mixture into each piece. Cover bowl or transfer to a resealable freezer bag. Seal bag and refrigerate overnight, or for up to 24 hours.

3. Preheat hot water bath to 167°F (75°C).

4. Rinse duck legs under cold running water. Pat dry with paper towels. Place legs, rendered fat and port (if using), in sous vide pouch and seal. Immerse in preheated water bath and cook for 18 to 24 hours.

5. Remove pouch from hot water bath. Increase temperature of bath to 190°F (87.8°C). Open pouch and pour duck mixture into a medium bowl. Let cool enough to handle.

## Tips

This recipe can also be made with a similar weight of goose legs. Refrigerate for 24 to 36 hours in Step 2. Increase the cooking time to 36 hours in Step 4.

Pork fat yields a firmer result and is actually preferable in this recipe.

6. Lift out duck pieces, leaving liquid in bowl. Remove bones from legs and discard. Using a fork and your hands, pull meat into shreds. Return to bowl with cooking liquid and toss to coat.

7. Spoon duck mixture into jars, leaving $\frac{1}{2}$ inch (1 cm) headspace. Wipe rims of jars thoroughly to ensure a good seal. Add lids and turn just until snug. Immerse jars in hot water bath and cook for $1\frac{1}{2}$ hours.

8. Remove jars from hot water bath. Immerse in a sink full of cold water and chill for 30 minutes. For best flavor, refrigerate for at least 1 to 2 weeks before serving, or for up to 2 months.

9. To serve, open jar and scoop duck mixture into a small bowl. Stir with a fork to incorporate surface fat and gelatinized liquid at bottom. Serve cold.

# Quail

Quails make a nice change from other poultry. Their diminutive size is handy as well — one is the perfect size for an appetizer and two or three make an enjoyable main course. They are tasty split and grilled over a fire with nothing more than salt, pepper and good olive oil. Because of their small bones, quails are usually eaten with your fingers.

For a more formal presentation, you need to either find a source for semi-boneless quail or bone the birds yourself. The technique for boning a quail is not so much difficult as it is slow. Working from within the cavity, you carefully turn the bird inside out, removing the bones with your hands as you go. The drumsticks and wings are left on so the finished product will maintain its birdlike appearance.

Semi-boneless quails are excellent filled with a savory stuffing. Stuffings made with rice or mushrooms are natural partners, as they complement the quail's delicate flavor. Filled with meat, a single quail can make a lovely entrée.

# Quails Filled with Chicken Mousse

These quails are filled with a lovely chicken forcemeat. Cooking them sous vide ensures that they are done evenly throughout; all they need is a quick browning of the skin and they are ready for the table. I like to serve these on mushroom risotto as a main course.

**MAKES 4 SERVINGS**

Freezer Bag Friendly

**Tip**

You can double this recipe, but halving it is difficult, since it's not easy to make a smaller amount of the mousse. If doubling, use 4 pouches.

▶ **Preheat hot water bath to 155°F (68.3°C)**
▶ **2 sous vide pouches**
▶ **Food processor**
▶ **Piping bag fitted with large plain tip, or freezer bag with one corner snipped off**

| | | |
|---|---|---|
| 6 oz | boneless, skinless chicken breast, diced and well chilled | 170 g |
| 1 tbsp | finely chopped shallot | 15 mL |
| ½ tsp | finely chopped garlic | 2 mL |
| ½ tsp | kosher salt | 2 mL |
| ¼ tsp | freshly ground black pepper | 1 mL |
| Pinch | ground nutmeg | Pinch |
| 1 | egg, chilled | 1 |
| 3 tbsp | heavy or whipping (35%) cream, well chilled | 45 mL |
| 4 | semi-boneless skin-on quails (see Tips, at right) | 4 |
| 3 tbsp | butter | 45 mL |

You can buy semi-boneless quails or do the boning yourself. Boning quail is a rite of passage for apprentices working in fine dining establishments. If you don't have time to do the work yourself, do buy them.

*To make ahead:* Prepare through Step 3. Remove pouches from hot water bath, transfer to an ice bath and chill for 30 minutes. Refrigerate sealed pouches for up to 5 days. To reheat from refrigerator temperature, preheat hot water bath to 122°F (50°C). Immerse pouches in preheated bath for 1 hour. Proceed with Step 4.

You can reserve any leftover chicken mixture for another use; Basic Chicken Thighs (page 145) is a good example. Alternatively, spoon small "dumplings" into boiling chicken broth to serve as chicken soup.

Use the cooking liquid in whatever you are serving with the quails, such as risotto.

1. In food processor fitted with the metal blade, combine chicken, shallot, garlic, salt, pepper and nutmeg. Pulse, stopping and scraping down sides periodically, until very well chopped. Add egg and pulse until smooth. With the motor running, slowly pour cream through feed tube, processing until thoroughly incorporated and mixture is smooth.

2. Spoon chicken mixture into piping bag. Pipe into quail cavities until birds are plump but not completely full (see Tips, at left). (The filling will expand slightly during cooking.)

3. Place 2 quails in each pouch and seal, using Delicate setting. Immerse pouches in preheated hot water bath and cook for 2 hours. (To make ahead, see Tips, at left.)

4. Remove pouches from hot water bath and let stand until slightly cooled. Open pouches and remove quails. Pat dry with paper towels. Reserve cooking liquid for use in preparing accompaniments (see Tips, at left).

5. In a large skillet, melt butter over medium heat until foaming. When foaming stops, add quails to pan. Brown, turning and basting with the butter, for 5 to 6 minutes, until skin is golden. Serve on warm plates.

## Variations

**Quail Filled with Chicken and Wild Mushroom Mousse:** Wild mushrooms such as chanterelles add wonderful texture and flavor to the mousse. Sauté 2 oz (60 g) coarsely chopped fresh wild mushrooms in 1 tbsp (15 mL) butter. Season to taste with salt and pepper and refrigerate until cold. Fold into mousse mixture. Proceed with Step 2, making sure that the piping tip or opening in the freezer bag is large enough to let the mushroom pieces pass through.

**Chicken Thighs Filled with Chicken Mousse:** The mousse mixture (with or without wild mushrooms) is wonderful in boneless chicken thighs. Place each of 4 large boneless chicken thighs between 2 pieces of plastic wrap. Using the flat side of a meat mallet or a rolling pin, gently pound to an even thickness. Spoon chicken mousse onto center of each thigh. Using bottom piece of plastic wrap to help, roll up thigh around filling. Pierce wrap around its circumference to release air and retighten slightly. Proceed with Step 3.

# Rabbit

Unlike other types of meat, which I prefer a little more rare, rabbit is best when fully cooked, so you don't need to be concerned about pathogens. Rabbit dishes are quite common in European cuisines, and the meat is becoming more readily available in North America. It is quite mild in flavor, so it needs some good seasoning. Assertive herbs such as sage and rosemary work well.

Domesticated rabbits are slaughtered when they are quite young, so their meat is very tender, lean and full of moisture. The flesh is so lean, however, that conventional cooking methods can make it dry out. Sous vide handles the task very well, but you can overdo it if you're not careful — because of the young age of commercial rabbits, the meat can become mushy if cooked for too long.

Cooking rabbit perfectly is tricky no matter which method you use, and sous vide is no exception. To achieve the delicious results that you get from braising or roasting, we will be using a sous vide cooking method known as "delta T." This simply means that the temperature in the hot water bath is hotter than the desired final core temperature, much more like conventional methods of roasting or pan-frying than the other recipes in this book, which set the water bath temperature to the desired final temperature for the dish (there's more about this on page 17). As a result, timing becomes more critical.

My recipes make use of all the parts of the rabbit and highlight several different techniques. Rabbit Saddle Wrapped in Bacon (page 183) is an example of "roasting," Rabbit Legs in Dijon Mustard Sauce (page 186) demonstrates braising, and Rabbit Rillettes (page 184) uses a long cooking method to prepare the front of the rabbit, which is generally considered too bony to serve whole. For more on how to cut and prepare a whole rabbit, see the box on page 185.

# Rabbit Saddle Wrapped in Bacon

If you prepare a whole small rabbit, you'll end up with enough delicious meat to cook a special meal for two. I suggest starting with this recipe, served as a warm salad with endive or radicchio, followed by Rabbit Legs in Dijon Mustard Sauce (page 186) with spaetzle. Both dishes are wonderful on their own, but you'll certainly create a night to remember with this combination!

| **MAKES 2 SERVINGS** |
|---|

Freezer Bag Friendly

## Tips

This recipe can be doubled easily. If you're doubling the recipe, use 2 pouches.

One rabbit saddle should be large enough to cut in half for this recipe.

If you like, add 2 prunes (pitted or whole) to the pouch along with the saddles. Serve them warm with the rabbit as an easy garnish.

*To make ahead:* Prepare through Step 2. Refrigerate sealed pouch for up to 5 days. Proceed with Step 3.

▸ **Preheat hot water bath to 167°F (75°C)**
▸ **Sous vide pouch**

| 2 | pieces bone-in rabbit saddle (each about 5 to 6 oz/140 g to 170 g; see box, page 185) | 2 |
|---|---|---|
|  | Salt and freshly ground black pepper |  |
| 2 | slices bacon | 2 |

1. Season saddle pieces to taste with salt and pepper. Wrap attached belly flaps around each piece, then wrap 1 slice bacon around each. Place side by side, without overlapping, in sous vide pouch and seal. Immerse in preheated hot water bath and cook for 45 minutes.

2. Remove pouch from hot water bath, transfer to an ice bath and chill for 30 minutes. (To make ahead, see Tips, at left.)

3. Open pouch and remove saddle pieces; discard cooking liquid. Pat meat dry with paper towels.

4. Preheat barbecue to Medium-High or preheat broiler. Place saddle pieces on grill of preheated barbecue or on a baking sheet under preheated broiler. Grill or broil, turning occasionally, until bacon is cooked to desired level of crispness, about 10 to 15 minutes. Serve on warm plates.

# Rabbit Rillettes

This is a great way to use up the bony parts of a rabbit. Like Potted Duck (page 178), these rillettes are a great addition to a charcuterie platter. Already packed in jars, rillettes are easily transportable and make great gifts. Serve with crusty bread, mustard and your favorite pickled vegetables.

**MAKES ABOUT
1 CUP (250 ML)**

Freezer Bag Friendly

## Tip

You can easily double or triple this recipe. If you're tripling it, use 2 bags. Make sure you have additional jars on hand.

▶ **Preheat hot water bath to 167°F (75°C)**
▶ **Large resealable freezer bag**
▶ **One 8 oz (250 mL) or two 4 oz (125 mL) straight-sided canning jars, with lids**

| | | |
|---|---|---|
| 1 to 1½ lbs | bone-in rabbit parts (see Tip, at right) | 450 to 675 g |
| 2 tsp | Spiced Salt (page 350) | 10 mL |
| ½ tsp | freshly ground black pepper | 2 mL |
| 3 | cloves garlic, coarsely chopped | 3 |
| 2½ tbsp | rendered pork fat (see box, page 177) | 37 mL |
| 1 | sprig fresh rosemary | 1 |
| | Chopped parsley, optional | |

1. Place rabbit pieces in a medium bowl. Sprinkle with spiced salt, pepper and garlic. Toss to combine.

2. Transfer rabbit mixture, pork fat and rosemary to freezer bag and seal. Immerse in preheated hot water bath and cook for 8 to 10 hours.

3. Remove bag from hot water bath. Let stand at room temperature until cool enough to handle. Increase temperature of hot water bath to 190°F (87.8°C).

4. Open bag and pour rabbit mixture into a medium bowl. Discard rosemary. Using your hands, remove bones and discard. Using a fork or your hands, pull rabbit meat into shreds. Feel around for any stray pieces of bone — rabbit bones can be very small and sneaky! Toss to coat meat with juices.

5. Spoon rabbit mixture into jars, leaving ½ inch (1 cm) headspace. Wipe rims of jars thoroughly to ensure a good seal. Add lids and turn just until snug. Immerse jars in hot water bath and cook for 1½ hours.

## Tip

In a professional kitchen this dish would typically be made with the rabbit parts that are too bony to serve on their own as a dish — in other words, the shoulders and maybe the racks. If you are a fan of this preparation, you can use the whole rabbit. Cut the rabbit into pieces no heavier than 3½ oz (100 g) with the bones in. Try to cut through the bones at the joints where you can, to avoid bone fragments. Be sure to use a cleaver or a knife that you care little about, since rabbit bones are surprisingly hard and will easily ruin the edge of a fine blade.

6. Remove jars from hot water bath. Immerse in an ice bath and chill for 30 minutes. For best flavor, refrigerate for at least 1 to 2 weeks before serving, or for up to 6 weeks.

7. To serve, open jar and scoop rabbit mixture into a small bowl. Stir with a fork to incorporate surface fat and gelatinized liquid at bottom. Serve cold, garnished with chopped parsley, if desired.

### How to Bone and Prepare a Whole Rabbit

Boning a whole rabbit is quite simple, though it takes a bit of getting used to. You will need a sharp boning knife and a small cleaver, since rabbit bones are very hard and will damage delicate knives.

- Lay the rabbit on its side on a cutting board. Using the boning knife, cut off the hind leg. Cut off the front leg, taking the shoulder blades with it. (The joints are quite loose, so you shouldn't need too much pressure to cut through them.) Turn the rabbit over and repeat on the opposite side.

- Turn the rabbit belly side up. Spread open the body cavity with your hands. Using the knife, remove the liver, which is halfway down the spine (I find the liver a little bitter, so I discard it).

- Using the cleaver, cut off the piece of spine protruding from where the hind legs were attached. Count 3 ribs up from that end; cut between the second and third ribs until you reach the spine. With the cleaver, chop through the spine.

- Cut the lower (loin) portion in half crosswise with the cleaver (or leave whole, if desired), leaving the belly flaps attached. This is your saddle.

The rack — the body portion that is left — and the front legs are bony. I recommend using them for rillettes.

# Rabbit Legs in Dijon Mustard Sauce

Dijon mustard and cream are a classic accompaniments for rabbit. The cream adds richness while the Dijon provides the needed piquancy. Simply cooked carrots and wilted greens lend color and round out this dish perfectly.

---

**MAKES
2 SERVINGS**

Freezer Bag Friendly

## Tips

This recipe can easily be halved or doubled. If you're doubling the recipe, use 2 bags.

*To make ahead:* Prepare through Step 2. Remove bag from hot water bath, transfer to an ice bath and chill for 1 hour, replenishing ice as necessary. Refrigerate sealed bag for up to 5 days. To reheat from refrigerator temperature, preheat hot water bath to 122°F (50°C). Immerse bag for 1 hour, then proceed with Step 3.

▶ **Preheat hot water bath to 167°F (75°C)**
▶ **Large resealable freezer bag**

| | | |
|---|---|---|
| ¼ cup | dry white wine | 60 mL |
| 2 tbsp | finely chopped shallots | 30 mL |
| ½ tsp | kosher salt (approx.) | 2 mL |
| 2 | rabbit hind legs (about 6 to 7 oz/ 170 to 200 g) | 2 |
| ⅔ cup | heavy or whipping (35%) cream | 150 mL |
| ½ cup | ready-to-use unsalted chicken broth | 125 mL |
| 1 | bay leaf | 1 |
| 1 tbsp | Dijon mustard | 15 mL |
| ⅛ tsp | ground white pepper | 0.5 mL |
| | Chopped fresh parsley, optional | |

1. In a small saucepan, combine wine, shallots and salt. Bring to a boil over medium heat. Reduce heat and simmer until liquid has almost evaporated and mixture has a slushy consistency, about 8 to 10 minutes.

2. Place rabbit legs in freezer bag. Add shallot mixture, cream, broth and bay leaf. Seal bag, immerse in preheated water bath and cook for 1 hour. (To make ahead, see Tips, at left.)

3. Remove bag from hot water bath, open bag and remove rabbit legs. Keep warm on a warm plate covered with foil and a folded kitchen towel. Pour cooking liquid from bag into a medium saucepan. Bring to a boil over medium heat. Lower heat and simmer until thickened and sauce-like, about 15 minutes. Whisk in mustard and white pepper. Season with additional salt if necessary.

4. Place rabbit legs on warm plates and pour sauce overtop. Garnish with parsley (if using).

# Foie Gras and Offal

# Foie Gras and Offal

Foie gras and offal, also known as variety meats or organ meats, have always been popular with professional chefs. Their tastes and textures are unique and offer a welcome change from chicken and beef. Offal is generally less expensive than traditional meats and frequently more nutrient-dense. Liver, for example, is nature's most concentrated source of vitamin A. Also, when you cook and eat offal, you are participating in the current trend of "nose to tail" (and Paleo) dining, where nothing edible goes to waste.

## The Basics

The preparation of offal can be more time-consuming and requires techniques unique to the particular cut. In North America these meats are not often cooked at home, so chefs put them on menus to offer their diners something different and show off their creativity in the process. Because the preparations for individual organs can be quite specific, there is less general introductory material in this chapter. In just about every case, sous vide techniques will help you achieve more precise and consistent results.

## Foie Gras

The first foie gras — fatty liver from specially raised geese — was developed by the Egyptians. More than 5,000 years later, foie gras became one of the first ingredients to be cooked sous vide in a modern professional kitchen. Cooking foie gras at a regulated low temperature controls the loss of its fat.

Many countries have at least a cottage industry that produces foie gras. France, Hungary, Israel, the United States and Canada immediately come to mind. If you first tried foie gras before about 1985, it is likely that you had a canned product from France. While it can be good, pasteurization in the canning process results in a product that doesn't compare to what you can enjoy in a fine restaurant or prepare yourself. I want the home chef to be able to replicate restaurant-quality foie gras dishes using this book, which means that none of them are pasteurized. Don't serve rare foie gras to young children, pregnant women or anyone with a compromised immune system (please refer to page 9 for more safety information).

## Grades of Foie Gras

Fresh foie gras is quite expensive. Raising ducks and geese with perfect livers is part art and part science. As a result, foie gras is usually available in three grades: A, B and C.

Grade A are the largest livers, up to 2 lbs (900 g), and the most expensive. I generally avoid those larger than 1½ lbs (675 g), as I find that they can render more fat, thus leaving you with less foie gras. They should be a pinkish creamy white color with no bruises or blemishes, well-rounded rather than flattened, and have a firm though not brittle texture. These are optimal for any preparation.

Grade B livers are smaller, typically 1 to 1½ lbs (450 to 675 g), and are about 20 percent less expensive. They are darker in color and may be a little flattened; they also frequently have a bruise or two and are softer. The best of grade B can be hard to distinguish from grade A, once cooked. Because they are smaller, I would not use them for the poached foie gras recipes here. Unless you can choose your grade B liver from several — finding the largest and palest, with maybe only one small bruise — I recommend sticking with grade A.

Grade C livers are smaller still and more bruised. They would be fine for Foie Gras Parfait (page 192) but they are not frequently available. That being said, I cannot recommend buying anything less than grade A, sight unseen. A good online US source for foie gras, both raw and prepared, is D'Artagnan, which also ships game, rendered duck fat and a variety of luxury ingredients. Their website, http://www.dartagnan.com/, also includes tips, information and recipes.

## Cleaning Foie Gras

Cleaning foie gras is a process of removing the veins that run through the liver without disturbing the bulk of it too much. This is important, because foie gras oxidizes easily and seems to render more fat if reduced to a paste while cleaning. The process is not difficult but it is somewhat slow. I suggest that you have someone show you how it's done or find a video on the Internet. Meanwhile, I will give you a few tips that may not be covered in the demonstration.

A lobe of foie gras has two parts: a larger outside piece and one slightly smaller piece that's nestled in behind. You always begin by separating the two. Remove the liver from the refrigerator and pull the pieces apart while it is still cold and firm. They are attached by a vein near the center. The smaller piece has more veins than the larger. If you are making Pomegranate-Poached Foie Gras (page 194), you will use only the larger piece, for that reason, and you'll need to leave it intact.

To remove the veins from either piece, you must let them come to room temperature so that they are soft. This will emphasize the contrast in texture between the liver and the veins so that you can easily find the veins. Take a small or medium cutting board and wrap it with plastic wrap. Lay it on the counter and place on it the foie gras you want to clean, rounded side down. Cover the liver with another sheet of plastic and let it warm up for about 1 hour. Remove the wrap and, using the dullest knife you have (I use a small butter knife), locate the exposed vein that attached the two pieces and gently follow its path through the liver, removing it as you go. The vein fans out both laterally and vertically through the liver and gets smaller as you progress from the exposed end. How extremely you clean is up to you — you will never get all the small veins. With experience, and depending on the recipe, you will learn how far you want to go. Only the largest veins will affect the texture; the smaller ones just mar the appearance of the finished dish. If the foie gras starts to get greasy because of the temperature of the room and the heat of your hands, cover it with plastic wrap and place it, still on the cutting board, in the refrigerator for 10 to 15 minutes to let it cool down a little before continuing.

Once you have finished, you will have a sheet of foie gras to use in your recipe. Cut the plastic wrap around the edges of the cutting board. You will now have a piece you can wrap the foie gras in to weigh it and thus determine the right amount of seasoning for your recipe. Proceed with your recipe or refrigerate it, wrapped, for no longer than 24 hours.

The current trend is to cook foie gras very little, if at all. To me the densest, purest foie gras is uncooked and cured with salt only. In this book, however, I present three recipes that are paradigms of their genre: one is a creamy spreadable product, the second is more like an elevated terrine, and the third is highly flavored and can be eaten like charcuterie.

## Sweetbreads

Sous vide is not an optimal technique for cooking sweetbreads. However, I feel that something would seem missing from this chapter without at least a mention of them. Sweetbreads are the thymus and pancreas glands of young cows or, very occasionally, lambs. The pancreas is larger and more evenly shaped and considered superior.

Whatever the final preparation, sweetbreads should be soaked under cold running water for a few hours, or they can be soaked in four or five changes of cold water. After soaking, they can then be stored in fresh water overnight to purge them of their fluids.

Frozen sweetbreads are fine; in fact, freezing helps to rid them of their fluids. Remove frozen sweetbreads from their wrappings and place them in a bowl of cold water; allow them to defrost overnight in the refrigerator. Change the water once or twice the following day before proceeding with the cooking process.

Argentines love their sweetbreads; they usually grill them, preferably over a wood or charcoal fire. The sweetbreads can be grilled immediately after soaking, but they are often simmered first in a court bouillon. To replicate that technique using sous vide, here is what I suggest:

1. Preheat hot water bath to 158°F (70°C).
2. Take onions, carrots and celery in a ratio of 3:2:1. Dice into $\frac{1}{2}$-inch (1 cm) or smaller pieces for your mirepoix. In a skillet over medium-low heat, cook the mirepoix in butter for about 15 minutes, until softened. Let cool.
3. Put the soaked sweetbreads in a resealable freezer bag. Add the mirepoix, a big pinch of salt and a good splash of tarragon vinegar. Seal and cook in preheated water bath for 3 to 4 hours.
4. Remove from hot water bath and chill in ice water for 30 minutes. Use immediately or refrigerate for up to 3 or 4 days. The sweetbreads are now ready for grilling, pan-frying or using in a terrine.

# Foie Gras Roulades

This preparation of foie gras is a subtly spiced stand-in for a terrine. It's cooked just enough to hold it together and renders very little fat as a result.

## Tips

If you prefer, you can make a half-portion of this recipe, though the small quantities of seasoning will require very careful measuring.

The foie gras is not pasteurized in this preparation. Please see page 20, if you have concerns.

The roulade will keep, refrigerated in its wrappings, for up to 6 days. Once opened, try to use it up within 2 days. It will keep about twice that long but will oxidize and the flavor and color will suffer.

A warm knife aids in getting a clean cut through the foie gras. Bring some water to a boil and transfer to a heatproof container deep enough to hold the knife blade, leaving the handle exposed. Remove hot knife from water and pat dry on paper towels. Slice foie gras, wipe blade and return to water, repeating as necessary.

- ▸ **Four 8-inch (20 cm) squares parchment paper**
- ▸ **Sushi mat (optional)**
- ▸ **Butcher's twine**

| | | |
|---|---|---|
| 2¼ lbs | cleaned grade A or B foie gras, at room temperature | 1 kg |
| 2 tsp | sweet white wine, such as Sauternes | 10 mL |
| 2 tsp | kosher salt | 10 mL |
| ¾ tsp | curing salt (see page 399) | 3 mL |
| ½ tsp | granulated sugar | 2 mL |
| 2½ tsp | Foie Gras Spice Blend (page 352) | 12 mL |

1. Place foie gras in a large mixing bowl. Add wine and turn to coat. In a small bowl, combine kosher salt, curing salt, sugar and spice blend. Sprinkle evenly over surface of foie gras and combine thoroughly with a spatula. Divide into 4 equal portions.

2. Working with one sheet at a time, place parchment paper on work surface. Place one portion of foie gras in center of parchment. Using your hands, form an even length of foie gras, leaving about 1 inch (2.5 cm) at each edge free (it should resemble a rough cylinder). Lift edge of parchment closest to you over the foie gras; using all your fingers, gently tighten to mold foie gras into an even cylinder (a sushi mat works well here) — it will squeeze out to the edges of the parchment, which is expected. Use a pin to release air bubbles in the parchment so you can see through the paper; tighten further. Finish by rolling parchment around cylinder so that it forms a double or triple thickness. Wrap tightly in plastic wrap. Twist both ends and tie tightly with butchers' twine. Wrap rolls in aluminum foil and twist ends to seal. Repeat with remaining foie gras and parchment. Refrigerate overnight, but not for more than 36 hours.

3. Preheat hot water bath to 180°F (82.2°C). Add cylinders and poach for 5 minutes. Immerse in a cold water bath for 15 minutes, drain and refrigerate overnight.

4. Unwrap and slice foie gras with a warm knife. Serve on warm or toasted baguette or brioche slices.

# Foie Gras Parfait

Parfait can mean a lot of different things, depending on what country you are in. In the United Kingdom it refers to a smooth meat paste, usually made from liver. This recipe is very similar to my Chicken Liver Mousse (page 198), but this version produces a more luxurious result because it replaces half the chicken livers with foie gras. I like to make a batch before Christmas and bring jars as gifts when I go to parties.

## MAKES ABOUT 8 CUPS (2 L)

## Tips

This recipe is great for a party, but if you want a smaller quantity, it is easy to halve.

*To trim chicken livers:* Rinse chicken livers under cold water and drain. One at a time, spread them open on a cutting board and, using a sharp knife, cut away and discard the connective membrane. Pat livers dry and set aside.

Curing salts are available online at Modernist Pantry (www. modernistpantry.com).

▸ **Preheat hot water bath to 152.6°F (67°C)**
▸ **Sixteen 4 oz (125 mL) or eight 8 oz (250 mL) canning jars, with lids**
▸ **Instant-read thermometer**
▸ **Food processor**
▸ **Fine-mesh sieve**

| | | |
|---|---|---|
| 1²⁄₃ cups | heavy or whipping (35%) cream | 400 mL |
| 1 tsp | honey | 5 mL |
| 3½ oz | rendered duck fat, chilled | 100 g |
| 3½ oz | butter, softened | 100 g |
| 17½ oz | trimmed chicken livers (see Tips, at left) | 500 g |
| 5 | egg yolks | 5 |
| 7 oz | cleaned foie gras (any grade) | 200 g |
| 1 tbsp | salt | 15 mL |
| 2 tsp | ground white pepper | 10 mL |
| ¾ tsp | curing salt (see page 399 and Tips, at left) | 3 mL |
| ¼ cup | sweet white wine, such as Sauternes | 60 mL |

1. In a small saucepan, heat cream and honey until bubbles form around the edges and temperature is slightly below boiling point, about 180°F (82.2°C). Remove from heat and let cool to room temperature.

2. In food processor fitted with the metal blade, process duck fat and butter until smooth. With the motor running, gradually add chicken livers, then egg yolks, one at a time through feed tube. Add cream mixture in a slow, steady stream. Stop motor and scrape down sides of bowl from time to time. Add foie gras, salt, pepper, curing salt and wine. Process until smooth.

*continued on page 193*

Sri Lankan Black Pork Curry (page 134)

Buttermilk Fried Chicken (page 152)

Drunken Duck Ramen with Sous Vide Egg (page 165)

Korean Duck Tacos (page 168)

Rabbit Rillettes (page 184)

Pomegranate-Poached Foie Gras (page 194)

Beef Heart Anticuchos (page 207)

The Most Delicious BBQ Salmon (page 222)

## Tips

Once opened, try and use up the parfait within 2 days. It will keep about for 4 days but will oxidize and the flavor and color will suffer. Unopened jars will keep for up to 6 days.

Four-ounce (125 mL) canning jars look great on a charcuterie platter. Each provides 3 to 4 servings.

If you are serving this out of the canning jars and want a special presentation, you can pour a thin layer of Cryo-clarified Pomegranate Aspic (page 396 — you will need a double batch) on top after Step 6.

3. Using a stiff rubber spatula, press mixture through fine sieve; discard any solids that don't pass through. Pack into jars, dividing equally and leaving ½ inch (1 cm) headspace. Make sure to wipe rims of jars thoroughly to ensure a good seal. Add lids and turn just until snug.

4. Immerse jars in preheated hot water bath and cook for 80 minutes.

5. Remove jars from hot water bath and immerse in an ice bath for 45 minutes, replacing ice as necessary. Refrigerate for at least 4 hours, until chilled, or for up to 7 days.

6. Open jars and, if desired, scrape off oxidized layer on top with a spoon.

7. Serve straight from jars or shape into quenelles, using two tablespoons, and serve on cool plates (see box below).

### Quenelles

Traditionally quenelles were elegant French dumplings made of minced meat, poultry, fish or even vegetables. Now it is common to see a quenelle defined by its shape rather than its ingredients. You'll recognize a quenelle by its small oval, football-like shape. Ice creams and sorbets are frequently quenelled onto dessert plates at fine-dining restaurants.

The key to making quenelles from liver is to use two identical spoons that have been warmed in hot water. Drag one spoon across the surface of the liver, filling it to a nice rounded shape. Transfer the mixture from spoon to spoon to refine its form. When you are satisfied, carefully slide the quenelle onto a plate with the help of the other spoon.

# Pomegranate-Poached Foie Gras

This is a variation on a recipe I developed more than ten years ago and still use. It's one of my favorite ways to cook foie gras. I like serving it as an appetizer, but it also makes an elegant salad garnish. Make sure to read my tip on how to use the rendered fat from this recipe — it's almost as flavorful as the foie gras.

**MAKES ABOUT 10 OZ (280 G), 4 TO 6 SERVINGS**

Freezer Bag Friendly

## Tips

You can easily double this recipe, dividing the ingredients equally between 2 bags.

The foie gras is not pasteurized in this preparation. Please see page 20, if you have concerns.

The reserved smaller lobe has too many veins running through it to use in this preparation. Use it for one of the other recipes in this book. Sealed well in a sous vide pouch to prevent oxidation or freezer burn, it can be refrigerated for 3 days or frozen for 3 to 4 months.

In this recipe the actual weight of the foie gras is not crucial. Just ensure that you have enough liquid to immerse the liver during marination and cooking.

▶ **Small resealable freezer bag**
▶ **Fine-mesh sieve**

| | | |
|---|---|---|
| 1 lb (approx.) | cleaned fresh grade A foie gras (the larger piece of one lobe; see page 189 and Tips, at left) | 450 g |
| 4 cups | fresh or unsweetened pomegranate juice | 1 L |
| 1 tbsp | salt | 15 mL |
| 1 tsp | whole white peppercorns | 5 mL |
| 1 | star anise pod | 1 |

1. Rinse foie gras briefly under cold running water and pat dry. Place on a plate and refrigerate.

2. Meanwhile, pour pomegranate juice into a saucepan and bring to a boil over high heat. Reduce heat and boil gently until reduced to just under half its original volume: slightly less than 1¾ cups (425 mL). Add salt, white peppercorns and star anise. Stir to dissolve the salt. Remove from heat and let cool to room temperature.

3. Place foie gras in a freezer bag just large enough to hold it. Using fine-mesh sieve, strain juice and pour into bag. Seal bag and refrigerate overnight, no longer than 24 hours.

4. Remove bag from refrigerator about 1 hour before you intend to cook it, to take the chill off the foie gras.

5. Meanwhile, preheat hot water bath to 129°F (53.9°C).

6. Immerse bag in hot water bath and cook for 10 minutes. Lower heat to 120°F (48.9°C) and cook for another 10 minutes.

## Tips

Expect to lose about 20% of the original weight of the foie gras to rendered fat.

*To reserve liquid for Cryo-clarified Pomegranate Aspic:* Transfer cooking liquid (juice and rendered fat) to a medium saucepan and bring to a simmer over medium heat; simmer to pasteurize, 2 to 3 minutes. Pour into an airtight container, cover and refrigerate overnight. Separate fat from liquid and refrigerate for 6 days or freeze for 6 months for future use (see recipe, page 396).

The foie gras will keep, refrigerated in its original bag, for up to 6 days. Once opened, try to use it up within 2 days. It will keep for about 4 days but will oxidize and the flavor and color will suffer.

7. Remove bag from hot water bath. Place bag in a colander in the sink and chill under cold running water for 20 minutes. Refrigerate for at least 3 hours or up to 6 days before proceeding (see Tips, at left).

8. Open bag and pour liquid contents into a bowl. Remove foie gras. Reserve cooking liquid for Cryo-clarified Pomegranate Aspic (page 396; see Tips, at left).

9. Pat foie gras dry with paper towels. Slice with a warm knife and serve on warm or toasted baguette slices or Melba toast.

### Rendered Fat

The fat rendered from the foie gras can be used in any recipe that calls for rendered chicken or duck fat. Rinse it well under cold tap water to remove any remnants of pomegranate juice. It will have taken on a slightly sweet, spiced taste, so keep that in mind when you're adding it to other dishes.

### How to Warm a Knife

A warm knife aids in getting a clean cut through foie gras. Bring some water to a boil and transfer it to a heatproof container deep enough to cover the knife blade, leaving the handle exposed. Remove hot knife from water and pat dry with paper towels. Slice foie gras, wipe blade and return to water, repeating as necessary.

# Chopped Liver Two Ways

Chopped liver is delicious and economical. Here are two versions: Jewish deli–style and Tuscan-style, a popular Italian approach. Both are delicious accompanied by crusty bread and pickled vegetables. Serve at room temperature or cold.

## Tips

*To trim chicken livers:* Rinse chicken livers under cold water and drain. One at a time, spread them open on a cutting board and, using a sharp knife, cut away and discard the connective membrane between the two lobes. Cut off any green parts and discard. Pat livers dry with paper towels and set aside.

If you don't want to prepare the hard-boiled eggs sous vide, you can cook them in a saucepan on the stove.

## Jewish Deli–Style

▸ **Preheat hot water bath to 154°F (67.8°C)**
▸ **Small resealable freezer bag**
▸ **Food processor**

| | | |
|---|---|---|
| 1 cup | rendered chicken or duck fat, divided | 250 mL |
| 2 | medium onions, sliced | 2 |
| 2 tsp | kosher salt | 10 mL |
| 1¼ lbs | trimmed chicken livers (see Tips, at left) | 565 g |
| 1 tsp | ground white pepper | 5 mL |
| ¼ tsp | dried thyme | 1 mL |
| 2 | hard-boiled eggs, cooled (see page 327) | 2 |

1. In a medium skillet, melt ½ cup (125 mL) chicken fat over medium heat. Add onions and salt; cook, stirring occasionally, until very soft but not brown, 30 to 40 minutes. Remove from heat and let cool.

2. In freezer bag, combine chicken livers, cooled onions, remaining ½ cup (125 mL) chicken fat, white pepper and thyme. Seal bag and immerse in preheated water bath. Cook for 1½ hours.

3. Remove bag from hot water bath, transfer to an ice bath and chill for 30 minutes.

4. Peel eggs and chop coarsely.

5. Place cooled cooked chicken liver mixture in food processor fitted with the metal blade. Pulse until almost smooth (a little texture is desirable). Add eggs and pulse 2 or 3 times, just until eggs are well combined but not puréed. Transfer to an airtight container, cover and chill for at least 5 hours before serving or for up to 6 days.

## Tips

You can easily halve
these recipes.

Frozen livers work well
for these recipes, though
I find the texture suffers
a bit.

## Tuscan-Style

▸ Preheat hot water bath to 154°F (67.8°C)
▸ Small resealable freezer bag
▸ Food processor

| ⅔ cup | olive oil, divided | 150 mL |
|---|---|---|
| 1 | medium onion, sliced | 1 |
| 1 tsp | kosher salt | 5 mL |
| 1 | medium celery stalk, finely chopped | 1 |
| 6 tbsp | dry white wine | 90 mL |
| 1¼ lbs | trimmed chicken livers (see Tips, page 196) | 565 g |
| 2 tbsp | drained capers, chopped | 30 mL |
| 5 | anchovy fillets, drained | 5 |
| ¼ cup | butter, softened | 60 mL |
| 1 tsp | freshly ground black pepper | 5 mL |

1. In a medium skillet, heat ⅓ cup (75 mL) olive oil over medium heat. Add onion and salt; cook, stirring occasionally, until very soft but not brown, 30 to 40 minutes. Add celery and wine; cook, stirring occasionally, until wine has evaporated, about 10 minutes. Remove from heat and let cool.

2. In freezer bag, combine trimmed chicken livers and cooled onion mixture. Seal bag and immerse in preheated hot water bath. Cook for 1½ hours.

3. Remove bag from hot water bath, transfer to an ice bath and chill for 30 minutes.

4. In food processor fitted with the metal blade, combine cooled cooked chicken liver mixture, capers, anchovies, butter, black pepper and remaining olive oil. Pulse until almost smooth (a little texture is desirable). Transfer to an airtight container, cover and chill for at least 5 hours before serving or for up to 6 days.

# Chicken Liver Mousse

This mousse gets as close to foie gras as you can without the expense. It is very lightly seasoned to let the pure flavors of the chicken livers come through. For best results, make sure that you use very fresh duck fat, which has a lovely sweet taste.

**MAKES ABOUT
4 CUPS (1 L)**

## Tips

You can easily double or triple this recipe, using more jars.

*To trim chicken livers:* Rinse chicken livers under cold water. One at a time, spread them open on a cutting board and, using a sharp knife, cut away and discard the connective membrane between the two lobes. Cut off any green parts and discard. Pat meat dry with paper towels and set aside.

*Mousse* is the typical name for this type of preparation. Odd as it may seem, this dish is — and should be — dense and unctuous.

▶ **Preheat hot water bath to 154.4°F (68°C)**
▶ **Eight 4 oz (125 mL) or four 8 oz (250 mL) canning jars, with lids**
▶ **Instant-read thermometer**
▶ **Food processor**
▶ **Fine-mesh sieve**

| | | |
|---|---|---|
| 1¼ cups | heavy or whipping (35%) cream | 300 mL |
| 3½ oz | butter, softened | 100 g |
| 3½ oz | rendered duck fat, chilled | 100 g |
| 9 oz | trimmed chicken livers (see Tips, at left) | 250 g |
| 3 | egg yolks | 3 |
| 1½ tsp | kosher salt | 7 mL |
| ½ tsp | curing salt (see page 399) | 2 mL |
| 1 tsp | freshly ground white pepper | 5 mL |
| 4 tsp | sweet white wine, such as Sauternes | 20 mL |
| 1 tbsp | cognac, Armagnac or brandy | 15 mL |

1. In a small saucepan, heat cream until bubbles form around the edges and temperature is slightly below the boiling point, about 180°F (82.2°C). Remove from heat and let cool to room temperature.

2. In food processor fitted with the metal blade, process butter and duck fat until smooth. With the motor running, gradually add chicken livers, then egg yolks, one at a time through feed tube, making sure each is incorporated before adding the next. Add cream in a slow, steady stream. Stop motor and scrape down sides of bowl as required. Add kosher salt, curing salt, white pepper, white wine and cognac. Process until smooth.

## Tips

Four-ounce (125 mL) jars of mousse look great on a charcuterie platter. Each provides 3 to 4 servings.

If you are serving this from the jars and want a special presentation, you can pour a thin layer of Cryo-clarified Pomegranate Aspic (page 396) on top after Step 6.

Once opened, this mousse is best consumed within 2 days. It will keep for about 4 days but it will oxidize and the flavor and color will suffer. Unopened jars will keep for up to 6 days.

**3.** Using a stiff rubber spatula, press mixture through fine-mesh sieve into a bowl; discard any pieces that won't pass through sieve. Pack into clean jars in equal amounts, leaving $\frac{1}{2}$ inch (1 cm) headspace. Make sure to wipe rims of jars thoroughly to ensure a good seal. Add lids and turn just until snug.

**4.** Immerse jars in preheated hot water bath and cook for $1\frac{1}{2}$ hours.

**5.** Remove jars from hot water bath, immerse in a sink full of ice water and chill for 45 minutes, replacing ice as necessary. Refrigerate for at least 4 hours before serving.

**6.** Open jars and, if desired, scrape off oxidized layer on top with a spoon.

**7.** Serve straight from the jar or shape into quenelles, using two tablespoons, and arrange on cool plates (see "Quenelles," page 193).

# Beef Liver Cooked in Milk

This recipe is good to try out on friends who tell you they don't like liver. I use baby beef liver here because the technique makes it taste almost like calf's liver, and it is less expensive and easier to find. Cooking the liver in milk with the aromatics gives it a mild and delicate flavor. The dish works well with mashed potatoes or root vegetables, French fries, grilled polenta or pickled or caramelized onions, as well as piquant garnishes such as Worcestershire sauce, mustard or peppercorn sauce, to name a few.

---

**MAKES
4 SERVINGS**

Freezer Bag Friendly

## Tips

You can easily halve this recipe. Doubling it is tricky because of the lightning-fast final preparation and the amount of skillet space needed. I am not fond of grilled liver, but you can grill this — one side only — over medium-high heat for the same amount of time. Brush the liver lightly with olive or vegetable oil before adding the pepper. Depending on the size of your grill, you may be able to double the recipe by using this technique.

Leeks can be tricky to clean. See page 400 for more information.

▸ **Preheat hot water bath to 140°F (60°C)**
▸ **2 large resealable freezer bags**

| | | |
|---|---|---|
| 1½ lbs | baby beef liver, sliced (see Tips, at right) | 675 g |
| 2 tbsp | butter, divided | 30 mL |
| 1 | small leek, white and light green parts only, finely chopped (see Tips, at left) | 1 |
| 2 | bay leaves | 2 |
| 1 tbsp | kosher salt | 15 mL |
| 1½ cups | whole milk | 375 mL |
| | Freshly ground black pepper | |
| 1 tbsp | vegetable oil | 15 mL |

1. Trim any sinew from liver and peel off any membrane on the outside. Set liver aside and discard trimmings.

2. In a medium skillet, heat half the butter over medium heat. Add leek and cook, stirring frequently, until soft, about 10 minutes. Add bay leaves, salt and milk. Bring to a simmer, stirring once to help salt dissolve. Remove from heat and let cool to room temperature.

## Tips

**3.** Divide liver pieces into 2 equal portions and place in separate freezer bags, arranging slices so they lie flat with no folds (they may overlap). Elevate the mouth of the bag by laying a thick cutting board flat in front of it and sliding just the opening of the bag over the edge of the board. Working with one bag at a time, carefully pour half the milk mixture into each bag and add a bay leaf. (Make sure the mouth of the bag stays elevated and the rest remains horizontal — if you lift up the whole bag, the liver will slump down to the bottom.) Press the bag against the meat to expel air, then carefully seal it. Carefully transfer packages to preheated water bath, making sure the liver doesn't curl up. Cook for 1½ hours.

**4.** Remove bags from hot water bath, transfer to an ice bath and chill for 20 minutes. (To make ahead, see Tips, at left.)

**5.** Open bags and transfer liver to a plate lined with paper towels to drain. Discard liquid in bags. With a knife or spoon, gently scrape off any bits of leek and bay leaf. Pat both sides of liver dry with paper towels. Grind some pepper over each side.

**6.** In one or two skillets large enough to hold the liver in one layer, heat vegetable oil over medium heat, making sure that it forms a thin, even layer in skillet. Once oil is hot, add remaining butter.

**7.** Once butter has melted and foam subsides, quickly add liver slices. Cook just until the underside starts to brown, about 90 seconds. Do not flip. Transfer to warm plates with the cooked side facing up. Serve immediately.

# Deviled Veal Kidneys with Caper Sultana Relish

Veal and lamb kidneys are considered a delicacy in Europe but are frequently overlooked in North America. The sous vide cooking method gives them a smooth texture and a pleasantly mild flavor. The Caper Sultana Relish, which is loaded with savory umami notes, has a piquancy that is a perfect foil for the rich-tasting meat. An endive salad dressed with walnut vinaigrette would be a great finish for this intriguing appetizer.

## Tip

Lamb kidneys also work nicely in this recipe. Because they are smaller, you need 1½ to 2 kidneys per person, and the cooking time in the hot water bath should be only 25 minutes. Once cooked, slice the kidneys in half lengthwise, respecting their natural curve. Apply the breading to the flat cut surface only, then complete Steps 8 and 9. Serve with the breaded side facing up.

▶ **Small resealable freezer bag**
▶ **Nonstick skillet**

| | | |
|---|---|---|
| 1 | whole veal kidney (about 1¼ lbs/ 550 g) | 1 |
| 2 cups | Spiced Brine (variation, page 350) | 500 mL |
| 1 tbsp | Spiced Salt (page 350) | 15 mL |
| 3 tbsp | milk | 45 mL |
| 3 tbsp | heavy or whipping (35%) cream | 45 mL |
| 1 tbsp | Dijon mustard | 15 mL |
| Dash | Worcestershire sauce | Dash |
| 1 cup | fresh bread crumbs (preferably sourdough; page 385) | 250 mL |
| 2 tbsp | butter | 30 mL |
| | Caper Sultana Relish (page 384) | |

1. Using a sharp knife, trim any sinew from kidney and peel off any membrane. Pour brine into a medium bowl and immerse kidney. Cover and refrigerate for 30 to 45 minutes.

2. Preheat hot water bath to 167°F (75°C).

3. Drain kidney, discarding brine. Pat dry with paper towels. Sprinkle meat with spiced salt.

4. Place kidney in freezer bag, add milk and seal. Immerse in hot water bath and cook for 50 to 60 minutes.

5. Remove bag from hot water bath, transfer to an ice bath and chill for 20 minutes. (To make ahead, see Tip, at right.)

*To make ahead:*
Prepare through Step 5.
Refrigerate sealed pouch
for up to 3 days, then
proceed with Step 6.

**6.** In a small bowl, combine cream, mustard and Worcestershire sauce; stir together until smooth. Slice kidney crosswise into slices $\frac{1}{2}$ inch (1 cm) thick. Add to cream mixture, turning to coat.

**7.** Spread out bread crumbs on a plate. Using a fork, lift one slice of meat from the cream mixture, shaking gently to remove excess. Press into bread crumbs, turning to coat. Repeat until all slices are coated. Discard any leftover cream mixture and crumbs. Cover and refrigerate for 30 minutes, until coating is firm, or for up to 4 hours.

**8.** In nonstick skillet, melt butter over medium-high heat. Fry kidney slices for 1 to $1\frac{1}{2}$ minutes per side or until golden brown. Transfer to a plate lined with paper towels and let drain.

**9.** Transfer kidney slices to warmed plates and serve relish alongside.

# Beef Tongue with Pastrami Flavors

If you've always been a bit apprehensive about tongue, consider trying this recipe. If you're already a fan of this frequently overlooked part of the cow, I guarantee you will love the rich flavors of this dish, which can be served hot or cold. It's great in sandwiches — I particularly like it as a replacement for corned beef in a Reuben — or try it cold and thinly sliced as part of a charcuterie platter. Serving it as a part of *bollito misto* or with mustard sauce are other good options.

**MAKES 8 TO 10 MAIN-COURSE SERVINGS OR 16 TO 20 SANDWICHES**

Freezer Bag Friendly

## Tip

Liquid smoke is available in the spice section of well-stocked grocery stores.

- ▶ **Large resealable freezer bag**
- ▶ **Metal skewer or Jaccard tenderizer**
- ▶ **Fine-mesh sieve**

### BRINE

| | | |
|---|---|---|
| 2 tbsp | rendered bacon fat or vegetable oil | 30 mL |
| 1 cup | each finely diced carrot, onion and celery | 250 mL |
| 1½ cups | hoppy beer, such as Pilsner | 375 mL |
| 3 tbsp | minced gingerroot | 45 mL |
| 3 tbsp | minced garlic | 45 mL |
| 6 | bay leaves, crumbled | 6 |
| 1 tbsp | liquid smoke (see Tip, at left) | 15 mL |
| ½ cup | kosher salt | 125 mL |
| ¼ cup | packed brown sugar | 60 mL |
| 2 tbsp | coriander seeds, crushed | 30 mL |
| 2 tbsp | mustard seeds, crushed | 30 mL |
| 2 tbsp | fresh black peppercorns, cracked | 30 mL |
| 1 | beef tongue (3 to 4 lbs/1.35 to 1.8 kg) | 1 |

1. *Brine:* In a large skillet over medium heat, melt bacon fat. Add carrot, onion and celery; cook, stirring often, until softened, about 15 to 20 minutes. Add beer, ginger, garlic, bay leaves, liquid smoke, salt, brown sugar, coriander seeds, mustard seeds and black pepper. Bring to a boil, reduce heat and simmer for 5 minutes. Remove from heat and let cool to room temperature. Transfer to an airtight container, cover and refrigerate until chilled, about 1 to 2 hours or overnight (see Tips, at right).

2. Rinse tongue briefly under cold water. With a skewer or needle, pierce tongue all over (roughly 70 to 80 times), especially through the tough skin. If you are using a Jaccard tenderizer, just press it into the tongue all over 7 or 8 times.

## Tips

There is no curing salt in this recipe, so the tongue will not have a rosy pink color. If desired, replace 1½ tbsp (22 mL) of the salt with 1 tbsp (15 mL) curing salt. Proceed with the rest of the recipe as directed.

Tongue is easiest to slice when chilled. If desired, reheat slices for 30 minutes in hot water bath preheated to 130°F (54.4°C).

**3.** Using a spoon, press brine through fine-mesh sieve into a large bowl. Discard solids. Add 3 cups (750 mL) cold water to brine. Transfer brine and tongue to freezer bag. Seal and refrigerate for 4 to 7 days.

**4.** Preheat hot water bath to 158°F (70°C).

**5.** Remove 1 cup (250 mL) brine from bag and discard. Add 1 cup (250 mL) cold water to bag and reseal.

**6.** Immerse bag in hot water bath and cook for 48 to 50 hours.

**7.** Remove bag from water bath and set aside until tongue is cool enough to handle, about 1 hour. Remove tongue from bag and discard liquid. Peel off tough outer skin of tongue and discard. Rinse meat briefly under cold running water and pat dry. Wrap tightly with plastic wrap and place in a covered airtight container. Refrigerate until chilled, at least 4 hours or up to 7 days, or freeze for up to 6 months.

**8.** Slice meat thinly or up to ½ inch (1 cm) thick, as desired.

## Variations

**Lamb Tongues with Pastrami Flavors:** Lamb tongues are absolutely delicious if you can get your hands on them. Omit the liquid smoke and cook for 24 to 25 hours.

**Simmered Tongue:** In Step 1, dissolve 1 tbsp (15 mL) salt in 1½ cups (375 mL) warm water. (This simple brine replaces the beer brine.) Refrigerate this brine until cold, about 20 to 30 minutes. Transfer tongue and brine to a large resealable freezer bag, seal and refrigerate overnight. Proceed with Step 6.

### Cooking Tongue

An interesting thing about cooking tongue is that the easiest way to determine when it is cooked is to try to remove the skin from the flesh. If it won't come off, then continue cooking. Traditionally you have to peel off the skin while the tongue is still hot. Cooking the tongue sous vide, though, means the skin will come off easily even when cold.

## Beef Heart

Beef heart is pure lean muscle, even though it's considered offal. It tastes like steak, only with a slightly more mineral flavor. Butchers routinely add it to ground beef, and it is not uncommon to see beef heart served as tartare in restaurants these days.

Cooking beef heart is a little like cooking squid — if you don't cook it briefly, you are obliged to cook it for a long time, or you will end up with something quite tough.

The following basic recipe tenderizes beef heart so that you can finish it stress-free. Count on ending up with about 60% of its original weight after you've cleaned and cooked the heart.

# Tender Beef Heart

Beef heart is surprisingly easy to cook. In this recipe there's no risk of its getting tough. The heart will then be ready for the following two recipes, or dream up one of your own. Beef heart chili, anyone? Even beef heart pasta carbonara would be worth a try. Get creative!

**MAKES ABOUT
1 LB (450 G)**

Freezer Bag Friendly

## Tips

This recipe can easily be scaled up or down to suit your needs.

Cooked heart can be refrigerated for up to 5 days or frozen for up to 6 months. Defrost in the refrigerator overnight before using.

▶ **Preheat hot water bath to 131°F (55°C)**
▶ **Paring knife**
▶ **Sous vide pouch**

| | | |
|---|---|---|
| 2 lbs | beef heart | 900 g |
| 2 tbsp | Worcestershire sauce | 30 mL |

1. With a paring knife, remove any fat from outer surface of heart. If heart is whole, slice it into four quarters. Trim away any tubes and fibrous tissue from the interior (it will be whitish gray as opposed to the very dark red of the meat — anything that doesn't look like flesh should be removed).

2. In a medium bowl, toss heart pieces with Worcestershire sauce. Place in pouch and seal. Immerse pouch in preheated hot water bath and cook for 18 to 20 hours.

3. Remove pouch from bath, immerse in an ice bath and chill for 20 minutes. Then proceed with Beef Heart Anticuchos (page 207) or Beef Heart Stroganoff (page 208), or refrigerate until ready to use.

# Beef Heart Anticuchos

Anticuchos are a popular Peruvian street food that can be made with any type of meat. The most popular are skewers of beef heart, and I can attest that this is one of the simplest and best ways to eat this delightful part of the cow. Ideally you would cook anticuchos over charcoal (it's the most authentic technique), but a gas grill on High works fine too. Serve with grilled corn or lightly grilled potatoes and pass the hot sauce.

**MAKES
4 SERVINGS**

## Tips

This recipe can easily be adapted to any quantity.

The skewers can be made up to a day in advance. Cover and refrigerate until ready to grill.

Chicken or duck hearts are also delicious prepared this way. Place whole raw hearts in marinade, cover and refrigerate for 3 to 5 hours. Cook for 8 to 10 minutes.

▸ **Four 8-inch (20 cm) bamboo skewers**

| | | |
|---|---|---|
| 1 | recipe Tender Beef Heart (page 206) | 1 |
| 1 cup | cider vinegar or white wine vinegar | 250 mL |
| ¼ cup | water | 60 mL |
| ½ cup | finely chopped white onion | 125 mL |
| 1 tbsp | olive oil | 15 mL |
| 1 tbsp | kosher salt | 15 mL |
| 1 tsp | freshly ground black pepper | 5 mL |
| ½ tsp | ground cumin | 2 mL |

1. Place skewers in cold water and let soak.

2. Dice cooked heart into ¾-inch (2 cm) cubes. Transfer to a non-metallic container or resealable freezer bag. Add cider vinegar, water, onion, olive oil, salt, black pepper and cumin. Stir ingredients until salt has dissolved. Cover container or seal bag and refrigerate for 3 to 5 hours.

3. Preheat grill to High or light charcoal. Drain the heart, discarding marinade. Thread meat evenly onto soaked skewers.

4. Grill skewers, turning occasionally, until sizzling, about 5 to 6 minutes. Serve hot.

# Beef Heart Stroganoff

Beef Stroganoff gets a bad rap because of those recipes found on soup-can labels that use so many processed ingredients, but it's a delicious and unabashedly rich meal. Heart works well because it only needs to be reheated, which doesn't dilute the sauce. It is best served with buttered and parsleyed egg noodles and sour cream. Your guests probably won't notice they're eating beef heart — they might even think they're eating steak.

---

**MAKES 4 SERVINGS**

## Tips

You can easily halve or double this recipe.

Low-fat sour cream can be used if desired.

| | | |
|---|---|---|
| 1 | recipe Tender Beef Heart (page 206) | 1 |
| 1½ tbsp | butter, divided | 22 mL |
| 1 cup | finely chopped white onion | 250 mL |
| 12 oz | sliced mushrooms (preferably cremini) | 340 g |
| ¼ cup | dry white wine | 60 mL |
| 1 | bay leaf | 1 |
| | Salt | |
| ½ tsp | freshly ground black pepper | 2 mL |
| 1 cup | sour cream (see Tips, at left) | 250 mL |
| 2 tsp | cornstarch | 10 mL |
| ¾ cup | ready-to-use or enriched beef broth (approx.) | 175 mL |
| 3 tbsp | chopped fresh dill, optional (see Tip, at right) | 45 mL |
| 2 tbsp | Dijon mustard | 30 mL |

1. Thinly slice heart into 1-inch (2.5 cm) strips. Set aside on paper towels.

2. In a large skillet or cast-iron frying pan, melt half the butter over medium heat. Add onion and cook, stirring often, until softened but not browned, about 10 minutes. Transfer to a bowl and set aside.

3. Increase heat to medium-high and add remaining butter and mushrooms. Cook, stirring, until mushrooms start to release their liquid. Add wine, bay leaf, onion, ½ tsp (2 mL) salt and black pepper. Increase heat to high and boil, stirring often, until pan is almost dry, about 10 minutes.

A pinch of dried thyme
works well if you're not
using dill.

**4.** Meanwhile, scoop sour cream into a small bowl. Using a whisk, gradually add cornstarch, combining until smooth.

**5.** Pour sour cream mixture into mushroom mixture and bring to a boil, stirring frequently. Reduce heat to a simmer and add enough broth to create a thick, sauce-like consistency (you may not need all the broth).

**6.** Stir dill (if using) and mustard into sauce. Add the heart and simmer briefly to reheat. Discard bay leaf. Season with salt to taste and serve hot.

# Pork Hearts with Sausage Stuffing

This is a variation on a British wartime dish called Mock Goose. It is hearty winter fare, suitable for a cold night, and stands up to big flavors such as rutabaga (see variation, page 312). Dijon mustard is a welcome accompaniment.

**MAKES
4 GENEROUS
SERVINGS**

Freezer Bag Friendly

## Tip

You can easily halve or double this recipe. If doubling, make sure to use 8 pouches.

▶ **Preheat oven to 275°F (135°C)**
▶ **4 sous vide pouches**
▶ **Butcher's twine**

| | | |
|---|---|---|
| 2 cups | cubed (½ inch/1 cm) day-old baguette | 500 mL |
| ¼ cup | butter | 60 mL |
| 8 oz | sweet Italian sausage (preferably with fennel), casing removed | 225 g |
| 1 cup | finely chopped onion | 250 mL |
| 2 tsp | minced garlic | 10 mL |
| ½ cup | finely chopped celery | 125 mL |
| ¾ cup | ready-to-use beef or chicken broth | 175 mL |
| ½ cup | chopped flat-leaf Italian parsley | 125 mL |
| 1 tbsp | chopped fresh thyme leaves | 15 mL |
| 1 tsp | rubbed dried sage or marjoram | 5 mL |
| 1 tsp | freshly ground black pepper | 5 mL |
| ½ tsp | kosher salt (approx.) | 2 mL |
| 4 | pork hearts | 4 |
| 2 tbsp | rendered pork, duck or chicken fat | 30 mL |

1. Spread bread cubes in a single layer on a baking sheet. Bake in preheated oven until dry, about 45 minutes. Let cool. Transfer to a large bowl.

2. In a large skillet over medium heat, melt butter. Break up sausage into small pieces and add to pan; cook, stirring occasionally, for 5 minutes. Add onion, garlic and celery; cook, stirring, until onion is softened but not brown, 5 to 7 minutes. Add broth, parsley, thyme, sage, black pepper and salt; bring to a simmer.

3. Pour sausage mixture over bread and mix together. Allow to cool and let bread soak up liquid. Make sure it is well combined and add salt to taste.

*To make ahead:* Prepare through Step 7. Chill pouches in an ice bath for 30 minutes, then refrigerate for up to 5 days or freeze for up to 6 months. To use frozen hearts, thaw overnight in the refrigerator. To reheat from refrigerator temperature, preheat hot water bath to 140°F (60°C) and immerse for 1 hour. Proceed with Step 8.

**4.** Preheat hot water bath to 141.8°F (61°C).

**5.** Place hearts in sink and rinse under cold running water for 10 to 15 minutes. Pat dry with paper towels. With a paring or boning knife, trim out any valves and blood vessels and slice through any internal muscles separating the heart into chambers. Rinse briefly and allow to drain in a colander.

**6.** Fill each heart loosely with sausage and bread mixture. If hearts have been sliced open, pack in the filling as much as you can, then tie with butcher's twine.

**7.** Place each heart in a separate pouch and seal. Immerse in hot water bath and cook for 12 hours. (To make ahead, see Tip, at left).

**8.** Remove hearts from pouches and discard liquid. Drain hearts on paper towels and pat dry.

**9.** Heat a large skillet over medium heat. Add pork fat. Once skillet is hot, add hearts and brown on all sides, for about 15 minutes. Serve hearts whole on warm plates for a stunning presentation, or slice crosswise into 1-inch (2.5 cm) pieces.

# French-Style Tripe

This is an iconic dish in France, where it is known as *tripes à la mode de Caen*. It is characterized by the classic French flavors of carrots, onions and wine, plus a dash of Calvados. Traditionally this dish is cooked slowly in a crock with its lid sealed with a flour-and-water paste. In my version I've replaced the Calvados with cider. Keep in mind that tripe shrinks a lot while cooking, and those who like it tend to eat large portions. It is typically served with boiled potatoes, but rice works well here too.

**MAKES 4 TO 6 SERVINGS**

Freezer Bag Friendly

## Tips

You can easily double this recipe, dividing the ingredients equally between 2 bags.

Leeks can be tricky to clean. See page 400 for more information.

A cow has four stomachs, each with its own texture and cooking requirements. You can use any kind of beef tripe for this recipe, but honeycomb works best for this timing (not to mention that it's the easiest to find).

▶ **Preheat hot water bath to 200°F (93.3°C)**
▶ **Large resealable freezer bag**
▶ **Butcher's twine**
▶ **Fine-mesh sieve**

| | | |
|---|---|---|
| 2 tbsp | lard or butter | 30 mL |
| 2½ cups | finely chopped carrots | 625 mL |
| 1½ cups | finely chopped onions | 375 mL |
| 1 cup | finely chopped leeks, white and green parts only (see Tips, at left) | 250 mL |
| 2 cups | dry alcoholic cider (sparkling or still) | 500 mL |
| 1½ tbsp | minced garlic | 22 mL |
| 2 cups | enriched beef stock (see page 399) | 500 mL |
| 2½ lbs | honeycomb beef tripe (see Tips, at left) | 1.125 kg |
| 3½ oz | raw pork rind | 100 g |
| 6 | sprigs fresh flat-leaf (Italian) parsley or basil leaves | 6 |
| 1 | celery stalk | 1 |
| 1 | whole clove | 1 |
| 1 | bay leaf | 1 |
| 1 tsp | chopped fresh thyme leaves | 5 mL |
| 1 tsp | kosher salt (approx.) | 5 mL |
| ½ tsp | freshly ground black pepper | 2 mL |
| 2 tsp | cider vinegar | 10 mL |
| | Sliced red onion, optional | |

1. In a medium skillet over medium heat, melt lard. Add carrots and onions; cook, stirring, until they start to soften, about 5 minutes. Add leeks and cook, stirring, for 5 minutes. Increase heat to high, stir in cider and garlic, and bring to a boil. Boil for 1 minute. Add stock and bring to a simmer. Remove from heat.

## Tips

Many people suggest that freezer bags will fail at this temperature for this length of time, but I have never found it an issue. Just make sure that you use a premium bag, or use a chamber vacuum sealer.

*To make ahead:* Prepare through Step 4. Chill in an ice bath for 20 minutes and transfer to the refrigerator for up to 5 days. To serve, reheat for 40 minutes in a preheated hot water bath set to 140°F (60°C). Proceed with Step 5.

I like to garnish this dish with raw sliced red onion to give it a little extra zip.

2. Rinse tripe and cut into 1-inch (2.5 cm) squares. Cut pork rind into strips about 1 inch (2.5 cm) long and $\frac{1}{8}$ inch (3 mm) wide. Set aside.

3. Pluck parsley leaves from stems, chop leaves and reserve. Press clove into inside surface of celery stalk and arrange parsley stems to fill the cavity. Tie tightly with butcher's twine. (Cut celery in half if it is too long to fit in freezer bag.)

4. Transfer tripe, pork rind, celery, bay leaf, thyme, carrot mixture and salt to freezer bag. Seal bag, immerse in preheated hot water bath and cook for 5 hours. Open bag and taste a piece. If it is still chewy, continue to cook, checking every 40 minutes, until tripe is firm but somewhat yielding (it can take up to 7 hours to cook). To make ahead, see Tips, at left.

5. Open pouch and pour cooking liquid through sieve into a medium saucepan. Set aside tripe and pork rind. Remove and discard celery bundle and bay leaf.

6. Bring cooking liquid to a boil over medium heat. Boil until reduced by half — it should start to become a little viscous and sticky. Add tripe, pork rind, chopped parsley leaves, black pepper and vinegar. Season to taste with salt, if necessary. Serve garnished with red onion, if desired.

# Drunken Pig Tails

Pig tails make a great snack or appetizer for a dinner party. The portions are small but they are great fun to nibble on. This recipe uses sherry, which gives the dish a Spanish accent. Pig tails can get messy, so make sure you have plenty of napkins!

**MAKES 2 TO 3 SNACK OR APPETIZER PORTIONS**

Freezer Bag Friendly

## Tips

You can easily double or triple this recipe. If tripling, use 2 bags.

*To make ahead:*
Prepare through Step 3. Chill in an ice bath for 30 minutes, then transfer to the refrigerator for up to 5 days or the freezer for up to 6 months. To use frozen tails, thaw overnight in the refrigerator. To reheat from refrigerator temperature, preheat hot water bath to 140°F (60°C) and immerse bag for 45 minutes prior to serving. Proceed with Step 4.

Don't throw out the cooking liquid. Use it when cooking to enhance beans or lentils.

▶ **Preheat hot water bath to 161.6°F (72°C)**
▶ **Small resealable freezer bag**

| | | |
|---|---|---|
| 1 lb | pig tails, cut into sections | 450 g |
| 1 tbsp | olive oil | 15 mL |
| 1 cup | dry sherry, preferably amontillado | 250 mL |
| 2 tsp | Spiced Salt (page 350) | 10 mL |
| 4 | green onions, cut in half | 4 |

1. Heat a medium skillet over medium-high heat. Add oil. Once the oil is hot but not smoking, add pig tails. Cook, stirring occasionally, until tails begin to brown, about 10 minutes. Reduce heat to medium and add sherry and spiced salt. Bring to a boil. Remove from heat and let cool.

2. Transfer pig-tail mixture to freezer bag, add green onions and seal.

3. Immerse bag in preheated hot water bath and cook for 24 hours. (To make ahead, see Tips, at left.)

4. Remove bag. If you want to reuse the cooking liquid, drain it through a fine-mesh sieve and reserve (see Tips, at left). Serve pig tails warm or at room temperature.

# Fish and Seafood

# Fish and Seafood

Fish is one of the best things to cook sous vide. The technique affords the precise control you need to keep fillets and steaks moist and supple. Also, fish is one of the quickest types of protein you can cook sous vide. Many recipes are done in an hour or less, so you can even squeeze them in on weeknights after work or school.

## The Basics

If you've cooked my meat and poultry recipes in the previous chapters, the temperature I use for fish may seem shockingly low — but the results will win you over. Fish are cold-blooded, unlike mammals, so their flesh cooks at a lower temperature than meat (this is also the reason that fish is more perishable). Something to keep in mind when you're using this technique is that fish served straight from the pouch may be cooler than you are used to. Make sure that you serve it on warm plates. And, unless you like a dish that's closer to room temperature, you might want to skip serving sous vide–cooked fish with cold salsa or a mayonnaise-based sauce, which will cool it further.

Another approach is to consider sous vide a precooking method for fish. Once it's cooked through, the warm fish can be finished on the grill, under the broiler or in a grill pan or skillet. This ensures that you have perfectly tender fish and lessens anxiety about overcooking, which is especially helpful when you're serving a special dinner to company.

One thing to remember: unless you add seasonings, such as a flavored oil, spice rub or seasoned broth, to the pouch along with the fish, your results will resemble plain poached fish. And while this is not the worst outcome — far from it! — you may want to prepare a complementary sauce while your fish is quietly cooking, to serve alongside.

## Selecting

In the past 10 to 15 years, our understanding of the earth's ocean ecosystems and the organisms they support has increased dramatically. In many cases, the stocks of fish, crustaceans, seabirds and aquatic mammals that we traditionally counted on have diminished to critical levels. This is caused by overfishing, habitat destruction or pollution, or a combination of all three. I used to adore cooking and eating skate, monkfish, many flatfish and grouper, but my concern for their sustainability has made me unable to enjoy or serve them anymore.

Thanks to good marine stewardship, however, many species have made a comeback in recent years. This makes choosing fish that you can consume in good conscience a bit of a moving target. There are many websites that offer reliable information about sustainable choices. In the United States, the Monterey Bay Aquarium has created the Seafood Watch program (www.seafoodwatch.org); in Canada, the Vancouver Aquarium has created the Ocean Wise program (www.oceanwise.ca). Both of their websites offer up-to-date information on the status of specific species so you can choose sustainable seafood confidently.

## Cooking

For cooking, fish are generally classified as fatty or lean. Fat content is the main factor that comes into play when choosing the cooking temperature. Once that baseline is determined, the total cooking time becomes a function of the thickness of the piece.

The temperatures for cooking fish sous vide lie between 105°F (40.6°C) and 145°F (62.8°C). Fatty fish, such as Atlantic salmon and mackerel, take a little longer to cook (and chill) and can tolerate higher temperatures than lean fish such as halibut and cod. However, things aren't cut-and-dried when it comes to a specific type. Two fishes of the same species can have different fat content, depending on where and at what point during their life cycle they were caught. Even a single fish can have different fat content throughout its body from head to tail. That's what makes cooking an adventure!

If there is a fish you like to cook that isn't included in the recipes in this book, don't worry. Start with the temperature from a recipe that uses a similar fish. The good news is that it's really hard to go wrong — doneness of fish is subjective, and you can enjoy it even if it's not exactly what you'd anticipated. For example, if you have opened the sous vide pouch or freezer bag to discover that the fish is a bit underdone for your taste, just cook it a little longer in a nonstick skillet with butter or oil. Get your chef's hat on and start experimenting.

## TIME AND TEMPERATURE

As you look through this chapter, you will see a narrow range of cooking times, with most being about 45 minutes. Because of the relatively low cooking temperatures, your fish can remain in the hot water bath for an additional 30 minutes without affecting taste or texture.

## Brining Fish

As you cook fish, a protein called albumin — the same protein that is in egg whites — squeezes out of the flesh and coagulates on the surface. It's white, so it's particularly noticeable when you're cooking a darker-fleshed fish such as salmon. You can eliminate this by brining the fish for 30 minutes or longer before cooking. A good and very simple example of this is Perfect "Poached" Salmon, on page 200.

Brining serves other functions as well. It firms up the flesh, making it less susceptible to damage when sealing the pouch. It also starts protein coagulation, which gets the fish on its way to being cooked; think of gravlax or pickled herring, which are uncooked but ready to eat, thanks to brining or salting. Brining also helps season your fish. Marinating fish in a sauce such as teriyaki or barbecue sauce serves the same purpose, so you can choose to do one or the other.

Brining is never essential — you can achieve delicious results without it — but it almost always results in a superior plate of fish.

## 3 Tips for Sealing Fish in Pouches

Although brining will firm up your fish a little, there are other precautions you should take when readying fish for sous vide cooking. Here are three things you need to do when you're prepping fish:

1. Portion fish before cooking. Cooked fish is difficult to cut cleanly and can tear and flake. Cutting it into serving-size portions alleviates this problem.
2. Wrap fish in plastic wrap before sealing in pouches. This allows a little cushion between the fish and the pouch and it keeps the flesh from sticking to the bag.
3. Use your sealer's Delicate setting. This will help keep the delicate flesh from crushing. If your sealer doesn't have a Delicate or Gentle setting, press Seal as soon as you see the pouch tighten around the fish. If you are combining fish with aromatics such as garlic cloves, olives or fennel slices, they will press an imprint into the fish as it cooks. A good alternative in this case is to use resealable plastic freezer bags, which I suggest in some of the recipes. The bags also allow you to add liquid ingredients to enhance the flavor of the fish.

## Fish Skin: On or Off?

I almost always cook fish with the skin on, even if I plan to take it off before serving. Cooking fish with the skin on is a good idea because there is a lot of flavor right underneath, and it helps hold fillets and steaks together during cooking. You can then leave it on the fish and crisp it up a little.

## CHOOSING SALMON

Salmon is the most widely consumed fresh fish in North America, and the vast majority of the salmon we eat is farmed Atlantic salmon. But, interestingly and controversially, Atlantic salmon is also farmed in the Pacific Ocean, which can lead to fish escaping and interbreeding with wild populations — an ecological disaster. Buy sustainable salmon to help protect the fish in our waters.

The wild species from the Pacific Ocean that you are likely to encounter at your supermarket are king (also known as chinook or spring), sockeye and coho. They are all leaner than Atlantic salmon, so they can dry out more easily during cooking. The temperatures I have used in my recipes are for Atlantic salmon but they also work well for wild Pacific salmon. You can experiment with lower temperatures down to about 110°F (43.3°C), if you like (see "Selecting," page 216).

Fish skin is soft when it emerges from the sous vide pouch. Crisping it can be difficult because it is quite wet; the time it takes to cook the moisture out increases the risk of overcooking the flesh. If you want to try browning the skin at this point, make sure that the cooked fish is as dry and cold as possible before you start. Cook the skin side at the highest temperature you can achieve, whether you're using a skillet or the barbecue. A propane torch also works well for this task, especially if you have only one or two portions to deal with. Another approach is to cook the skin separately, as you would chicken skin (see box, below). Either way, it adds crunch and savory taste to dishes.

## Pasteurization and Fish

Many fish dishes cooked sous vide will not be pasteurized. Select fish that you would feel comfortable eating raw. Since there is no set standard for "sushi grade," however, I suggest that you shop at a fish supplier that has high turnover and sells to sushi bars and restaurants. See "Make It the Way You Like It" on page 221 for more information

---

### CRISPY FISH SKIN: TWO METHODS FOR SUCCESS

Crispy fish skin makes a delightful contrast to tender fillets. Here are two methods that will yield the results you desire. Start with sous vide–cooked fish that has been chilled until cold. Pat it dry with paper towels before beginning.

- **In a skillet:** Add a small amount of a neutral oil, such as corn, grapeseed or sunflower, to skillet and heat over high heat. Place sous vide–cooked skin-on fish in skillet, skin side down. Cook until skin is browned and crisp. Alternatively, you can peel the skin off the fish and cook it on its own in the skillet. Slice the crispy skin and sprinkle it over the fish as a garnish.

- **In the oven:** Preheat oven to 350°F (180°C). Peel the skin off sous vide–cooked fish. Place skin in a single layer on a baking sheet lined with parchment paper; season very lightly to taste with salt and pepper. Cover with a second sheet of parchment paper and weigh down with a second baking sheet (to keep the skin from buckling). Bake in preheated oven for 15 to 20 minutes or until skin is browned and crisp. Drain on a plate lined with paper towels. Slice the crispy skin and sprinkle it over the fish as a garnish.

# Perfect "Poached" Salmon

This recipe is adaptable — you can eat the fish as is or finish it in a skillet, on the barbecue or under the broiler. Straight out of the pouch, the salmon will have the tender texture of fish that has been very carefully poached. If that's the way you like it, slip it onto warm plates and serve it promptly. Hollandaise Sauce (page 332) or Egg and Lemon Sauce (page 334) makes an excellent accompaniment.

---

**MAKES
2 SERVINGS**

Freezer Bag Friendly

## Tips

You can adapt this recipe to the number of guests you're having. Plan on serving one piece of salmon fillet or steak per person. Just make sure to cook each piece in its own sous vide pouch.

For salmon more than 2 inches (5 cm) thick, add 15 minutes to the cooking time.

If you are in a hurry, a 30-minute brining period is enough to keep the albumin at bay. See box, page 237.

▶ **2 sous vide pouches**

| 2 | pieces skin-on salmon fillet or steaks, each about 5 to 6 oz (140 to 170 g) | 2 |
| ½ | recipe Fish Brine (page 354) | ½ |
| 1 tbsp | olive or vegetable oil | 15 mL |

1. Place salmon in a medium non-reactive dish or resealable plastic freezer bag. Add brine, turning to coat. Cover and refrigerate for at least 4 hours or up to 8 hours (see Tips, at left).

2. Preheat hot water bath to desired temperature (see "Make It The Way You Like It," page 221).

3. Remove salmon from brine and pat dry with paper towels. Discard brine.

4. Brush oil all over salmon. Wrap each piece separately in plastic wrap. Place each wrapped piece in a separate sous vide pouch and seal, using the Delicate setting (see Tips, at left). Immerse in preheated water bath and cook for 45 minutes. (To make ahead, see Tips, at right.)

5. Remove pouches from hot water bath. Open pouches, remove salmon and remove plastic wrap. Remove skin if desired. Serve immediately on warm plates.

### Packaging Fish

If your sealer doesn't have a Delicate setting, press Seal as soon as you see the pouch begin to tighten around the fish.

## Tips

*To make ahead:* Prepare through Step 4. Remove pouches from hot water bath, transfer to an ice bath and chill for 40 minutes. Refrigerate sealed pouches for up to 5 days. To reheat from refrigerator temperature, preheat hot water bath to the temperature the salmon was cooked at. Immerse pouches in preheated bath for 20 to 30 minutes, then proceed with Step 5.

You can also reheat or finish the salmon by other means. Unwrap it and let it stand briefly at room temperature while you preheat the barbecue, a skillet or a griddle to medium-high (or preheat the broiler). Cook for 1 to 2 minutes per side, until the outside takes on a little color.

### Make It the Way You Like It

I like to cook "poached" salmon at 125°F (51.7°C) — this temperature yields a soft "fancy restaurant" texture. If you prefer your fish firmer, increase the heat to 130°F (54.4°C). To yield fully cooked salmon, or if you want your salmon to behave more like canned salmon for salads and other dishes, cook it at 140°F (60°C). Cooked for 1 hour at this temperature, the fish will be pasteurized. In fact, this combination of time and temperature will pasteurize any single-serving-size fish fillet. If you plan to grill (or otherwise cook) the salmon later, turn down the heat to 110°F (43.3°C). The initial brining and light cooking at this ultra-low temperature will firm and set the flesh so the center won't have a raw texture after grilling.

# The Most Delicious BBQ Salmon

This recipe is all about the delicious marinade. Marinated for about four hours, the fish will have a subtle planked salmon–style flavor. Marinated overnight, it will take on a teriyaki-like intensity. In either case, coleslaw makes an excellent side dish.

## Tips

You can adapt this recipe to the number of guests you're having. Plan on serving one piece of salmon fillet or steak per person. Just make sure to put each piece in its own sous vide pouch.

For salmon more than 2 inches (5 cm) thick, add 15 minutes to the cooking time.

Use the highest-quality frozen orange juice concentrate you can buy. The flavor of the marinade will be much better.

If you don't feel like making the marinade from scratch, substitute 1⅓ cup (75 mL) of your favorite store-bought teriyaki or barbecue sauce.

▶ **4 sous vide pouches**

| | | |
|---|---|---|
| 2 tbsp | frozen orange juice concentrate (see Tips, at left), thawed | 30 mL |
| 1 tbsp | oyster sauce | 15 mL |
| 1 tbsp | dark soy sauce | 15 mL |
| 1 tbsp | Worcestershire sauce | 15 mL |
| ½ tsp | onion powder | 2 mL |
| ½ tsp | garlic powder | 2 mL |
| ½ tsp | chipotle chile powder | 2 mL |
| Pinch | freshly ground black pepper | Pinch |
| 4 | pieces skin-on salmon fillet or steaks, each about 5 to 6 oz (140 to 170 g) | 4 |

1. In a small bowl, stir orange juice concentrate well to ensure that no ice crystals remain. Stir in oyster sauce, soy sauce, Worcestershire sauce, onion powder, garlic powder, chipotle chile powder and black pepper.

2. Place salmon in a medium non-reactive dish and rub all over with orange juice mixture. Cover and refrigerate for at least 4 hours or up to 12 hours.

3. Preheat hot water bath to 110°F (43.3°C).

4. Remove salmon from marinade and pat dry with paper towels (do not rinse). Discard marinade.

5. Wrap each piece separately in plastic wrap. Place each wrapped piece in a separate sous vide pouch and seal, using the Delicate setting (see Tips, at right). Immerse in preheated water bath and cook for 45 minutes. (To make ahead, see Tips, at right.)

## Tips

If your sealer doesn't have a Delicate setting, press Seal as soon as you see the pouch begin to tighten around the fish.

*To make ahead:* Prepare through Step 5. Remove pouches from hot water bath, transfer to an ice bath and chill for 40 minutes. Refrigerate sealed pouches for up to 5 days. To reheat from refrigerator temperature, preheat hot water bath to 110°F (43.3°C). Immerse pouches in preheated bath for 20 to 30 minutes, then proceed with Step 6.

6. Remove pouches from hot water bath. Let stand for 30 minutes.

7. Preheat grill to Medium.

8. Remove salmon from pouches and remove plastic wrap. Remove skin from fish, if desired. Place on grill of preheated barbecue. Grill, turning often, for about 5 minutes or until browned on all sides. Serve immediately on warm plates.

### Protect Your Fish

The plastic wrap will keep the delicate fish from sticking to the sous vide pouch. After you remove the fish from the pouch, unwrap it carefully.

# Seared Salmon in Southeast Asian–Style Broth

I love fish served in an aromatic broth. Salmon has enough flavor to stand up to this assertive preparation, which is sweet, sour and a little spicy. Feel free to substitute another fish fillet, such as striped bass, if you prefer. This dish is best served in wide pasta bowls.

---

**MAKES
2 SERVINGS**

Freezer Bag Friendly

## Tips

You can easily double this recipe. Just make sure to put each piece of salmon in its own sous vide pouch.

For salmon more than 2 inches (5 cm) thick, add 15 minutes to the cooking time.

If you are in a hurry, a 30-minute brining period is enough to keep the albumin at bay. See box, page 237.

If you like your salmon more well-done or want to pasteurize it, see "Make It the Way You Like It" (page 221).

If you are lucky enough to have two sous vide machines, you can save time by setting one at the lower temperature for the salmon and the second at the higher temperature for the Jerusalem artichokes. That way, everything will be ready at the same time.

▶ **Preheat hot water bath to 203°F (95°C)**
▶ **3 sous vide pouches**
▶ **Small cast-iron skillet (optional)**

| | | |
|---|---|---|
| 2 | pieces skin-on salmon fillet, each about 5 to 6 oz (140 to 170 g) | 2 |
| ½ | recipe Fish Brine (page 354) | ½ |
| 3 | Jerusalem artichokes (unpeeled), scrubbed and halved (see Tips, at right) | 3 |
| 5 tsp | vegetable oil, divided | 25 mL |
| | Salt | |
| 1 | plum (Roma) tomato, quartered | 1 |
| 1 | jalapeño pepper | 1 |
| 3 | whole okra pods | 3 |
| 1½ cups | ready-to-use reduced-sodium chicken or fish broth | 375 mL |
| 2 | cloves garlic, chopped | 2 |
| 1 tsp | chopped gingerroot | 5 mL |
| 1 cup | coarsely chopped watercress (leaves and stems) | 250 mL |
| ½ cup | coarsely chopped fresh cilantro (leaves and tender stems) | 125 mL |
| 5 | large fresh mint leaves, chopped | 5 |
| | Grated zest and juice of 1 lime | |
| 1 tsp | fish sauce (approx.) | 5 mL |
| 1 tsp | granulated sugar | 5 mL |
| ¼ tsp | ground white pepper | 1 mL |

1. Place salmon in a medium non-reactive dish or resealable plastic freezer bag. Add brine, turning to coat. Cover and refrigerate for at least 4 hours or up to 8 hours (see Tips, at left).

## Tips

Jerusalem artichokes (also called sunchokes) are tubers that are native to northeastern North America. They have a nutty, sweet taste. Substitute fingerling potatoes if they are not available, reducing the hot water bath temperature to 194°F (90°C) and the cooking time to about 45 to 60 minutes. The size of the potatoes will determine the cooking time.

If your sealer doesn't have a Delicate setting, press Seal as soon as you see the pouch begin to tighten around the fish.

*To make ahead:* Prepare through Step 6. Remove pouches from hot water bath, transfer to an ice bath and chill for 40 minutes. Refrigerate sealed pouches for up to 5 days. To reheat from refrigerator temperature, preheat hot water bath to 110°F (43.3°C). Immerse for 20 minutes, then proceed with Step 7.

2. Meanwhile, in a small bowl, combine Jerusalem artichokes and 2 tsp (10 mL) oil. Season to taste with salt. Toss to coat. Place in sous vide pouch and seal (see Tips, page 224). Immerse in preheated hot water bath and cook for 1 hour.

3. Remove pouch from hot water bath. Reduce temperature of water bath to 110°F (43.3°C). Transfer pouch to a bowl of cold water and chill until cool enough to handle. Remove Jerusalem artichokes from pouch and set aside.

4. Meanwhile, heat cast-iron skillet over high heat or preheat broiler. Add tomato and jalapeño to skillet or place on a baking sheet. Cook or broil, turning, until vegetables are lightly charred all over, about 4 to 5 minutes. Transfer to a cutting board and let cool enough to handle. Coarsely chop tomato and jalapeño. Set aside.

5. Remove salmon from brine and rinse under cold running water. Pat dry with paper towels. Discard brine.

6. Brush remaining oil all over salmon. Wrap each piece separately in plastic wrap. Place wrapped pieces in separate sous vide pouches and seal, using the Delicate setting (see Tips, at left). Immerse in preheated hot water bath and cook for 45 minutes. (To make ahead, see Tips, at left.)

7. Remove pouches from hot water bath. Let stand at room temperature until slightly cooled.

8. Remove stems from okra and split pods in half lengthwise. Place broth in a medium skillet and bring to a boil over medium heat. Add okra, garlic, ginger and Jerusalem artichokes. Boil for 2 minutes.

9. Meanwhile, preheat a large skillet or griddle to medium-high, or preheat broiler. Remove salmon from pouches. Remove plastic wrap and skin. Place in preheated pan or on a baking sheet under preheated broiler. Sear or broil for 1 to 2 minutes per side, until outside takes on a little color. Place in warm bowls.

10. Add watercress, cilantro, mint, lime juice and zest, fish sauce, sugar and white pepper to broth. Cook, stirring, for 30 seconds. Season to taste with additional fish sauce if desired. Pour over salmon in bowls, distributing vegetables evenly. Serve immediately.

# Herb-"Crusted" Salmon

As you can see from my recipes, I believe that salmon can stand up to bold, assertive flavors. This dish is no exception. The "crust," applied before the salmon goes into the hot water bath, captures all the savory juice that comes out of the fish as it cooks. Broiling it before serving crisps up the crust a bit and gives it a nice color. Serve this dish with asparagus and beets for an attractive and tasty dinner.

## MAKES 4 SERVINGS

**Freezer Bag Friendly**

## Tips

You can easily double this recipe. Just make sure to put each piece of salmon in its own sous vide pouch.

You can seal any leftover bread mixture in an airtight container and freeze for up to 1 month. The flavor and color will diminish, but, fried lightly in butter, it becomes a delicious filling for omelets. It can also be worked into a traditional turkey stuffing or used as a topping for broiled clams if you add melted butter.

▸ **Preheat hot water bath to 120°F (48.9°C)**
▸ **4 sous vide pouches**
▸ **Food processor**
▸ **Baking sheet, lined with aluminum foil and buttered or oiled**

| | | |
|---|---|---|
| 4 | pieces skin-on salmon fillet, preferably center-cut, each about 2 inches (5 cm) thick and weighing 5 to 6 oz (140 to 170 g) | 4 |
| 1 | recipe Fish Brine (page 354), optional | 1 |
| 2 tbsp | prepared horseradish | 30 mL |
| 3½ cups | diced crustless day-old white bread (½-inch/1 cm cubes) | 875 mL |
| 3 tbsp | chopped fresh cilantro | 45 mL |
| 3 tbsp | chopped fresh flat-leaf (Italian) parsley | 45 mL |
| 3 | green onions (white and green parts), coarsely chopped | 3 |
| 1½ tsp | Dijon mustard | 7 mL |
| 1 tsp | Worcestershire sauce | 5 mL |
| ½ tsp | freshly ground black pepper | 2 mL |
| | Extra virgin olive oil | |

1. If brining, place salmon in a medium non-reactive dish or resealable plastic freezer bag. Add brine, turning to coat. Cover and refrigerate for at least 4 hours or up to 8 hours.

2. Meanwhile, spoon horseradish onto a clean tea towel. Cover and squeeze out moisture. Set aside.

3. In food processor fitted with the metal blade, pulse bread into ragged pea-size pieces. Add horseradish, cilantro, parsley, green onions, mustard, Worcestershire sauce and pepper. Pulse until mixture is finely chopped and comes together like a loose pie dough.

## Tips

When sealing the sous vide pouches, this is a special case. You want the sealer to push the bread mixture firmly onto the salmon without the force being so great that it crushes the fish. Once you are familiar with your sealer, you will have a better idea of what setting to use.

You can use a torch to lightly brown the crust instead of broiling it.

4. Remove salmon from brine and pat dry with paper towels. Discard brine.

5. Place 1 piece of the salmon, skin side down, on a long piece of plastic wrap. Press about one-quarter of the bread mixture firmly onto salmon to adhere (pick up any mixture that falls off and press to make an even surface). Pull up plastic wrap around salmon and wrap snugly. Repeat with remaining salmon pieces and bread mixture. (You might not need all the bread mixture; save remainder for another use. See Tips, page 226.)

6. Place each wrapped piece in a separate sous vide pouch and seal (see Tips, at left). Immerse in preheated hot water bath and cook for 45 minutes.

7. Preheat broiler.

8. Remove pouches from hot water bath. Remove salmon from pouches and remove plastic wrap. Wipe any stray bits of crust off sides. Hold each piece in your hand and carefully peel skin off bottom of fillet. Place salmon on prepared baking sheet, crust side up.

9. Broil for 3 to 4 minutes or until crust is light golden. Serve on warm plates. Pass olive oil at the table for drizzling.

# Salmon Coulibiac

Coulibiac is now an obscure dish but was adored in pre-revolutionary Russia, where the czars imported chefs from France to cook grandiose dishes such as this one. It is an involved dish, but impressive and worth the trouble. I remember making it in a large restaurant in the 1980s, where we would bake 10 portions at a time. I have simplified the recipe a little and cooked the salmon sous vide so it has the ideal texture. Sugar snap or snow peas make a nice accompaniment. Serve with rich Hollandaise Sauce (page 332) or the lighter Egg and Lemon Sauce (page 334), passing it separately at the table.

Freezer Bag Friendly

## Tips

You can scale up this recipe to make 2 coulibiacs. Just make sure to use 2 separate freezer bags. This is a great meal for a crowd because there is so little last-minute cooking.

Since you are going to all this trouble, spring for the pricier and more sumptuous king salmon.

Besides the 3 baking sheets, you will need 2 pastry brushes (one for the egg wash and one to brush off flour) and plenty of parchment paper.

The plastic wrap will keep the delicate fish from sticking to the sous vide pouch. After you remove the fish from the pouch, unwrap it carefully.

▸ **2 sous vide pouches**
▸ **3 baking sheets, lined with parchment paper**
▸ **Instant-read thermometer**

| | | |
|---|---|---|
| 1 | piece skin-on salmon fillet of even thickness (not from the tail end), 1½ to 2 lbs (675 to 900 g; see Tips, at left) | 1 |
| 1½ | recipes Fish Brine (page 354) | 1½ |
| 2 tbsp | olive oil | 30 mL |
| 3½ oz | smoked salmon, coarsely chopped | 100 g |
| ¼ cup | chopped fresh dill | 60 mL |

**RICE**

| | | |
|---|---|---|
| ½ cup | long-grain brown rice | 125 mL |
| ½ | bay leaf | ½ |
| ¼ tsp | salt | 1 mL |
| 1½ tsp | butter | 7 mL |

**DUXELLES**

| | | |
|---|---|---|
| 1½ tbsp | butter | 22 mL |
| 1 | large shallot, finely chopped | 1 |
| 8 oz | white mushrooms, finely chopped | 225 g |
| ¾ tsp | kosher salt | 3 mL |
| 1 tsp | lemon juice | 5 mL |
| ½ tsp | freshly ground black pepper | 2 mL |

**PASTRY**

| | | |
|---|---|---|
| 1 | package (14 oz/397 g) frozen puff pastry, thawed, at refrigerator temperature | 1 |
| | All-purpose flour | |
| 1 | egg | 1 |
| Pinch | salt | Pinch |

## Tips

If your sealer doesn't have a Delicate setting, press Seal as soon as you see the pouch begin to tighten around the fish.

If you have rice mixture left over, save it for another use. I like to add it to chicken broth to create a simple chicken and rice soup.

The object here is to cook the pastry fully without overcooking the salmon. That's why it goes straight from the refrigerator into an oven at a relatively high temperature. It is hard to overcook a pastry stuffed with such a moist filling, but it is easy to overcook salmon. It is better to start the coulibiac at a high temperature and lower it as the pastry cooks and takes on color.

1. Carefully inspect salmon, removing any scales and pin bones. Cut fish crosswise into 2 equal pieces; place in a medium non-reactive dish or resealable plastic freezer bag. Add brine, turning to coat. Cover and refrigerate for at least 4 hours or up to 8 hours.

2. Remove salmon from brine and rinse under cold running water. Pat dry with paper towels. Discard brine.

3. Preheat hot water bath to 110°F (43.3°C).

4. Brush oil all over salmon. Wrap each piece separately in plastic wrap. Place each wrapped piece in a separate sous vide pouch and seal, using the Delicate setting (see Tips, at left). Immerse in preheated water bath and cook for 45 minutes.

5. Remove pouches from hot water bath, transfer to an ice bath and chill for 30 minutes. Refrigerate until ready to use, for up to 2 days.

6. *Rice:* In a medium saucepan, bring water to a boil over high heat. Add rice, bay leaf and salt. Reduce heat to low, cover and simmer according to package instructions, until rice is tender and no liquid remains. Transfer to a large bowl and gently stir in butter. Set aside.

7. *Duxelles:* In a large skillet, melt butter over medium heat, until foaming. When foaming stops, add shallot. Cook, stirring, until shallot pieces are soft, about 2 to 3 minutes. Increase heat to high and add mushrooms and salt. Cook, stirring constantly, for 8 to 10 minutes or until mushrooms have released their liquid and are starting to get dry. Stir in lemon juice and pepper. Reduce heat to medium and cook, stirring, for 5 to 6 minutes or until no liquid remains. Scrape mixture onto a prepared baking sheet, spread out and let cool.

8. Add cooled duxelles, smoked salmon and dill to rice; stir gently to combine. Cover and refrigerate until ready to use, for up to 2 days.

9. *Pastry:* Divide puff pastry into 2 equal pieces. Dust a cool, dry work surface with flour and roll out 1 piece until it is 3 inches (7.5 cm) longer and wider than one piece of the salmon (this will be the bottom of the coulibiac). Transfer to a prepared baking sheet and refrigerate.

*continued on next page*

## Tips

You can turn off the oven, leave the door ajar and let the freshly baked coulibiac stand in it for 30 to 40 minutes before serving.

Coulibiac is even more delicious made with yeast-based brioche dough instead of puff pastry. Since it is generally unavailable in ready-made form, I've opted for the simpler puff pastry. If you have access to or can make brioche dough, you are in for an extra-special treat. Use 16 oz (450 g) brioche dough and proceed with recipe.

Store any leftover coulibiac in the refrigerator for up to 3 days. You might want to discard the pastry, which can get mushy as it stands, and just eat the filling. It is delicious at room temperature.

**10.** Roll out remaining pastry until it is 5 inches (12.5 cm) longer and wider than salmon (this will be the top of the coulibiac). Transfer to remaining prepared baking sheet and refrigerate until ready to use.

**11.** Remove salmon from pouches. Remove plastic wrap and skin. Pat dry with paper towels.

**12.** In a small bowl, using a fork, beat egg with salt. Remove baking sheet with bottom pastry from refrigerator. Center 1 piece of salmon, flesh side up, on pastry. Top with rice mixture, making a layer ¾ inch (2 cm) deep (you may not need all the rice mixture). Gently place remaining salmon on top of rice, flesh side down, making the coulibiac as even and flat as possible. Brush off any rice mixture that has fallen out of the stack.

**13.** Remove top pastry from refrigerator. Gently brush off any remaining flour. Brush some of the egg mixture over exposed edges of bottom pastry. Carefully invert top pastry over stack and press edges down onto bottom pastry to seal. Fold bottom edges up over edges of top pastry and crimp with a fork to seal.

**14.** Brush off any flour remaining on top of coulibiac. Brush remaining egg mixture all over top. Using a small, sharp knife, make 4 or 5 small slits in top to act as steam vents. Refrigerate on baking sheet for at least 20 minutes or up to 4 hours.

**15.** Preheat convection oven to 400°F (200°C) or conventional oven to 425°F (220°C) and place rack in center position.

**16.** Remove coulibiac from refrigerator. Re-cut steam vents if they have closed. Bake for 45 minutes. If the pastry starts to over-brown, switch off convection fan and/or lower temperature by 25°F (15°C.) Insert thermometer through a steam vent into center of coulibiac; it should read about 125°F (51.7°C). If pastry is not fully cooked and/or center isn't at least 110°F (43.3°C), reduce oven temperature to 275°F (140°C) and continue cooking until correct temperature is achieved and pastry is well browned (see Tips, at left). Remove from oven and let stand for 5 minutes.

**17.** Using a serrated knife, cut coulibiac crosswise into slices. Serve on warm plates.

# Salmon Gravlax

Gravlax is cured salmon, so you won't need your sous vide device for this recipe. However, a home vacuum sealer makes gravlax a snap — it's tidy, less expensive and tastier. This is probably my favorite way to eat salmon, and the only way I enjoy Atlantic salmon. I have chosen a size that makes the measuring easy, but you can adjust the proportions for larger or smaller fillets if you have a scale (see Tips, below). Gravlax Salad with Cucumbers, New Potatoes and Crispy Gravlax Skin is a delicious way to enjoy this fish and the skin.

## MAKES ABOUT 1¾ LBS (800 G)

**Freezer Bag Friendly**

## Tips

To make gravlax you can use as little as 1 lb (450 g) salmon or as much as a whole fillet. To scale the recipe up or down, weigh the salmon. Use ¼ oz (7.5 g) sugar and ½ oz (15 g) kosher salt for each 1 lb (450 g) salmon. Adjust pepper and dill accordingly.

Turbinado sugar has crystals that are similar in size to those of kosher salt, so they mix very evenly. It can be a nice substitute for the granulated sugar if you have it.

This is a fairly light cure, so it will be hard to over-cure the salmon. I usually take out my fish after 3 days unless the fillet is very large. If I plan to serve it on day 4 or 5, I just leave it in the pouch until then.

Don't discard the skin! Seal it in a pouch and freeze until needed.

▸ **Sous vide pouch**

| | | |
|---|---|---|
| 1 | piece (2 lbs/900 g) skin-on salmon fillet (preferably not from the tail end) | 1 |
| 3 tbsp | kosher salt | 45 mL |
| 1½ tbsp | granulated sugar (see Tips, at left) | 22 mL |
| 1½ tbsp | cracked black peppercorns | 22 mL |
| 1½ cups | fresh dill, chopped | 375 mL |

1. Carefully inspect salmon, removing any scales and pin bones. Set aside. In a small bowl, stir together salt, sugar and peppercorns.

2. Cut a piece of plastic wrap long enough to wrap the salmon comfortably. Lay on the work surface. Sprinkle half the salt mixture down center of wrap, approximately the length and width of the salmon. Top with half of the dill. Arrange salmon, skin side down, on top. Top with remaining dill. Sprinkle with remaining salt mixture.

3. Pull up plastic wrap around salmon to enclose. Place wrapped salmon in sous vide pouch and seal. Refrigerate for at least 3 days or up to 5 days, turning over pouch daily (see Tips, at left).

4. Open pouch and remove salmon. Remove plastic wrap and dill. Carefully remove any pepper embedded in salmon. Wipe with paper towels.

5. To serve, slice salmon very thinly crosswise. Cut through the flesh down to the skin, then cut slices off skin, leaving skin intact in a single piece. Re-wrap leftover salmon (skin on) and seal in a clean sous vide pouch. Store in refrigerator for up to 1 week or freeze sealed pouch for up to 2 months, thawing overnight in refrigerator before using.

# Gravlax Salad with Cucumbers, New Potatoes and Crispy Gravlax Skin

This is an colorful, elegant dish of contrasts — crispy and supple, hot and cold, salty and a little sweet. I created it to show off crispy gravlax skin, which tastes like a cross between dill pickle potato chips and crispy bacon (believe me, it's better than it sounds). I first had warm gravlax decades ago, at the fantastic restaurant Le Bernardin in New York. It was a revelation. Warming gravlax brings all its flavors forward — try it in an omelet.

---

**MAKES 4 APPETIZER SERVINGS**

**Tip**

You can easily double this recipe for a larger group. Just make sure to divide the potatoes between 2 pouches.

▶ **Preheat hot water bath to 140°F (60°C)**
▶ **2 sous vide pouches**
▶ **Mandoline or food processor**
▶ **2 baking sheets, 1 lined with parchment paper**

| | | |
|---|---|---|
| 1 | piece salmon skin from 2 lbs (900 g) Salmon Gravlax (page 231) | 1 |
| ½ | large English cucumber | ½ |
| | Salt | |
| 2 tsp | granulated sugar | 10 mL |
| 1 tsp | unseasoned rice vinegar | 5 mL |
| 1 lb | small white new potatoes or fingerling potatoes | 450 g |
| 1 tbsp | olive oil | 15 mL |
| | Freshly ground black pepper | |
| ¼ tsp | ground white pepper | 1 mL |
| ½ cup | sour cream | 125 mL |
| 1 | green onion (white and green parts), finely chopped | 1 |
| 12 | slices Salmon Gravlax (page 231) | 12 |

1. Pat salmon skin dry with paper towels. Lay flat in a sous vide pouch and seal. Immerse in preheated hot water bath and cook for 30 minutes.

2. Remove pouch from hot water bath, transfer to a bowl of cold water and chill for 10 minutes. Increase temperature of hot water bath to 194°F (90°C).

## Tip

Fingerling potatoes cook more quickly than regular new potatoes. Cook for 40 to 45 minutes, depending on size. Red-skinned new potatoes are the most difficult to overcook (and thus safest for beginners); they can stay in the hot water bath for 60 minutes.

3. Meanwhile, using mandoline or food processor fitted with the thin slicing disc, slice cucumber thinly. In a medium bowl, toss together cucumber, 2 tsp (10 mL) salt, sugar and vinegar. Let stand at room temperature for 30 minutes or cover and refrigerate for up to 5 hours.

4. Scrub potatoes well and cut each in half (or quarters if large). In another medium bowl, toss potatoes with oil to coat. Season to taste with salt and pepper. Spoon into second sous vide pouch and seal. Immerse in preheated water bath and cook for 45 to 60 minutes, depending on size (see Tip, at left).

5. Meanwhile, preheat oven to 325°F (160°C).

6. Remove salmon skin from pouch. Using the back (dull side) of a knife, gently scrape off any fat or flesh clinging to skin. Using a sharp chef's knife, cut skin into strips 1/2 inch (1 cm) wide. Arrange strips on prepared baking sheet in a single layer. Cover with a second sheet of parchment paper and weigh down with second baking sheet, to keep the strips from curling.

7. Bake in preheated oven for 15 to 20 minutes or until crisp. Transfer strips to a plate lined with paper towels and let drain.

8. Drain cucumbers, reserving liquid (you should have a little more than 2 tbsp/30 mL). Rinse cucumbers under cold running water and drain again. Transfer to a bowl and sprinkle with white pepper. Cover and refrigerate until ready to use, for up to 5 hours.

9. In a small bowl, stir together reserved cucumber liquid, sour cream and green onion. Season to taste with additional salt if necessary.

10. Remove potato pouch from hot water bath. Open pouch and divide potatoes equally among 4 plates. Lay gravlax slices over potatoes to warm them. Arrange 3 small mounds of cucumber on each plate, without touching potatoes. Drizzle sour cream mixture all over salad. Scatter salmon skin overtop. Serve immediately.

# Smoky Arctic Char with Radishes and Mint

This is a delicious dish full of contrasts. The fish is warm and the garnishes are cool. Here the char resembles smoked salmon and is very gently cooked. The radishes, watercress and mint lend freshness, while the pumpkinseed oil unifies the dish with its rich, nutty notes.

## Tips

You can easily double this recipe for a large group, dividing the fish equally between 2 pouches.

The brine and the refrigerated resting time are essential to cure the char so that it's ready for cooking at a low temperature. It also firms up the flesh.

▶ **Sous vide pouch**

| | | |
|---|---|---|
| ½ | recipe Fish Brine (page 354) | ½ |
| 2 tsp | liquid smoke | 10 mL |
| 1 | piece skinless arctic char fillet (1 lb/450 g) | 1 |
| 1 tbsp | olive oil | 15 mL |
| 2 tsp | smoked paprika | 10 mL |
| 1 | bunch watercress, large stems removed | 1 |
| 12 | red radishes, trimmed and quartered | 12 |
| 6 | large fresh mint leaves, finely sliced | 6 |
| 2 tbsp | cold-pressed pumpkinseed oil, preferably Austrian (see box, at right) | 30 mL |
| 2 tsp | large-flake sea salt, such as Maldon | 10 mL |

1. Stir liquid smoke into brine. Immerse char in brine, turning to coat. Cover and refrigerate for at least 4 hours or up to 8 hours (see Tips, at left).

2. Remove char from brine and rinse briefly under cold running water. Pat dry with paper towels. Discard brine.

3. Brush olive oil all over fish. Sprinkle both sides with paprika and wrap in plastic wrap. Place wrapped char in sous vide pouch and seal, using the Delicate setting (see Tips, at right). Refrigerate for 8 to 12 hours.

4. Preheat hot water bath to 110°F (43.3°C).

## Tips

If your sealer doesn't have a Delicate setting, press Seal as soon as you see pouch begin to tighten around the fish.

The plastic wrap will keep the delicate fish from sticking to the sous vide pouch. After you remove the fish from the pouch, unwrap it carefully.

5. Immerse pouch in preheated bath and cook for 30 minutes. Remove from bath, open pouch and remove char and plastic wrap. Using the dull side of a knife, gently scrape off paprika. Break fish into chunks.

6. Divide watercress equally among 4 plates. Arrange char overtop. Top with radishes and sprinkle with mint. Drizzle pumpkinseed oil over each of the salads and sprinkle with sea salt.

---

### Pumpkinseed Oil

In the southeast corner of Austria and into Slovenia, there is a culture of using pumpkinseed oil as a seasoning and in vinaigrettes. The oil from this region is the best that I have ever tasted. Look for Styrian pumpkinseed oil in specialty grocery stores.

# Warm Trout and Escarole Salad with Bacon Vinaigrette

Gently cooked fish works really well in warm salads. Trout fillets are readily available in most supermarkets and go very nicely with a warm bacon vinaigrette and slightly bitter escarole.

**MAKES 4 APPETIZER SERVINGS**

Freezer Bag Friendly

## Tip

You can easily double or halve this recipe. If you double it, divide the escarole and dressing ingredients in half and toss in 2 batches. Use 2 or 4 sous vide pouches.

▶ **1 or 2 sous vide pouches**

| | | |
|---|---|---|
| 8 oz | skin-on trout fillets (1 large or 2 small) | 225 g |
| ½ | recipe Fish Brine (page 354) | ½ |
| 1 tbsp | olive or vegetable oil | 15 mL |
| 4 | slices bacon, cut into ½-inch (1 cm) pieces | 4 |
| 8 cups | torn escarole or frisée, tough stems removed | 2 L |
| 2 tbsp | minced shallots | 30 mL |
| 2 tsp | minced garlic | 10 mL |
| ¼ cup | extra virgin olive oil | 60 mL |
| 3 tbsp | red wine vinegar | 45 mL |
| | Salt and freshly ground black pepper | |

1. Place trout in a medium non-reactive dish or resealable plastic freezer bag. Add brine, turning to coat. Cover and refrigerate for at least 4 hours or up to 8 hours (see box, at right).

2. Preheat hot water bath to 130°F (54.4°C).

3. Remove trout from brine and rinse briefly under cold running water. Pat dry with paper towels. Discard brine.

4. Brush olive or vegetable oil all over trout. Wrap in plastic wrap (individually, if using 2 fillets) and place each piece in a sous vide pouch. Seal pouch(es), using the Delicate setting (see Tips, at right). Immerse in preheated hot water bath and cook for 30 minutes.

5. Meanwhile, in a large skillet over medium heat, cook bacon, stirring often, for 5 to 7 minutes or until starting to crisp. Remove from heat and set skillet aside.

## Tips

If your sealer doesn't have a Delicate setting, press Seal as soon as you see the pouch begin to tighten around the fish.

The plastic wrap will keep the delicate fish from sticking to the sous vide pouch. After you remove the fish from the pouch, unwrap it carefully.

**6.** Remove pouch(es) from hot water bath. Open each pouch and remove trout. Remove plastic wrap and carefully remove skin. Place fish on a plate lined with paper towels and set aside.

**7.** Place escarole in a large bowl. Set aside. Return skillet with bacon to medium heat and heat until sizzling. When hot, stir in shallots and garlic. Pour hot bacon mixture over escarole and toss well to coat. Add extra virgin olive oil and red wine vinegar; toss again. Season to taste with salt and pepper.

**8.** Divide salad equally among 4 warm plates. Using your hands, break trout into bite-size pieces and scatter over salad. Serve immediately.

### Brine in a Hurry

The brine firms up the flesh and keeps that unattractive white film of albumin from appearing on the surface of the trout as it cooks. If you are in a hurry, a 30-minute brining period is enough to keep the albumin at bay. Refrigerate any unused brine for up to 1 month. Discard any that has come in contact with fish.

# "Canned" Tuna

Most of the canned tuna these days is packed in water or broth, which is a shame if you care about flavor. The canning process and shelf-life considerations mean that this type of commercial tuna is super-cooked and dry. However, using the sous vide technique, you can carefully and fully cook tuna in olive oil, yielding fish that is supple and delicious. You'll also end up with an aromatic oil to use in other recipes.

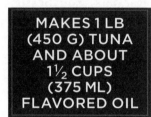

**MAKES 1 LB (450 G) TUNA AND ABOUT 1½ CUPS (375 ML) FLAVORED OIL**

Freezer Bag Friendly

## Tips

Yellowfin tuna is likely what you will find at the fish counter, and it yields terrific results. If you like albacore tuna, you can use it here instead.

If you want to make sure the tuna is pasteurized, increase the cooking time to 4 hours.

▶ **2 small resealable freezer bags**

| | | |
|---|---|---|
| 1 lb | fresh tuna steak, any species, in 1 piece (see box, page 239, and Tips, at left) | 450 g |
| 1 | recipe Fish Brine (page 354) | 1 |
| 1½ cups | olive oil | 375 mL |
| 2 | cloves garlic, thinly sliced | 2 |
| 2 | dried japones chiles, optional (see Tips, at right) | 2 |
| 1 | bay leaf, broken in half | 1 |

1. Cut tuna into 2 equal pieces, making them as close to a cube shape as possible. Place in a medium non-reactive dish or resealable plastic freezer bag. Add brine, turning to coat. Cover and refrigerate for at least 8 hours or up to 12 hours.

2. Remove tuna from brine and rinse under cold running water. Pat dry with paper towels. Discard brine.

3. Preheat hot water bath to 133°F (56.1°C).

4. Divide oil, garlic, chiles and bay leaf halves between 2 freezer bags. Place 1 piece of tuna in each bag and seal. Immerse in preheated hot water bath and cook for 1 hour.

5. Remove bags from hot water bath, transfer to an ice bath and chill for 1 hour, replenishing ice as necessary. Serve immediately or refrigerate sealed pouches until ready to use (see Tips, at right).

## Tips

Japones chiles are small dried red chiles that you commonly find in Asian or Latin American grocery stores.

The oil in the freezer bag can be used in other fish recipes or to make a flavorful homemade mayonnaise. It can also be used in vinaigrettes.

The tuna will keep in the refrigerator for up to 10 days in oil or for 5 days, wrapped, out of the oil. You can also freeze the tuna in oil for up to 3 months. On its own, the oil can be refrigerated in a well-sealed container for up to 10 days or frozen for up 3 months.

## Choosing Tuna

Tuna, like salmon, actually comprises several species lumped together under one name. It is prized largely for its silky texture and mild flavor. When cooked like steak, tuna can be appealing anywhere on the doneness scale, from raw to fully cooked. Well-done tuna is strongly flavored and tastes like canned tuna, which is also well-done.

You are likely to encounter the yellowfin and bigeye species at the fish counter. These are quite similar to one another and can be used interchangeably. Depending on where you live, you may find either of these species labeled "ahi tuna," the fish's Hawaiian moniker. Alas, bluefin, the king of tunas, is no longer a sustainable option, so it's best avoided.

Albacore, another species of tuna, has become increasingly available recently, but it almost always arrives to market frozen. It is an interesting choice, with pale, mild flesh — I characterize it as the veal of the tuna family. Pescetarians will be glad to know that Vitello Tonnato (veal with tuna sauce, page 85) can be turned into Tonno Tonnato, or tuna with tuna sauce, using albacore in place of the veal. Even though it looks different, treat albacore as you would the more common red tuna.

Tuna is low in fat and most delicious when lightly cooked. The one exception is "Canned" Tuna, which yields fully cooked tuna that's head-and-shoulders better than the commercial version. It's no bargain, but it will be the best "canned tuna" that you have ever eaten.

# Tuna Salade Niçoise

This recipe demonstrates how a modular dish that includes many components can be cooked easily using a sous vide machine. Salade niçoise has many variations. This one includes all the elements that I consider essential.

## Tips

You can easily halve or double this recipe. If doubling, use 2 bags.

This recipe can, of course, be made with commercial canned tuna. Try to buy tuna packed in oil, but drain the oil from the can and discard it. Use plain extra virgin olive oil in place of the seasoned oil in the recipe.

If you don't want to prepare the hard-boiled eggs sous vide, you can cook them in a saucepan on the stove.

▶ **Preheat hot water bath to 203°F (95°C)**
▶ **Large resealable freezer bag**

### ARTICHOKES AND POTATOES

| | | |
|---|---|---|
| 1 lb | baby artichokes | 450 g |
| 3 tbsp | lemon juice, divided | 45 mL |
| ¼ cup | olive oil from "Canned" Tuna (page 238) | 60 mL |
| ¼ cup | ready-to-use unsalted chicken broth | 60 mL |
| 2 tsp | kosher salt | 10 mL |
| ½ tsp | freshly ground black pepper | 2 mL |
| ½ | bay leaf | ½ |
| 10 oz | small white-skinned new potatoes, scrubbed | 280 g |

### GREEN BEANS

| | | |
|---|---|---|
| 4 oz | green beans, stem ends removed | 115 g |
| 2 tsp | olive oil from "Canned" Tuna (page 238) | 10 mL |
| | Salt and freshly ground black pepper | |

### VINAIGRETTE

| | | |
|---|---|---|
| 1 tbsp | each Dijon mustard and red wine vinegar | 15 mL |
| 2 tsp | finely chopped drained capers | 10 mL |
| 2 tsp | finely chopped shallot | 10 mL |
| 1 tsp | finely chopped garlic | 5 mL |
| 4 | leaves romaine lettuce, coarsely chopped or torn | 4 |
| 1 | recipe "Canned" Tuna (page 238), broken into chunks, at room temperature | 1 |
| 8 | cherry tomatoes, halved, or 1 or 2 large ripe tomatoes, cut into wedges | 8 |
| 6 | red radishes, trimmed and halved | 6 |
| 1 cup | olives (with pits), preferably niçoise | 250 mL |

## Tips

*To make ahead:*
Prepare through Step 4. Remove bag from hot water bath, transfer to an ice-water bath and chill for 30 minutes. Refrigerate bag for up to 2 days. Before serving, allow to return to room temperature, about 90 minutes. Proceed with Step 5.

To me this salad tastes best when the vegetables are still a little tepid from cooking and the tuna is at room temperature.

| 3 | hard-boiled eggs (page 327), quartered | 3 |
|---|---|---|
| 2 tbsp | coarsely chopped flat-leaf (Italian) parsley | 30 mL |

1. *Artichokes and Potatoes:* Prepare artichokes according to instructions on page 398. Set aside in water acidulated with 2 tbsp (30 mL) lemon juice while preparing the rest.

2. Place remaining lemon juice, olive oil, broth, salt, pepper and bay leaf in freezer bag. Drain artichokes and add to bag, along with potatoes, and seal. Immerse pouch in preheated hot water bath and cook for 1 hour.

3. *Green Beans:* Meanwhile, in a small bowl, toss beans with olive oil to coat. Season lightly to taste with salt and pepper. Set aside until 15 minutes before the artichoke-potato bag is ready.

4. Remove artichoke bag from water bath and open carefully (bag will be very hot). Place beans in bag with artichokes and potatoes, pushing them down into the liquid, and seal. Return bag to hot water bath and cook for 15 minutes longer. (To make ahead, see Tips, at left.)

5. Remove bag from hot water bath. Place a sieve or colander over a medium bowl. Open bag and pour cooking liquid through sieve. Discard bay leaf. Set aside vegetable mixture while preparing vinaigrette.

6. *Vinaigrette:* Add mustard, vinegar, capers, shallot and garlic to vegetable liquid in bowl. Whisk to combine and season to taste with salt.

7. Divide romaine evenly among 4 plates. Top with vegetable mixture. Scatter tuna overtop. Garnish with tomatoes, radishes and olives. Arrange 3 egg quarters on each plate. Whisk vinaigrette to recombine and drizzle over salad. Sprinkle with parsley and serve immediately.

# Rare Seared Tuna

This dish is a restaurant favorite. It is tricky to get right, because a hard sear will create a heavy layer of well-done tuna that can mar the delicate flavor and texture of the rare fish in the center. The following method uses your sous vide device and your freezer to get excellent results.

**MAKES 2 MAIN-COURSE SERVINGS OR 4 APPETIZER SERVINGS**

Freezer Bag Friendly

## Tips

You can easily halve or double this recipe. If doubling, use 4 pouches.

Yellowfin tuna is likely what you will find at the fish counter, and it yields good results. Bigeye tuna is usually a little brighter red and more tender. Tuna cooked rare like this demands the best-quality fish you can find. If it isn't shiny and a bright pink-red, choose another recipe.

If you prefer your tuna more well-done, increase the temperature of the hot water bath to a maximum of 131°F (55°C). Cooking tuna at this temperature for 3 hours (for steaks 1 inch/2.5 cm thick) or 4 hours (for steaks 1½ inches/4 cm thick) will pasteurize the fish.

▶ **2 sous vide pouches**

| 2 | pieces fresh tuna steak, each 1 to 1½ inches (2.5 to 4 cm) thick and weighing about 7 oz (200 g; see Tips, at left) | 2 |
| ½ | recipe Fish Brine (page 354) | ½ |
| 2 tbsp | olive oil | 30 mL |

1. Place tuna in a medium non-reactive dish or resealable plastic freezer bag. Add brine, turning to coat. Cover and refrigerate for at least 4 hours or up to 8 hours.

2. Preheat hot water bath to 110°F (43.3°C). Remove tuna from brine and rinse under cold running water. Pat dry with paper towels. Discard brine. Place fish on a plate and freeze for 15 minutes.

3. Heat a heavy-bottomed skillet over high heat. Remove tuna from freezer and again pat dry with paper towels. Add oil to skillet and heat until very hot (almost smoking). Immediately add tuna to pan and sear for 1 minute. Turn and sear for 1 minute on opposite side. Transfer to a clean plate and place in the freezer for 5 to 10 minutes or until chilled.

4. Place each piece of seared tuna in a separate sous vide pouch and seal, using the Delicate setting (see Tips, page 245). Immerse in preheated water bath and cook for 45 minutes if tuna is 1 inch (2.5 cm) thick or 90 minutes if 1½ inches (4 cm) thick.

5. Remove pouches from hot water bath. Open pouches and serve tuna immediately on warm plates.

### Versatile Tuna

All kinds of sauces go well with seared tuna, and even foie gras makes a tasty topping. Keep in mind that the tuna will not be piping hot. If you use room-temperature sauces or salsas, you will be serving a room-temperature dish.

# Asian-Style Whole "Steamed" Fish

It is common in many parts of Asia to serve simply steamed whole fish finished with a drizzle of soy sauce and oil. This is a gorgeous and delicious dish that you can easily make using your sous vide device. I serve the fish with plain steamed white rice and wilted greens.

**MAKES
2 SERVINGS**

## Tips

You can cook a single larger fish to serve 2 people, as long as it will fit in your hot water bath. Triple the cooking time in this case.

I recommend snapper, porgy, sea bass or sea bream for this preparation. Ask your fishmonger for cleaned fish, which have been gutted and scaled. They won't require preparation at home and will be ready to cook.

Fish are cooked when their eyes become opaque. Check the eyes before opening the pouch. If they are not opaque, cook the fish for an additional 15 to 20 minutes.

▶ **Preheat hot water bath to 140°F (60°C)**
▶ **2 sous vide pouches**

| | | |
|---|---|---|
| 2 | whole fish, cleaned, each 12 oz to 1 lb (340 to 450 g; see Tips, at left) | 2 |
| 3 tbsp | corn oil or peanut oil, divided | 45 mL |
| 6 | green onions | 6 |
| 6 | slices (½ inch/1 cm) gingerroot | 6 |
| 1 tbsp | hot water | 15 mL |
| 2 tsp | granulated sugar | 10 mL |
| 2 tbsp | soy sauce | 30 mL |
| 4 | sprigs fresh cilantro | 4 |

1. Rinse fish under cold running water. Pat dry, inside and out, with paper towels. Using a sharp knife, make 3 vertical slits in fattest part of each side of fish. Brush 1 tbsp (15 mL) oil over both fish.

2. Separate white and green parts of green onions; julienne both. Julienne 2 slices of ginger. Using the back of the knife, smash remaining ginger slices.

3. In the cavity of each fish, place 2 smashed ginger slices and half of white parts of onions. Push julienned gingerroot into slits on both sides of each fish. Place fish in separate sous vide pouches and seal, using the regular setting (not Delicate). Immerse in preheated water bath and cook for 30 minutes (see Tips, at left).

4. Meanwhile, in a small saucepan, stir together hot water and sugar until sugar is dissolved. Stir in soy sauce. Keep warm over low heat.

5. Remove pouches from hot water bath. Open pouches and transfer fish to warmed deep plates, discarding cooking juices. Garnish with green parts of onions and cilantro.

6. In a small skillet, heat remaining oil over medium heat for 3 to 4 minutes, until very hot but not smoking. Immediately pour over fish. Drizzle warm soy sauce mixture overtop.

# Fresh Cod with Chorizo Vinaigrette

Fresh cod is very mild, so this dish takes on the robust flavor of the chorizo. I like to pair it with mashed potatoes or lightly wilted spinach — or both!

## Tips

You can easily halve or double this recipe. Use 1 pouch for each piece of cod.

The cod can be replaced with almost any lean white-fleshed fish, such as lingcod or halibut from the west coast or porgy. Sea scallops from the east coast will also work, but cook them for 25 minutes.

▶ **4 sous vide pouches**

| | | |
|---|---|---|
| 4 | pieces fresh cod fillet, each about 4 oz (115 g) | 4 |
| 1 | recipe Fish Brine (page 354) | 1 |
| 1½ tbsp | vegetable or olive oil | 22 mL |
| 3½ oz | dry-cured chorizo, sliced into ⅛-inch (3 mm) rounds (see Tips, at right) | 100 g |
| 2 tbsp | finely chopped shallots | 30 mL |
| 1½ tbsp | extra virgin olive oil (see Tips, at right) | 22 mL |
| 2 tbsp | finely chopped fresh chives | 30 mL |
| 1 tbsp | sherry vinegar | 15 mL |

1. Place cod in a medium non-metallic container or resealable plastic freezer bag. Add brine, turning to coat. Cover and refrigerate for at least 4 hours or up to 8 hours.

2. Preheat hot water bath to 125°F (51.7°C).

3. Remove cod from brine and rinse under cold running water. Pat dry with paper towels. Discard brine.

4. Brush vegetable oil on both sides of cod. Wrap each piece separately in plastic wrap. Place each wrapped piece in a separate sous vide pouch and seal, using the Delicate setting (see Tips, at right). Immerse in preheated water bath and cook for 45 minutes.

5. Meanwhile, heat a small skillet over medium heat. Add chorizo, shallots and extra virgin olive oil. Cook, stirring often, for 10 to 15 minutes or until shallots start to turn golden. Remove from heat and set skillet aside.

## Tips

For the vinaigrette in this recipe, use the best extra virgin olive oil you have available. You will notice the difference.

If your sealer doesn't have a Delicate setting, press Seal as soon as you see the pouch begin to tighten around the fish.

The plastic wrap will keep the delicate fish from sticking to the sous vide pouch. After you remove the fish from the pouch, unwrap it carefully.

6. Remove pouches from hot water bath. Open pouches and remove cod and plastic wrap (see Tips, at left). Keep fish warm on a warm plate covered with foil and a folded kitchen towel. Pour any liquid from pouches into chorizo mixture.

7. Return skillet with chorizo mixture to medium heat. When it starts to bubble, stir in chives and sherry vinegar. Place cod on warm plates and drizzle with warm vinaigrette. Serve immediately.

### Chorizo

Chorizo is a spicy sausage made in Spain and parts of Latin America. The chorizo in this recipe is the Spanish dry-cured type, which is often smoked. It can be quite pungent, so use a smaller quantity or cut the rounds ¼ inch (0.5 cm) thick, if desired. Latin American chorizo is a raw pork sausage that requires cooking — it's not the same and you can't substitute it for the dry-cured version.

# Salt Cod with Onions and Olives

I adore salt cod. I like it puréed on toast or even raw, a typical Catalan and Portuguese preparation. Here is a go-to traditional recipe for those who are new to salt cod. Polenta works perfectly as an accompaniment. This dish is rich but I find that I can eat a lot of it — because it's incredibly delicious.

## Tips

You can easily halve or double this recipe. If doubling, use 4 bags.

Try to get canned Spanish or Portuguese black olives; pitted black olives such as niçoise or kalamata can also be used in a pinch. The green olives can be jarred or packaged from bulk in the supermarket. Buy pitted olives so that you can easily slice them. Be sure to rinse well after slicing to remove any excess salt.

▶ **2 small resealable freezer bags**
▶ **Large skillet with lid**

| | | |
|---|---|---|
| 1 | piece boneless salt cod fillet (7 oz/200 g) | 1 |
| 2 tbsp | olive oil | 30 mL |
| 2 | onions, thinly sliced | 2 |
| Pinch | salt | Pinch |
| ⅓ cup | sliced drained canned Spanish black olives (see Tips, at left) | 75 mL |
| ⅓ cup | sliced drained canned green olives | 75 mL |
| 3 | cloves garlic, halved and sliced thinly | 3 |
| ½ tsp | freshly ground black pepper | 2 mL |
| Pinch | saffron threads | Pinch |
| 2 | bay leaves | 2 |
| 1 tbsp | coarsely chopped fresh flat-leaf (Italian) parsley | 15 mL |

1. Two days before you plan to serve this dish, place cod in a medium bowl. Place bowl in the sink and run cold water over it for 2 to 3 hours (see Tips, at right). Drain and place in a clean bowl; cover with fresh cold water. Cover and refrigerate overnight. Repeat entire process on the second day.

2. Early on the third day, taste a bit of the raw cod. If it is salty, drain and refill the bowl with fresh cold water. Place cod in bowl and run cold water over it for another hour or two. If it tastes salted but not salty, drain and refill bowl with cold water; add cod and set aside until ready to use.

## Tips

If you want to conserve water, instead of running the water for 2 to 3 hours, place the cod in an ice-water bath for 2 to 3 hours, replenishing the water every 30 minutes. Proceed with the rest of Step 1.

Cooked (or bottled) artichoke hearts are a welcome addition to this dish. In Step 3, add 3 pieces per bag to the onion mixture along with the olives.

**3.** In a large skillet, heat olive oil over medium heat. Add onions, sprinkle with salt and cover. When pan starts to sizzle, uncover and stir. Reduce heat to low and cook, uncovered, stirring occasionally, until onions are wilted and soft but not colored, about 10 minutes. Remove from heat. Stir in black and green olives, garlic, pepper, saffron and bay leaves. Let stand for about 20 minutes or until cooled.

**4.** Preheat hot water bath to 132°F (55.6°C).

**5.** Remove cod from soaking water and cut into 2 equal pieces. Place each piece in a separate freezer bag. Add half of the onion mixture and 1 bay leaf to each, then seal. Immerse in preheated hot water bath and cook for 1 hour.

**6.** Remove bags from hot water bath. Open bags and discard bay leaves. Serve cod on warm plates, topped with onion mixture. Garnish with parsley.

# Swordfish Steaks with Charred Eggplant Relish

Swordfish has a similar texture to beef steak and is definitely the most "meaty" type of fish. It needs to be cooked past rare to be tasty. This dish is perfect for fall, when the weather is cool and eggplants are at their peak. On the eastern seaboard it's also when swordfish is the most readily available. I first learned this stovetop eggplant-charring technique from Marcella Hazan, when I cooked with her in Mexico.

**MAKES
2 SERVINGS,
PLUS 2 CUPS
(500 ML)
RELISH**

Freezer Bag Friendly

## Tips

You can easily halve or double this recipe. If doubling, use 4 pouches and make 1½ times the relish recipe (or double it and enjoy the leftover relish).

*To toast cumin seeds:* Place in a small, dry frying pan over medium-low heat and stir constantly until fragrant, about 3 to 4 minutes. Let cool about 5 minutes. Grind in a spice or coffee grinder or use a mortar and pestle.

If you want to pasteurize your swordfish, increase the cooking time to 3 hours for steaks 1 inch (2.5 cm) thick or 4 hours for steaks 1½ inches (4 cm) thick.

▶ **Preheat hot water bath to 132°F (55.6°C)**
▶ **2 sous vide pouches**

| | | |
|---|---|---|
| 2 | swordfish steaks, skinless or skin-on, each about 6 to 7 oz (170 to 200 g) and 1 to 1½ inches (2.5 to 4 cm) thick (see Tips, at right) | 2 |
| 2 tbsp | coarse pickling salt (see box, page 249) | 30 mL |
| 1 tbsp | olive oil | 15 mL |

CHARRED EGGPLANT RELISH

| | | |
|---|---|---|
| 2 | medium Italian eggplants | 2 |
| 1 | jalapeño pepper | 1 |
| 1 | green onion, finely chopped | 1 |
| 3 tbsp | extra virgin olive oil | 45 mL |
| 2 tbsp | chopped flat-leaf (Italian) parsley | 30 mL |
| 1 tbsp | red wine vinegar | 15 mL |
| 1 tsp | finely chopped garlic | 5 mL |
| ½ tsp | kosher salt | 2 mL |
| ½ tsp | dried oregano | 2 mL |
| ¼ tsp | freshly ground black pepper | 1 mL |
| ¼ tsp | toasted ground cumin (see Tips, at left) | 1 mL |

**1.** If swordfish has skin, remove with a sharp knife and discard. Place fish on a plate and sprinkle pickling salt over both sides. Refrigerate for 15 to 20 minutes.

## Tips

You can char the eggplants and jalapeño on a barbecue that has been preheated to High or on a baking sheet under a preheated broiler. Broil the eggplants for about 10 minutes or grill for 20 to 25 minutes over high heat. The jalapeño will take 5 to 6 minutes under a broiler or 10 to 12 minutes on the barbecue.

*To make relish ahead:* Prepare through Step 5. The relish will keep in the refrigerator for up to 5 days. Bring to room temperature or gently warm in a skillet over low heat. Proceed with Step 6.

Cooked swordfish can be kept for up to 4 days. Remove from hot water bath, chill in ice bath for 30 minutes then refrigerate. To reheat, preheat hot water bath to 130°F (54.4°C); immerse pouches for 30 minutes. Proceed with Step 6.

This swordfish is delicious lightly grilled before serving. Remove the pouches from the bath and let them cool slightly while you preheat the barbecue or a grill pan to High. Remove fish from pouch and pat dry with paper towels. Grill for 1 minute per side. Serve on warm plates with the relish.

2. Rinse swordfish under cold running water. Pat dry with paper towels. Brush olive oil all over fish. Place each piece in a separate sous vide pouch and seal, using the Delicate setting. Immerse in preheated hot water bath and cook for 45 minutes if 1 inch (2.5 cm) thick or 90 minutes if $1\frac{1}{2}$ inches (4 cm) thick.

3. *Charred Eggplant Relish:* Meanwhile, adjust 2 burners of a gas stove to medium heat (see Tips, at left). Using tongs, place eggplants directly on burners and cook, turning often, for 15 to 20 minutes or until charred and collapsed. Remove from stove and place in an airtight container. Cover and let steam for 15 to 20 minutes.

4. Using tongs, place jalapeño pepper directly on a burner and cook, turning often, for 8 to 10 minutes or until charred and collapsed. Remove from stove and place in another airtight container. Cover and let steam for 15 to 20 minutes.

5. Remove stem ends from eggplants. Cut in half lengthwise. Using a spoon, scrape flesh away from skin. Discard skin. Chop eggplant flesh coarsely and add to a medium bowl. Remove skin and stem from jalapeño and discard. Coarsely chop jalapeño. Pat dry with paper towels and add to eggplant. Stir in green onion, oil, parsley, vinegar, garlic, salt, oregano, pepper and cumin. Set aside until ready to serve. (To make relish ahead, see Tips, at left.)

6. Remove pouches from hot water bath (see Tips, at left). Open pouches and place swordfish on warm plates. Top with large spoonfuls of eggplant relish and serve immediately. (Leftover relish is also delicious as a spread on crusty bread or pita.)

### Pickling Salt

Pickling salt is used here because its coarse crystals dissolve slowly and salt the swordfish more gently. However, kosher salt can replace the coarse pickling salt. Use $1\frac{1}{2}$ tbsp (22 mL) kosher salt and refrigerate the fish in Step 1 for no more than 15 minutes.

# Haddock Hash with Leek and Potato

Haddock is a member of the cod family and, like cod, is very mild-tasting. The fillets can be very fragile and flaky, so they are ideal for hash. This makes a nice weekend breakfast or brunch dish and is terrific with a poached egg on top.

**MAKES
4 SERVINGS**

Freezer Bag Friendly

## Tips

Any flaky white fish, such as lingcod, can be substituted for the haddock.

▶ **Preheat hot water bath to 203°F (95°C)**
▶ **Large resealable freezer bag**
▶ **Fine-mesh sieve**
▶ **Blender**

| | | |
|---|---|---|
| 1 | leek (white and light green parts only), split lengthwise (see Tips, at left) | 1 |
| 3 cups | diced (½-inch/1 cm cubes) peeled russet or yellow-fleshed potatoes | 750 mL |
| 1½ cups | table (18%) cream (see Tips, at right) | 375 mL |
| 1 tsp | kosher salt | 5 mL |
| ½ | bay leaf | ½ |
| 12 oz | fresh or thawed frozen skinless haddock fillet | 340 g |
| 2 tbsp | butter | 30 mL |
| | Freshly ground black pepper | |

PARSLEY SAUCE

| | | |
|---|---|---|
| 1 cup | loosely packed curly parsley leaves | 250 mL |
| ½ tsp | finely chopped garlic | 2 mL |
| Pinch | freshly grated nutmeg | Pinch |
| | Salt and freshly ground black pepper | |

**1.** Cut leek crosswise into ½-inch (1 cm) pieces. Place in a colander and wash well under cold running water to remove any grit. Drain well.

**2.** Place leek, potatoes, cream, salt and bay leaf in freezer bag and seal. Immerse in preheated hot water bath and cook for 30 minutes.

**3.** Remove bag from hot water bath. Place sieve over a medium bowl and drain potato mixture, reserving liquid. Discard bay leaf. Set freezer bag aside.

In place of the table cream, you can use 1 cup (250 mL) heavy or whipping (35%) cream mixed with ½ cup (125 mL) water.

This hash tastes good warm or at room temperature. Serve within 3 hours.

**4.** Reduce temperature of hot water bath to 115°F (46.1°C). You can let it cool or add cold water to speed up the process.

**5.** Place haddock in reserved freezer bag along with reserved vegetable cooking liquid and seal. Immerse in hot water bath and cook for 30 minutes.

**6.** Remove bag from hot water bath. Open bag and remove haddock. Pour cooking liquid into a heatproof glass measuring cup. Set aside.

**7.** In a large nonstick skillet over medium heat, melt butter until foaming. Add potato mixture and cook, stirring, for 6 to 7 minutes or until mixture dries out slightly. Flake haddock into skillet and lightly season to taste with pepper. Add all but ½ cup (125 mL) reserved cooking liquid and stir to combine. Set aside remaining cooking liquid. Reduce heat to medium-low and cook, without stirring, until mixture begins to form a crust on bottom of pan, about 8 to 10 minutes.

**8.** *Parsley Sauce:* Meanwhile, in blender, combine remaining cooking liquid, parsley, garlic and nutmeg. Blend at low speed, then gradually increase to high speed and blend until smooth. Season to taste with salt and pepper. Pour into a small saucepan. Heat over low heat for 3 to 4 minutes or until heated through.

**9.** When hash has formed a solid crust and slides easily in pan, slide out onto a large plate. Invert back into skillet, crust side up. (If hash does not hold together or sticks to pan, lightly scrape to detach it and cook for a few more minutes, until crust is solid.) Cook hash until bottom is golden and crisp, 10 to 15 minutes.

**10.** Spoon hash onto warm plates. Serve immediately with warm parsley sauce.

# Halibut with Duck-Fat Potatoes and Brava Sauce

Halibut is delicious any way you prepare it. Here is a twist on fish and chips that features the bold Spanish flavors of brava sauce.

## Tips

You can coordinate making the Duck-Fat Potato Wedges with cooking the halibut for this recipe. While the halibut is brining (Step 1), prepare the potato recipe through Step 2. Once the fish is in the hot water bath (Step 4), complete the potato recipe.

The brine is an important step in this recipe because it simultaneously firms and seasons the halibut.

Halibut cooked at this temperature will have just started to flake when it's finished. If you prefer a flaky fish, increase the temperature of the hot water bath to 130°F (54.4°C). For pasteurized halibut, cook it at 130°F (54.4°C) for 90 minutes.

If your sealer doesn't have a Delicate setting, press Seal as soon as you see the pouch begin to tighten around the fish.

▸ **4 sous vide pouches**

| | | |
|---|---|---|
| 4 | pieces skin-on halibut fillet, each 5 to 6 oz (140 to 170 g) | 4 |
| 1 | recipe Fish Brine (page 354) | 1 |
| 1 | batch Duck-Fat Potato Wedges to Make You Crazy (page 298; see Tips, at left) | 1 |
| 1 tbsp | olive oil | 15 mL |
| ¼ | recipe Brava Sauce (page 371), at room temperature | ¼ |

1. Place halibut in a medium non-reactive dish or resealable plastic freezer bag. Add brine, turning to coat. Cover and refrigerate for at least 4 hours or up to 8 hours (see Tips, at left).

2. Preheat hot water bath to 125°F (51.7°C).

3. Remove halibut from brine and rinse under cold running water. Pat dry with paper towels.

4. Brush oil all over fish. Wrap each piece separately in plastic wrap. Place each wrapped piece in a separate sous vide pouch and seal, using the Delicate setting (see Tips, at left). Immerse in preheated water bath and cook for 45 minutes.

5. Remove pouches from hot water bath, open and remove halibut. Remove plastic wrap, then remove skin. Arrange on warm plates and surround with potato wedges. Drizzle potatoes with brava sauce.

# Miso-Maple Marinated Sea Bass

This dish, popularized by the famed chef Nobu Matsuhisa, is based on a traditional Japanese preparation in which fish is marinated in the lees of sake. My take works equally well for both Chilean sea bass and sablefish (also known as black cod) — sablefish has a finer flavor while sea bass has a slightly firmer texture. Both have been on and off the seafood watch lists, so check your source before choosing to ensure that you're getting a sustainable option.

## MAKES 2 SERVINGS

## Tips

You can easily double or triple this recipe. Use one pouch for each pair of fillets.

If your sealer doesn't have a Delicate setting, press Seal as soon as you see the pouch begin to tighten around the fish.

*To make ahead:* Prepare through Step 5. Remove fish from pouch and remove plastic wrap. Scrape off miso mixture. Cover and refrigerate for up to 3 days, then proceed with Step 6.

If your oven doesn't have a convection setting, bring the fish to approximately room temperature. Preheat broiler and broil fish until browned, about 4 to 5 minutes. You can also use a torch to brown the fish, but start with warm fish straight from the hot water bath. Torch the fleshy side and serve.

▶ Sous vide pouch
▶ Baking sheet lined with parchment paper

| | | |
|---|---|---|
| 3 tbsp | white miso paste | 45 mL |
| 2 tbsp | pure maple syrup | 30 mL |
| 2 | pieces skinless sea bass or sablefish fillet, each about 4 to 5 oz (115 to 140 g) | 2 |

1. In a small bowl, stir miso paste with maple syrup until smooth and well combined.

2. On work surface, lay out a piece of plastic wrap large enough to envelop the fish. Thinly spread half the miso mixture in center of plastic, to approximately same size as fish pieces. Place fish fillets side by side on top of miso mixture. Spread remaining miso mixture evenly overtop. Pull up plastic around fish and wrap snugly, ensuring that fillets are not overlapping. Place in sous vide pouch and seal, using the Delicate setting (see Tips, at left). Refrigerate overnight or up to 24 hours.

3. Preheat hot water bath to 167°F (75°C).

4. Immerse pouch in preheated water bath and cook for 45 minutes.

5. Remove pouch from hot water bath, transfer to an ice bath and chill for 30 minutes. (To make ahead, see Tips, at left).

6. Meanwhile, preheat convection oven to 425°F (220°C). (If you do not have a convection oven, see Tips, at left.)

7. Remove fish from pouch and remove plastic wrap. Gently scrape off most of the miso mixture, leaving a thin coating. Place fish on prepared baking sheet. Bake in preheated oven for 8 to 10 minutes or until browned. Serve immediately.

# Octopus

Octopuses are mysterious creatures, both in our oceans and in our kitchens. For the first half of my career, they were the most confounding food to cook properly. Every country that features octopus in its repertoire has a different method for cooking them properly and making them tender. I think I tried them all — beating them, massaging them with grated daikon radish, simmering them with wine corks — and none of the methods helped.

Then I learned a Japanese method from master sushi chef Hiro Yoshida in Toronto about 15 years ago. He told me to immerse the octopus in a bowl of dashi with sake and a little sugar, then put the bowl inside a large steamer (the kind you use to steam buns for dim sum). This method gives your octopus a decidedly Japanese flavor, which is great sometimes, but I wanted to adapt it for other types of cuisines. I decided to try cooking it in the steamer straight, without any accoutrements. Bingo! I got perfect, unadulterated octopus that was ready for further preparation.

Octopus has become very popular in restaurants, especially in the past 10 years with the resurgence of Spanish cuisine. One of my favorite ways of eating octopus is in paella — drop pieces cooked with the master recipe into the paella about halfway through the cooking time. Except among households with an Asian or Mediterranean background, octopus is rarely cooked at home in North America. As I said, octopus is mysterious . . .

Octopuses are found in oceans and seas all over the world. There are at least 300 species, ranging in size from smaller than a lime to over 100 pounds (45 kg). Octopuses are graded by size: T-3 is 4 to 5 lbs (1.8 to 2.25 kg), T-5 is 2 to 3 lbs (900 to 1.35 kg), and so on. I recommend that you get the largest size that you can use. The yield will be the same, but larger octopuses have more impressive arms and are somewhat quicker to work with. If you plan to put them on the grill, you'll certainly want larger specimens, so they won't fall through the openings in the rack. These sizes are also the most user-friendly for home and sous vide purposes. Very small Mediterranean octopuses can be grilled straight from raw, but generally octopus need to be precooked.

As with most seafood, freshest is best. If you are fortunate enough to live near the coast, then you may have access to fresh octopus. If you do, by all means buy it. Most octopuses, however, are sold frozen or previously frozen, which is not a concern. In fact, the freezing process tenderizes them somewhat. Some octopuses are mechanically tenderized, which both shortens cooking time and increases yield.

I recommend buying frozen octopuses from Spain and Morocco. They are fished from the same waters and are of high quality. Octopuses are never inexpensive and their yield is low; expect cooked octopus to be 35% to 40% of its raw weight. I must add that most octopuses are fished unethically — the methods used to catch them cause ocean habitat destruction. If you can find a source that can assure you that the octopus is by-catch (caught accidentally while netting other fish), you should opt for it.

When it comes to cooking, doneness is highly subjective. The Japanese, in my opinion, are the masters of cooking octopus: they cook it quickly to firm it up for sashimi or simmer it until it is yieldingly tender. In Italy I had to cook it so completely that the suction cups and all the skin would come off. This method gives a very small yield, and I find that octopus cooked that way tastes a little like canned tuna.

## CLEANING OCTOPUS

The only inedible parts of an octopus are the beak, the eyes and the viscera (which are in the head). I have encountered viscera only in fresh, not commercially frozen octopus. Under running water, turn the head inside out, grab the viscera (everything inside the head) and tear them out. Give the inside of the head a good rinse and turn it right side out again. The eyes are dark spots on either side of the head; cut these out with a utility or boning knife. The beak is on the underside, where the arms converge. Dig it out with a paring knife, using a twisting motion as if removing the stem end of a tomato. If you have a frozen octopus, I recommend cooking it straight from frozen, and do any cleaning after cooking. Otherwise, do it when the octopus is raw.

## TEMPERATURES FOR COOKING OCTOPUS

You can cook octopus at any temperature at or above 175°F (80°C) for any size from 3½ oz (100 g) to the largest that you can bag and fit in your hot water bath. Very large octopuses can be cut up to fit into bags.

## GRILLING OCTOPUS

Once you have a cooked octopus, grilling it will seem straightforward. Somehow the flavor of octopus is especially enhanced by being grilled over live fuel, so if you have a charcoal grill, I suggest using it here. You want to grill it quite quickly to avoid drying out, so you will need to use medium-high heat with gas or be 3 to 4 inches (7.5 to 10 cm) from the coals. Cut up your octopus into manageable pieces and bring it to room temperature, about 30 minutes. Lightly coat it with olive oil and season very lightly with salt, freshly ground pepper and oregano (fresh or dried), if desired, and get grilling.

# Octopus Confit

This is a great way to add a little extra flavor to your octopus for salads and cold preparations. The garlic- and ginger-flavored oil gives it an Asian twist that is delightfully tangy. You also extend the storage time by cooking it in a jar.

## Tips

You can easily double or triple this recipe by using more jars. Do not use larger canning jars — stay with the 2-cup (500 mL) size.

Alter the ingredients to suit yourself. This version is just one of many possibilities. For a Mediterranean version, you might use olive oil, garlic and bay leaves, for example.

Remove from the refrigerator 30 minutes before needed, so the oil will become less viscous.

▶ **Preheat hot water bath to 170°F (76.7°C)**
▶ **One 2-cup (500 mL) canning jar, with lid**

| | | |
|---|---|---|
| 1 | recipe cooked octopus, from fresh (page 259) or frozen (page 258) | 1 |
| 10 | cloves garlic, halved | 10 |
| 5 | slices fresh gingerroot, about ½ inch (1 cm) thick | 5 |
| 1 cup | vegetable oil | 250 mL |

1. Cut octopus into serving-sized pieces (I like them about the size of cherry tomatoes).

2. Place octopus pieces in jar, followed by garlic and ginger. Top with oil, leaving ½ inch (1 cm) headspace (you may not need all the oil). Make sure you wipe the rim of the jar thoroughly to ensure a good seal. Add lid and turn just until snug.

3. Place jar in preheated hot water bath. Cook for 90 minutes.

4. Remove jar and let cool for 45 minutes. Serve immediately or refrigerate sealed jar for up to 2 weeks.

# Octopus Confit Salad with Avocado, Kale and Ponzu Vinaigrette

Here's a great way to make a little octopus go a long way. Impress dinner-party guests by serving this as an elegant, simple (and healthy!) appetizer before ramen noodles or shabu-shabu (hotpot). I would serve a junmai sake, well chilled, with it to complete the meal.

**MAKES 4 APPETIZER PORTIONS**

## Tips

You can easily halve or double this recipe.

*Fleur de sel* is French for the highest-quality sea-salt flakes. Maldon salt, a fleur de sel from England, is a favorite among chefs because it is very light, flaky and clean-tasting.

You can strain and store the oil from the confit for future octopus preparations or to use in vinaigrettes for seafood. The oil can be refrigerated on its own in a well-sealed container for up to 10 days or frozen for up 3 months.

| | | |
|---|---|---|
| 1 | recipe Octopus Confit (page 256) | 1 |
| 2 tbsp | unseasoned rice vinegar | 30 mL |
| ½ tsp | toasted sesame oil | 2 mL |
| 3 tbsp | Key Lime Ponzu Sauce (page 358) | 45 mL |
| 1 | large Hass avocado | 1 |
| 6 cups | baby kale | 1.5 L |
| 2 | green onions, finely sliced | 2 |
| ½ cup | coarsely chopped cilantro | 125 mL |
| ¾ cup | fresh pomegranate seeds | 175 mL |
| | Fleur de sel (see Tips, at left) | |

1. Bring octopus confit to room temperature, about 30 minutes. Strain oil from jar into a measuring cup and allow it to settle (there will be octopus juices under the oil that you can discard).

2. In a small bowl, combine vinegar, sesame oil and Key Lime Ponzu Sauce. Add ¼ cup (60 mL) oil from the octopus confit (see Tips, at left).

3. Halve and peel avocado. Remove seed and slice halves crosswise, ¼ inch (0.5 cm) thick.

4. Divide kale between 4 room-temperature or chilled dinner plates. Scatter avocado slices and then arrange octopus, green onions and cilantro on top. Whisk vinaigrette and drizzle over salad. Garnish with pomegranate seeds and sprinkle with a little fleur de sel.

# Octopus Two Ways

It took me half my career to figure out how to cook octopus easily: steaming it in a big Chinese steamer with no seasoning. Sous vide best replicates that technique. I have included two recipes here so that you can cook octopus from frozen or fresh or defrosted. Try it hot or cold. If serving the octopus cold, I recommend serving it with Key Lime Ponzu Sauce (page 358). If you decide to finish the octopus on the grill, try it with Saffron Cauliflower with Sultanas (page 309) or Balsamic Pearl Onions (page 314), also reheated on the grill. Chimichurri Sauce (page 370) would be the perfect finishing touch.

---

| **MAKES 2 SERVINGS** |
|:---:|

Freezer Bag Friendly

## Tips

Very small octopuses — about 6 to 8 oz (170 g to 225 g) — can cook is as short a time as 30 minutes. Octopuses as large as 5 lbs (2.25 kg) can take 8 to 9 hours.

The octopus will be moist when you take it out of the hot water bath for the first time, so you can't put it back in a sous vide pouch. I find that a large resealable freezer bag works nicely here.

Cooked octopus will keep in the refrigerator for up to 4 days.

### From Frozen

▶ **Preheat hot water bath to 180°F (82.2°C)**
▶ **Sous vide pouch**
▶ **Large resealable freezer bag**

| 1½ lbs | octopus, in one piece | 675 g |
|---|---|---|

1. Place octopus in sous vide pouch and seal.

2. Immerse bag in preheated water bath. Cook for 2½ hours.

3. Remove pouch from hot water bath. Open carefully, since it will be very hot. With a fork or skewer, pierce the octopus. If the meat pierces easily, it has finished cooking. If it needs more cooking, transfer to freezer bag and seal (see Tips, at left). If possible, keep sealed end of bag out of the water to help protect against possible bag failure. Continue cooking and testing for doneness every 30 minutes.

4. Once octopus has finished cooking, remove bag from hot water bath. Let stand for 30 minutes. Transfer to an ice-water bath for 30 minutes, then refrigerate.

5. Remove octopus from bag. Clean, if necessary, by removing eyes and beak (see "Cleaning Octopus," page 255).

6. Butcher octopus by removing arms at the head. Cut arms and head into pieces of desired size. If grilling, you can grill the arms and head as is or cut into smaller pieces and thread on skewers (see "Grilling Octopus," page 255). Octopus is naturally salty and therefore needs little or no extra seasoning.

Freezer Bag Friendly

## Tips

Very small octopuses — about 6 to 8 oz (170 to 225 g) — can cook in as short a time as 30 minutes. Octopuses as large as 5 lbs (2.25 kg) can take 8 to 9 hours.

*To make ahead:* Prepare through Step 5. Cooked octopus will keep in the refrigerator for up to 4 days. Proceed with Step 6.

### From Fresh or Defrosted

▶ **Preheat hot water bath to 180°F (82.2°C)**
▶ **Large resealable freezer bag**

| 22 oz | octopus, in one piece | 630 g |
| 3 tbsp | water | 45 mL |

**1.** Clean octopus (see page 255).

**2.** Place octopus in freezer bag. Add water to bag (to aid in forming a good seal) and seal.

**3.** Immerse bag in preheated hot water bath and cook for 90 minutes. If possible, keep sealed end of bag out of the water (to help protect against possible bag failure).

**4.** Start testing for doneness after 90 minutes: Remove bag from hot water bath. Open carefully (bag will be very hot). With a fork or skewer, pierce octopus. When the meat pierces easily, it has finished cooking — likely after 2 to 3 hours for an octopus of this size. If further cooking is required, reseal bag and return to hot water bath. Repeat testing every 30 minutes until done.

**5.** Remove bag from hot water bath. Let stand on counter for 30 minutes. Transfer to an ice-water bath for 30 minutes, then refrigerate. (To make ahead, see Tips, at left.)

**6.** Butcher octopus by removing arms at the head. Cut arms and head into pieces of desired size. If grilling, you can grill the arms and head as is or cut into smaller pieces and thread on skewers (see "Grilling Octopus," page 255). Octopus is naturally salty and therefore needs little or no extra seasoning.

# Squid Filled with Orzo and Olives

It's hard for me to resist the temptation to fill squid with something tasty when
I plan to cook them slowly for a long time. Gently cooking them sous vide in a
pouch or freezer bag helps keep the filling inside the squid. This recipe brings to
life the flavors of Greece, with feta cheese, olives, parsley and olive oil. I like to
serve these squid with diced ripe tomatoes tossed with capers, olive oil and garlic.

**MAKES 4 LIGHT
MAIN-COURSE
SERVINGS**

Freezer Bag Friendly

## Tip

You can easily halve or
double this recipe, using
4 squid per bag.

▸ **Preheat hot water bath to 140°F (60°C)**
▸ **2 sous vide pouches**

| | | |
|---|---|---|
| 8 | cleaned squid bodies, with tentacles, each 5 to 8 inches (12.5 to 20 cm) long | 8 |
| ⅔ cup | dry orzo pasta | 150 mL |
| 2 tbsp | extra virgin olive oil | 30 mL |
| ⅔ cup | pitted kalamata olives, coarsely chopped | 150 mL |
| ⅔ cup | crumbled feta cheese | 150 mL |
| 6 tbsp | chopped flat-leaf (Italian) parsley | 90 mL |
| ¼ cup | chopped green onion | 60 mL |
| 1 tsp | freshly ground black pepper | 5 mL |
| 1 tsp | finely chopped garlic | 5 mL |
| | Salt | |

## Tips

If your sealer doesn't have a Delicate setting, press Seal as soon as you see the pouch begin to tighten around the squid.

*To make ahead:* Prepare through Step 6. Chill pouches in an ice-water bath for 20 minutes and refrigerate for up to 4 days. To reheat from refrigerator temperature, preheat hot water bath to 130°F (54.4°C) and immerse pouches for 20 minutes. Proceed with Step 7.

Leftover orzo mixture can be stirred into chicken broth and simmered until the orzo is al dente, to serve as a light soup.

1. If still attached, separate squid bodies from tentacles. Slice about ¼ inch (0.5 cm) off very ends of bodies (so you can run water through the tubes and to make it easier to fill them later).

2. Rinse bodies and tentacles under cold running water. Set tentacles aside in a sieve or colander to drain. Run some water through the bodies to make sure there is no debris left inside. Drain. Coarsely chop tentacles.

3. Meanwhile, bring to a boil a medium pot of lightly salted water.

4. Once water is boiling, add orzo and chopped tentacles; blanch for 1 to 2 minutes. Drain in a sieve or colander and transfer to a medium bowl. Toss orzo and tentacles with olive oil. Add olives, feta cheese, parsley, green onion, pepper, garlic and salt to taste. Stir to combine.

5. With a teaspoon, carefully fill squid bodies with orzo mixture until they are about half full (orzo will expand during the cooking process and bodies will shrink slightly). You may not need all of the mixture (see Tips, at left).

6. Carefully slide 4 squid into each pouch, horizontally and in one layer. Seal using the Delicate setting (see Tips, at left). Immerse in preheated water bath and cook for 90 minutes. (To make ahead, see Tips, at left.)

7. Remove pouches from bath. Open pouches and slide squid onto room-temperature plates. Either leave whole or carefully slice into 1½-inch (4 cm) sections.

---

### Cooking Squid

The current wisdom is to cook squid quickly for a short time or slowly for a long time. While commercially available squid that have been frozen and defrosted are quite unlikely to be tough, I tend to adhere to this principle. Cooking squid quickly usually involves sautéing, deep-frying or grilling. Slow cooking is braising or simmering. Sous vide improves on both of these methods. Aside from controlling the temperature, cooking squid in a pouch keeps the fragile filling stable, should you decide to stuff them.

# Lobster

Lobster is considered a great luxury, but it was not always so. Up until about 150 years ago, along the east coast of the United States and Canada, lobster was considered food for the poor and was served to servants and in jails.

"Lobster" technically refers to a family of crustaceans with claws that includes langoustines. The type most common in North America is known as Maine lobster. From a culinary perspective, Maine lobster can be grouped with its distant relative the spiny lobster (also known as rock lobster or Cuban lobster). Since rock lobsters are clawless, they are usually sold as frozen tail meat only. Maine lobster can also be processed this way, and meat from the knuckles and claws may end up in cans. It is generally considered superior and more reliable than rock lobster because it lives in cold water; its texture is better than in lobsters that come from warmer waters. Here we will be using the tails of Maine and rock lobsters, which from a cooking perspective are interchangeable.

Frozen tails are usually graded by size: 2 to 3 oz (55 to 85 g); 3 to 4 oz (85 to 115 g); and so on. If you have tails that weigh more than 4 oz (115 g), they are almost certainly from rock lobsters. Since lobster is quite rich and usually served with butter, 5 oz (140 g) of tail will make a meal for one, with accompaniments. Commercially frozen tails are dipped in water prior to freezing to give them a thin coating of ice, thus inhibiting freezer burn.

## COOKING LOBSTER

Most recipes suggest defrosting lobster tails overnight in the refrigerator prior to cooking. The low temperatures of sous vide cooking plus the protective layer of plastic make this unnecessary. Because we are cooking from frozen, the shell will further protect the delicate flesh. The temperatures for cooking lobster range from 130° to 140°F (54.4° to 60°C), depending on your taste and the planned use. If you are making sushi or dropping the lobster into a cream sauce for pasta, opt for a lower temperature. If you want the tail to have a texture resembling boiled lobster, go higher. A temperature of 135°F (57.2°C) will give you a tender cooked texture.

A further advantage to cooking lobster sous vide is that you can cook it with the butter right in the pouch. This can lead to endless variations, as the following recipe suggests.

## COOKING LOBSTER TAILS WITHOUT THE SHELLS

If you want to cook lobster tails without the shells, you have to blanch them before removing the shells; otherwise the shell will cling to the flesh. Allow the tails to defrost in the refrigerator overnight. Wrap each one tightly in two layers of plastic wrap. Blanch in a pot of boiling water for 2 minutes, then immediately plunge into an ice bath; let stand for 4 to 5 minutes. Remove tails from ice bath and unwrap. With kitchen scissors, cut through the top and bottom of each shell from end to end. Carefully pry the shells away from the flesh. Return to the refrigerator and use within 1 day. Defrosted tails at refrigerator temperature cook in one-third the time of frozen tails. If using them in Lobster Tails with Tarragon and Butter (page 264), reduce the cooking time to 20 minutes.

# Lobster Tails with Tarragon and Butter

Lobster seems to have an affinity for tarragon's subtle licorice notes. Because lobster is such a luxury, I cook it with the best cultured butter I can find. The tarragon here would not be out of place in a surf-and-turf dinner (think Béarnaise sauce). Instead of scorching your precious lobster on the grill, try this method instead.

**MAKES
2 SERVINGS**

Freezer Bag Friendly

## Tips

You can easily scale this recipe up or down as required. Package the tails individually so they cook evenly.

The lobster in this recipe is not pasteurized; it should not be served to young children, the elderly, pregnant women or people who have a compromised immune system. See page 20 for more information. For pasteurized lobster, triple the cooking time.

For larger tails (about 5 oz/140 g), double the seasonings — the tails should be well bathed in the buttery cooking liquid — and increase the cooking time by 15 minutes. For smaller tails, keep the seasoning amounts the same and reduce the time by 15 minutes.

▸ **Preheat hot water bath to 135°F (57.2°C)**
▸ **2 small resealable freezer bags**
▸ **Fine-mesh sieve**

| | | |
|---|---|---|
| 2 | frozen lobster tails, each about 4 oz (115 g; see Tips, at left) | 2 |
| 2 tbsp | salted cultured butter (see box, at right) | 30 mL |
| 2 tsp | tarragon vinegar | 10 mL |
| | Finely ground black pepper | |
| | Hot pepper sauce, such as Tabasco | |

**1.** Place frozen lobster tails in separate freezer bags. To each bag add 1 tbsp (15 mL) butter, 1 tsp (5 mL) tarragon vinegar, a pinch of pepper and a dash of hot pepper sauce. Seal and immerse bags in preheated water bath; cook for 1 hour.

**2.** Remove bags and let cool for 3 to 4 minutes. Open bags, remove tails and set aside. Pour liquid contents into a small saucepan. Bring to a boil over medium-high heat; cook until desired salt level is reached and volume is reduced to about 2 tbsp (30 mL).

**3.** Meanwhile, cut tops of shells vertically from end to end. Remove lobster meat from shells or leave in, if desired.

**4.** Strain hot liquid through fine-mesh sieve, pouring evenly over tails. Serve immediately.

## Tips

Maine lobster tends to be saltier than rock lobster. If using rock lobster, add a pinch of salt to each pouch.

If you are using unsalted butter, add a big pinch of salt to each pouch.

For a more intense tarragon flavor, include a small sprig of tarragon in each pouch.

You may substitute white or rice wine vinegar for the tarragon vinegar, if desired.

## Variations

**Curried Lobster Tails:** Replace the tarragon vinegar with 2 tsp (10 mL) curry powder. Omit the pepper. This is particularly good with Curried Quinoa Salad (page 395).

**Kimchi Lobster Tails:** Kimchi butter is easy to make and lends a mildly assertive Korean flavor to lobster. Replace the butter with 2 tbsp (30 mL) Kimchi Butter (page 368); omit the tarragon vinegar and hot pepper sauce.

### Cultured Butter

Cultured butter is made from cultured cream and has a more developed, tangier flavor. Use the best butter that you can find for this recipe — you will be rewarded.

# Scallops

Scallops are a family of bivalves that live throughout the oceans. They are unusual because most are free-swimming, which means they can propel themselves through the water by rapidly opening and closing their shells. It is not uncommon to see them sold in the shell with the edible roe, known as "coral," attached. In North America, however, most scallops are shucked at sea and only the pale adductor muscle is kept for sale.

At the fish counter, scallops are divided into sea scallops and the much smaller bay scallops. Bay scallops are frequently enjoyed raw on the half shell or cooked very briefly, so there is no sous vide application for them. The larger sea scallops are sold fresh or IQF (individually quick frozen) and are graded according to size. U10 scallops — meaning less than 10 to a pound (450 g) — are the largest, and very expensive. You are most likely to find the 20/30 size in restaurants and fish stores, and they are reasonable in price.

## DRY VERSUS SOAKED SCALLOPS

In the seafood industry scallops are processed in two ways: dry and soaked. The latter are frequently soaked in water containing sodium tripolyphosphate. The phosphate causes the scallops to absorb water, which increases their shelf life but leaves them with a subtle chemical taste. I try to avoid soaked scallops, even though they are easier to find and less expensive.

Dry scallops are not treated and smell and taste more of the sea. They are also easier to sear, since you won't end up with a puddle of liquid in your skillet as they cook. Keep in mind that soaked scallops are not labeled "soaked," since it is the accepted industry standard; dry scallops, however, are usually marketed as such because of their higher price. Have a discussion with your fishmonger about which types are available. See if dry scallops can be ordered in advance and consider asking if the frozen scallops are labeled (so you can avoid buying soaked ones). If you are buying fresh dry scallops, make sure to buy them on the day that you plan to cook them.

# Seared Scallops with Kimchi Butter

I use my sous vide machine to prepare scallops even if I plan to cook them again. It firms them up and they lose less moisture during their final sear. Sous vide cooking has the added advantage of being able to infuse scallops with flavor in the pouch. The kimchi butter I've suggested for this recipe is only slightly spicy. These scallops are great as a warm salad or served simply with wilted greens or asparagus and steamed white rice.

| MAKES |
| --- |
| 2 SERVINGS |

## Tips

You can easily halve or double this recipe. If doubling, use 2 pouches.

The scallops in this recipe are not pasteurized; they should not be served to young children, the elderly, pregnant women or people who have a compromised immune system. See page 20 for more information.

If working with fresh scallops, seal in the pouch using the Delicate setting (or press Seal as soon as you see the pouch begin to tighten around them). In Step 2, cook for 20 minutes.

If working with fresh dry scallops, brine with Fish Brine (page 354) for 10 minutes before cooking. Drain and pat dry, then proceed with Step 1.

▸ **Sous vide pouch**
▸ **Preheat hot water bath to 122°F (50°C)**

| 8 oz | frozen scallops (20/30 size) | 225 g |
| --- | --- | --- |
| ¼ cup | Kimchi Butter (page 368) | 60 mL |
| | Salt | |

1. Place scallops and butter in pouch. Arrange in one layer and seal.

2. Immerse pouch in hot water bath. Cook for 30 minutes.

3. Remove pouch and chill in an ice bath for 15 minutes. (To make ahead, see Tips, page 268.)

4. Open pouch and scrape any kimchi clinging to scallops into a small saucepan. Set aside scallops. Transfer kimchi butter and any liquid from pouch to saucepan; warm over low heat, about 2 to 3 minutes. Remove from heat and set aside.

5. Place over medium-high heat a dry skillet large enough to hold scallops in one layer. When skillet is hot, quickly add scallops and cook briefly, turning once, until they take on a little color, about 1 minute per side.

*continued on next page*

## Tips

*To make ahead:*
Prepare through Step 3. Refrigerate for up to 2 days. To reheat from refrigerator temperature, let stand at room temperature for 30 minutes, then proceed with Step 4.

If your scallops are larger than those indicated in the recipe, add 10 minutes to the respective fresh and frozen cooking times.

For fully cooked scallops for salads, soup garnishes and open-faced sandwiches, preheat the hot water bath to 128°F (53.3°C), then proceed with Step 1. Omit the kimchi butter if desired.

For a more neutral flavor, substitute 2 tbsp (30 mL) olive or vegetable oil for the butter and season lightly with salt and pepper.

**6.** Season scallops with salt to taste. Serve immediately, with warm kimchi butter sauce drizzled on top.

## Variation

**Scallops for Ceviche:** Even scallops for ceviche benefit from the cooking treatment in this recipe, because it firms them up. Brine fresh scallops in Fish Brine (page 354) for 10 to 20 minutes. Drain and seal in pouch with a neutral oil such as grapeseed (or olive oil, if you prefer) instead of butter. Cook for 20 minutes, then chill in an ice bath for 15 minutes. Proceed with your favorite ceviche recipe.

---

### Compound Butters

You can use any compound butter that you like: umami (page 367), parsley, basil, cilantro and dill butters all taste great with scallops.

# Shrimp

Shrimp, the beloved crustaceans also known as prawns, are found worldwide. There are even freshwater species! Since they are very perishable, they are usually sold headless and frozen. Wild shrimp are usually processed at sea. Expect to see better-quality shrimp frozen into blocks rather than IQF, which prevents freezer burn. Most of the shrimp that you see at the fish counter will have been defrosted by your fishmonger.

Shrimp are sized like scallops, with numbers indicating how many there are per pound (450 g); usually the larger the shrimp, the higher the cost. For a nice size of shrimp for cocktails, salads and rice dishes, I choose the 16/20 size, but the 20/30 size are less expensive and only a little smaller.

The best shrimp come from cooler waters in both hemispheres. There are lots of high-quality shrimp available from Argentina, Chile and Alaska. Wild white Gulf of Mexico shrimp are also very good, and I generally choose them. Most farmed shrimp come from equatorial countries where the supply chain is so complicated it is hard to know whether you are buying ethically farmed shrimp or not. For this reason, I buy wild shrimp exclusively.

No matter what kind of shrimp you choose, always buy shrimp with their shells on. This helps ensure that any freezer burn will be minimal. Whenever possible, I cook shrimp with the shells on to buffer them slightly from the heat and to extract added flavor from the shell.

## ETHICAL SHRIMP

Per capita consumption of shrimp has doubled in the United States since the early 1980s — it has even surpassed American consumption of salmon! This has put a lot of pressure on global shrimp suppliers. Both farmed and wild shrimp are fraught with ethical issues. Fishing for wild shrimp has an unusually high by-catch rate (the amount of unintended sea life caught in nets and usually discarded). Sea turtles are particularly vulnerable. Farming shrimp produces a lot of effluent that can contaminate bodies of water or land and cause habitat damage. Slave labor has also been reported at some Southeast Asian shrimp farms in the past few years. The best way to navigate your shrimp purchase — and all other fish and seafood ethical issues — is through the Seafood Watch (www.seafoodwatch.org) and Ocean Wise (www.oceanwise.ca) websites.

# Shrimp Escabeche

*Escabeche* is a Spanish word for food that is lightly cooked with an acidic liquid. It was originally created to extend food longevity before refrigeration. Today we continue the tradition less for its practical application and more for the unique, lightly pickled flavor. A great and improved alternative to shrimp cocktail, these are tasty in salads or alone — no cocktail sauce required! I developed Curried Quinoa Salad (page 395) to work as a side.

---

**MAKES
2 PORTIONS**

Freezer Bag Friendly

## Tips

You can easily double or triple this recipe. Use 2 or 3 jars, as required.

Peeled or smaller shrimp can be used in this recipe without any adjustments.

If you want cooked shrimp without the vinegar and spices, add 1 tsp (5 mL) salt and 1 bay leaf to 1 cup (250 mL) water and bring to a simmer. Transfer to a 1-quart (1 L) canning jar, with lid. Bring to room temperature, either by chilling in an ice-water bath or letting stand for 1 hour. Proceed with recipe, using this mixture to replace Basic Pickling Liquid.

*To make ahead:* In Step 2, transfer chilled jar of shrimp to refrigerator for up to 2 days (they will start to get mushy after that). They are best served the same day, either tepid or chilled.

▶ **Preheat hot water bath to 130°F (54.4°C)**
▶ **One 1-quart (1 L) canning jar, with lid**

| | | |
|---|---|---|
| 8 oz | shell-on shrimp (16/20 or 20/30 size), fresh or defrosted (see Tips, at left) | 225 g |
| 1 | recipe Basic Pickling Liquid (page 355) | 1 |

1. Place shrimp in canning jar. Pour in cold or room-temperature pickling liquid, leaving ½ inch (1 cm) headspace. Make sure to wipe the rim of the jar thoroughly to ensure a good seal. Add lid and turn just until snug. Immerse in preheated hot water bath and cook for 30 minutes.

2. Remove jar from bath and let stand until cooled slightly, about 30 minutes. Serve shrimp immediately or, if desired, chill in an ice bath for 40 minutes and serve cold. Peel shrimp or leave guests to do it, as desired. (To make ahead, see Tips, at left.)

---

### Salt Wash for Shrimp

Here's a technique that I have used for many years to improve the texture of frozen shrimp. I call it salt-washing. For each 1 pound (450 g) of shrimp, peeled or unpeeled (I usually do this just before peeling), eyeball an equal quantity of ice. Place ice and shrimp in a large bowl and sprinkle in 1 tbsp (15 mL) salt. Stir to distribute and let stand for 15 to 20 minutes (the ice will be mostly melted by then). Peel shrimp and rinse quickly under cold water, then proceed with your recipe. You will find that the shrimp are juicier and have a firmer texture.

---

# Ground Meat and Fish

# Ground Meat and Fish

This short chapter focuses on the preparation of ground meat and fish, with a couple of my own twists. Sous vide gives you the opportunity to cook food safely without having to resort to the higher temperatures that are traditionally used. Packaging and seasoning ground meats and fish allows the home cook to have great control over these dishes and requires special consideration.

## The Basics

Grinding meat takes tough or oddly shaped cuts and makes them easier to use. It is usually done with a meat grinder. This machine pushes the chunks of meat onto a blade against a plate that has machined openings — the size of these holes determines the fineness of the final grind. This process can also be done by hand or in a food processor, and both of these methods can create a variety of different textures. In this chapter I use the term "grind" interchangeably for both hand-chopping and machine processing. No matter which method you use, the meat or fish should be very well chilled so the fat doesn't break down and smear, ruining texture and juiciness. When I use a meat grinder, I refrigerate it or place it in a bowl of ice water to chill before using; just be sure to dry it well before adding the meat.

Grinding meat makes it more tender and pleasant to eat. It is less common to see ground fish, however, because few fish are actually tough to begin with. However, it is a convenient way to use small or oddly shaped pieces. Salmon tails, for instance, vary in thickness and can be difficult to grill, but they are well suited to grinding because they are boneless and contain a bit more protein and less fat than the rest of the fish. This extra protein helps the fish hold together well after grinding.

## Selecting

If this weren't a sous vide book, I might suggest selecting medium ground beef for burgers, because health departments in many jurisdictions require restaurants to cook hamburgers to 160°F (71°C), or well-done. To a degree, the fattier meat prevents you from ending up with a dry burger. However, with the sous vide device you can cook at a lower temperature, so even a well-done burger will stay juicy. So buy your ground beef (or other meats) with the level of fat that you like.

## Pasteurizing Ground Meat and Fish

With the exception of poultry and pork, it's generally considered that whole cuts of meat and saltwater fish are safe to eat without pasteurizing them to the core. That's why many people feel comfortable eating rare grilled steak or a leg of lamb cooked traditionally rare. The meat is considered safe to eat even uncooked, and a brief cooking takes care of any pathogens that may be on the surface. We are less sure about the outside of the meat because, in the process of slaughtering and butchery, it goes through many hands and comes in contact with a lot of surfaces.

Because grinding causes any bacteria present on the surface to end up mixed throughout the meat or fish, we must ensure that the entire portion is pasteurized. The good news is that we can pasteurize at temperatures as low as 130°F (54.4°C) — roughly medium-rare — if we hold that temperature long enough. At 130°F (54.4°C), a hamburger 1 inch (2.5 cm) thick takes about 2 hours to pasteurize to the core (remember, cooking times depend on thickness, not overall size). As we increase the temperature of the water bath, the times shorten considerably. In a nutshell, this means that ground beef and lamb will have the same cooking considerations as a pork chop or chicken breast.

Unless you want to pasteurize your ground fish preparation, choose fish that you would happily eat as sashimi. It should smell of the ocean (rather than "fishy"), which is a sign of freshness and quality. As a final caveat, freshwater fish can contain parasites that are not present in saltwater fish, which is why you don't see rainbow trout sashimi in Japanese restaurants. If you want to prepare trout, pike or freshwater bass, make sure you pasteurize it. Fortunately, sous vide gives you the option.

## Packaging

Ground meats also require special consideration when it comes to packaging for cooking sous vide. If you take a burger and seal it in a pouch, it will be compressed, making it dense and a little tough. The compression will also round out its edges, creating a misshapen burger. There are a few ways to avoid this.

The first option is to package each portion of meat or fish individually in resealable freezer bags and seal them using the water displacement method that's described on page 15. You will end up with nicely shaped burgers and meatballs that have the consistency you are accustomed to.

A second, more refined approach is to form your burgers in some sort of circular mold. This can be as simple as the aluminum foil ring described in the Salmon Burgers recipe (page 278). For reusable rings, I suggest using tuna cans with both ends cut out. (However, these days many tuna cans have rounded bottom edges to make them stackable, and I haven't figured out a way — yet! — to cut out the bottoms cleanly.) Baking rings for making English muffins or crumpets would also work well. Well-stocked kitchen supply stores that cater to professionals carry stainless-steel rings in all heights and diameters that will last forever. They help weigh the burgers down in the hot water bath as they cook, which is an added advantage. If you plan on making a lot of burgers, I recommend buying some.

A third and final suggestion, which I recommend only for making burgers ahead of time, is to form them and freeze them before packaging. You can then store the burgers in the freezer for up to 3 months and cook them from frozen, as desired.

With the exception of the first method, you can use your sealer and pouches rather than freezer bags. To avoid compression, use the Delicate setting on your sealer and press Seal as soon as you see the pouch tighten around the product. Make sure you use a firm ring rather than foil, to ensure nicely shaped meat and fish. You can then slide two burgers into each pouch side by side, if desired.

## Burgers

With ground meat (or fish) you have the option to add whatever seasoning you want; egg, bread crumbs, salt, herbs, spices, onions and sauces are all common. While they have their place in meatloaf and meatballs, I am a purist when it comes to hamburgers, so I add just a small amount of salt. Adding salt to the ground meat gives them a bouncier texture. Make sure you are judicious with the amount that you use, or you will end up with burgers with a sausage-like texture. And be careful not to handle the meat too much as you distribute the salt; you could wind up with a dense, chewy patty.

Once you have your burgers seasoned and formed, you have the option of freezing them for convenience and economy. When fresh ground meat goes on sale, you can stock up. You can also choose to freeze cooked or raw burgers. Scientifically it is better to freeze cooked meat rather than raw, because there is less moisture in cooked meat. Moisture creates ice crystals that pierce cells, causing further moisture loss. To me the differences are negligible. Freezing raw meat allows you to use the easy packaging method described above and gives you the option to defrost a few burgers or make chili, for example, without going to the grocery store. To cook frozen burgers from raw, add

an extra 30 minutes to the cooking time in the hot water bath. Cooking your burgers first and then freezing them is perfect for taking them to a picnic or vacation home. They will slowly defrost in a cooler and you will only need to reheat them.

When browning burgers, it important that they not be fresh from the hot water bath. Burgers of any kind are fairly small and you risk overcooking during the browning stage. The solution: let them rest and cool down for a while before creating that delicious crust. Open the pouch or bag, set the burgers on a plate lined with paper towels and let them cool while you prepare the barbecue, skillet or broiler. The paper towels will wick away any surface moisture, which will allow the patties to brown more quickly. To ensure the best results, brown burgers over the highest possible heat for the shortest possible time.

For beef burgers I give you three cooking temperatures to choose from: one for medium-rare, one for medium to medium-well, and one for well-done. Just before serving, you'll brown them in the usual fashion, either on the barbecue or in a skillet. This is good news if you like your burgers well-done: it requires less last-minute cooking, which is great when you are serving a crowd. Cooking burgers in advance to finish them later means you can concentrate on heating and browning them before serving without wondering if they are fully cooked. Finally, sous vide works best with burgers that are 3/4 to 1 1/4-inch (2 to 3 cm) thick. Cook thinner burgers conventionally.

# Feta-Stuffed Lamb Burgers

Full disclosure: I am not a big fan of traditional cheeseburgers. I much prefer a plain hamburger, selectively topped. On occasion, however, I like a little cheese tucked into the center of a ground meat mixture — such as burgers stuffed with a chunk of Roquefort cheese. Here I've added some crumbled feta (preferably made with sheep's milk).Garlic-laden grilled or pickled eggplant makes a nice topping.

| MAKES 2 BURGERS |
|---|

Freezer Bag Friendly

## Tips

You can make your burgers any weight and diameter you like, but I find that burgers between ¾ and 1¼ inch (2 to 3 cm) thick make the best use of sous vide techniques.

This recipe makes a burger that is cooked to medium. If you prefer your burgers well-done, increase the temperature of the hot water bath to 150°F (65.6°C) and cook for 1 hour.

*To make ahead:* Prepare through Step 2. Remove bag from hot water bath, transfer to an ice bath and chill for 10 minutes. Refrigerate sealed bag for up to 4 days. Open bag and transfer burgers to a plate lined with paper towels. Let burgers stand at room temperature for 20 to 30 minutes. Pat dry on both sides with paper towels before proceeding with Step 4.

▶ **Preheat hot water bath to 135°F (57.2°C)**
▶ **2 small resealable freezer bags**

| 12 oz | ground lamb | 340 g |
|---|---|---|
| 1½ oz | feta cheese | 45 g |
| | Salt and freshly ground black pepper | |
| | Olive or vegetable oil (optional) | |
| 2 | hamburger buns (optional), split and toasted or grilled | 2 |

1. Divide lamb into 4 equal portions. Using damp hands, pat out each to ½ inch (1 cm) thick. Place on a cutting board or plate. Make a small indentation in the tops of 2 of the patties. Crumble half of the cheese into each indentation. Top each with one of the remaining patties and pinch edges to seal cheese inside.

2. Lightly season both sides of each burger with salt to taste. Place each in a separate freezer bag and seal. Immerse in preheated hot water bath and cook for 1¼ hours. (To make ahead, see Tips, at left.)

3. Remove bags from hot water bath. Open bags and transfer burgers to a plate lined with paper towels. Let cool for 20 to 30 minutes, turning once to dry both sides and replacing paper towels if necessary.

4. Meanwhile, preheat grill (if using) to High.

5. Place burgers on preheated barbecue and grill for 1 minute. Flip and season tops with salt and pepper to taste. Cook for 1 minute more, or until lightly browned on both sides. Alternatively, pour enough oil (if using) into a heavy cast-iron skillet to come ⅛ inch (0.25 cm) up sides. Heat over high heat just until oil begins to smoke lightly. Add burgers and cook for 1 minute. Flip and season tops with salt and pepper to taste. Cook for 1 minute more, or until lightly browned on both sides. Serve immediately on buns (if using).

# Beef Burgers

I've created this recipe for a single burger, using a specific ratio of salt to meat to ensure that the patty tastes really good and has a great texture. You can scale up the recipe to make as many burgers as you need, using these proportions. Just place each one in an individual freezer bag.

---

**MAKES
1 BURGER**

Freezer Bag Friendly

Can Be Scaled Up

## Tips

Technically you can make your burgers any weight and diameter you like. However, I find that burgers between ¾ and 1¼ inches (2 to 3 cm) thick make the best use of sous vide techniques.

You can use any type of ground beef that you like, but I prefer medium.

*To make ahead:* Prepare through Step 2. Remove bag from hot water bath, transfer to an ice bath and chill for 30 minutes. Refrigerate sealed bag for up to 4 days or freeze for up to 3 months. Defrost in the refrigerator overnight, if needed. Open bag and transfer patty to a plate lined with paper towels. Let stand at room temperature for 20 to 30 minutes. Pat dry with a paper towel on both sides before proceeding with Step 4.

▶ **Preheat hot water bath to**
- 130°F (54.4°C) for medium-rare
- 138°F (59°C) for medium or medium-well
- 150°F (65.6°C) for well-done

▶ **Small resealable freezer bag**

| 6 to 8 oz | ground beef (see Tips, at left) | 170 to 225 g |
| ½ tsp | kosher salt | 2 mL |
| | Salt and freshly ground black pepper | |
| | Vegetable oil (optional) | |
| | Hamburger bun (optional), split and toasted or grilled | |

1. In a medium bowl, gently mix beef with salt, if desired (if not, set salt aside). Gently shape into a patty ¾ to 1 inch (2 to 2.5 cm) thick. Lightly season both sides of patty with salt if not already added.

2. Place burger in freezer bag and seal. Immerse in preheated hot water bath and cook for 2 hours at 130°F (54.4°C) for medium-rare, 1¼ hours at 138°F (59°C) for medium to medium-well, or 1 hour at 150°F (65.6°C) for well-done. (To make ahead, see Tips, at left.)

3. Remove bag from hot water bath, open bag and transfer patty to a plate lined with paper towels. Let cool for 20 to 30 minutes, turning once to dry both sides and replacing paper towels if necessary.

4. Meanwhile, preheat grill to High, if using.

To make cheeseburgers, place a slice of your favorite cheese on the patty immediately after flipping it. Depending on how salty the cheese is, you may not need to season the patty with additional salt. Sprinkle the pepper either under or over the cheese.

**5.** Place patty on preheated barbecue and grill for 1 minute. Flip and season top with salt and pepper to taste. Cook for 1 minute more, or until lightly browned on both sides. Alternatively, pour enough oil (if using) into a heavy cast-iron skillet to come ⅛ inch (0.25 cm) up sides. Heat over high heat just until oil begins to smoke lightly. Add patty and cook for 1 minute. Flip and season top with salt and pepper to taste. Cook for 1 minute more, or until lightly browned on both sides. Serve immediately on bun (if using).

## Variations

**Pork Burgers:** These burgers are cooked long enough to pasteurize them, so it's safe to substitute ground pork for the beef. Or use a mixture of pork and beef.

**Chicken or Turkey Burgers:** Substitute ground chicken or turkey for the beef. Cook using either of the two higher temperatures and their respective times — either 138°F (59°C) for $1\frac{1}{4}$ hours, or 150°F (65.6°C) for 1 hour.

### Packaging Burgers

When scaling up recipes, make sure to package each burger individually.

# Salmon Burgers

Salmon burgers need a little help seasoning-wise to taste good. These are delicately flavored with a little green onion and celery, which don't overpower the fish. This recipe uses a couple of tricks to help the burger hold together. The first is processing about one-third of the fish until it's almost a purée, and the second is adding miso paste, which helps bind the mixture. The miso also adds umami and some saltiness. Try topping these burgers with kimchi or seaweed salad for an Asian accent. For a Mediterranean twist, try them with a garnish of tarragon mayonnaise or tapenade.

## MAKES
## 2 BURGERS

Freezer Bag Friendly

## Tips

You can easily scale up this recipe to make as many burgers as you want. Just make sure you use a separate bag for each burger.

These burgers are not cooked long enough to pasteurize the fish. If you want to pasteurize them, increase the cooking time to 2 hours.

You can make the burgers larger or smaller in weight and diameter if desired. However, I find that 5 oz (140 g) is a good size for salmon burgers.

▶ **Preheat hot water bath to 130°F (54.4°C)**
▶ **Food processor**
▶ **Can or jar about 3½ inches (8.5 cm) in diameter, such as a tuna can**
▶ **Tape or stapler**
▶ **2 small resealable freezer bags**

| | | |
|---|---|---|
| 10 oz | skinless salmon fillet (see Tips, at left) | 280 g |
| 2 tbsp | white miso paste | 30 mL |
| 2 tbsp | minced celery | 30 mL |
| 2 tbsp | minced green onion | 30 mL |
| | Salt and freshly ground black pepper | |
| | Olive or vegetable oil (optional) | |
| 2 | hamburger buns (optional), split and toasted or grilled | 2 |

1. Inspect salmon carefully and remove any scales, bits of bone or skin. Cut into ¾-inch (2 cm) cubes. Spread out cubes on a plate or a baking sheet lined with plastic wrap. Freeze for 20 minutes or until just starting to firm up. At the same time, place food processor work bowl and metal blade in freezer to chill along with the salmon.

2. Meanwhile, cut two pieces of foil 5 inches (12.5 cm) long. Fold each piece several times to make a strip that is as wide as the thickness of the burgers you will be making. Wrap each strip around can, using it as a mold to form a supporting ring. Slide off can and tape or staple to secure. Set aside.

## Tips

The temperature in this recipe make a burger that is cooked to medium-rare. If you prefer your salmon burgers medium or well-done, increase the temperature of the hot water bath to 140°F (60°C) and cook the burgers for 1 hour.

*To make ahead:* Prepare through Step 6. Remove bags from hot water bath, transfer to an ice bath and chill for 10 minutes. Refrigerate sealed bags for up to 4 days. Open bag and transfer burger to a plate lined with paper towels. Let stand at room temperature for 20 to 30 minutes. Pat dry on both sides with paper towels before proceeding with Step 8.

**3.** Remove salmon, work bowl and blade from freezer. In cold food processor fitted with the metal blade, combine about one-third of the salmon with miso paste. Pulse 10 to 12 times, stopping motor and scraping down sides of bowl several times, until coarsely puréed (mixture should not be perfectly smooth).

**4.** Add celery, green onion and remaining salmon. Pulse 5 or 6 times, stopping motor and scraping down sides of bowl between pulses, until very roughly chopped, with some chunks remaining. If chunks are not well distributed, transfer mixture to a bowl and stir gently with a rubber spatula.

**5.** Place each foil ring on a separate square of parchment paper. Divide salmon mixture between rings and pat down lightly so there are no air pockets and tops are even.

**6.** Carefully slide each burger, with foil ring and parchment paper, into a separate freezer bag and seal. Immerse in preheated hot water bath and cook for 1 hour. (To make ahead, see Tips, at left.)

**7.** Remove bags from hot water bath. Open bags and transfer burgers to a plate lined with paper towels. Remove paper and foil rings. Let cool for 20 to 30 minutes, turning once to dry both sides and replacing paper towels if necessary.

**8.** Meanwhile, preheat grill (if using) to High.

**9.** Place burgers on preheated barbecue and grill for 1 minute. Flip and lightly season tops with salt and pepper. Cook for 1 minute more, or until lightly browned on both sides. Alternatively, pour enough oil (if using) into a heavy cast-iron skillet to come $\frac{1}{8}$ inch (0.25 cm) up sides. Heat over high heat just until oil begins to smoke lightly. Add burgers and cook for 1 minute. Flip and season tops with salt and pepper to taste. Cook for 1 minute more, or until lightly browned on both sides. Serve immediately on buns (if using).

# Catalan Giant Meatballs

I discovered these in Barcelona and recreated them back in Toronto at my former restaurant, Cava. They are called *pilotas*, named after the ball used in a traditional Catalan game. They are usually served on Christmas day, made from leftovers from the Christmas Eve dinner of boiled meats, blood sausage and vegetables. In this recipe I'm starting from scratch and filling the meatballs with blood sausage. I like to serve them warm, right from the sous vide pouch, in seasoned broth with chickpeas or pasta shells, and garnished with lots of chopped fresh parsley. They're also delicious as part of an assortment of boiled meats.

**MAKES
6 LARGE
MEATBALLS**

## Tips

You can easily double this recipe. Just make sure you use 6 sous vide pouches.

You'll find blood sausage in grocery stores that specialize in Spanish or Portuguese products. It is a cooked sausage.

If you like, you can replace the ground chicken thighs with ground skinless chicken breast, ground veal or a mixture of ground beef and pork.

Mushroom duxelles, made from either wild or cultivated mushrooms, can be substituted for the blood sausage with delicious results. Just make sure they are well seasoned and cooked.

▶ **Preheat hot water bath to 140°F (60°C)**
▶ **3 sous vide pouches**

| | | |
|---|---|---|
| 2 tbsp | olive oil | 30 mL |
| ½ cup | minced onion | 125 mL |
| ¼ cup | dry red wine | 60 mL |
| 1½ tbsp | finely chopped garlic | 22 mL |
| 1 tsp | kosher salt | 5 mL |
| 2 tsp | smoked paprika | 10 mL |
| 6 oz | ground boneless, skinless chicken thighs (see Tips, at left) | 170 g |
| 6 oz | medium ground beef | 170 g |
| 6 oz | medium ground pork | 170 g |
| ¼ cup | fresh bread crumbs (see page 385) | 60 mL |
| 3 tbsp | grated manchego cheese | 45 mL |
| 1 tsp | anchovy paste or finely chopped anchovies | 5 mL |
| 6 oz | blood sausage (see Tips, at left) | 170 g |

1. In a small skillet, heat oil over medium heat. Add onion and cook, stirring frequently, for 5 minutes or until softened. Add wine, garlic and salt. Cook, stirring, until almost no liquid remains and mixture is slushy, about 10 minutes. Remove from heat. Stir in paprika and let cool.

2. In a medium bowl, combine onion mixture, chicken, beef, pork, bread crumbs, cheese and anchovy paste. Mix until well blended, taking care not to overwork the ground meat. Divide into 6 equal portions. Remove casing from sausage, divide sausage meat into 6 portions and form each into a ball.

## Tips

If your sealer doesn't have a delicate setting, press Seal as soon as you see the pouch begin to tighten around the meat.

*To make ahead:* Prepare through Step 4. Remove pouches from hot water bath, transfer to an ice bath and chill for 30 minutes. Refrigerate sealed pouches for up to 5 days or freeze for up to 3 months. Defrost in the refrigerator overnight, if needed. To reheat from refrigerator temperature, preheat hot water bath to 130°F (54.4°C). Immerse the pouches in preheated bath for 30 minutes, then proceed with Step 5.

**3.** Place a 12-inch (30 cm) piece of plastic wrap on work surface. Moisten hands and pat out 1 portion of ground meat mixture into a 4-inch (10 cm) circle on plastic. Place 1 ball of sausage meat in center and, using the edges of the wrap to help, pull up ground meat mixture around sausage to enclose it and form a large ball. Pull plastic around the ball and twist to compress the meat mixture. Prick the plastic wrap several times with a pin to remove any air bubbles. Repeat with remaining meat mixture and sausage.

**4.** Place wrapped *pilotas* in pairs in separate sous vide pouches and seal using the Delicate setting. Immerse in preheated hot water bath and cook for 2 hours. (To make ahead, see Tips, at left.)

**5.** Remove pouches from hot water bath. Open pouches, remove plastic wrap and transfer *pilotas* to warmed shallow bowls. Serve immediately.

# Spicy Meatloaf Roulade

There is no particular culinary advantage to cooking meatloaf sous vide, but it will free up your oven for other dishes or keep you from heating up your kitchen on a hot day. Happily, you don't have to make any adaptations (or own a loaf pan) to cook your favorite meatloaf recipe. In case you don't have one, here's mine. Gelatin helps the meatloaf hold on to its natural moisture, so it's lovely and juicy.

## Tips

You can easily halve or double this recipe. If doubling, use 2 additional pouches.

If you can't find chipotle purée, buy a can of chipotle chiles in adobo sauce and purée the contents in a mini food processor. Measure out 2 tbsp (30 mL) and refrigerate or freeze the rest for another use.

Gelatin helps the meatloaf stay moist and holds the meat mixture together.

If you don't have homemade black garlic on hand, substitute 3 cloves fresh garlic, finely chopped.

▶ **Preheat hot water bath to 145°F (62.8°C)**
▶ **2 sous vide pouches**
▶ **Food processor**

| | | |
|---|---|---:|
| 2 tbsp | chipotle purée (see Tips, at left) | 30 mL |
| 2 tbsp | sour cream | 30 mL |
| 1 tbsp | fish sauce | 15 mL |
| 1 tbsp | light soy sauce | 15 mL |
| 1 tbsp | Worcestershire sauce | 15 mL |
| 1 tbsp | ketchup | 15 mL |
| 1 | envelope (¼ oz/7 g) unflavored gelatin powder (see Tips, at left) | 1 |
| 1¼ lbs | lean or medium ground beef | 565 g |
| 12 oz | medium ground pork | 340 g |
| 2 tbsp | butter | 30 mL |
| ¾ cup | chopped onion | 175 mL |
| ½ cup | chopped carrot | 125 mL |
| ¼ cup | chopped celery | 60 mL |
| 4 oz | white or cremini mushrooms, sliced | 115 g |
| 6 | cloves 40 Days and 40 Nights Black Garlic (page 388), finely chopped (see Tips, at left) | 6 |
| 1 tsp | kosher salt | 5 mL |
| 1 tsp | freshly ground black pepper | 5 mL |
| 1 cup | dry bread crumbs (see Variation, page 385) | 250 mL |
| ¼ cup | grated Pecorino Romano cheese | 60 mL |
| ¼ cup | chopped fresh parsley | 60 mL |

1. In a large bowl, whisk together chipotle purée, sour cream, fish sauce, soy sauce, Worcestershire sauce and ketchup. Sprinkle gelatin overtop and whisk to combine. Add beef and pork and mix thoroughly. Set aside.

## Tips

This meatloaf is quite spicy. If you want to make a milder one, halve the amount of chipotle purée and increase the ketchup to 2 tbsp (30 mL).

You can also cook the meatloaf in a 4-cup (1 L) loaf pan. Gently pack down and level the mixture to ensure that there are no air pockets. Seal each pan in a separate sous vide pouch and cook as directed.

*To make ahead:* Prepare through Step 6. Transfer to an ice bath and chill for 30 minutes. Refrigerate sealed pouch for up to 7 days or freeze for up to 3 months. Defrost in the refrigerator overnight, if needed. To reheat from refrigerator temperature, preheat hot water bath to 130°F (54.4°C). Immerse pouches in preheated bath for 60 minutes. Proceed with Step 7.

This dish can also be served cold.

2. In a large skillet, melt butter over medium heat. Add onion, carrot and celery. Cook, stirring occasionally, for 10 minutes or until vegetables are starting to soften.

3. Increase heat to medium-high and add mushrooms. Cook, stirring often, until mushrooms are cooked and some of their juices have evaporated, about 5 minutes. Add garlic, salt and pepper; cook, stirring, for 5 minutes. Remove from heat and let cool slightly.

4. Scrape vegetable mixture into food processor fitted with the metal blade and pulse until finely chopped. Add to meat mixture and pulse 4 to 5 times to combine, stopping motor and scraping down sides of bowl several times, as necessary. Add bread crumbs, cheese and parsley; pulse to combine.

5. Place a large piece of plastic wrap on work surface. Scoop half the meat mixture onto plastic and roll into a cylinder about 2 inches (5 cm) in diameter. Pull up plastic wrap around log and twist to compress meat mixture. Prick plastic all over with a pin to remove any air bubbles. Repeat with rest of meat mixture.

6. Place wrapped cylinders in separate sous vide pouches and seal (see Tips, at left). Immerse in preheated hot water bath and cook for 7 to 8 hours. (To make ahead, see Tips, at left.)

7. Remove pouches from hot water bath. Open pouches and remove plastic wrap. Transfer roulades to a serving platter, slice and serve immediately on warm plates.

# Country Pork Terrine

Cooking terrines sous vide allows you to use your oven for other preparations, which is terrific if you're hosting a party and juggling a lot of different dishes. Most terrine recipes will work well in the sous vide machine, but here's one of my favorites, which uses a little-known technique. It's called *gratin* in French, and it means that a part of the mixture that includes liver (chicken liver, in this case) is lightly cooked and incorporated into the main mixture before the final cooking step, creating a super-silky texture.

---

**MAKES
2 TERRINES,
OR 12 TO
15 APPETIZER
SERVINGS**

Freezer Bag Friendly

## Tip

You can easily double this recipe. Just make sure to package the molds or pans individually.

▶ **Preheat hot water bath to 145°F (62.8°C)**
▶ **2 or 3 sous vide pouches**
▶ **Food processor**
▶ **2 terrine molds, each 11¾ by 2½ inches (29 by 6 cm), or 3 mini loaf pans, each 5½ by 3 inches (14 by 7.5 cm)**

### SEASONINGS

| | | |
|---|---|---|
| 1½ tbsp | kosher salt | 22 mL |
| 1 tbsp | chopped fresh thyme | 15 mL |
| 1½ tsp | freshly ground black pepper | 7 mL |
| ¾ tsp | ground nutmeg | 3 mL |
| ¼ tsp | ground cloves | 1 mL |
| ¼ tsp | ground ginger | 1 mL |

### GRATIN

| | | |
|---|---|---|
| 2 tbsp | rendered duck or pork fat or butter | 30 mL |
| 8 oz | rindless pork belly, cut into ½-inch (1 cm) cubes | 225 g |
| ½ cup | finely chopped carrot | 125 mL |
| ½ cup | finely chopped shallots | 125 mL |
| 4 oz | button mushrooms, sliced | 115 g |
| 5½ oz | trimmed chicken livers (see Tips, at right) | 155 g |
| 1 | bay leaf | 1 |
| 7 tbsp | Madeira or medium-dry sherry | 105 mL |
| 7 tbsp | heavy or whipping (35%) cream | 105 mL |
| 1 tbsp | finely chopped garlic | 15 mL |
| 1 | envelope (¼ oz/7 g) unflavored gelatin powder | 1 |
| 2 lbs | medium coarsely ground pork | 900 g |
| | Salt, optional | |

## Tips

*To trim chicken livers:*
Rinse chicken livers under cold water and drain. One at a time, spread them open on a cutting board and, using a sharp knife, cut away and discard the connective membrane between the two lobes. Cut off any green parts and discard. Pat meat dry and set aside.

*To make ahead:*
Prepare through Step 8. Refrigerate sealed bag for up to 10 days or freeze for up to 3 months. Defrost in the refrigerator overnight and proceed with Step 9.

1. *Seasonings:* In a small bowl, stir together salt, thyme, pepper, nutmeg, cloves and ginger. Set aside.

2. *Gratin:* In a large skillet, melt rendered duck fat over medium heat. Add pork belly, carrot and shallots; cook, stirring often, until vegetables are starting to soften, about 5 minutes. Increase heat to high and add mushrooms and chicken livers. Cook, stirring, for 2 minutes. Add bay leaf, Madeira, cream and garlic and bring to a boil. Boil for 1 minute (the livers should remain soft).

3. Remove *gratin* from heat and stir in seasonings. Sprinkle gelatin over mixture and let cool.

4. Discard bay leaf. Scrape cooled *gratin* mixture into food processor fitted with the metal blade. Pulse until coarsely chopped.

5. In a large bowl, mix ground pork with chopped *gratin*. In a small skillet over medium heat, cook a spoonful of the meat mixture for 4 to 5 minutes or until no longer pink. Taste and check the seasoning, keeping in mind that when cold, the terrine will taste less salty. If mixture is not salty enough, season to taste with additional salt.

6. Divide meat mixture between terrine molds. Lightly pack down and level mixture to ensure that there are no air pockets.

7. Place each mold in a separate sous vide pouch and seal. Immerse in preheated hot water bath and cook for 7 to 8 hours.

8. Remove pouches from hot water bath. Let stand at room temperature for 1 hour. Refrigerate overnight. (To make ahead, see Tips, at left.)

9. Open pouches and unmold terrines onto plates or small platters. Serve cold.

# Jarred Salmon "Loaf"

This recipe is basically a salmon terrine, and it can be the template for a terrine made from any firm, not-too-oily fish fillets. Cod and halibut are other delicious choices. Eggs are traditionally included in fish terrines, but because this terrine is cooked at a temperature lower than the one you need to cook eggs, I have omitted them. Instead I've substituted sodium caseinate, a milk protein sold in powdered form. While not essential, it results in a creamier terrine. Slice this dish and serve as you would any other terrine, or use it as a sandwich filling. Accuracy is paramount in this recipe, so the salmon and crème fraîche are measured by weight rather than volume. A digital scale with a tare button is a must for weighing these ingredients.

**MAKES 1 CUP (250 ML), OR 3 TO 4 SERVINGS**

## Tips

This recipe can easily be doubled or tripled. Use 1 jar for each recipe.

Salmon tails are great for this recipe because they have a slightly higher protein and lower fat content than the middle of the fish.

Sodium caseinate is available online at Modernist Pantry (modernistpantry.com).

▶ **Preheat hot water bath to 139°F (59.4°C)**
▶ **8 oz (250 mL) straight-sided canning jar, with lid**
▶ **Food processor**
▶ **Digital scale**

| | | |
|---|---|---|
| 4.2 oz | skinless salmon fillet (see Tips, at left) | 120 g |
| ¾ tsp | kosher salt | 3 mL |
| 1 tsp | sodium caseinate, optional | 5 mL |
| ¼ tsp | finely ground white pepper | 1 mL |
| ¼ tsp | hot pepper sauce, such as Tabasco | 1 mL |
| Pinch | ground nutmeg | Pinch |
| 3½ oz | crème fraîche | 100 g |
| 1 tbsp | finely chopped chives | 15 mL |
| 1 tbsp | finely chopped tarragon | 15 mL |

1. Inspect salmon carefully and remove any scales, bits of bone or skin. Cut into 1-inch (2.5 cm) cubes. Spread out on a plate and freeze for 30 minutes or until just starting to firm up. At the same time, place food processor work bowl and metal blade in freezer to chill along with the salmon.

## Tip

You can serve this "loaf" warm or cold. If you're serving it warm, plate it right after cooking, because reheating is difficult. If you're serving it cold, prepare through Step 4 and refrigerate up to 5 days if desired.

**2.** Remove salmon, work bowl and blade from freezer. In cold food processor fitted with the metal blade, pulse salmon 2 to 3 times, stopping motor and scraping down sides of bowl as necessary. Add salt, sodium caseinate (if using), pepper, hot sauce and nutmeg. Pulse 2 to 3 times, stopping motor and scraping down sides of bowl several times, as necessary. Gradually add crème fraîche, one-third at a time, pulsing 2 to 3 times between additions and stopping motor to scrape down sides of bowl as necessary. Add chives and tarragon; pulse 2 to 3 times to combine.

**3.** Using a rubber spatula, pack salmon mixture into canning jar, leaving $1/2$ inch (1 cm) headspace. Make sure you wipe the rim of the jar thoroughly to ensure a good seal. Add lid and turn just until snug. Immerse jar in hot water bath and cook for 2 hours.

**4.** Remove jar from hot water bath and let cool slightly, about 15 minutes. If serving cold, transfer to an ice bath for 30 minutes.

**5.** To serve, open jar and run a slender knife around edges. Invert jar over a plate and lightly tap bottom — the salmon should slide onto the plate. Using a sharp knife, slice into wedges or $1/2$-inch (1 cm) vertical or horizontal slices.

# Simple Sausages

Sausages are one of the easiest things to cook sous vide. They come already seasoned, and many varieties are available at the supermarket. Those that are already vacuum-sealed can go straight into your hot water bath to cook. If you are buying fresh sausages at a butcher shop, ask your butcher to vacuum-seal them in pouches (without any butcher paper) in the quantity you desire. Since sausages contain ground meat (often pork), they need to be pasteurized. This is a very simple recipe — just one ingredient!

---

**MAKES
4 SAUSAGES**

Freezer Bag Friendly

## Tips

You can adjust the number of sausages to suit your needs. Just make sure they are not overlapping, to ensure even cooking.

You can substitute small resealable plastic freezer bags for the sous vide pouch. Package sausages in pairs and seal.

*To make ahead:* Prepare through Step 1. Remove pouch from hot water bath, transfer to an ice bath and chill for 30 minutes. Refrigerate sealed pouch for up to 5 days or freeze for up to 3 months. Defrost in the refrigerator overnight, if needed. Open bag and transfer sausage to a plate lined with paper towels. Let stand at room temperature for 5 minutes. Pat dry on both sides with paper towels before proceeding with Step 3.

▸ **Preheat hot water bath to 140°F (60°C)**
▸ **Sous vide pouch**

| 4 | fresh sausages, such as Italian (sweet or hot), garlic or breakfast | 4 |
| | Oil | |

1. Place sausages in a single layer in sous vide pouch and seal (see Tips, at left). Immerse in preheated hot water bath and cook for 2 hours. (To make ahead, see Tips, at left.)

2. Remove pouch from hot water bath. Open pouch and remove sausages. Pat dry with paper towels. Let stand at room temperature for 10 to 20 minutes or until slightly cooled.

3. Meanwhile, preheat grill to High, preheat broiler or place a large skillet over high heat.

4. Lightly brush sausages with oil. Place sausages on grill, on a baking sheet or in skillet. Grill, broil or pan-fry sausages, turning often, until casings are browned and crisp, about 4 to 5 minutes.

---

## Variation

Prepare the sausages through Step 2 and then slice them to add to stews or pasta sauces. You may find the casings tough if they haven't been browned. Remove them after Step 2, if desired.

---

### Cooking Sausages from Frozen

Sausages, like many other meats, can be cooked directly from frozen. Immerse the sausage pouch in a preheated hot water bath and add 30 minutes to the original cooking time.

---

Fresh Cod with Chorizo Vinaigrette (page 244)

Octopus Confit Salad with Avocado, Kale and Ponzu Vinaigrette (page 257)

Catalan Giant Meatballs (page 280)

Barigoule of Artichokes (page 316)

Aloo Gobi (page 320)

Perfect Poached Egg (page 325)

Chawanmushi (page 331)

Crème Brûlée (page 336)

# Vegetables

# Vegetables

## The Basics

Cooking vegetables is quite different from cooking meat and fish sous vide. Vegetables contain starch and pectin, rather than protein, which both need higher temperatures than meat or eggs to cook. Starches begin this transformation at a temperature of 175°F (79.4°C). Pectin, found in non-starchy vegetables such as carrots and asparagus, transforms from raw to cooked at slightly higher temperatures.

The second major difference is that vegetables are less dense than meat, and frequently less dense than water. This means that some of them are likely to float in the hot water bath, resulting in uneven cooking. Adding to this problem, vegetables are not as evenly shaped as pieces of meat or fish, which makes it difficult to remove air from the bag using the water displacement method. If the vegetable is to be cooked in liquid within the bag, the liquid will displace the air, making it easier to achieve a bag that will stay immersed in the hot water bath.

Vegetables cooked sous vide have more intense flavor and retain more nutrients, because neither is washed away by the water they are cooking in. Green vegetables will not be as bright as they are when blanched in boiling water, because the chlorophyll-damaging acids and enzymes in their cells will not be diluted.

## Packaging

Using a home sealer is the best strategy for sealing and cooking vegetables that are to be cooked dry or with just a small amount of butter or liquid. With more than about 2 tsp (10 mL) of liquid you need a different approach. To avoid sucking the liquid into your sealer, you can either freeze the liquid if you can plan ahead, or use a pouch about 8 inches (20 cm) longer than its contents. To use this "long pouch" method, bring your sealer up to the edge of the counter, place the pouch opening in the sealer with the bag hanging down off the counter, and seal, using the Moist or Delicate/Gentle setting. (If your sealer doesn't have a Delicate or Gentle setting, press Seal as soon as you see the pouch tighten around the food.) The air will be evacuated from the pouch and the bag will be sealed before the liquid can reach the sealing mechanism. A more costly option that avoids all these complications is to use a chamber vacuum sealer (see page 14).

Vegetables that are soft and malleable, such as the eggplant in Caponata (page 306), or those that are cooked in plenty of liquid can be placed in resealable freezer bags, with one caveat — these bags are not designed for cooking and have been known to fail when immersed in high-temperature water. While this has never happened to me, I try not to cook vegetables in freezer bags at temperatures higher than 185°F (85°C). When I must, then I use a larger bag than necessary and keep the zip closure out of the water. Make sure that you use the heaviest-gauge bags you can find, and don't reuse them, just for extra security. Also see "Weigh Down Those Bags" on page 317.

# White Asparagus

White asparagus is a special treat and a culinary sign of spring throughout Europe. Peru produces large quantities for the North American market, and it can be very good. The small amount of sugar in the recipe guards against any bitterness. This asparagus is also delicious with Hollandaise Sauce (page 332). I like to serve it as an appetizer because it is so special, but it will also turn Veal Tenderloin with Exotic Mushroom Sauce (page 46) into a black-tie dinner.

**MAKES 2 SERVINGS**

Freezer Bag Friendly

## Tips

You can easily double this recipe.

The bottom half of asparagus tends to have a stringy exterior. Peeling is essential for white asparagus because it allows the whole spear to be tender from end to end.

*To make ahead:* Prepare through Step 2. Chill bag in an ice bath for 20 minutes, then refrigerate for up to 4 days. Reheat in hot water bath, if desired, at 130°F (54.4°C) for 15 minutes, then proceed with Step 3.

▸ **Preheat hot water bath to 194°F (90°C)**
▸ **Large resealable freezer bag**

| | | |
|---|---|---|
| ½ tsp | kosher salt | 2 mL |
| ½ tsp | granulated sugar | 2 mL |
| 1 cup | water | 250 mL |
| ½ lb | white asparagus, trimmed and peeled | 225 g |

1. In a small saucepan over low heat (or in a microwave), dissolve salt and sugar in water. Transfer asparagus and resulting brine to freezer bag and seal.

2. Immerse bag in preheated hot water bath. Cook for 45 to 60 minutes, depending on thickness and desired doneness (I find white asparagus is best when fully cooked and tender). Check pouch after 45 minutes, giving asparagus a squeeze to check doneness. Be careful when handling the bag — you are cooking at a high temperature, so it will be hot. Remove bag from hot water bath. (To make ahead, see Tips, at left.)

3. Open bag and remove asparagus, discarding liquid. Serve immediately.

# White Asparagus with Ricotta

After cooking white asparagus in milk, you can turn the milk into ricotta, thus capturing the flavor that would normally be lost in water. I use it as a base for saucing the asparagus, flavoring it with a little pesto. You can just as easily stir in some freshly chopped herbs instead.

---

**MAKES
2 PORTIONS**

Freezer Bag Friendly

## Tips

You can easily double this recipe.

Fresh chives and mint, in combination or alone, make a great substitute for the pesto. Chop them and mix in with the ricotta. Add a big pinch of salt and some freshly ground pepper to adjust the seasoning.

---

▶ **Preheat hot water bath to 194°F (90°C)**
▶ **Large resealable freezer bag**
▶ **Small fine-mesh sieve**

| | | |
|---|---|---|
| ½ tsp | kosher salt | 2 mL |
| ½ tsp | granulated sugar | 2 mL |
| 1 cup | whole milk | 250 mL |
| ½ lb | white asparagus, trimmed and peeled (peelings reserved) | 225 g |
| 1 to 2 tbsp | plain yogurt | 15 to 30 mL |
| 1 tbsp | pesto (store-bought or homemade; see Tips, at right) | 15 mL |

1. In a small saucepan over low heat (or in a microwave), dissolve salt and sugar in milk. Transfer asparagus, asparagus peelings and milk to freezer bag and seal.

2. Immerse bag in preheated hot water bath. Cook for 45 to 60 minutes, depending on thickness and desired doneness (I find white asparagus is best when fully cooked and tender). Check pouch after 45 minutes, giving asparagus a squeeze to check doneness. Be careful when handling the bag — you are cooking at a high temperature, so it will be hot. Remove bag from hot water bath. (To make ahead, see Tips, at right.)

3. Drain liquid from asparagus into a small saucepan, discarding peelings. Transfer asparagus to a plate; cover with foil and a folded kitchen towel to keep warm while preparing the sauce.

## Tips

I designed this recipe to be made using traditional basil pesto, but if you are feeling adventurous, try it with Pistachio Mint Pesto (page 369).

*To make ahead:* Prepare through Step 2. Chill bag in an ice bath for 30 minutes, then transfer to the refrigerator for up to 4 days. Reheat asparagus in hot water bath at 160°F (71.1°C) for 5 minutes, then proceed with Step 3.

**4.** To prepare the sauce, stir 1 tbsp (15 mL) yogurt into saucepan and bring to a boil over medium-high heat. The milk should separate. If it doesn't, stir in a little more yogurt and continue cooking. Pour liquid through fine-mesh sieve and allow to drain — do not press on solids, as you want the ricotta to stay moist. Discard liquid. Transfer ricotta to a small bowl and stir in pesto.

**5.** Place asparagus on warm plates, garnish with ricotta and serve immediately. The dish will be only slightly warm, which is intended (and preferred).

### Don't Forgot to Peel

The bottom half of asparagus tends to have a stringy exterior. Peeling allows the whole spear to be tender from end to end, which is essential for white asparagus.

# Asparagus Plain and Simple

The two highly seasonal vegetables that I most anticipate each year are tomatoes, to serve raw in late summer, and asparagus, simply prepared in the spring. As the season progresses I look for more exotic preparations, but for the first few asparagus feeds I want it plain and simple. The color will not be as bright as when you boil the asparagus, but the intensity of flavor more than makes up for it.

## Tips

You can easily double this recipe. Just make sure you arrange the spears in one layer, or use two pouches if necessary.

The bottom half of asparagus tends to have a stringy exterior. Peeling allows the whole spear to be tender from end to end.

If you only have unsalted butter on hand or are using olive oil, add a big pinch of salt and proceed with the recipe.

Doneness of asparagus is highly subjective and also takes a little practice when cooking sous vide. I find that underdone asparagus has no flavor, so you have to catch it at that "sweet spot." When you squeeze the asparagus through the pouch, it should be yielding but not soft.

▸ **Preheat hot water bath to 185°F (85°C)**
▸ **Sous vide pouch**

| | | |
|---|---|---|
| ½ lb | green asparagus, trimmed and peeled (see Tips, at left) | 225 g |
| 1 tbsp | butter, preferably salted, or olive oil (see Tips, at left) | 15 mL |

1. In a sous vide pouch, arrange the asparagus spears in one layer. Add the butter in one piece and seal.

2. Immerse pouch in preheated hot water bath. Cook thin spears for 15 to 30 minutes and thick spears for 30 to 45 minutes, depending on desired doneness. Squeeze asparagus through the bag to check (see Tips, at left) — be careful while handling hot pouch. Remove pouch from hot water bath. (To make ahead, see Tips, at right.)

3. Serve immediately or chill in an ice bath for 20 minutes, then transfer to the refrigerator and serve cold, if desired.

## Variation

**Asparagus with Gorgonzola:** If you like blue cheese, try replacing the butter with 1 tbsp (15 mL) Gorgonzola. Serve hot.

## Tips

*To make ahead:* Prepare through Step 2. Chill pouch in an ice bath for 30 minutes, then refrigerate for up to 3 to 4 days. Serve cold.

If serving the asparagus cold, substitute olive or vegetable oil for the butter. Flavored oils such as lemon-infused olive oil or nut oils can be interesting here.

## Timing Asparagus and Sauce

Asparagus is also delicious with Hollandaise Sauce (page 332) or, for a lighter version, with Egg and Lemon Sauce (page 334). Cook the asparagus first and set it aside on the counter while making the sauce. Ten minutes before the sauce has finished cooking, return the asparagus pouch or bag to the water bath to reheat. Open pouch and bag(s) and serve warm.

## Cooking Asparagus in a Freezer Bag

To cook the asparagus in a resealable freezer bag, I recommend adding a light brine; otherwise the asparagus will float and not cook evenly. To make the brine, dissolve ¼ tsp (1 mL) kosher salt in ½ cup (125 mL) water; a microwave oven works well, or you can heat it in a saucepan over low heat. Transfer spears and brine to bag and proceed with the recipe, adding 5 minutes to the cooking time if the brine isn't hot when it goes into the water bath. Drain asparagus and discard brine. Toss asparagus in melted unsalted butter in a bowl or skillet and serve.

# Savoy Cabbage with Chestnuts

I developed this hearty side dish for venison, but it also makes an excellent accompaniment for pork or game birds such as squab and pheasant.

---

**MAKES
4 SERVINGS**

Freezer Bag Friendly

## Tips

You can easily halve or double this recipe.

Regular green cabbage can be substituted for the savoy. Slice it extremely finely, using a mandoline or similar slicing device, and cook for 15 minutes longer.

Pre-peeled chestnuts in small pouches have become increasingly available and are a great time-saver. Just make sure they are unsweetened.

*To make ahead:* Prepare through Step 2. Chill bag in an ice bath for 30 minutes, then refrigerate for up to 5 days. Reheat cabbage in hot water bath at 130°F (54.4°C) for 30 minutes, then proceed with Step 3.

▸ **Preheat hot water bath to 200°F (93.3°C)**
▸ **Large resealable freezer bag**

| | | |
|---|---|---|
| 4 cups | finely sliced savoy cabbage leaves, large ribs removed (about ½ medium cabbage; see Tips, at left) | 1 L |
| 12 | chestnuts, roasted and peeled (see Tips, at left) | 12 |
| 1 cup | low-sodium ready-to-use chicken broth | 250 mL |
| 2 tbsp | finely chopped shallots | 30 mL |
| 1 tbsp | unsalted butter | 15 mL |
| ½ tsp | freshly ground black pepper | 2 mL |
| ½ tsp | freshly ground caraway seeds | 2 mL |
| ½ tsp | kosher salt | 2 mL |

1. In this order, place cabbage, chestnuts, broth, shallots, butter, pepper, ground caraway seed and salt in freezer bag (make sure the salt goes in last). Let stand for 30 minutes, until cabbage is slightly wilted.

2. Roll up bag to expel as much air as possible and seal. Immerse bag in preheated water bath and cook for 30 minutes, checking bag after 15 minutes. If it has expanded with air, carefully remove bag, remove air using the water displacement method, and reseal. Return bag to hot water bath and cook for 15 minutes more. Remove bag from bath. (To make ahead, see Tips, at left.)

3. Cut open bag and strain liquid into a medium non-reactive skillet. Transfer cabbage mixture to a warm bowl.

4. Over high heat, boil liquid in skillet until reduced to 2 tbsp (30 mL). Pour over cabbage mixture and serve.

# Buttery New Potatoes

Cooking new potatoes sous vide offers no culinary advantage. However, cooked potatoes sealed in a pouch are very handy to take to a vacation home or a barbecue. You can serve these straight from the pouch or reheat them on the grill or in the oven.

## MAKES 4 SERVINGS

## Tips

You can easily halve or double this recipe.

If your potatoes are on the larger side, cut them in half.

If using rosemary, I prefer to keep the leaves on the sprigs so they can easily be removed after the cooking process.

If you plan to serve the potatoes cold or at room temperature, use olive oil rather than butter.

Other aromatics, such as whole garlic cloves, diced double-smoked bacon or saffron, can be added to the pouch for additional flavor.

*To make ahead:* Prepare through Step 2. Remove pouch and chill in an ice bath for 20 minutes, then refrigerate for up to 6 days. Reheat potatoes in hot water bath, if desired, at 140°F (60°C) for 30 minutes, then proceed with Step 3.

▶ **Preheat hot water bath to 190°F (87.8°C)**
▶ **Sous vide pouch**

| | | |
|---|---|---|
| 1 lb | medium new potatoes | 450 g |
| 3 tbsp | butter, melted, or olive oil (see Tips, at left) | 45 mL |
| 1 tsp | kosher salt | 5 mL |
| ½ tsp | freshly ground black pepper | 2 mL |
| | Fresh herbs such as rosemary, dill, parsley or chives, optional (see Tips, at left) | |

1. In a medium bowl, toss potatoes with butter, salt and pepper. Add herbs, if using.
2. Transfer potatoes to pouch, arrange in one layer and seal. Immerse in preheated water bath and cook for 60 to 70 minutes — cooking time will be determined by size and variety of potatoes. Remove pouch from hot water bath. (To make ahead, see Tips, at left.)
3. Open and discard herbs, if desired. Serve immediately.

### Clean Your Potatoes

New potatoes are small and can be difficult to scrub, but you need to do that thoroughly, under running water, to prevent them from tasting like the dirt clinging to them.

# Duck-Fat Potato Wedges to Make You Crazy

This recipe relies on a technique used by Heston Blumenthal, a world-famous chef, to create the best fried potatoes you've ever tasted. Normally I peel potatoes to make french fries, but here the skin adds a nice texture. Use older Yukon Gold or other yellow-fleshed potatoes if you can, although Kennebec potatoes are also a good option.

---

**MAKES 2 SERVINGS**

Freezer Bag Friendly

## Tips

You can easily double or triple this recipe. If you double it, you don't have to double the duck fat — use the amount called for and fry the potatoes in 2 batches. If you triple the recipe, increase the duck fat to 2 cups (500 mL), use a larger pan and fry the potatoes in 2 batches.

This is a simple recipe, so ingredient quality is paramount. That means you'll have to choose different potato varieties at different times of the year, depending on what's in season and what looks good.

▶ **Preheat hot water bath to 203°F (95°C)**
▶ **Large resealable freezer bag**
▶ **Candy/deep-fry, instant-read or infrared thermometer**
▶ **Wire skimmer (optional)**

| | | |
|---|---|---|
| 4 cups | warm water | 1 L |
| 4 tsp | kosher salt | 20 mL |
| 1 lb | yellow-fleshed potatoes (see Tips, at left), each cut lengthwise into 8 to 12 wedges | 450 g |
| 1½ cups | rendered duck fat (see Tips, at left) | 375 mL |
| | Salt or Brava Sauce (page 371), optional | |

1. In a medium bowl, stir salt into water until dissolved.

2. Place potatoes in freezer bag, top with brine and seal. Immerse in preheated water bath and cook for 30 minutes.

3. Remove bag from hot water bath. Drain potatoes in a colander and pat dry. Discard liquid. Let potatoes dry completely. (To make ahead, see Tips, at right.)

4. In a large, deep skillet or Dutch oven, heat duck fat over medium heat until thermometer reads 350°F (177°C). Using wire skimmer or a slotted spoon, lower potatoes into fat, increasing heat as necessary to maintain temperature. Fry, turning often, for 4 to 5 minutes or until potatoes are golden brown and crisp.

5. Using skimmer or slotted spoon, transfer potatoes to a plate lined with paper towels and let drain. Salt lightly or serve with brava sauce.

## Tips

The potatoes need to dry well before frying, to ensure a golden, crispy finish. Chef Blumenthal dries them in a chamber vacuum sealer, but I've found a simple method that works well for small quantities: simply place the potatoes on a rack in front of a small fan and leave them there for 1 hour, turning occasionally.

*To make ahead:* Prepare through Step 3. Transfer dry potatoes to a resealable freezer bag or cover and refrigerate for up to 3 days. The key to the potatoes' texture is their dryness, so repeat the drying step before you fry the potatoes to ensure that any moisture has dissipated. Proceed with Step 4.

You can reuse the fat once with good results if you don't heat it to more than 400°F (200°C). Strain and refrigerate, if possible, between uses.

### Buying Duck Fat

You can buy duck fat from specialty purveyors such as D'Artagnan (www.dartagnan.com) or render your own. Both will work fine. If you want to branch out, try a blend of pork fat and vegetable oil; in Belgium, horse fat is the traditional choice. Corn or sunflower oil also works well but doesn't taste as special as duck fat. Avoid canola oil, which gives potatoes an unpleasant flavor.

### Frying Safety

Great care must be exercised when frying in a pot with this amount of oil. If you have a deep-fryer, I suggest that you use it for this recipe. In a pot, a thermometer with a digital timer and a remote probe is handy and adds an element of safety. Set the temperature alert to the temperature specified in the recipe. That way, the alarm will ring when the temperature is reached.

# Georgian-Style Green Beans with Lamb

Georgians love beans, both green and dried. Combining a small amount of meat with vegetables is a common practice in the Caucasus. Serve this dish topped with an egg (such as Japanese Hot-Spring Egg, page 326) and some rice and you'll have a healthy, delicious and inexpensive dinner. Georgians like their beans tender. If you prefer al dente, reduce the cooking time to 20 minutes.

**MAKE 2 TO 3 SERVINGS**

Freezer Bag Friendly

## Tips

You can easily halve or double this recipe. If doubling, use 2 bags.

For more information on grinding your own meat, see page 272.

▶ **Preheat hot water bath to 190°F (87.8C)**
▶ **Meat grinder (optional)**
▶ **Small resealable freezer bag**

| | | |
|---|---|---|
| 5 oz | ground lamb or chilled boneless lamb shoulder, cubed (see Tips, at left) | 140 g |
| ½ cup | white or cremini mushrooms, finely chopped if necessary (optional) | 125 mL |
| 1½ tbsp | olive oil (see box, at right) | 22 mL |
| ½ cup | finely chopped onion | 125 mL |
| 1 tbsp | finely chopped garlic | 15 mL |
| 2 tsp | kosher salt | 10 mL |
| ¼ tsp | sweet Hungarian paprika | 1 mL |
| Pinch | ground cinnamon | Pinch |
| Pinch | ground cumin | Pinch |
| 1 cup | whole canned tomatoes, with juice | 250 mL |
| 1 lb | green beans, trimmed | 450 g |
| | Coarsely chopped fresh flat-leaf (Italian) parsley or cilantro | |

1. If grinding the lamb yourself, put chilled meat through grinder fitted with the coarse cutting plate. If you are adding mushrooms, you can put them through the grinder after the lamb.

## Tip

*To make ahead:* Prepare through Step 4. Remove bag from hot water bath and chill in an ice bath for 20 minutes, then refrigerate for up to 6 days. Reheat in hot water bath at 125°F (51.7°C) for 30 minutes, then proceed with Step 5.

**2.** In a medium skillet, heat oil over medium heat. Cook onion, stirring, until just starting to brown, about 10 minutes. Increase heat to high and add lamb; cook, stirring frequently to break it up, until meat starts to brown, about 10 minutes. Add garlic, salt, paprika, cinnamon and cumin. Cook, stirring occasionally, for 3 to 4 minutes. Add tomatoes, reduce heat to medium and boil gently, stirring occasionally to break up tomatoes, for 15 minutes. Set aside to cool slightly.

**3.** Add beans to freezer bag. Add lamb mixture and seal.

**4.** Immerse bag in preheated water bath and cook for 70 to 80 minutes. (To make ahead, see Tip, at left).

**5.** Remove bag from hot water bath and let stand for 5 to 10 minutes. Open bag and serve contents warm, garnished with parsley or cilantro.

---

### Sunflower Oil

In Georgia, sunflower oil would be used for cooking and as a condiment. If you can find cold-pressed sunflower oil, use it in place of the olive oil in all Georgian dishes.

# Leeks with Goat Cheese

This is as satisfying as it is simple. Make sure you use the best olive oil available and mop it up with a crusty sourdough loaf, which brings these elements together. I like my leeks fully cooked and very tender, but shorten the time to 40 minutes if you prefer them al dente. This dish can be enjoyed warm or at room temperature.

---

> MAKES
> 4 APPETIZER
> OR 8 SMALL-
> BITE SERVINGS

## Tips

You can easily halve or double this recipe.

A chamber vacuum sealer is particularly good for this recipe because it helps force the cheese into the leeks. A home sealer also works well.

*To make ahead:* Prepare through Step 3. Chill pouch in an ice bath for 10 minutes, then refrigerate for up to 5 days or freeze for up to 3 months. To reheat from refrigerator temperature, preheat hot water bath to 130°F (54.4°C) and immerse pouch for 20 minutes, then proceed with Step 4.

▸ **Preheat hot water bath to 190°F (87.8°C)**
▸ **Sous vide pouch**

| 4 | medium-large leeks, dark leaves removed | 4 |
| ½ cup | soft goat cheese | 125 mL |
| | Coarsely ground black pepper | |
| | French-style sourdough loaf | |
| | Salt | |
| | Extra virgin olive oil | |

1. Split washed leeks lengthwise, keeping the halves intact by not cutting off the root ends (trim off any long roots and dirt). Drain on paper towels.

2. Trim tops of leeks so they are tidy and will fit into pouch. On a cutting board, arrange split leeks flat side up. Spread 1 tbsp (15 mL) goat cheese on each side. Sprinkle with pepper. Reassemble leeks by pushing them together like a sandwich.

3. Arrange leeks in one layer in sous vide pouch and seal. Immerse in preheated water bath and cook for 50 to 60 minutes. (To make ahead, see Tips, at left.)

4. Remove pouch from hot water bath and let stand for 15 minutes.

5. Open pouch and serve one leek per person, as an appetizer with crusty bread or cut into rounds and served on toast as canapés. Salt lightly and liberally drizzle with olive oil.

# Cashew Portobello Mushrooms

This is an interesting and versatile vegan recipe that's an umami bomb of flavor. Serve as canapés or as appetizer salads, surrounded by greens dressed in a light vinaigrette.

## Tips

You can easily halve or double this recipe.

If you don't have homemade black garlic, you can find the Korean version at specialty markets or well-stocked grocery stores.

*To make ahead:* Prepare through Step 3. Chill pouch in an ice bath for 10 minutes, then refrigerate for up to 4 days or freeze for up to 3 months. Defrost for 1 hour at room temperature, if necessary, then proceed with Step 4.

Here's an interesting fact: one whole portobello mushroom cap prepared with this recipe yields about 16 grams of protein — more than 2 eggs provide.

▶ **Preheat hot water bath to 185°F (85°C)**
▶ **Sous vide pouch**
▶ **Mini food processor or mini chopper**

| | | |
|---|---|---|
| 2 | portobello mushrooms, caps about 4 inches (10 cm) in diameter | 2 |
| 6 tbsp | nutritional yeast | 90 mL |
| ¼ cup | unsalted, unsweetened cashew butter | 60 mL |
| 2 tbsp | white miso paste | 30 mL |
| 2 tbsp | tahini | 30 mL |
| ½ tsp | rubbed dried marjoram | 2 mL |
| 4 | black garlic cloves (store-bought or homemade, see page 388), optional | 4 |

1. Remove stems from mushrooms and discard or reserve for another use. With a spoon, scrape out gills on underside of mushroom caps and discard.

2. In food processor fitted with the metal blade, combine nutritional yeast, cashew butter, miso paste, tahini, marjoram and black garlic, if using. Process to a smooth paste.

3. With a palette knife or butter spreader, spread paste evenly on undersides of mushroom caps. Arrange mushrooms in one layer in sous vide pouch and seal. Immerse pouch in preheated water bath and cook for 30 to 40 minutes. Remove pouch from hot water bath. (To make ahead, see Tips, at left.)

4. Open pouch and place mushrooms, rounded side down, on paper towels to drain; discard liquid from pouch.

5. Preheat broiler.

6. Arrange mushrooms, rounded side down, on a baking sheet. Broil until cashew butter mixture starts to brown, about 2 to 3 minutes.

7. Serve hot or let cool slightly. Cut each into 6 wedges and serve as an appetizer or pass around as canapés.

# Turbo Broccoli

My assistant introduced me to nutritional yeast. I know the name doesn't conjure up visions of yumminess, but you will be surprised when you try it. The yeast in the Umami Butter amplifies the flavor of vegetables and adds a slightly cheesy tang. Turbocharged!

| MAKES |
| :---: |
| **MAKES 2 SERVINGS** |

## Tip

You can easily halve or double this recipe. If doubling, use 2 pouches.

▶ **Preheat hot water bath to 185°F (85°C)**
▶ **Sous vide pouch**

| 1 | large head broccoli with stem, or 2 smaller heads | 1 |
| 2 tbsp | Umami Butter (page 367) or salted butter | 30 mL |

1. With a paring knife or vegetable peeler, peel stem of broccoli up to the head. Slice head and stalk in half lengthwise. If using smaller heads, just peel stems.

2. Arrange broccoli in sous vide pouch, alternating directions to make a tidy package. Add umami butter to pouch and seal.

3. Immerse pouch in preheated water bath and cook for 30 to 35 minutes. If pouch floats, weigh it down with a heavy object such as a small cast-iron skillet.

4. Remove pouch from hot water bath. Open pouch and serve broccoli on warm plates. Drizzle some or all of the liquid overtop.

# Corn on the Cob

Like most vegetables, corn has more flavor when cooked sous vide. The umami butter adds an extra layer of intensity.

Freezer Bag Friendly

## Tips

You can easily halve or double this recipe. If doubling, use 2 pouches.

Kimchi Butter (page 368) is also great on corn. Substitute the same amount for the umami butter.

To use freezer bags for this recipe, slip 2 or 3 stainless-steel spoons into the bag along with the corn. They will keep the bags from floating. See "Weigh Down Those Bags" (page 317) for more details.

▶ **Preheat hot water bath to 185°F (85°C)**
▶ **Sous vide pouch**

| 1½ tbsp | Umami Butter (page 367) or salted butter, softened | 22 mL |
| 2 | ears of corn, shucked, silk removed | 2 |

1. With a palette knife or a rubber spatula, spread butter evenly over corn.
2. Place corn in sous vide pouch in a single layer and seal.
3. Immerse pouch in preheated hot water bath and cook for 20 minutes. If pouch floats, weigh down with a heavy object such as a small cast-iron skillet.
4. Remove pouch from hot water bath. Open pouch and serve corn warm. Drizzle liquid from pouch overtop, if desired.

# Caponata

Eggplant is very popular around the Mediterranean. Here's a recipe that I like from Sicily. Served hot, it's terrific with lamb. At room temperature it's fabulous as part of a mezze platter. Caponata is also good in sandwiches and can even be tossed with pasta or put in omelets.

## Tips

You can easily double this recipe. Use 2 bags to ensure even cooking.

I use Japanese eggplants because they cook quickly and are never bitter. Substitute one Italian eggplant in their place if you wish. Cut into ¾-inch (2 cm) dice and give it a little longer frying time, about 10 minutes.

▶ **Preheat hot water bath to 194°F (90°C)**
▶ **Large resealable freezer bag**
▶ **Large nonstick skillet**

| | | |
|---|---|---|
| 2 tbsp | cornstarch | 30 mL |
| 2 tsp | kosher salt | 10 mL |
| 2 | Japanese eggplants, cut into ¾-inch (2 cm) dice (see Tips, at left) | 2 |
| ¼ cup | olive oil | 60 mL |
| 2 tbsp | extra virgin olive oil | 30 mL |
| 1 cup | finely chopped onion | 250 mL |
| 1 cup | coarsely chopped celery | 250 mL |
| 1 tbsp | finely chopped garlic | 15 mL |
| 1 | plum (Roma) tomato, peeled and seeded, cut into ½-inch (1 cm) dice | 1 |
| 1 | red or yellow bell pepper, cut into ½-inch (1 cm) dice | 1 |
| 2 tbsp | brined capers, drained | 30 mL |
| 2 tbsp | red wine vinegar | 30 mL |
| 1 tbsp | tomato paste | 15 mL |
| 1 tbsp | granulated sugar | 15 mL |
| 1 tsp | freshly ground black pepper | 5 mL |
| | Toasted pine nuts, optional | |
| | Flat-leaf (Italian) parsley, coarsely chopped, optional | |
| | Whole anchovy fillets, drained, optional | |

**1.** In a medium bowl, combine cornstarch and salt. Add eggplant and toss to coat. Let stand for 3 to 4 minutes, then toss again.

## Tips

Because of the high temperature involved, I cook the caponata with the zip closure of the bag hanging outside the water. This prevents the risk of bag failure.

*To make ahead:* Prepare through Step 4. Chill bag in an ice bath for 30 minutes, then refrigerate for up to 6 days or freeze for up to 3 months. To reheat from refrigerator temperature, preheat hot water bath to 130°F (54.4°C) and immerse pouch for 20 minutes, then proceed with Step 5.

Olives are frequently added to caponata. After cooking, add up to ½ cup (125 mL) Gaeta or Cerignola olives. Don't forget to warn your guests about the pits!

**2.** In a large nonstick skillet, heat olive oil over high heat. When oil is hot, add eggplant and cook, stirring occasionally, until tender but not collapsing, about 7 to 8 minutes (cook in batches if necessary). Transfer to a plate lined with paper towels to drain.

**3.** Meanwhile, in a medium skillet over medium heat, heat extra virgin olive oil. Add onion and cook, stirring occasionally, until it starts to soften, about 5 minutes. Add celery and garlic; cook, stirring, until celery is cooked but still crunchy, about 4 to 5 minutes. Remove from heat.

**4.** Transfer eggplant, celery-onion mixture, tomato, bell pepper, capers, vinegar, tomato paste, sugar and pepper to freezer bag and seal. Immerse bag (see Tips, at left) in preheated water bath and cook for 1 hour. (To make ahead, see Tips, at left.)

**5.** Remove bag from hot water bath and let cool briefly.

**6.** Open bag and serve caponata warm. Garnish with pine nuts, parsley and/or anchovies, if desired.

All the vegetables in the following recipes are flavored in some way. They are great on their own or, after cooking them separately, you can warm them together as a medley, with each retaining its own distinctive taste. Because most of the recipes contain a small amount of liquid and the vegetables are firm and oddly shaped, they are hard to seal in freezer bags. Use a chamber vacuum sealer if possible, or refer to "Packaging" on page 290 to learn how to seal pouches containing small amounts of liquid with a conventional home sealing unit.

# Okra with Preserved Lemon

Okra is an underappreciated vegetable that people often complain is slimy. If you keep the okra whole, you can avoid this texture and get a wonderful flavor somewhere between asparagus and green beans. I like this recipe as a side with lamb, but it's also great with Filipino Pork Belly Adobo (page 120).

**MAKES 4 TO 6 SERVINGS**

## Tips

You can easily halve or double this recipe.

*To make ahead:* Prepare through Step 4. Chill pouch in an ice bath for 20 minutes, then refrigerate for up to 5 days. Preheat hot water bath to 150°F (65.6°C) and immerse pouch for 15 minutes, then proceed with Step 5.

▷ **Preheat hot water bath to 185°F (85°C)**
▷ **Sous vide pouch**

| | | |
|---|---|---|
| ¼ | preserved lemon (store-bought or homemade, page 386) | ¼ |
| 24 | whole okra pods | 24 |
| ½ tsp | freshly ground black pepper | 2 mL |

1. Using your fingers, remove and discard flesh of preserved lemon. Rinse skin and chop finely.

2. Trim about ¼ inch (0.5 cm) off each okra stem, without cutting into body of vegetable.

3. In a large bowl, toss okra with lemon and pepper. Transfer to pouch, arranging in neat rows so that they won't deform while cooking.

4. Immerse pouch in preheated hot water bath and cook for 30 minutes. (To make ahead, see Tips, at left.)

5. Remove pouch from hot water bath. Open and serve immediately.

# Saffron Cauliflower with Sultanas

This cauliflower comes out a bright yellow, and sous vide cooking really amplifies its taste. I like this dish warm with lamb or at room temperature as part of a vegetable antipasto. Serve hot or cold, as you prefer.

**MAKES 4 TO 6 SERVINGS**

## Tips

You can easily double this recipe.

A chamber vacuum sealer is particularly good for this recipe because it helps force the saffron liquid into the cauliflower. A home sealer also works well.

*To make ahead:* Prepare through Step 3. Chill pouch in an ice-water bath for 20 minutes, then refrigerate for up to 6 days. To reheat from refrigerator temperature, preheat hot water bath to 130°F (54.4°C) and immerse pouch for 30 minutes, then proceed with Step 4.

The liquid from the bag can be added to the water or broth used for cooking rice, if desired.

▶ **Preheat hot water bath to 185°F (85°C)**
▶ **Sous vide pouch**

| | | |
|---|---|---|
| 2 tbsp | unseasoned rice vinegar | 30 mL |
| 1 tbsp | olive oil | 15 mL |
| 1½ tsp | Saffron Salt (page 351) | 7 mL |
| 3 tbsp | sultana raisins | 45 mL |
| ½ tsp | ground white pepper | 2 mL |
| 1 | medium cauliflower, cut into florets, stems cut into 1-inch (2.5 cm) dice | 1 |
| | Salt | |
| | Chopped flat-leaf (Italian) parsley, optional | |

1. In a small saucepan over low heat, combine rice vinegar and olive oil and heat (or use a bowl in the microwave). Remove from heat and whisk in saffron salt until dissolved. Stir in raisins and white pepper.

2. In a medium bowl, combine raisin mixture and cauliflower. Toss to coat cauliflower. Place in pouch and seal, using the "long pouch" method (page 290).

3. Immerse pouch in preheated water bath and cook for 45 minutes. (To make ahead, see Tips, at left.)

4. Remove pouch from hot water bath. Open pouch and drain liquid (see Tips, at left). Add salt to taste and garnish with parsley, if desired. To serve cold, first chill in an ice bath for 20 minutes.

## Variation

**Cauliflower with Capers:** Omit rice vinegar, saffron salt and raisins. Drain 2 tbsp (30 mL) brined capers (do not rinse), reserving 2 tbsp (30 mL) brine. Add capers and brine to 1 tbsp (15 mL) olive oil and ½ tsp (2 mL) ground white pepper. Proceed with Step 2, substituting capers for raisins.

# Carrots with Orange and Ginger

This is an easy recipe that gives carrots a little extra zing. The flavor is much more subtle than the ingredient list would suggest. I serve this dish as an accompaniment to beef and lamb, especially lamb shanks. It's particularly nice with Osso Bucco (page 90) as well.

**MAKES 3 TO 4 SERVINGS**

Freezer Bag Friendly

## Tips

You can easily double this recipe. If doubling, use 2 pouches.

This time and temperature work for medium-size carrots and result in a tender-crisp texture. If you are using large storage carrots, increase the hot water bath temperature to 190°F (87.8°C) and cook for 90 minutes. For smaller young carrots, use the temperature in the recipe but reduce the cooking time to 75 minutes.

If you are using a freezer bag instead of a pouch, allow the frozen orange juice concentrate to defrost before sealing the bag.

▶ **Preheat hot water bath to 185°F (85°C)**
▶ **Sous vide pouch**

| | | |
|---|---|---|
| 2 cups | carrot pieces (see Tips, at left) | 500 mL |
| 1 tsp | freshly squeezed lemon juice | 5 mL |
| ¾ tsp | kosher salt | 3 mL |
| ¼ tsp | ground white pepper | 1 mL |
| ¼ tsp | ground ginger | 1 mL |
| ¼ tsp | ground cumin | 1 mL |
| 1 tbsp | frozen orange juice concentrate (see Tips, at right) | 15 mL |
| 2 tbsp | butter | 30 mL |
| | Chopped fresh chives, optional | |

1. In a medium bowl, combine carrots, lemon juice, salt, pepper, ginger and cumin.

2. Place carrot mixture, frozen orange juice concentrate and butter in sous vide pouch and seal. Immerse in preheated water bath and cook for 85 minutes. (To make ahead, see Tips, at right.)

3. Remove pouch from hot water bath. Open and serve immediately. Garnish with chives, if desired.

## Tips

Use the best-quality frozen orange juice concentrate you can find. It will make a difference.

*To make ahead:* Prepare through Step 2. Chill pouch in an ice bath for 20 minutes, then refrigerate for up to 7 days. Preheat hot water bath to 150°F (65.6°C) and immerse pouch for 20 minutes, then proceed with Step 3.

For glazed carrots, place contents of pouch in a small skillet after removing from hot water bath. Bring mixture to a boil over medium-high heat. Cook, basting carrots continuously with cooking juices, until liquid is thickened and carrots are glazed, about 3 to 4 minutes. Serve immediately.

### Persistent Firmness

"Persistent firmness" is a chemical reaction that takes place in some vegetables — such as potatoes, sweet potatoes, carrots and beets — when you precook them between about 130° and 140°F (54° to 60°C). The pectin in the vegetables binds with an enzyme that makes them resistant to further breakdown. This can be useful for tapered vegetables that are difficult to cook evenly, such as carrots, when you want to glaze them with broth and butter afterwards. The carrots will retain a nice dense, meaty texture from end to end. Using your hot water bath allows you to reach and hold this temperature accurately during the precooking stage.

To cause this reaction, precook the vegetables sous vide for 30 minutes at 140°F (60°C) before proceeding with your recipe. This is a handy method for root vegetables that are intended for a stew, because it will keep them from getting mushy.

### Carrots: Restaurant-Style

You can cut the carrots into bite-size rounds or pieces or use a fancier roll cut for a restaurant-style presentation. Place peeled carrot on work surface and, using a sharp chef's knife held at an angle, cut a thick slice. Roll carrot about a quarter-turn and cut again. Repeat down length of carrot. This creates chunky and more irregular but attractive pieces.

# Turnips with Honey and Lemongrass

These turnips make a nice accompaniment for roast duck and also work well in vegetable medleys. Serve hot or cold.

**MAKES 4 SERVINGS**

## Tips

You can easily double this recipe.

A chamber vacuum sealer is particularly good for this recipe because it helps force the liquid into the turnips. A home sealer also works well.

*To make ahead:* Prepare through Step 4. Chill pouch in an ice bath for 15 minutes, then refrigerate for up to 7 days. Preheat hot water bath to 130°F (54.4°C) and immerse pouch for 20 minutes, then proceed with Step 5.

The liquid from the turnips can be added to the sauce of any meat you are serving them with, to enrich the flavor.

These turnips are equally delicious served cold with cured meats or hard cheese. To sharpen up their flavor a bit, sprinkle on a little more vinegar and salt before serving.

▶ **Preheat hot water bath to 185°F (85°C)**
▶ **Sous vide pouch**

| | | |
|---|---|---|
| 3 to 4 | white turnips | 3 to 4 |
| 2 | stalks fresh lemongrass | 2 |
| 1 tbsp | liquid honey | 15 mL |
| 1 tsp | cider vinegar | 5 mL |
| ½ tsp | kosher salt | 2 mL |

1. Peel turnips and slice vertically into wedges, depending on size. For turnips the size of a lime, you should get about 6 wedges from each. For turnips the size of a lemon, you'll have about 8 wedges. You should end up with 2 to 3 cups (500 to 750 mL) in total.

2. Cut off and discard tops of lemongrass, leaving 7-inch (18 cm) stalks. Discard roots and split each stalk down the center. Cut each stalk crosswise into 2 or 3 smaller pieces. (Keep in mind that you will be picking this out after cooking, so don't cut into very small pieces.)

3. In a large bowl, toss turnips with lemongrass, honey, cider vinegar and salt.

4. Transfer to pouch, arranging wedges in one layer, and seal. Immerse pouch in preheated water bath and cook for 45 minutes. (To make ahead, see Tips, at left.)

5. Remove pouch from hot water bath and let cool slightly, about 10 minutes. Open pouch, pick out lemongrass pieces and discard. Salt to taste and serve immediately or refrigerate, covered, and serve cold.

--------------------------------------------------------------

## Variation

**Rutabaga with Honey:** To prepare the rutabaga, peel and cut into ¾-inch (2 cm) dice. Omit lemongrass but add a big pinch of black pepper. Transfer to pouch, seal and cook at 185°F (85°C) for 90 to 100 minutes. You can use truffle honey instead of regular honey or add a splash of truffle oil, which goes well with this lowliest of root vegetables. Serve warm or cold with a splash of cider vinegar and salt, as above.

# Fennel with Apple and Dill

Fennel is another oft-forgotten vegetable. It's very versatile and can be served raw, cooked al dente or roasted until it is soft and creamy. By cooking it with apple juice, this recipe brings out fennel's latent sweetness, while its anise tones are enhanced with a little dill.

**MAKE 3 TO 4 SERVINGS**

## Tips

You can easily double or triple this recipe. Just ensure that each fennel bulb gets its own pouch.

Black garlic (page 388) will add a more subtle flavor than raw garlic. Use 5 cloves, coarsely chopped.

A chamber vacuum sealer is particularly good for this recipe because it helps force the juice into the fennel. A home sealer also works well.

*To make ahead:* Prepare through Step 4. Chill pouch in an ice bath for 15 minutes, then refrigerate for up to 6 days. Preheat hot water bath to 130°F (54.4°C) and immerse pouch for 20 minutes, then proceed with Step 5.

▶ **Preheat hot water bath to 190°F (87.8°C)**
▶ **Sous vide pouch**

| | | |
|---|---|---|
| 1 | medium fennel bulb | 1 |
| ½ cup | loosely packed chopped fresh dill | 125 mL |
| ½ cup | unsweetened apple juice | 125 mL |
| 3 | garlic cloves, halved (see Tips, at left) | 3 |
| 1 tsp | kosher salt | 5 mL |
| ¼ tsp | freshly ground black pepper | 1 mL |

1. Place fennel bulb on a cutting board and cut off stalks about 1 inch (2.5 cm) above bulb. You can chop the stalks and fronds and add them to the pouch for additional flavor.

2. Trim any discolored parts from the base of the bulb. Slice into 6 to 8 vertical wedges.

3. Transfer fennel to pouch and add dill, apple juice, garlic cloves, salt and pepper, plus chopped stalks and fronds, if desired. Arrange wedges in one layer and seal.

4. Immerse pouch in preheated water bath and cook for 55 to 60 minutes. (To make ahead, see Tips, at left.)

5. Remove pouch from hot water bath. Open pouch, discarding liquid, any added stalks and fronds and garlic. Using a knife, scrape dill off fennel bulb. Add salt to taste and serve immediately.

# Balsamic Pearl Onions

These pearl onions taste delicious at room temperature. They make a wonderful addition to an appetizer spread or a picnic as a garnish for cured meats or hard cheese. They can also be added to any stew.

---

**MAKES 1 CUP (250 ML)**

## Tips

You can easily double or triple this recipe. Try to keep the onions in one layer; use additional pouches if necessary.

A chamber vacuum sealer is particularly good for this recipe because it helps force the vinegar into the onions. A home sealer also works well.

If using a home sealer, you will need to use the "long pouch" method described on page 290.

▷ **Preheat hot water bath to 190°F (87.8°C)**
▷ **Sous vide pouch**

| | | |
|---|---|---|
| 1 cup | pearl onions | 250 mL |
| 3 tbsp | balsamic vinegar | 45 mL |
| 1½ tsp | kosher salt | 7 mL |

1. To peel onions, submerge in a bowl of warm water for 15 to 20 minutes (the water will soften the papery outer layers, making them easier to remove). Trim off root ends and slip off papery skin.

2. Place onions, vinegar and salt in pouch. Arrange onions in one layer and seal.

3. Immerse pouch in preheated water bath and cook for 55 to 60 minutes.

4. Remove pouch from hot water bath and chill in ice water for 10 minutes. Open pouch and serve, reserving liquid (see Tips, at right).

---

## Variation

**Balsamic Cipolline:** Cipolline are flat, chestnut-sized onions that make a great garnish for cold meat and cheese plates. Cipolline cook a little more quickly than pearl onions because they are less dense. Substitute 12 to 14 cipolline for the pearl onions, making sure they are arranged in one layer. Cook at 190°F (87.8°C) for 50 minutes.

## Tips

The onions, sealed in the pouch, will keep well for up to 1 month in the refrigerator. Once the pouch is opened, try to use up the onions within 7 days.

The leftover vinegar mixture can be used to enliven sauces or vinaigrettes, especially with warm salads.

## Variations

**Buttery Pearl Onions:** Buttery pearl onions stewed with fresh garden peas are a springtime treat. Prepare the onions using the recipe to the left, substituting 2 tbsp (30 mL) salted butter for the vinegar and salt. These are also perfect for coq au vin and beef bourguignon.

**Vegetable Medley:** Once you have a variety of cooked vegetables, you can combine them to make a colorful, flavorful combination. The vegetables can then be gently reheated together, with each retaining its own character. Here are some combinations that I like:

- Carrots with Orange and Ginger (page 310), Turnips with Honey and Lemongrass (page 312) and Buttery Pearl Onions (above), garnished with chopped fresh mint.
- Saffron Cauliflower with Sultanas (page 309) plus Carrots with Orange and Ginger (page 310), garnished with chopped fresh chives.
- Cauliflower with Capers (variation, page 309) with Balsamic Pearl Onions (left), garnished with chopped fresh parsley.

# Barigoule of Artichokes

A barigoule is a Provençal vegetable stew that traditionally contains artichokes, onions and garlic, but I've added carrots for color and some sweetness. The potato isn't a customary ingredient either, but it provides a little starch and helps to lightly thicken the sauce. Strain out the potato after you finish the sauce or leave it in, if desired.

---

**MAKES
2 SERVINGS**

Freezer Bag Friendly

## Tips

You can easily double or triple this recipe. If you triple the recipe, split the ingredients equally between 2 bags.

To prepare the onions, submerge in a bowl of water for 15 to 20 minutes before peeling. The water will soften the papery skin, making it easier to handle. Trim off root ends and slip off the skins.

Because of the high temperature involved, I cook the barigoule with the zip closure of the bag hanging outside the water. This helps avoid the risk of bag failure.

▶ **Preheat hot water bath to 194°F (90°C)**
▶ **Large resealable freezer bag**
▶ **Cheesecloth**
▶ **Butcher's twine**
▶ **Fine-mesh sieve**

| | | |
|---|---|---|
| 2 | medium artichokes (or 6 small) | 2 |
| 1 | medium carrot | 1 |
| 1 | small baking potato | 1 |
| 4 | garlic cloves, split in half | 4 |
| 3 | fresh thyme sprigs | 3 |
| 1 | bay leaf | 1 |
| ⅓ cup | unsalted ready-to-use broth (chicken, beef or lamb) | 75 mL |
| ⅓ cup | olive oil | 75 mL |
| ⅓ cup | dry white wine | 75 mL |
| 1½ tsp | kosher salt | 7 mL |
| ½ tsp | freshly ground black pepper | 2 mL |
| 8 | pearl onions, peeled (see Tips, at left) | 8 |
| 2 tbsp | chopped flat-leaf (Italian) parsley | 30 mL |
| 1 tbsp | chopped mint | 15 mL |

1. Prepare artichokes according to instructions on page 398.

2. Cut carrot into bite-sized pieces or roll-cut (see Tips, at right). Peel potato and cut into ½-inch (1 cm) dice.

3. Cut two pieces of cheesecloth, one large enough to enclose potato and one to hold garlic, thyme and bay leaf. Rinse cloths briefly under cold water and squeeze dry. Place potato in one piece and tie with twine to secure. Repeat with garlic, thyme and bay leaf to make a second bundle.

## Tips

You can cut the carrots into bite-size rounds or pieces or do a fancier roll cut for a restaurant-style presentation. Place peeled carrot on work surface and, using a sharp chef's knife held at an angle, cut a thick slice. Roll carrot about a quarter-turn and cut again. Repeat down the length of the carrot. This creates chunky and more irregular but attractive pieces.

Fennel can be added, if desired. Cut the bulb into ½-inch (1 cm) slices and place in the bag in Step 5.

*To make ahead:* Prepare through Step 6. Chill bag in an ice bath for 15 minutes, then refrigerate for up to 3 days (any longer and the artichokes will start to turn black). Reheat barigoule in a large saucepan over medium heat for about 10 minutes. Proceed with Step 7.

**4.** In a small saucepan, combine broth, olive oil, white wine and herb bundle. Bring to a boil over high heat. Stir in salt and pepper and remove from heat.

**5.** Add a weight to freezer bag (see box, below). Place artichokes, carrot, onions and potato bundle in bag. Add broth mixture, including herb bundle, and seal.

**6.** Immerse bag in preheated water bath and cook for 1 hour. (To make ahead, see Tips, at left.)

**7.** Pour bag contents through sieve into a medium skillet (off the heat). Remove herb bundle and discard. Remove potato from cheesecloth and add to broth mixture. Transfer remaining vegetables to a warm platter while you prepare sauce.

**8.** Bring broth mixture to a boil over high heat. Reduce heat and boil gently until liquid is reduced by about half or until it starts to look a little creamy, about 10 minutes. Pour through fine-mesh sieve over other vegetables, straining out potato, if desired. Garnish with parsley and mint and serve immediately.

### Weigh Down Those Bags

Vegetables are not as dense as meat, nor are they as smooth-sided. Sealing a resealable freezer bag with the water displacement method can often result in a bag that floats, meaning that your food will not cook properly. A crafty method that works in a lot of cases is to place dense, inert objects, such as a couple of stainless-steel spoons, inside the bag before adding the vegetables. The spoons will help the bag to sink (nestle them together so they don't take up too much space). This works well for recipes such as Barigoule of Artichokes because there is enough liquid in the recipe to bathe the artichokes properly in spite of the spoons. It doesn't work for recipes such as Saffron Cauliflower with Sultanas (page 309), because the small amount of liquid in the recipe will settle around the spoons instead of the cauliflower, where it needs to be.

# "Braised" Red Cabbage

Inexpensive and delicious, this is another tangy vegetable that I like to eat straight from the fridge (although I admit it's better warmed). I serve it alongside roast pork, pork chops or duck. The most basic method for this recipe is given here, but if you're short on time, refer to the Tips to save a few hours.

**MAKES 6 TO 8 SERVINGS**

Freezer Bag Friendly

## Tips

You can easily halve or double this recipe. If doubling, use 2 bags.

To save time, you can blanch the cabbage for 2 minutes in boiling salted water, drain and then proceed with the recipe. The cabbage will collapse somewhat and there will be less air in the bag. It will cook in about 4 hours. Be sure to deflate the bag occasionally while cooking.

▶ **Preheat hot water bath to 194°F (90°C)**
▶ **Large resealable freezer bag**
▶ **Cabbage shredder or mandoline (optional)**

| | | |
|---|---|---|
| 1 | small red cabbage, about 2 lbs (900 g) | 1 |
| 1 cup | unsweetened apple juice | 250 mL |
| ¾ cup | cider vinegar | 175 mL |
| ¼ cup | finely chopped shallots | 60 mL |
| ¼ cup | apricot jam | 60 mL |
| ¼ cup | frozen orange juice concentrate | 60 mL |
| 3 tbsp | finely chopped fresh gingerroot | 45 mL |
| 1 tbsp | kosher salt | 15 mL |
| 2 tsp | ground white pepper | 10 mL |
| ¼ tsp | ground cloves | 1 mL |
| 2 | bay leaves | 2 |

1. Using a sharp knife, cut cabbage into quarters, remove core and slice thinly, preferably with a cabbage shredder or mandoline (by hand is the last resort). You should end up with about 8 cups (2 L).

2. Transfer cabbage, apple juice, cider vinegar, shallots, apricot jam, orange juice concentrate, ginger, salt, white pepper, ground cloves and bay leaves to a freezer bag and seal (try to squeeze out as much air as possible).

## Tips

If you have a chamber vacuum sealer, follow the recipe and seal the pouch. The vacuum will compress the cabbage and the bag will sink and cook evenly in about 4 hours. You won't need to check every hour and there's an added bonus: your kitchen will not smell of cabbage.

*To make ahead:* Prepare through Step 3. Chill bag in ice water for 30 minutes, then refrigerate for up to 10 days or freeze for up to 3 months. To reheat cabbage from refrigerator temperature, preheat hot water bath to 140°F (60°C). Immerse bag for 30 minutes, then proceed with Step 4.

3. Immerse bag in preheated hot water bath. It will float because of trapped air, so weigh it down by placing an object such as a cast-iron skillet on top. Cook for 6 to 7 hours, until cabbage is tender. The bag will inflate as air inside expands with the heat. Every hour, remove bag and, with a towel (bag will be hot), open bag, tighten up cabbage and squeeze out as much air as possible, then reseal. Slightly shift around contents of bag so all the cabbage has a turn being submerged in the juices. (To make ahead, see Tips, at left.)

4. Remove bag from hot water bath. Open bag and serve immediately. Alternatively, chill bag in an ice bath for 30 minutes, then transfer to the refrigerator. Serve cold, if desired.

# Aloo Gobi

For me, aloo gobi is a non-negotiable must-order dish when I am eating Indian food. It's a wonderful complement to butter chicken. I have used coconut milk in this recipe, which gives the dish a luscious creaminess.

**MAKES 4 TO 6 SERVINGS**

## Tips

You can easily halve or double this recipe. If you are doubling the recipe, use 2 pouches.

For the vegetables to cook evenly, you need to remove all the air from the pouch, using a chamber vacuum sealer or home sealer. With a home sealer, it is most effective to freeze the liquid first in order to keep it from getting sucked into the machine.

*To make ahead:* Prepare through Step 4. Chill pouch in ice water for 20 minutes, then refrigerate for up to 5 days. Preheat hot water bath to 125°F (51.7°C) and immerse pouch for 30 minutes, then proceed with Step 5.

▷ **Preheat hot water bath to 190°F (87.8°C)**
▷ **Coffee grinder or spice grinder**
▷ **Sous vide pouch**

| | | |
|---|---|---|
| 4 tsp | coriander seeds | 20 mL |
| 1 tsp | cumin seeds | 5 mL |
| ½ tsp | ground turmeric | 2 mL |
| 2 tsp | kosher salt | 10 mL |
| 3 tbsp | vegetable oil | 45 mL |
| 2 tbsp | finely chopped garlic | 30 mL |
| 2 tbsp | finely chopped fresh gingerroot | 30 mL |
| 1 | medium cauliflower, core removed, cut into 1½- to 2-inch (4 to 5 cm) florets | 1 |
| 2 | medium russet potatoes, peeled and cut into 1-inch (2.5 cm) dice | 2 |
| 2 | jalapeño peppers or serrano chiles, chopped | 2 |
| 1 cup | coconut milk (or ¾ cup/175 mL water), frozen into cubes | 250 mL |
| | Coarsely chopped cilantro, optional | |

1. In coffee or spice grinder, combine coriander seeds, cumin seeds, turmeric and salt. Grind to a powder.

2. In a small saucepan, heat oil over medium heat. Add garlic and ginger. Cook, stirring often, for 4 to 5 minutes, until fragrant. Add spice mixture and cook, stirring, for 4 minutes. Remove from heat.

3. Place cauliflower, potatoes, jalapeños and spice mixture in pouch. Add frozen coconut milk cubes and seal.

4. Immerse pouch in preheated water bath and cook for 70 to 80 minutes. (To make ahead, see Tips, at left.)

5. Remove pouch from hot water bath and let stand for 5 to 10 minutes. Open pouch and serve warm, garnished with cilantro, if desired.

# Eggs and Sweets

# Eggs

## The Basics

Chances are very good that you've cooked something sous vide long before buying this book, without knowing it. Can you guess? It's soft-boiled eggs. The general definition of sous vide is cooking at a specific temperature in a sealed container — the eggshell. Soft-boiled eggs are actually a form of sous vide preparation.

Eggs are one of the easiest and most satisfying foods that you can cook sous vide, and they require no sealer. Around 2005, when sous vide circulators were becoming more common in restaurant kitchens, eggs were one of the first foods that chefs started playing with. Since eggs are relatively inexpensive, you can have fun experimenting with your device too, so you can see how temperature affects the coagulation of the various proteins. But before you get cooking, let's review a little egg chemistry first.

When I refer to eggs in this book, I mean chicken eggs. However, I have also provided cooking instructions for quail and duck eggs in the Tips section of the relevant recipes.

## The Anatomy of an Egg

There are three parts to an egg that matter for our purposes: the yolk, the thick white surrounding it, and the thin white, next to the shell.

The yolk makes up a little more than one-third of the total weight of a shelled egg, but it contains about three-quarters of the calories. It also contains about 40% of the egg's protein and all of its fat. At 150°F (65.6°C) the proteins start to thicken. At 158°F (70°C), the yolk becomes firm and set. Finally, at 170°F (76.7°C), the yolk starts to get crumbly.

The white makes up the rest of the egg's weight and is about 90% water. There are about a dozen different proteins in the white, but only three comprise the bulk (over 75%) of this protein. You're probably wondering why I'm telling you all this. It's because the

## SIZE MATTERS

Chicken eggs graded as large weigh about 2 oz (55 g), and extra-large weigh 2.2 oz (60 g). Over the years I have found that the "extra" in extra-large eggs is mostly white, while the yolks are about the same size as those in large eggs. I use large eggs for these recipes, but you can substitute extra-large if you prefer.

properties of these proteins determine how your egg cooks, so it's important stuff! The main protein in the thin white coagulates at about 180°F (180°C) — way higher than we want for cooking our yolk. The thick white starts to coagulate at 145°F (62.8°C) and becomes firm but tender at 150°F (65.6°C), which is in the same range as for the yolk. As you can see, the temperatures are quite precise.

By regulating time and temperature, you have far more control with the sous vide device than you could ever have with a pot on the stove. It takes about 45 minutes for any water temperature in a sous vide device to reach the center of the yolk. Pulling your eggs out of the hot water bath before that means that the yolk will be cooler, and therefore less cooked than the white. Since everyone is quite particular about the doneness of their eggs, take the time to figure out which timing and temperature works best for you. (All the recipes in this chapter presume that the eggs come straight from the refrigerator.)

## POACHED AND HARD-BOILED EGGS

When we want to precisely cook eggs sous vide in the shell, we often have to sacrifice the thin white for the sake of getting the thick white and the yolk the way we want them. It's important to always use fresh eggs when cooking sous vide, because as an egg ages, water leaches out of the thick white into the thin white. At sous vide temperatures, the thin white thickens only slightly and will run off as you shell the egg. Therefore, shell your eggs as you would raw eggs — have a dish ready to catch the thin white. Interesting fact: the white that spreads through the water when you're poaching eggs traditionally is the thin white.

Sous vide offers precise results for hard-boiled eggs as well. In order to get the thin white cooked solid so you can peel the egg the traditional way, you need to blanch the eggs in boiling water on the stove for 2 minutes before proceeding. Incidentally, if you're a fan of the classic 3-minute soft-boiled egg, keep doing what you're doing! However, keep in mind that eggs cooked this way are not pasteurized. With sous vide equipment you can now pasteurize eggs first, while still raw, and then proceed with making your soft-boiled eggs (see Pasteurized "Raw" Egg, page 324).

# Pasteurized "Raw" Egg

If you are concerned about pathogens in raw eggs, I suggest you try this recipe. It's ideal if you're looking to add eggs to a Caesar salad or are making homemade mayonnaise. You can store the eggs in the refrigerator until the best-before date on the carton and use them as needed.

**MAKES
1 SERVING**

Can Be Scaled Up

## Tips

The egg white will be a little runnier than you're used to. If you plan on using the egg in a meringue, it will take a little more beating to aerate.

Marking a pasteurized egg with a felt-tipped pen will allow you to identify it in a carton of other eggs.

▷ **Preheat hot water bath to 135°F (57.2°C)**

| 1 | egg | 1 |
|---|-----|---|

1. Immerse egg in preheated hot water bath and cook for 75 minutes (see Tips, at left).

2. Remove egg using a slotted spoon and let cool, about 10 minutes. Serve immediately or return to carton and refrigerate until needed (see Tips, at left).

- - - - - - - - - - - - - - - - - - - - - - - - - - - - - - - - - - - - - - - - - -

## Variations

**Pasteurized "Raw" Quail Egg:** Immerse egg in hot water bath and cook for 40 minutes.

**Pasteurized "Raw" Duck Egg:** Immerse egg in hot water bath and cook for 100 minutes.

# Perfect Poached Egg

This is a great way to get ahead of Sunday brunch for a crowd. The egg cooks for a relatively short time, which sets the thick white but leaves the yolk quite runny. Aki Kamozawa and H. Alexander Talbot first wrote about this now widely publicized method in *Ideas in Food*. These eggs are also perfect for garnishing a bowl of ramen.

## Tip

This egg is not pasteurized. If you have safety concerns about raw egg, start with eggs that you have previously pasteurized (opposite).

▶ **Preheat hot water bath to 167°F (75°C)**

| 1 | egg | 1 |

1. Immerse egg in preheated hot water bath and cook for 13 minutes. Using a slotted spoon, remove from water bath.
2. Crack the egg as you would a raw egg, into a warm bowl. With a tablespoon, lift egg out of bowl, leaving any remnants of thin white behind. Serve immediately.

## Variations

**Poached Quail Egg:** Preheat hot water bath to 146.3°F (63.5°C) and immerse egg for 15 minutes. Serve immediately or chill in an ice bath for at least 5 minutes before transferring to the refrigerator. Because the shell of a quail egg can be quite tough and leathery, open it by placing the egg on a folded kitchen towel and giving it a light rap with the sharp edge of a knife. There will be very little egg white left on the yolk.

**Poached Duck Egg:** Preheat hot water bath to 150°F (65.6°C) and immerse egg for 30 minutes. Serve immediately or chill in an ice bath for at least 10 minutes before transferring to the refrigerator.

# Japanese Hot-Spring Egg

*Onsen tamago* is Japanese for "hot-spring egg." It's a popular dish in Japan that's traditionally served at hot-spring spas. The eggs are cooked at a low temperature in the spring, resulting in a very tender white and a barely solidified yolk. They are both conceptually and physically the opposite of poached eggs. I describe the yolk texture as similar to ripe Camembert.

## MAKES 1 SERVING

Can Be Scaled Up

## Tips

The nature of the proteins in quail and duck eggs makes it not possible to prepare them this way.

This egg is pasteurized.

I like to serve this dish in small rice bowls like those used in Chinese restaurants.

*To make ahead:* Prepare through Step 1. Remove egg from hot water bath and chill in an ice bath for at least 10 minutes. Cover and refrigerate for up to 7 days. To reheat, preheat hot water bath to 140°F (60°C) and immerse egg for 15 minutes. Proceed with Step 2.

In Japan this type of egg is garnished with some broth or soy sauce. I like it with a sprinkle of dried bonito flakes or smoked salt and a few drops of Tabasco.

▶ **Preheat hot water bath to 150°F (65.6°C)**

| 1 | egg | 1 |
|---|---|---|
| | Optional garnishes: | |
| | Dashi (page 356) or Bacon Dashi (variation, page 357) | |
| | Soy sauce | |
| | Bonito flakes | |
| | Smoked salt | |
| | Hot pepper sauce, such as Tabasco | |

1. Immerse egg in preheated hot water bath and cook for 90 minutes. (To make ahead, see Tips, at left.)

2. Using a slotted spoon, remove egg from water bath and set aside until cool enough to handle, about 3 to 4 minutes.

3. Carefully crack about one-third of shell from end to end. Over a warm bowl, peel away enough of the shell that egg falls out into bowl. Some of the thin white will cling to the shell; it may be discarded.

4. Garnish egg as desired and serve immediately (see Tips, at left).

# Hard-Boiled Eggs

If you've ever been frustrated by having to cook a large number of hard-boiled eggs for entertaining, I suggest you try this recipe. It's ideal for making dishes for a crowd, such as deviled eggs or egg salad. You'll end up with perfectly cooked, stress-free eggs.

**MAKES 12 SERVINGS**

## Tips

This recipe can easily be scaled up or down.

Boiling the eggs first firms up the whites and facilitates peeling. The whites of these eggs are slightly more tender than the whites of hard-boiled eggs cooked using traditional methods. If you boil the eggs for 2 minutes instead of 1, the whites will be indistinguishable from what you are used to. You can dispense with the boiling if you aren't concerned about some of the white sticking to the shell. In that case, add 3 minutes to the cooking time in the hot water bath.

*To make ahead:* Prepare through Step 3. After chilling eggs in ice bath, cover and refrigerate for up to 7 days.

▶ **Preheat hot water bath to 180°F (82.2°C)**

| 12 | eggs | 12 |

1. Bring a large pot of water to a boil. Add eggs and boil for 1 minute.

2. Using a slotted spoon, immediately transfer eggs to preheated hot water bath and cook for 30 minutes.

3. Using slotted spoon, remove eggs from hot water bath. Transfer to an ice bath and chill thoroughly for at least 30 minutes, to facilitate peeling. (To make ahead, see Tips, at left.)

4. Peel eggs, rinse and serve or use in your recipe.

## Variations

**Hard-Boiled Quail Eggs:** Preheat hot water bath to 167°F (75°C). Proceed with Step 1. Immerse eggs in preheated hot water bath for 25 minutes. Using a slotted spoon, remove eggs from bath and chill in ice water for 15 minutes. Proceed with peeling when desired.

**Hard-Boiled Duck Eggs:** Preheat hot water bath to 167°F (75°C). Proceed with Step 1. Immerse eggs in preheated hot water bath for 1 hour. Using a slotted spoon, remove eggs from bath and chill in ice water for 30 minutes. Proceed with peeling when desired.

# French-Style Scrambled Eggs

These eggs are very rich and elegant, with an almost sauce-like consistency. Scrambled eggs like this suggest accompaniments such as asparagus, smoked salmon or black truffles — not your usual breakfast eggs!

## Tips

This recipe can be scaled up as desired. Add 5 minutes of cooking time for each additional egg. Use up to 5 eggs in one small bag, and ensure that the bags are not touching each other in the hot water bath.

Half of the cream can be replaced with milk, if desired.

*To make ahead:* Prepare through Step 2. Chill bag in an ice bath for 10 minutes. Refrigerate sealed bag for up to 5 days. To reheat from refrigerator temperature, preheat hot water bath to 160°F (71.1°C) and immerse bag for 15 minutes (add 4 minutes for each additional egg). Proceed with Step 3.

▷ **Preheat hot water bath to 170°F (76.7°C)**
▷ **Small resealable freezer bag**

| | | |
|---|---|---|
| 2 | eggs | 2 |
| 2 tbsp | heavy or whipping (35%) cream (see Tips, at left) | 30 mL |
| ¼ tsp | kosher salt | 1 mL |
| ⅛ tsp | freshly ground black pepper | 0.5 mL |
| 1 tbsp | butter | 15 mL |

**1.** In a small bowl, combine eggs, cream, salt and pepper. Whisk together. Pour into freezer bag. Add butter to bag and seal.

**2.** Immerse bag in preheated water bath and cook for 30 minutes, removing it at 10-minute intervals to break up curds — wrap the bag in a towel, because it will be a little hot. (To make ahead, see Tips, at left.)

**3.** Remove bag from hot water bath and serve eggs immediately.

# Mushroom Omelet

Sous vide omelets have perfect texture, though their shape is a little compromised because they take the shape of the bag they are cooked in. This is great for a crowd who want a choice of flavorings in their omelets; here we are using mushrooms. Keep in mind that the "filling" is distributed throughout the eggs rather than tucked into the center.

**MAKES
1 SERVING**

Freezer Bag Friendly

## Tips

This recipe makes a tender omelet. If you like yours firmer, increase the cooking time to 30 minutes. If you prefer it firmer still, increase the temperature of the bath to 170°F (76.7°C).

You can make many omelets at once, as long as the bags are not touching each other in the hot water bath.

*To make ahead:* Prepare through Step 3. Remove bag from hot water bath and transfer to an ice bath for 15 minutes. Refrigerate sealed bag for up to 5 days. To reheat from refrigerator temperature, preheat hot water bath to 160°F (71.1°C) and immerse bag for 15 minutes. Proceed with Step 4.

▶ **Preheat hot water bath to 167°F (75°C)**
▶ **Small resealable freezer bag**

| | | |
|---|---|---|
| 1 tbsp | butter | 15 mL |
| 1 tbsp | chopped shallot, optional | 15 mL |
| ¼ tsp | freshly ground black pepper | 1 mL |
| 1 tsp | chopped fresh thyme (or pinch dried thyme) | 5 mL |
| 1 cup | sliced white or cremini mushrooms | 250 mL |
| 3 | eggs | 3 |
| ½ tsp | kosher salt | 2 mL |

1. In small skillet, melt butter over medium heat. When foam subsides, add shallot (if using), pepper, thyme and mushrooms. Cook, stirring, until mushrooms are tender and lightly browned, about 8 to 10 minutes. Remove from heat and let cool.

2. Crack eggs into a medium bowl. Add salt and beat with a fork until mixed. Add mushroom mixture and stir briefly to combine.

3. Pour egg mixture into freezer bag. Immerse bag in preheated hot water bath and cook for 25 minutes.

4. Remove bag from bath and lay it on the counter. With scissors, carefully cut open upper side of bag. Transfer omelet to a warm plate and serve immediately.

### Omelets Your Way

You can substitute many other ingredients for the mushrooms. Keep in mind that wet ingredients such as tomatoes will dilute the eggs and compromise cooking, so I suggest using them judiciously. I recommend chopped herbs, chopped ham, green onions or grated hard cheese such as Gruyère or Parmesan.

# Potato Chip Tortilla Española

Tortilla española is a classic in the canon of Spanish dishes. This recipe is a cheeky twist on it that is simple but requires a bit of advance planning — be sure to start the day before you want to serve it. For a group, serve with other tapas selections such as anchovies, marinated mushrooms and cheese. As a main course, serve with a green salad.

**MAKES
6 APPETIZER
OR 2
MAIN-COURSE
SERVINGS**

## Tips

I find that ridged potato chips work best for this recipe because they are sturdier than regular potato chips.

Regular potatoes can be used in place of the potato chips. Boil 1 medium baking potato in salted water until tender, about 40 minutes. Peel, if desired. Cut into ½-inch (1 cm) slices (it is okay if they break up a bit). Season with salt and fry slices in 2 tbsp (30 mL) olive oil until cooked but not brown, about 6 minutes. Let cool. Stir into egg mixture along with ½ tsp (2 mL) salt. Proceed with Step 3.

*To make ahead:* Prepare through Step 3. Freeze container for up to 2 weeks. Proceed with Step 4.

▸ Sous vide pouch
▸ 4-cup (1 L) plastic storage container, with lid

| | | |
|---|---|---|
| 2½ tbsp | olive oil, divided | 37 mL |
| ½ cup | finely chopped onion | 125 mL |
| 2 cups | crushed potato chips (see Tips, at left) | 500 mL |
| ¼ tsp | freshly ground pepper | 1 mL |
| 1 tsp | chopped fresh thyme | 5 mL |
| 5 | eggs, beaten | 5 |

1. In a small skillet, heat 2 tbsp (30 mL) olive oil over medium heat. Add onion and cook, stirring occasionally, until soft but not brown, about 5 to 6 minutes. Set aside to cool.

2. In a medium bowl, combine onion, potato chips, pepper, thyme and eggs.

3. Brush plastic container with remaining oil. Pour egg mixture into container and freeze overnight or until firm, about 6 hours. (To make ahead, see Tips, at left.)

4. Preheat hot water bath to 176°F (80°C).

5. Remove egg mixture from freezer and run hot water around bottom of container to loosen. Unmold egg mixture, place in pouch and seal.

6. Place pouch in preheated water bath. It will float, so cover bath to create a warm environment for top of mixture. Cook for 45 minutes.

7. Open cover of water bath and flip over pouch to cook other side. Cover bath and cook for another 15 minutes.

8. Remove pouch from hot water bath and let cool for 15 minutes. Open pouch and place tortilla on a cutting board. Cut into pieces and serve. Tortilla española is typically served at room temperature.

# Chawanmushi

Chawanmushi, a Japanese steamed savory custard, can be cooked perfectly sous vide. Traditionally it is made and served in specially designed porcelain cups with lids. Here we use individual canning jars with their tight-fitting lids to recreate this impressive dish at home.

---

**MAKES
2 SERVINGS**

## Tips

You can easily double or triple this recipe.

For a non-traditional twist, substitute Bacon Dashi (variation, page 357) for the regular dashi.

Chawanmushi is infinitely adaptable to its ingredients. Peeled uncooked small shrimp, oysters, freshly cooked crab, lightly cooked chicken and most mushrooms make excellent additions.

It is best to serve the chawanmushi promptly. If you need to wait for 45 minutes or so before serving, remove the jars from the hot water bath and turn off the sous vide machine. Set the temperature of the bath to 185°F (85°C) and leave the jars immersed for 10 minutes. Serve immediately.

▸ **Preheat hot water bath to 185°F (85°C)**
▸ **Two 8 oz (250 mL) straight-sided canning jars, with lids**
▸ **Blender or immersion blender**
▸ **Fine-mesh sieve**

| | | |
|---|---|---|
| 1½ cups | dashi (store-bought or homemade, page 356), at room temperature | 375 mL |
| 2 | eggs | 2 |
| 1 | shiitake mushroom, stem removed and cap sliced | 1 |
| 1 | 4-inch (10 cm) piece imitation crab leg, diced (see Tips, at left) | 1 |
| 1 tbsp | minced green onion | 15 mL |

1. In a blender or using an immersion blender in a tall container, blend eggs with dashi.

2. Divide mushroom and imitation crab equally between jars. Using a spoon, press egg mixture through fine-mesh sieve into jars; strain liquid into jars, leaving ½ inch (1 cm) headspace. Wipe rims of jars thoroughly to ensure a good seal. Add lids and turn just until snug. Immerse jars in preheated water bath and cook for 20 minutes.

3. Remove jars from hot water bath and let cool slightly, about 5 minutes. Open jars and garnish with green onion. Serve immediately.

---

### For Tradition's Sake

If you have real chawanmushi cups or 8 oz (250 mL) cups that you would like to use, improvise a rack in your water bath that will allow the water to come up to but not over the rim of the cups. Check the minimum water level requirement for your equipment. Before you start heating the bath, set up the rack and all the cups you plan to use (fill them with water so they won't float) to determine how much water to use. Seal the cups tightly with plastic wrap before cooking.

# Hollandaise Sauce

Hollandaise sauce needs no introduction. Often thought of as a tricky dish to master at home, it is easy to make sous vide, and it can even be made ahead of time and reheated when desired. I love serving this sauce in the spring on top of salmon with asparagus. This recipe makes enough for about 6 servings.

## Tip

The shallots will disappear into the sauce while it's blending. If you're using an immersion blender or want to ensure a perfectly smooth sauce, use a fine-mesh sieve to strain the shallots out of the vinegar before proceeding with Step 3. Be sure to press down hard on the solids with a spoon to extract as much vinegar as possible.

▶ **Preheat hot water bath to 165°F (73.9°C)**
▶ **Small resealable freezer bag**
▶ **Instant-read thermometer**
▶ **Blender or immersion blender**

| | | |
|---|---|---|
| 2 tbsp | finely chopped shallots | 30 mL |
| 2½ tbsp | white wine vinegar | 37 mL |
| 1 cup | butter | 250 mL |
| 1½ tbsp | water | 22 mL |
| 2 tsp | lecithin granules (see box, at right) | 10 mL |
| 4 | egg yolks, at room temperature | 4 |
| 1 tbsp | freshly squeezed lemon juice | 15 mL |
| 1½ tsp | kosher salt | 7 mL |
| Dash | hot pepper sauce, such as Tabasco | Dash |

1. In a small saucepan, combine shallots and vinegar. Bring to a boil over medium-high heat. Remove from heat.

2. Melt butter by floating it in a bowl in the preheating water bath, or use the microwave or stove. Butter should be between 100° and 140°F (38° to 60°C).

3. In blender or using immersion blender in a tall container, combine shallot and vinegar mixture, water, lecithin granules, egg yolks, lemon juice, salt and hot pepper sauce. Blend for 2 to 3 minutes, until lecithin is combined. Stop the motor and scrape down sides of container as required.

4. With motor running, add melted butter in a continuous stream through hole in lid. Blend until consistency resembles that of heavy cream, about 2 minutes.

## Tip

*To make ahead:* Prepare through Step 5. Remove bag from hot water bath and transfer to a cold water bath for 15 minutes. Refrigerate sealed bag for up to 3 days. To reheat from refrigerator temperature, preheat hot water bath to 150°F (65.6°C) and immerse bag for 15 minutes. Proceed with Step 6.

**5.** Transfer mixture to freezer bag. Immerse bag in preheated water bath and cook for 30 minutes. (To make ahead, see Tip, at left.)

**6.** To serve, open bag and stir briefly with a spoon to remove any air bubbles.

## Variation

**Béarnaise Sauce:** Béarnaise sauce is a kissing cousin of hollandaise that is great with steaks, fish or chicken. Replace the white wine vinegar and lemon juice with the same quantity of tarragon vinegar. Prior to serving, stir in 1 tbsp (15 mL) freshly chopped tarragon and 2 tsp (10 mL) coarsely ground black pepper.

### Lecithin Granules

Lecithin is a natural emulsifier that is present in eggs. It helps create a stable emulsion without using extra yolks. While not absolutely necessary, the lecithin provides a further level of assurance that the sauce will not break. It is available in most health food stores.

# Egg and Lemon Sauce

This is a lighter, fresher variation of Hollandaise Sauce (page 332). Using olive oil to replace one-third of the butter gives it a Mediterranean accent, and replacing another third with chicken broth makes it less rich and more versatile. Try this sauce with vegetables, fish and chicken. The recipe makes enough for 4 to 5 servings.

**MAKES ABOUT 1½ CUPS (375 ML)**

## Tips

You can easily double this recipe.

You can make the butter mixture in the microwave instead of a saucepan, if you desire.

*To make ahead:* Prepare through Step 3. Remove bag and chill in an ice bath for 15 minutes, then refrigerate for up to 3 days. To reheat from refrigerator temperature, preheat hot water bath to 140°F (65.6°C) and immerse bag for 15 minutes.

You can hold the sauce for up to 3 hours at the reduced water bath temperature. For quality and safety reasons, it should be discarded after being held for 3 hours.

▶ **Preheat hot water bath to 165°F (73.9°C)**
▶ **Small resealable freezer bag**
▶ **Blender**

| | | |
|---|---|---|
| ⅓ cup | unsalted butter | 75 mL |
| ⅓ cup | olive oil (see Tips, page 335) | 75 mL |
| ⅓ cup | ready-to-use reduced-sodium or unsalted chicken broth | 75 mL |
| Pinch | grated lemon zest | Pinch |
| 2 tbsp | freshly squeezed lemon juice | 30 mL |
| 5 | drops hot pepper sauce, such as Tabasco | 5 |
| Pinch | ground white pepper | Pinch |
| Pinch | salt | Pinch |
| 2 | egg yolks, at room temperature | 2 |
| 1 tsp | lecithin granules (see box, page 333) | 5 mL |

1. In a medium saucepan, combine butter, olive oil and chicken broth. Heat over medium-low heat, stirring, for about 5 minutes or until butter is melted (see Tips, at left). Stir in lemon zest, lemon juice, hot pepper sauce, pepper and salt. Keep warm over low heat so butter remains liquid.

2. Place egg yolks and lecithin granules in blender. With motor running, whisk butter mixture and slowly pour through hole in lid. Blend until smooth and well combined.

3. Pour mixture into freezer bag and seal. Immerse in preheated water bath and cook for 30 minutes. (To make ahead, see Tips, at left.)

4. Remove bag from hot water bath, open bag and stir sauce. Season to taste with additional salt, if necessary. Use immediately or reduce temperature of hot water bath to 140°F (60°C), reseal bag, immerse and hold for up to 3 hours.

# Olive Oil "Cream"

This is a variation of a sauce that I developed for my first restaurant, Avalon. It's similar to hollandaise sauce but is emulsified with olive oil rather than butter — and it's great with braised lamb shoulder. Just keep in mind that its flavor depends on the quality of your stock. This recipe makes enough for 6 to 8 servings.

**MAKES 2 CUPS (500 ML)**

Freezer Bag Friendly

## Tips

It is hard to make less than this amount but easy to double this recipe. Blend in one batch and then divide between 2 small resealable freezer bags. You can reheat a double batch in one bag.

Use your favorite olive oil, since the flavor really comes through here.

*To make ahead:* Prepare through Step 4. Remove bag from bath and chill in an ice bath for 15 minutes. Refrigerate for up to 3 days. To reheat from refrigerator temperature, preheat hot water bath to 140°F (65.6°C) and immerse bag for 15 minutes.

You can hold the sauce for up to 3 hours. Reduce the temperature of the bath to 140°F (60°C) after Step 4 and store the sauce in the bath. It should be discarded after being held for 3 hours.

▶ **Preheat hot water bath to 165°F (73.9°C)**
▶ **Small resealable freezer bag**
▶ **Instant-read thermometer**
▶ **Blender or immersion blender**

| | | |
|---|---|---|
| ⅓ cup | extra virgin olive oil (see Tips, at left) | 75 mL |
| 1 cup | enriched beef broth (page 401) | 250 mL |
| 2 | egg yolks, at room temperature | 2 |
| 1 tbsp | lecithin granules (see box, page 333) | 15 mL |
| 3 tbsp | freshly squeezed lemon juice | 45 mL |
| ¼ tsp | freshly ground black pepper | 1 mL |

1. In a small saucepan over low heat, combine and heat olive oil and broth (or use the microwave). The temperature should be between 100° and 140°F (38° to 60°C).

2. In blender or using immersion blender in a tall container, combine egg yolks, lecithin and lemon juice.

3. With motor running, pour broth mixture in a steady stream through hole in lid. Blend for 2 to 3 minutes, stopping motor periodically to scrape down the sides, until lecithin is fully incorporated. Add pepper; blend for 1 minute.

4. Transfer mixture to freezer bag and seal. Immerse bag in preheated water bath and cook for 30 minutes. (To make ahead, see Tips, at left.)

5. Remove bag from hot water bath, open bag and stir sauce. Add salt to taste.

> ### Tailor-Made "Cream"
>
> Feel free to customize this sauce to its use. For example, you can substitute a strong fish stock for the beef broth if you want to use it with fish, and so on.

## Sweets

Most of these dessert recipes involve eggs, because the precision of sous vide affords assurance of success in these otherwise somewhat tricky preparations. Sous vide also turns cooking fruit into a tidy, trouble-free endeavor. While it is technically possible to cook flour-based desserts and quick breads with your hot water bath set to the highest setting, I see no practical advantage to doing so. You lose the opportunity for browning, not to mention missing the lovely aromas in your kitchen that you get from baking.

# Crème Brûlée

Crème brûlée is always the most popular dessert on restaurant menus, and it's easy to make at home using your sous vide device. Small canning jars make the perfect portion size — you can torch the sugar and serve them right in the jar. Bring the prepared dessert to a dinner party along with your torch and look like a hero.

---

**MAKES
4 SERVINGS**

## Tips

You can easily double or triple this recipe.

I recommend using brand-new jars that have not previously been heat stressed.

▸ **Preheat hot water bath to 176°F (80°C)**
▸ **Four 4 oz (125 mL) glass canning jars, with lids**
▸ **Fine-mesh sieve**
▸ **Propane or butane torch**

| | | |
|---|---|---|
| 1 cup | whole milk | 250 mL |
| ⅔ cup | heavy or whipping (35%) cream | 150 mL |
| 2 | egg yolks | 2 |
| 1 | whole egg | 1 |
| 2 tbsp | granulated sugar | 30 mL |
| 1 tsp | vanilla extract | 5 mL |
| ¼ cup | granulated sugar, divided | 60 mL |

1. In a small saucepan, combine milk and cream. Bring to a simmer, stirring, over medium heat. Remove from heat.

2. In a medium bowl, whisk together egg yolks, egg, 2 tbsp (30 mL) sugar and vanilla, until well blended. Gradually whisk in milk mixture. Strain through fine-mesh sieve into a liquid measuring cup. (To make uncooked custard ahead, see Tips, at right.)

## Tips

*To make uncooked custard ahead:* Prepare through Step 2. Transfer mixture to an airtight container, cover and refrigerate for up to 2 days. Proceed with Step 3.

*To make cooked custard ahead:* Prepare through Step 4. Refrigerate for up to 3 days. Proceed with Step 5.

**3.** Pour equal amounts of mixture into jars, leaving $\frac{1}{2}$ inch (1 cm) headspace. Wipe rims of jars thoroughly to ensure a good seal. Add lids and turn just until snug. Immerse jars in preheated hot water bath and cook for 50 minutes. (To make cooked custard ahead, see Tips, at left.)

**4.** Remove jars from bath and let cool for 20 to 30 minutes. Refrigerate for 1 hour or up to 3 days.

**5.** When ready to serve, open jars and spread 1 tbsp (15 mL) sugar evenly over surface of each custard. With torch at full blast, holding it 2 to 3 inches (5 to 7.5 cm) from surface, wave it over sugar. Keep torch moving constantly to avoid blackening sugar — you want a deep golden brown. Each custard will take about 2 minutes to complete. Let cool for 3 to 4 minutes, then serve.

# Crème Caramel

Crème caramel is a simple dessert but it has its pitfalls: it is easy to either over- and undercook. The sous vide cooking technique helps you get around those challenges, and the little canning jars these desserts are made in are very cute. You could easily bring them to a dinner party as gifts.

## Tips

You can easily double or triple this recipe.

I recommend using brand-new jars that have not previously been heat stressed.

▸ **Preheat hot water bath to 176°F (80°C)**
▸ **Four 4 oz (125 mL) glass canning jars, with lids**
▸ **Candy/deep-fry or instant-read thermometer**
▸ **Fine-mesh sieve**

### CARAMEL

| | | |
|---|---|---|
| ½ cup | granulated sugar | 125 mL |
| 3 tbsp | water | 45 mL |

### CUSTARD

| | | |
|---|---|---|
| 3 | eggs | 3 |
| 2 tbsp | granulated sugar | 30 mL |
| 1 tsp | vanilla extract | 5 mL |
| 1½ cups | whole milk | 375 mL |
| | Whipped cream, sweetened, if desired, optional | |

1. Place jars on a small baking sheet or in a skillet. (This ensures that they will be contained if they crack when the hot caramel is added.)

2. *Caramel:* In a small, heavy-bottomed saucepan, combine sugar and water. Let stand for 1 minute or until sugar is moistened. Bring to a boil over medium heat. Boil, without stirring, until caramel is a medium-dark color and temperature reads 338° to 340°F (170° to 171°C). Pour about 2 tbsp (30 mL) caramel into each jar. Let cool.

3. *Custard:* In a small bowl, whisk together eggs, sugar and vanilla until blended. Set aside. (To make uncooked custard ahead, see Tips, at right.)

4. Meanwhile, in a medium saucepan over medium heat, bring milk to a simmer. Remove from heat. Gradually pour about ½ cup (125 mL) hot milk into egg mixture, whisking constantly. Then, whisking constantly, gradually pour egg mixture into remaining milk.

## Tips

*To make uncooked custard ahead:* Prepare through Step 3. Transfer mixture to an airtight container, cover and refrigerate for up to 2 days. Proceed with Step 4.

*To make cooked custard ahead:* Prepare through Step 6. Refrigerate for up to 3 days. Proceed with Step 7.

5. Strain custard through fine-mesh sieve into a bowl. Ladle over caramel in jars, leaving $\frac{1}{2}$ inch (1 cm) headspace. Wipe rims of jars thoroughly to ensure a good seal. Add lids and turn just until snug. Immerse jars in preheated water bath and cook for 50 minutes. (To make cooked custard ahead, see Tips, at left.)

6. Remove jars from hot water bath and let stand at room temperature for 20 to 30 minutes. Refrigerate overnight.

7. Open jars. Slide a thin-bladed knife around edge of each custard and invert onto a plate, letting caramel pool around custard. (You may need to jiggle the custards a bit to get them to slide out.) Garnish with whipped cream, if using.

-----------------------------------------------------------------

## Variation

**Bonet:** This Italian (Piedmontese, to be specific) chocolate and hazelnut crème caramel is one I frequently serve at parties. Omit the vanilla. In Step 3, add to the egg mixture $3\frac{1}{2}$ tbsp (52 mL) unsweetened hazelnut paste, 1 tbsp (15 mL) amber or dark rum (optional), and 4 tsp (20 mL) unsweetened cocoa powder. Whisk until smooth. Proceed with Step 4.

# Vanilla Ice Cream

I make ice cream that has a butterfat content between 10% and 19%, depending on whether I am serving it in a cone or cup or garnishing a dessert with a little ice cream quenelle. This recipe calls for equal parts milk and cream to create a richer, restaurant-style ice cream.

**MAKES ABOUT 5 CUPS (1.25 L) ICE CREAM BASE**

Freezer Bag Friendly

## Tips

You can easily halve or double this recipe.

For a lighter ice cream with a butterfat content of about 10%, use 1 part cream to 3 parts milk. In this recipe that would be 1 cup (250 mL) cream and 3 cups (750 mL) whole milk.

▶ **Preheat hot water bath to 180°F (82.2°C)**
▶ **Large resealable freezer bag**
▶ **Blender or immersion blender**
▶ **Fine-mesh sieve**
▶ **Ice-cream maker**

| | | |
|---|---|---|
| 2 cups | whole milk (see Tips, at left) | 500 mL |
| 2 cups | heavy or whipping (35%) cream | 500 mL |
| 8 | egg yolks (see Tips, at right) | 8 |
| 1 cup | granulated sugar | 250 mL |
| 1 | vanilla bean, split lengthwise | 1 |

1. In blender or using immersion blender in a tall cup, combine milk, cream, egg yolks and sugar. Blend until smooth.

2. Pour mixture into freezer bag, add vanilla bean and seal. Immerse bag in preheated water bath and cook for 1 hour.

3. Open bag and strain mixture through fine-mesh sieve into a large bowl. If desired, use the tip of a small, sharp knife to scrape vanilla seeds into mixture; whisk to combine. (Discard vanilla pod or save for another use; see box, page 342.)

4. Place bowl in a larger bowl filled with ice water and stir until chilled, about 15 minutes. Cover and refrigerate overnight or for up to 3 days.

5. Pour mixture into ice-cream maker and freeze according to manufacturer's instructions.

## Tips

Leftover egg whites can be frozen for up to 1 year in a well-sealed airtight container. In fact, they make more stable meringues than fresh whites, at the expense of some volume.

Keep in mind that frozen food tastes less sweet than food at room temperature. Try this experiment: taste the mix before and after freezing to see if you notice the difference.

### Vanilla Ice Cream and Crème Anglaise — Same Thing!

Vanilla ice cream is basically frozen crème anglaise, a French custard sauce whose name means "English cream." I call for whole milk in both recipes, but you can use a lower-fat milk if you like. The cooked egg yolks thicken the custard and give it a voluptuous texture. The proteins in the yolk begin to set at 150°F (65.6°C), so if you take your custard past about 185°F (85°C), you risk creating grainy curds.

Traditionally this mixture is cooked on the stove and stirred constantly, because the cook has to judge the right moment to stop and transfer it to another container to halt the cooking process (this ensures the egg mixture doesn't scramble at the bottom). By cooking it sous vide, however, you can set the hot water bath temperature to 180°F (82.2°C) and let your custard cook without overseeing the process.

### Stone Fruit Purées

Apricots, plums, peaches and nectarines can easily be turned into purées for making ice cream, sorbet or frozen drinks — peach daiquiris, anyone? To turn any of these fruits into a purée, preheat hot water bath to 190°F (87.8°C). Halve fruits and remove stones. Arrange in a sous vide pouch in a single layer and seal. Immerse in hot water bath for 30 minutes. The pouch may float, so place a heavy object like a small cast-iron skillet on top so that the fruit is submerged and cooks evenly. Remove pouch and let cool, about 20 minutes. Open pouch and transfer fruit to a blender or food processor, in batches if necessary, and purée. Using a stiff rubber spatula, force purée through a fine-mesh sieve into a bowl to remove the skins. Refrigerate for up to 3 days or freeze for up to 3 months. Freeze in ice-cube trays for blending into drinks.

# Crème Anglaise

Crème anglaise is the most basic and versatile of dessert sauces. This recipe is identical to the base for Vanilla Ice Cream (page 340) but contains a larger number of egg yolks — ideal for a large group. The extra yolks result in a thicker sauce with a more custardy flavor. Serve it with poached fruit, meringues or chocolate cake.

---

**MAKES ABOUT 5 CUPS (1.25 L)**

Freezer Bag Friendly

## Tips

You can easily halve or double this recipe.

I like to use crème anglaise as a base for ice cream made with stone fruits such as peaches or apricots (see "Stone Fruit Purées," page 341). The richer base compensates for all the fruit. Use equal quantities of fruit purée and crème anglaise and adjust to taste, adding slightly more crème anglaise or purée as desired.

▸ **Preheat hot water bath to 180°F (82.2°C)**
▸ **Large resealable freezer bag**
▸ **Blender or immersion blender**
▸ **Fine-mesh sieve**

| | | |
|---|---|---:|
| 2 cups | whole milk | 500 mL |
| 2 cups | heavy or whipping (35%) cream | 500 mL |
| 12 | egg yolks (see Tips, page 341) | 12 |
| 1 cup | granulated sugar | 250 mL |
| 1 | vanilla bean, split lengthwise | 1 |

**1.** In blender or using immersion blender in a tall cup, combine milk, cream, egg yolks and sugar. Blend until smooth.

**2.** Pour mixture into freezer bag, add vanilla bean and seal. Immerse bag in preheated water bath and cook for 1 hour.

**3.** Open bag and strain mixture through fine-mesh sieve into a large bowl. If desired, use the tip of a small, sharp knife to scrape vanilla seeds into mixture; whisk to combine. (Discard vanilla pod or save for another use; see box, below.)

**4.** Place bowl in a larger bowl filled with ice water and stir until chilled, about 15 minutes. Cover and refrigerate overnight or for up to 4 days.

---

### Reusing Vanilla Beans

If desired, you can reuse the vanilla pod. It will be slightly reduced in strength but still good. Rinse and set aside on a plate to dry for 24 hours. Then bury it in 1 cup (250 mL) granulated sugar. Set aside until ready to use. Add the vanilla pod and sugar to your next batch.

---

# Dulce de Leche

Dulce de leche is a confection popular all over Latin America. It is made from sweetened milk that is slowly simmered until it has a nutty caramel color and flavor. (In Mexico it's called *cajeta* and is made from goat's milk instead of cow's milk.) This recipe uses an old trick — a can of sweetened condensed milk. I suggest cooking it in a freezer bag, because it can be hazardous making it in the can. Use dulce de leche to fill profiteroles or sandwich cookies, or in Caramel Rice Pudding (page 344).

**MAKES 14 OZ (300 ML)**

Freezer Bag Friendly

## Tips

You can easily double or triple this recipe using one bag.

Dulce de leche makes a great, inexpensive and healthier alternative to chocolate hazelnut spread. Spread it straight onto toast or blend it with an equal quantity of nut or seed butter — pumpkinseed butter is a favorite of mine.

▶ **Preheat hot water bath to 200°F (93.3°C).**
▶ **Large resealable freezer bag**

| 1 | can (14 oz/300 mL) sweetened condensed milk | 1 |

1. Open can. Using a rubber spatula, transfer contents to freezer bag and seal.
2. Place bag in preheated water bath with zip seal hanging outside the bath. Cook for 8 to 10 hours.
3. Remove bag from bath and let cool, about 2 hours.
4. Serve immediately or store in the refrigerator for up to 7 days.

### Dulce de Leche Whipped Cream

Dulce de leche whipped cream is great on ice cream, with roasted bananas or as a quick cake frosting. Adding dulce de leche to whipping cream makes a slightly denser but more stable cream. To make 1 cup (250 mL), place 2 tbsp (30 mL) dulce de leche in a chilled bowl with 2 tbsp (30 mL) chilled heavy or whipping (35%) cream. Whisk until well combined, about 2 minutes. Add 6 tbsp (90 mL) more cream and whisk vigorously until thickened and almost doubled in volume, about 4 to 5 minutes. Store in an airtight container in the refrigerator for up to 24 hours.

# Caramel Rice Pudding

Rice pudding is polarizing — you either love it or hate it. I like it but rarely go to the trouble of making this inexpensive dessert. However, with sous vide, there is very little cleanup and you don't have to worry about scorching the rice. This recipe combines two Latin American favorites in one dessert: rice pudding and dulce de leche. Feel free to enhance it with some raisins or toasted slivered almonds.

**MAKES
4 SERVINGS**

## Tip

Rice absorption and time to doneness depend on the variety and age of the rice. For this recipe I have had the best results with sushi rice grown in the United States, but most other short-grain rice works here too. Avoid rice with large grains, such as Arborio, because it takes too long to cook.

▸ **Preheat hot water bath to 200°F (93.3°C)**
▸ **1-quart (1 L) canning jar, with lid**

| | | |
|---|---|---|
| 3 cups | water | 750 mL |
| ¾ cup + 2 tbsp | American sushi rice (see Tips, at left) | 205 mL |
| 2½ cups | whole milk, divided | 625 mL |
| 6 tbsp | dulce de leche (page 343) | 90 mL |
| ¼ tsp | kosher salt | 1 mL |
| ¼ tsp | ground cinnamon | 1 mL |
| ¼ tsp | ground cardamom | 1 mL |
| ¼ tsp | vanilla extract | 1 mL |

1. In a medium saucepan, bring water to a boil over medium-high heat. Add rice and blanch for 3 minutes. Drain in a colander.

2. Place rice in jar. Add 1½ cups (375 mL) milk and stir to combine. Wipe rim of jar thoroughly to ensure a good seal. Add lid and turn just until snug. Immerse jar in preheated water bath and cook for 30 minutes.

3. Using tongs, remove jar. Using a clean kitchen towel, open jar carefully (it will be hot). Stir in dulce de leche until thoroughly combined. Add salt, cinnamon, cardamom, vanilla and ½ cup (125 mL) milk; stir well. Wipe rim and reseal jar. Return to hot water bath and cook for 30 minutes.

If you like, stir in raisins after cooking and/or top with toasted slivered almonds when serving.

**4.** Using tongs, remove jar. Using kitchen towel, open jar. Add remaining $\frac{1}{2}$ cup (125 mL) milk and stir well. Wipe rim and reseal jar. Return to water bath and cook for 30 minutes.

**5.** Using tongs, remove jar. Using kitchen towel, open jar. Stir rice and taste to check for doneness. If it is still al dente and all the milk has been absorbed, add 2 to 3 tbsp (30 to 45 mL) more milk or water, leaving at least $\frac{1}{2}$ inch (1 cm) headspace. Wipe rim, reseal jar and cook for 15 minutes longer.

**6.** Remove jar from bath and let stand, unopened, until cool, about 2 hours. Refrigerate or serve at room temperature. The pudding will keep in the refrigerator for up to 5 days.

# Pears in Red Wine

This is an easy classic. Poaching whole pears in red wine gives you a striking presentation — bright red on the outside but still ivory colored on the inside. Make sure to halve the pears before serving them, alongside vanilla ice cream or whipped cream.

## Tips

You can easily halve or double this recipe. Use a separate bag for each set of pears.

White wine works equally well for this recipe, although you won't get the same color effect for a striking presentation.

Substitute half a vanilla bean for the cinnamon, if you prefer.

To cook properly, pears should be slightly under-ripe and firm. Other varieties of pears will work but their cooking times will vary.

*To make ahead:*
Prepare through Step 3. Refrigerate for up to 5 days. Proceed with Step 4.

Dulce de Leche Whipped Cream (see box, page 343) would be an excellent garnish here.

▶ **Preheat hot water bath to 180°F (82.2°C)**
▶ **2 small resealable freezer bags**

| | | |
|---|---|---|
| 2 cups | fruity dry red wine, such as Gamay (see Tips, at left) | 500 mL |
| ½ cup | granulated sugar | 125 mL |
| 1 | 2-inch (5 cm) piece cinnamon stick (see Tips, at left) | 1 |
| 4 | firm medium Bartlett pears, peeled (see Tips, at left) | 4 |
| | Sweetened whipped cream or ice cream, optional | |

1. In a small saucepan, combine wine, sugar and cinnamon. Bring to a boil over medium-high heat. Set aside to cool slightly.

2. Place 2 pears in each freezer bag. Discard cinnamon, divide wine mixture equally between bags and seal. Immerse bags in preheated water bath and cook for 50 minutes.

3. Remove bags from hot water bath and let cool slightly, about 10 minutes. (To make ahead, see Tips, at left.)

4. Open bags and pour liquid into a small saucepan. Bring to a boil over medium heat and boil until liquid is reduced to 1½ cups (375 mL), about 10 minutes. Remove from heat and let cool slightly.

5. Meanwhile, halve pears vertically. Using a melon baller or small spoon, scoop out seed cavity and discard.

6. Serve pear halves warm or cold, accompanied by the poaching liquid plus whipped cream and/or ice cream, if desired.

# Pears with Dried Cranberries

Pears and dried fruit are a natural combination and make an easy lunch or brunch dessert, or even a midnight snack. These pears are very lightly sweetened and their juice plumps the cranberries as they cook. They can also be diced and served, with the cranberries, as a topping for hot cereal, such as No-Mess Perfect Steel-Cut Oatmeal (page 389), or as a savory garnish for Venison Sauerbraten (page 102; see Tips, below). It's a very versatile dish!

MAKES
2 SERVINGS

## Tips

You can easily halve or double this recipe. If doubling, use 2 pouches.

To cook properly, pears should be slightly under-ripe and firm. Other varieties of pears will work but their cooking times will vary.

Substitute other dried fruits, such as raisins or prunes, if desired.

If you will be adding the pears to oatmeal, double the sugar (if desired). If using the pears as a garnish for venison, replace the sugar with a pinch of salt.

*To make ahead:* Prepare through Step 3. Refrigerate for up to 5 days. Proceed with Step 4.

▶ **Preheat hot water bath to 180°F (82.2°C)**
▶ **Sous vide pouch**

| | | |
|---|---|---|
| 2 | firm medium Bartlett pears, peeled, halved and cored (see Tips, at left) | 2 |
| 2 tsp | granulated sugar | 10 mL |
| 3 tbsp | dried cranberries (see Tips, at left) | 45 mL |

1. In a medium bowl, toss pears with sugar to coat.

2. Place cranberries in pouch. Arrange pear halves in a single layer in pouch and seal. Immerse pouch in preheated water bath and cook for 40 minutes.

3. Remove pouch from hot water bath and let cool slightly, about 10 minutes. (To make ahead, see Tips, at left.)

4. Open pouch and serve.

### Apples and Pears

Apples and pears are interchangeable in many desserts. However, there is one significant difference when it comes to cooking them sous vide — apples float and pears sink. (I guess that's why you never hear about bobbing for pears at Halloween.)

Since the air inside the flesh of apples is a poor conductor of heat, they take quite a bit longer to cook than pears. And because they float, you'll have to use my "spoon technique" (page 317) for submerging the pouches or bags.

# Buttery Apples

These lemony, buttery apples are adaptable. Serve them with yogurt for breakfast or with crème fraîche for dessert. I also like them as an accompaniment to Duck Confit (page 176) or roast pork.

---

**MAKES
4 SERVINGS**

Freezer Bag Friendly

## Tips

You can easily halve or double this recipe. Use one pouch per apple.

To use resealable freezer bags, melt butter in a small saucepan over low heat or in the microwave. Pour melted butter over apples in Step 2 and seal, then cook as directed. Don't forget to include spoons in the bags.

Other varieties of apples can be used, though their cooking times will vary.

These apples are only lightly sweetened. Double the sugar if desired.

Feel free to substitute brown sugar for the white sugar for a slight caramel flavor, or use maple syrup instead.

Check doneness after 90 minutes by gently squeezing the pouch. Use a towel, as the contents will be hot.

*To make ahead:*
Prepare through Step 3. Refrigerate for up to 5 days. Proceed with Step 4.

▶ **Preheat hot water bath to 180°F (82.2°C)**
▶ **2 sous vide pouches**

| | | |
|---|---|---|
| 2 | large Granny Smith apples, peeled, halved lengthwise and cored | 2 |
| 2 tbsp | granulated sugar (see Tips, at left) | 30 mL |
| 1 tsp | grated lemon zest | 5 mL |
| 1 tbsp | freshly squeezed lemon juice | 15 mL |
| ¼ tsp | ground nutmeg | 1 mL |
| Pinch | salt | Pinch |
| 3 tbsp | butter, chilled | 45 mL |

**1.** Slice each apple half into 3 smaller wedges. Place in a medium bowl. Add sugar, lemon zest, lemon juice, nutmeg and salt. Toss to coat.

**2.** Nest 2 or 3 teaspoons in the bottom of each sous vide pouch (to prevent the pouches from floating while cooking). Evenly divide apple mixture and butter between pouches and seal. Immerse pouches in preheated water bath and cook for 2 hours.

**3.** Remove pouches from hot water bath and let cool slightly, about 15 minutes. (To make ahead, see Tips, at left.)

**4.** Open pouches and pour contents into a medium skillet (pick out spoons with kitchen tongs). Bring to a boil over high heat. Baste the apples with a spoon as the liquid reduces, glazing them with a smooth, shiny coating, for about 5 to 7 minutes. Serve hot.

# Sauces and Sundries

This chapter consists mostly of support recipes such as sauces and pantry staples for the rest of the book. Most of these do not require sous vide equipment and can be used as base recipes in your general repertoire. I've also included some infusions and outliers — such as yogurt and oatmeal — that don't fit in elsewhere. The purpose of this chapter is to set you up for success.

If you have time, skim through the recipes. Many of them, including Spiced Salt, keep for quite a while, and they are handy to have available before you dive into other parts of this book.

# Spiced Salt

This seasoned salt was originally created for making duck confit, but it is excellent in many other recipes. It can also be used to make a wonderful spiced brine for meats (see Variation, below).

**MAKES 1 CUP (250 ML)**

### Tip

This recipe can easily be doubled or tripled.

| | | |
|---|---|---|
| ½ cup | kosher salt | 125 mL |
| 2 tbsp | granulated sugar | 30 mL |
| 2 tbsp | chopped shallots | 30 mL |
| 1½ tbsp | chopped fresh thyme | 22 mL |
| 1 tbsp | cracked black pepper | 15 mL |
| 1 tbsp | chopped garlic | 15 mL |
| 3 | bay leaves, finely crumbled | 3 |

1. In a medium bowl, stir together salt, sugar, shallots, thyme, pepper, garlic and bay leaves. Use immediately or freeze in an airtight container for up to 6 months.

### Variation

**Spiced Brine:** In a large bowl, stir ½ cup (125 mL) Spiced Salt into 1 cup (250 mL) hot water until dissolved. Stir in 3 cups (750 mL) cold water. Cover and refrigerate until chilled. Use within 5 days. Makes 4 cups (1 L). Make sure to never reuse brine. Always make a fresh batch for each dish you cook, in order to avoid cross-contamination.

# Saffron Salt

Saffron is as hard to measure as it is expensive. Here's a way to get the best use out of a little that will also give you a powder that's easy to measure. It works well in Saffron Cauliflower with Sultanas (page 309) and can also be used in risottos and paellas.

**MAKES 3 TBSP
(45 ML)**

## Tips

You can easily double or triple this recipe. Make it in batches that you can use up in 1 or 2 months.

I like to add this toward the end of preparation when I'm cooking traditionally, such as for rice dishes. I find that I get a purer, stronger flavor that way.

▶ **Spice grinder or coffee grinder**

| | | |
|---|---|---|
| 2 tsp | saffron threads | 10 mL |
| ¼ cup | kosher salt | 60 mL |

1. In a small skillet over low heat, combine saffron and salt. Warm gently, stirring constantly with a wooden spoon, until just hot to the touch (130° to 140°F/ 54.4° to 60°C), about 2 or 3 minutes.

2. Allow to cool slightly. In spice grinder, process mixture into a powder. Store, covered, in a cool, dark place.

# Foie Gras Spice Blend

This mixture is quite subtle. If you are grinding your own spices, I recommend aging the blend for a few days prior to use, so the spices can mellow and their aromas meld.

**MAKES
6¾ TBSP
(100 ML)**

## Tips

You can halve this recipe.

This mixture can also be used for pâtés and terrines made from pork.

It isn't absolutely essential to grind all your own spices for this recipe. For instance, grinding small quantities of cloves can be difficult in a coffee grinder. If you have a reasonably fresh jar of ground cloves, go ahead and use it. You must, however, grind the spices individually before measuring.

The blend will keep for up to 4 months if well stored.

| | | |
|---|---|---|
| 6½ tsp | ground white pepper | 32 mL |
| 5 tsp | freshly grated nutmeg | 25 mL |
| 2½ tsp | ground ginger | 12 mL |
| 2½ tsp | freshly ground allspice | 12 mL |
| 2½ tsp | freshly ground Ceylon cinnamon (see box, below) | 12 mL |
| 1¼ tsp | freshly ground cloves | 6 mL |

1. In a small bowl, combine white pepper, nutmeg, ginger, allspice, cinnamon and cloves. Transfer to an airtight container, cover and store in a cool, dark place.

### Ceylon Cinnamon

Ceylon cinnamon, also known as true cinnamon, is a little different from the product that's usually marketed as cinnamon, which is cassia, a relative. True cinnamon has a gentler and more complex flavor than cassia, and it is softer and easier to grind. Look for it in Latin American and Asian grocery stores.

# Pork Brine

This recipe makes enough brine for about 1½ lbs (675 g) of pork. When you use it, be sure that the brine is cold and that the pork is completely submerged before refrigerating. To ensure accuracy, it is best to weigh rather than measure powders such as salts and sugars. This guarantees that you'll get the right proportions of all the elements.

---

**MAKES
4 CUPS (1 L)**

## Tips

You can easily make more or less of the brine to suit your needs.

The sugar counteracts the hardening effect of salt on the meat. Brown or turbinado sugar can be substituted, if desired.

If you are in a hurry, you can use ice cubes in place of the remaining 2 cups (500 mL) cold water. After Step 1, pour unstrained brine into a 4-cup (1L) measuring cup. Add ice until the liquid reaches the 4-cup (1 L) mark. Stir occasionally until the ice melts.

You can omit the curing salt if it is unavailable or not desired, but you will lose the lovely rosy hue that it gives to pork. Replace the curing salt with kosher salt.

Curing salt is available online at Modernist Pantry (www. modernistpantry.com).

The chilled brine will keep in the refrigerator for up to 7 days.

▶ **Fine-mesh sieve**

| | | |
|---|---|---|
| 4 cups | cold water, divided | 1 L |
| 1 oz | kosher salt (about 2½ tbsp/37 mL) | 30 g |
| ⅓ oz | granulated sugar (about 2 tsp/10 mL) | 10 g |
| ⅓ oz | curing salt (about 2 tsp/10 mL; see Tips, at left) | 10 g |
| 1 tsp | cracked black peppercorns | 5 mL |
| 3 | cloves garlic, thinly sliced | 3 |
| 2 | bay leaves | 2 |
| 2 | sprigs fresh thyme or ⅛ tsp (0.5 mL) dried thyme | 2 |

1. In a medium saucepan, combine 2 cups (500 mL) water, kosher salt, sugar, curing salt, cracked pepper, garlic, bay leaves and thyme. (Keep remaining water cold.) Bring pan to a simmer over medium heat. Reduce heat to low and simmer, stirring occasionally, for 4 to 5 minutes or until salts and sugar have dissolved.

2. Remove from heat and stir in remaining cold water. Transfer to a medium bowl. Cover and refrigerate until well chilled before using, about 2 hours. Strain through sieve before use; discard solids.

# Fish Brine

Brining fish serves several purposes. While seasoning the fish slightly, it also firms up the flesh a little, thus making it less susceptible to crushing when sealing it in pouches. It also keeps the albumin in the fish from collecting on the surface and leaving a milky residue, which is especially noticeable on darker-fleshed fish such as salmon and char. When using it, be sure that the brine is cold and the fish is completely submerged before refrigerating. This recipe is easy to make and gives you enough brine for 4 to 6 portions of fish.

**MAKES
4 CUPS (1 L)**

## Tips

*To prepare fish:*
Immerse fish in brine and refrigerate for 4 to 8 hours. Remove from brine and pat dry. Discard brine and proceed with your recipe.

Fish can be brined and drained up to 36 hours ahead of cooking.

The sugar counteracts the hardening effect of salt on the fish. The ratio I use is 6% salt and 3% sugar compared to the weight of the water — in other words, 60 g salt and 30 g granulated sugar for each liter of water (which weighs 1,000 g). Scale up or down as desired.

The brine cannot be reused. However, any leftovers will keep for up to 7 days in the refrigerator.

| | | |
|---|---|---|
| 4 cups | cold water, divided | 1 L |
| ⅓ cup | kosher salt | 75 mL |
| 3 tbsp | granulated sugar | 45 mL |

1. In a medium saucepan, combine 2 cups (500 mL) water, salt and sugar. (Keep remaining water cold.) Bring to a simmer over medium heat. Simmer, stirring, until salt and sugar are dissolved, about 1 to 2 minutes.

2. Transfer to a container and add remaining 2 cups (500 mL) water. Allow to cool for 20 to 30 minutes, then refrigerate until cold, about 1 to 2 hours.

# Basic Pickling Liquid

I have used this recipe for many years to lightly pickle fish or vegetables. Like many other basic recipes in this book, it is highly adaptable. I have added fresh ginger, horseradish, carrots and whole cloves to the liquid, either together or individually, for various dishes. Depending on what you're cooking, get creative!

**MAKES ABOUT 10 OZ (300 ML)**

## Tips

You can easily double or triple this recipe.

I sometimes like to use the red onions as a garnish for whatever I am pickling.

This pickling liquid will keep for up to 5 days in the refrigerator.

▶ **Fine-mesh sieve**

| | | |
|---|---|---|
| ½ cup | unseasoned rice vinegar | 125 mL |
| ⅓ cup | water | 75 mL |
| 1½ tbsp | granulated sugar | 22 mL |
| 1 tsp | kosher salt | 5 mL |
| 4 | allspice berries | 4 |
| 1 tsp | black peppercorns | 5 mL |
| 1 | bay leaf | 1 |
| ½ cup | finely sliced red onion | 125 mL |

1. In a small saucepan, combine vinegar, water, sugar, salt, allspice, peppercorns and bay leaf. Bring to a simmer over medium heat. Simmer, stirring to dissolve sugar and salt, for 2 to 3 minutes. Remove from heat and let cool slightly, about 5 minutes.

2. Place onion in a small bowl. Strain warm liquid through sieve into the bowl, covering onions. Let cool to room temperature, cover and refrigerate.

### Easy Pickling 101

If you have a chamber vacuum sealer, you can use Basic Pickling Liquid to lightly vacuum-pickle vegetables such as cucumbers. Using a mandoline, thinly slice cucumbers and place in a sous vide pouch. Cover with pickling liquid. Seal pouch, using the highest setting. Refrigerate for at least 2 hours. The pickled cucumbers will keep for 3 to 4 days in the refrigerator.

# Dashi

Sous vide is a great technique for making dashi, the workhorse stock used in Japanese cooking. You may not have heard of it before, but dashi is the base for some of the most well-known Japanese dishes, such as miso soup, noodle broths and *okonomiyaki*. Homemade dashi isn't as popular as it used to be, but it's well worth the extra effort if you have the time. You'll notice very delicate flavor nuances that are lacking in store-bought versions.

---

**MAKES
4 CUPS (1 L)**

## Tips

You can easily double or triple this recipe. Use 2 or 3 jars, respectively.

Soft water results in more flavorful dashi. If your tap water is very hard, add some distilled water or use reverse-osmosis filtered water.

▶ **1-quart (1 L) canning jar, with lid**
▶ **Fine-mesh sieve**

| ½ oz | kombu (see box, page 358) | 15 g |
| 4 cups | cold water (see Tips, at left) | 1 L |
| 1 oz | katsuobushi (see box, at right) | 30 g |

1. Lightly wipe kombu sheet with a paper towel to remove any dust or foreign particles. The dry white powder clinging to the seaweed contains much of the flavor — try not to wipe that off.

2. Place kombu in jar, cutting to fit as required. Pour water overtop, making sure kombu is completely immersed and leaving ½ inch (1 cm) headspace. Wipe rim of jar thoroughly to ensure a good seal. Add lid and turn just until snug.

3. Place jar in unheated water bath and add enough water to match level of water in the jar. Heat hot water bath to 149°F (65°C).

4. Once water bath reaches desired temperature, start timing. Cook for 1 hour.

5. Using fine-mesh sieve, strain liquid into a medium saucepan; discard solids. Bring liquid to a simmer over medium heat. Add katsuobushi and remove from heat. Allow katsuobushi to settle and infuse, about 5 minutes. Using sieve, strain liquid into a bowl or clean jar; discard solids. Use immediately or refrigerate for up to 3 days.

## Tips (Variation)

You will likely want to use the broth and the rendered bacon fat for separate purposes. After refrigerating, the fat can be easily removed from the surface of the broth.

If not using the dashi immediately, leave the fat on to help seal and preserve the broth. But remember, fat picks up refrigerator odors like a sponge. Be sure to seal the container once it has chilled completely.

Stored in an airtight container, this heartier dashi will keep in the refrigerator for up to 4 days covered with its fat.

## Variation

Bacon Dashi: The famous New York–based chef David Chang introduced the world to bacon dashi, in which bacon stands in for the katsuobushi. This is a very robust broth, suitable for ramen dishes. I also use it to moisten sauerkraut.

After Step 4, strain broth, discarding spent kombu. Add 8 oz (225 g) finely diced bacon to jar — European-style smoked slab bacon works particularly well here; leave the rind on if present. Top up with kombu broth, leaving $1/2$ inch (1 cm) headspace. You will have a small amount of broth left over; refrigerate it and use for another purpose or add it back into the dashi after final straining. Wipe rim of jar to ensure a good seal; screw lid just until snug. Continue cooking in hot water bath set to 149°F (65°C) for 5 to 10 hours. Using fine-mesh sieve, strain, discarding solids.

### Katsuobushi

Katsuobushi is dried, salted and smoked bonito, a variety of tuna. It is generally served shaved and is a common ingredient in Japanese cuisine. It can be purchased in Asian grocery stores. Store, tightly sealed, in a cool, dark place, and don't buy more than you can use in 2 or 3 months.

# Key Lime Ponzu Sauce

Ponzu is a cold citrus-flavored, soy-based dipping sauce. It is excellent with chilled octopus and tasty with grilled squid. Traditionally the citrus is either yuzu or sudachi, fruits that can be difficult to source. I find that key limes make a good substitute.

**MAKES 1½ CUPS (375 ML)**

## Tips

You can easily double this recipe.

Try to find organic key limes, since you are infusing the skin oils into the sauce.

If you have access to sudachis, by all means use them in place of the key limes. Substitute 6 sudachis for the limes and use the juice of 3 of them in Step 6.

The unjuiced limes can be juiced and the juice frozen in ice-cube trays for future use. Remember that key limes are not quite as sour as Persian limes.

This will keep for 12 months in the freezer, and a little goes a long way. The sauce may or may not freeze solid, depending on the temperature of your freezer and the salinity of the soy sauce. If it does, you will have to defrost it before use. Transfer to the refrigerator overnight or leave on the counter for a few hours.

▸ **Preheat hot water bath to 149°F (65°C)**
▸ **1-quart (1 L) canning jar, with lid**
▸ **Fine-mesh sieve**
▸ **Cheesecloth (optional)**

| | | |
|---|---|---|
| 8 | key limes (see Tips, at left) | 8 |
| 1¼ cups | low-sodium Japanese soy sauce | 300 mL |
| 1 | piece kombu, 1 by 2 inches (2.5 by 5 cm; see box, below) | 1 |
| 1 | big pinch katsuobushi (see box, page 357) | 1 |

1. Scrub limes with a brush or green scouring pad. Wipe dry with paper towels.

2. Place limes, soy sauce, kombu and katsuobushi in jar. Wipe rim of jar thoroughly to ensure a good seal. Add lid and turn just until snug.

3. Place jar in preheated water bath and cook for 1 hour. Using a towel, remove jar from bath and shake to redistribute ingredients (be careful — the jar will be hot). Cook for 1 hour longer.

4. Remove jar from bath and let cool for at least 1 hour or up to 12 hours.

5. Open jar and strain contents through fine-mesh sieve, preferably lined with cheesecloth, into a clean jar.

6. Rinse limes and then juice 4 of them (see Tips, at left). Strain juice through sieve into soy mixture and stir to combine. Use sauce immediately or store in a glass jar in the freezer.

### Kombu

Kombu is an edible variety of dried kelp, a sea vegetable. It is most commonly used in dashi, the Japanese stock that is fundamental to miso soup. It can be found in grocery stores catering to an Asian clientele. Sold dry, it will keep for years.

# Barbecue Pork Rib Rub

This spice blend is designed for ribs but works equally well for unbrined pork belly. You can even use it for barbecue-style chicken that will be finished on the grill. It keeps quite well and is sufficient for 8 or 16 pounds (3.6 kg or 7.25 kg) of ribs, depending on how you finish them.

**MAKES 1 CUP (250 ML)**

## Tips

You can easily halve or double this recipe.

For a light cure when you plan to glaze the ribs with barbecue sauce before serving, use 1 tbsp (15 mL) rib rub for each 1 lb (450 g) of ribs. Double that amount if you are planning to finish the ribs without further seasoning.

The flavors of this rub are especially potent if you grind the whole spices yourself rather than using ready-ground. If you decide to start from whole spices, grind them individually so you can measure them accurately.

If you are a fan of monosodium glutamate (MSG), this is a place where you can use it, in controlled quantities. Add up to 2 tbsp (30 mL) to the spice mixture for an enhanced umami note.

▶ **Small fine-mesh sieve or food processor**

| | | |
|---|---|---|
| 3 tbsp | kosher salt | 45 mL |
| 2 tbsp | packed brown sugar | 30 mL |
| 2 tbsp | garlic powder | 30 mL |
| 2 tbsp | dry mustard | 30 mL |
| 2 tbsp | freshly ground black pepper | 30 mL |
| 2 tbsp | chipotle chile powder | 30 mL |
| 1 tbsp | smoked sweet paprika | 15 mL |
| 1 tbsp | onion powder | 15 mL |
| 1 tsp | ground dried thyme | 5 mL |
| 1 tsp | ground cumin | 5 mL |
| 1 tsp | ground coriander | 5 mL |
| 1 tsp | ground turmeric | 5 mL |

**1.** In a small bowl, whisk together salt, brown sugar, garlic powder, mustard, pepper, chile powder, paprika, onion powder, thyme, cumin, coriander and turmeric. If powder is lumpy, spoon into fine-mesh sieve and sift into an airtight container, pressing to break up any lumps of sugar. Alternatively, combine all ingredients in food processor fitted with the metal blade and process until well combined. Use immediately or store in a cool, dark place for 3 to 4 months.

# Chinese Black Bean Pork Seasoning

This seasoning paste is terrific on Pork Ribs (page 116) or pork belly. The quantity here is sufficient for about 2 lbs (900 g) of pork back or side ribs or 1 to 1½ lbs (450 to 675 g) of pork belly (rind on or off). The seasoning recreates the flavor of the black bean ribs you get for dim sum at Chinese restaurants.

**MAKES ABOUT
1½ CUPS
(375 ML)**

## Tip

Salted fermented black beans are sold damp in cellophane packages in Chinese grocery stores. They have the consistency of hard-boiled egg yolk. Although they are very salty and are frequently soaked before use, here we use them unsoaked to capture all their flavor.

▶ **Food processor**

| | | |
|---|---|---|
| ¼ cup | salted fermented black beans | 60 mL |
| 4 tsp | finely chopped gingerroot | 20 mL |
| 1 tsp | finely chopped garlic | 5 mL |
| ½ tsp | hot pepper sauce, such as Tabasco sauce | 2 mL |
| ½ tsp | finely ground white pepper | 2 mL |
| 4 | green onions, chopped | 4 |
| 1 cup | loosely packed fresh cilantro (leaves and stems) | 250 mL |
| 1 tbsp | soy sauce | 15 mL |
| ½ tsp | unseasoned rice vinegar | 2 mL |

1. In food processor fitted with the metal blade, combine black beans, ginger, garlic, hot pepper sauce and white pepper. Pulse, periodically stopping motor and scraping down sides of bowl, until coarsely chopped.

2. Add green onions, cilantro, soy sauce and vinegar; continue pulsing. Stop the motor and scrape down sides of bowl as required. Process until a slightly coarse paste forms.

3. Use immediately or transfer to a bowl, cover and refrigerate for up to 1 week.

# Thai Pork Barbecue Seasoning

I love the fresh, citrusy flavors of this seasoning paste. Brighter than the other seasonings in this book, it works well in a Thai-inspired meal as a contrast to rich coconut milk–based curries. Try this on pork belly or Pork Ribs (page 116). This recipe makes enough to season about 2 lbs (900 g) of pork back or side ribs or 1 to 1½ lbs (450 to 675 g) of pork belly (rind on or off).

**MAKES ABOUT 1 CUP (250 ML)**

▶ **Food processor**

| | | |
|---|---|---|
| 3 tbsp | chopped trimmed fresh lemongrass (light-colored part only) | 45 mL |
| 3 tbsp | gingerroot, chopped across the grain | 45 mL |
| 2 tbsp | granulated sugar | 30 mL |
| 2 tbsp | chopped shallots | 30 mL |
| 8 | fresh kaffir lime leaves, finely sliced | 8 |
| 1 tbsp | chopped garlic | 15 mL |
| ¼ cup | fish sauce | 60 mL |
| 1½ tbsp | freshly squeezed lime juice | 22 mL |
| 1 tsp | ground white pepper | 5 mL |

1. In food processor fitted with the metal blade, combine lemongrass, ginger, sugar, shallots, lime leaves and garlic. Pulse, periodically stopping motor and scraping down sides of bowl, until finely chopped.

2. Add fish sauce, lime juice and white pepper. Continue pulsing, periodically stopping motor and scraping down sides of bowl, until a medium-textured paste forms. (There should be no pieces larger than a grain of rice.)

3. Use immediately or transfer to a bowl, cover and refrigerate for up to 5 days.

# Tamarind Chipotle Seasoning Paste

This mixture gives you every flavor you could want in a seasoning: sweet, sour, salty, smoky and spicy. It is delicious on Pork Ribs (page 116) or pork belly. I learned this combination in the 1980s when I was working for chef Mark Miller at the famous Coyote Café in Santa Fe, New Mexico. It's been my go-to recipe for pork belly or ribs ever since. This recipe makes enough to season about 2 lbs (900 g) of pork back or side ribs or 1 to 1½ lbs (450 to 675 g) of pork belly (rind on or off).

---

### MAKES ABOUT ¾ CUP (175 ML)

**Tip**

If you can't find chipotle purée, buy a can of chipotle chiles in adobo sauce. Purée the contents of the can in a mini food processor until smooth, then measure out 5 tsp (25 mL).

▶ **Mini food processor**

| | | |
|---|---|---|
| 1 | head 40 Days and 40 Nights Black Garlic (page 388), peeled | 1 |
| ⅓ cup | prepared tamarind paste (see box, page 135) | 75 mL |
| ¼ cup | packed brown sugar | 60 mL |
| 2 tbsp | chopped drained sun-dried tomatoes | 30 mL |
| 5 tsp | chipotle purée (see Tip, at left) | 25 mL |
| 1½ tsp | salt | 7 mL |
| 1 tsp | freshly ground black pepper | 5 mL |

1. In food processor fitted with the metal blade, combine black garlic, tamarind paste, brown sugar, sun-dried tomatoes, chipotle purée, salt and pepper. Pulse until a paste forms.

2. Use immediately or transfer to a small bowl, cover and refrigerate for up to 1 week.

# Garlic Oil

Garlic oil is handy to have around. I like to add a bit to vinaigrettes or brush it over food before it goes on the grill.

**MAKES**
**¾ CUP (175 ML)**

## Tip

Store garlic oil in the freezer between uses.

▸ **Preheat hot water bath to 140°F (60°C)**
▸ **8 oz (250 mL) canning jar, with lid**
▸ **Fine-mesh sieve**

| | | |
|---|---|---|
| 1 | head garlic | 1 |
| ¾ cup | olive oil | 175 mL |

1. Separate garlic into cloves and peel. Cut each clove in half and remove bitter germ. Place garlic halves in jar and pour in oil, leaving ½ inch (1 cm) headspace. Wipe rim of jar thoroughly to ensure a good seal. Add lid and turn just until snug.

2. Immerse jar in preheated water bath and cook for 1 hour.

3. Remove jar from hot water bath and let cool to room temperature.

4. Place sieve over a large glass measuring cup. Strain oil into cup and discard garlic. Pour oil into a clean jar. Use immediately or store in the freezer for up to 6 months.

# Base Sauce for Coq au Vin, Beef Bourguignon, Lamb Shanks and Short Ribs

From a sauce perspective, the only difference between coq au vin and beef bourguignon is the addition of a little tomato paste to the latter. I've used xanthan gum as a thickener in this recipe because it doesn't need simmering to thicken and cook out the starch. As an added bonus, it's also gluten-free.

**MAKES
4 SERVINGS**

## Tips

You can easily halve or double this recipe.

Use chicken broth for Coq au Vin and beef broth for Beef Bourguignon, lamb shanks and short ribs.

A regular blender works well here if you don't have an immersion blender. Using a low speed, start the blender before taking out the plug in the lid, then sprinkle the xanthan gum through the hole.

▸ **Fine-mesh sieve**
▸ **Immersion blender**

| | | |
|---|---|---|
| 2 cups | unsalted chicken or beef broth (see Tips, at left) | 500 mL |
| 1 cup | dry red wine | 250 mL |
| 12 | button mushrooms, stems trimmed, removed and reserved | 12 |
| ½ | bay leaf | ½ |
| 5 oz | slab pancetta or salt pork | 140 g |
| 2 tbsp | butter | 30 mL |
| | Salt and freshly ground black pepper | |
| 2 tsp | chopped garlic | 10 mL |
| 2 tsp | tomato paste, optional | 10 mL |
| ½ tsp | xanthan gum (see page 400) | 2 mL |
| 1 | recipe Balsamic Pearl Onions, drained (page 314) | 1 |
| 1 tsp | chopped fresh thyme | 5 mL |

1. In a medium saucepan, combine broth, wine, mushroom stems and bay leaf. Bring to a boil over medium heat. Reduce heat and boil gently until reduced to 1⅓ cups (325 mL), about 30 minutes. Strain through fine-mesh sieve into a small bowl and let cool; discard solids.

2. Cut pancetta into ½-inch (1 cm) dice. In a saucepan of unsalted boiling water, blanch pancetta for 1 minute. Drain and refresh under cold water, transfer to a bowl and set aside.

**3.** In a large skillet, melt butter over medium heat. Cook mushroom caps, stirring, for 10 minutes, until tender. Season with salt and pepper. Add garlic and cook, stirring, for 1 minute. Set aside.

**4.** Transfer wine mixture and tomato paste (if using) to a tall beaker or similar vessel. Using immersion blender, blend for 30 seconds while carefully sprinkling in xanthan gum, stopping to scrape down sides of container, if necessary.

**5.** Add onions, pancetta and thyme to mushrooms in bowl. Using fine-mesh sieve, strain wine mixture over mushroom mixture; stir to combine. (To make ahead, see Tip, at left.)

# Juniper Butter

This easy-to-make butter is excellent with big-flavored game meats such at venison and elk, served piping hot from the grill. It also enhances bison burgers. This recipe makes enough for 10 to 12 servings.

**MAKES 1 CUP (250 ML)**

## Tip

This recipe can be easily doubled.

▶ **Food processor**

| | | |
|---|---|---|
| 1 cup | softened butter | 250 mL |
| 2 tbsp | finely chopped shallots | 30 mL |
| 1 tbsp | dried juniper berries, ground | 15 mL |
| 1 tsp | freshly ground black pepper | 5 mL |
| 1 tsp | Worcestershire sauce | 5 mL |
| 1 tsp | soy sauce | 5 mL |
| ½ tsp | kosher salt | 2 mL |
| ¼ tsp | ground cumin | 1 mL |

1. Cut butter into ½-inch (1 cm) cubes and place in food processor fitted with the metal blade. Add shallots, ground juniper berries, pepper, Worcestershire sauce, soy sauce, salt and cumin. Process, stopping motor occasionally to scrape down sides of bowl, until well incorporated.

2. Place a long piece of parchment paper or plastic wrap on work surface. Spoon butter onto paper. Using the paper or plastic wrap to help, roll butter mixture into a cylinder ¾ inch (2 cm) in diameter.

3. Wrap paper or plastic wrap tightly around roll and refrigerate for 2 to 3 hours or until firm. Refrigerate butter, well sealed, for up to 10 days or freeze for up to 3 months.

# Umami Butter

Here's a compound butter to use with fish or vegetables such as broccoli (see page 304). Unlike other compound butters, it is not meant to add much of its own flavor. The nutritional yeast, anchovy and soy sauce are full of umami, bringing out the flavor of the foods it is used with.

(see page 304)

**MAKES ½ CUP (125 ML)**

## Tip

If you want a vegetarian butter, omit the anchovy and increase the salt by ¼ tsp (1 mL).

This recipe can be easily doubled.

▶ **Mini food processor**

| | | |
|---|---|---|
| ⅓ cup | softened butter | 75 mL |
| ⅓ cup | nutritional yeast | 75 mL |
| 1 tsp | soy sauce | 5 mL |
| 1 tsp | freshly squeezed lemon juice | 5 mL |
| ¾ tsp | kosher salt | 3 mL |
| ½ tsp | ground white pepper | 2 mL |
| ¼ tsp | hot pepper sauce, such as Tabasco | 1 mL |
| 1 | canned anchovy fillet, drained (or 2 tsp/10 mL anchovy paste) | 1 |

1. In food processor fitted with the metal blade, combine butter, nutritional yeast, soy sauce, lemon juice, salt, white pepper, hot sauce and anchovy. Process, periodically stopping to scrape down sides of container, until smooth.

2. Serve immediately or refrigerate butter, well sealed, for up to 7 days or freeze for up to 3 months.

# Kimchi Butter

I dreamed up this compound butter for scallops, but it also tastes great with lobster and corn on the cob. The butter tones down the spiciness of the kimchi and the kimchi adds flavor-boosting umami to the butter — a win-win situation!

**MAKES 2 CUPS (500 ML)**

## Tip

You can easily halve this recipe. Use a mini food processor instead of the full-size one.

▶ **Food processor**

| | | |
|---|---|---|
| 1 cup | napa cabbage kimchi, drained | 250 mL |
| 1 cup | butter, cut into ½-inch (1 cm) cubes | 250 mL |

1. Using paper towels, squeeze any excess liquid from kimchi; discard liquid. Transfer kimchi to food processor fitted with a metal blade and pulse, periodically stopping to scrape down sides of bowl, until shredded.

2. Add butter and process, periodically stopping to scrape down sides of bowl, until mixture is fairly smooth, with only fine pieces of kimchi visible.

3. Serve immediately or refrigerate butter, well sealed, for up to 10 days or freeze for up to 3 months.

# Pistachio Mint Pesto

This pesto is delightful on lamb, especially chops, where it cuts the richness of the meat. It also goes well with vegetables such as artichokes and makes a great spread for lamb sandwiches. This recipe makes enough for about 8 servings.

**MAKES ⅔ CUP (150 ML)**

## Tips

This recipe can be doubled or tripled easily.

The cheese for this recipe needs to be very finely grated, and it needs to be fresh off the block of cheese, not pre-grated, for the best flavor. A sharp-toothed rasp grater (like the ones made by Microplane) does a magnificent job of grating hard cheeses such as Grana Padano.

When serving this pesto with warm dishes, bring it to room temperature before using. That way it will give better flavor and won't cool down the food.

You can use a mortar and pestle in lieu of the food processor if you prefer. Add the ingredients to the mortar in the same order as indicated for the food processor.

▶ **Food processor**

| | | |
|---|---|---|
| ½ cup | finely grated Grana Padano cheese (see Tips, at left) | 125 mL |
| 1 tsp | freshly squeezed lemon juice | 5 mL |
| 1 | clove garlic, halved lengthwise and thinly sliced | 1 |
| 1 cup | loosely packed fresh peppermint or spearmint leaves | 250 mL |
| ¼ cup | ground unsalted pistachios | 60 mL |
| ¼ cup | extra virgin olive oil | 60 mL |
| | Salt and freshly ground black pepper | |

1. In food processor fitted with the metal blade, combine cheese, lemon juice and garlic. Pulse until a coarse paste forms. Add mint and pistachios; pulse until mint is finely chopped. With the motor running, pour in oil through the feed tube and purée until smooth. Season to taste with salt and pepper.

2. Use immediately or transfer to an airtight container and refrigerate for up to 1 week.

### Hard Cheeses of Italy

Pecorino Romano makes a wonderful alternative to Grana Padano in this pesto. It's also a nice choice thematically, bringing together a sheep's cheese and lamb. Parmigiano-Reggiano will work as well, but the expense isn't justified.

# Chimichurri Sauce

Chimichurri is an Argentinean sauce often served with grilled beef. It's delicious with Matambre (page 68). The best part is that it's very simple to make in a food processor and keeps quite well. Bold and a little brash, it's perfect to serve at an outdoor gathering. This recipe makes enough for about 6 servings.

**MAKES
1 CUP (250 ML)**

## Tips

This recipe can easily be halved or doubled.

Chimichurri is versatile. Try it with simply grilled lamb, fish, chicken or octopus.

Parsley and cilantro (especially the latter) can be gritty. Make sure you wash the leaves very well and dry them before packing them into the measuring cup. A salad spinner is great for this task.

A food processor is easiest, but you can use your blender or a mortar and pestle to make chimichurri. If you use a blender, first place all the ingredients in the container, in the order specified, and then blend, stopping periodically to scrape down the sides of the jar.

▶ **Food processor**

| | | |
|---|---|---|
| 1½ | cloves garlic, peeled, halved and germ removed | 1½ |
| 1 | jalapeño pepper, halved and seeded | 1 |
| ¾ tsp | kosher salt | 3 mL |
| 1 cup | loosely packed fresh flat-leaf (Italian) parsley leaves (see Tips, at left) | 250 mL |
| 1 cup | loosely packed fresh cilantro (leaves and tender stems) | 250 mL |
| 6 tbsp | olive oil | 90 mL |
| 3 tbsp | red wine vinegar | 45 mL |
| 1 tsp | dried oregano | 5 mL |
| 1 tsp | freshly ground black pepper | 5 mL |

1. In food processor fitted with the metal blade, combine garlic, jalapeño pepper and salt. Pulse until coarsely chopped.

2. One small handful at a time, add parsley and cilantro to food processor. Pulse until reduced to a coarse paste.

3. With the motor running, slowly pour oil, then vinegar, through feed tube until a paste forms. Add oregano and pepper. Process just until combined.

4. Serve immediately at room temperature or transfer to an airtight container and refrigerate until ready to serve, or for up to 1 week.

# Brava Sauce

I think of brava sauce as Spanish ketchup. It's great with eggs and an essential condiment for *patatas bravas*, which are deep-fried potato wedges or cubes. I sometimes even slip in a little when steaming mussels. Serve hot or cold.

**MAKES 4 CUPS (1 L)**

## Tips

You can easily double this recipe.

If you want to store the sauce for longer than 10 days, you can freeze it. The frozen sauce will keep well for up to 6 months.

▶ **Blender**

| | | |
|---|---|---|
| 2 tbsp | olive oil | 30 mL |
| 1 | onion, finely chopped | 1 |
| 2 | cloves garlic, chopped | 2 |
| 1 | can (28 oz/796 mL) plum (Roma) tomatoes, with juice | 1 |
| 1 tbsp | hot pepper flakes, optional | 15 mL |
| 1 tbsp | smoked sweet Spanish paprika | 15 mL |
| 2 tsp | salt | 10 mL |
| 1 tsp | freshly ground black pepper | 5 mL |
| 1 tbsp | sherry vinegar | 15 mL |
| 1 tbsp | liquid honey | 15 mL |

1. In a medium skillet, heat oil over medium heat. Add onion and cook, stirring often, for 4 to 5 minutes or until softened but not colored. Add garlic and cook, stirring, for 2 to 3 minutes.

2. Stir in tomatoes, hot pepper flakes (if using), paprika, salt, pepper, vinegar and honey. Reduce heat and simmer, stirring occasionally, until tomatoes have broken down and sauce has thickened, about 45 minutes. Remove from heat. Let cool for 30 minutes.

3. Pour mixture into blender and purée until smooth. Serve immediately or transfer to an airtight container and refrigerate for up to 10 days.

# Sauce Robert

This sauce, like Lingonberry Cream Sauce (page 373) and Morel Mushroom Cream Sauce (page 374), is French in approach. All these sauces come together fairly quickly and are superb on Basic Pork Chops or Basic Pork Tenderloin (page 114). The recipe dates so far back — more than 500 years — that no one can agree on its exact origin. But no matter where it comes from, this sauce is savory and delicious and keeps beautifully. Try it with rabbit too. This recipe makes enough for about 8 servings.

**MAKES
ABOUT 2 CUPS
(500 ML)**

## Tips

You can easily halve or double this recipe.

Sauce Robert is often given a sweet-and-sour flavor by adding a little granulated sugar. If you are keen to try this, add 1 to 2 tsp (5 to 10 mL), to taste.

To add a little extra richness, stir in 1 to 2 tbsp (15 to 30 mL) crème fraîche or sour cream along with the mustard.

*To make ahead:* Let sauce cool completely, then refrigerate in an airtight container for up to 1 week. Reheat in a saucepan over medium-low heat.

| | | |
|---|---|---|
| 1 tbsp | butter | 15 mL |
| 2 cups | finely chopped onions | 500 mL |
| 1 tbsp | all-purpose flour | 15 mL |
| 1 cup | ready-to-use reduced-sodium beef broth or homemade beef or pork stock, at room temperature | 250 mL |
| 1 tbsp | good-quality red wine vinegar or tarragon vinegar | 15 mL |
| 1 tbsp | Dijon mustard | 15 mL |
| ½ tsp | freshly ground black pepper | 2 mL |
| | Salt | |
| | Chopped fresh parsley, optional | |

1. In a medium heavy-bottomed skillet, melt butter over low heat. Add onions and cook, stirring often, for 30 minutes or until soft and tender.

2. Sprinkle flour over onions. Increase heat to medium and cook, stirring often, for 10 minutes. Gradually add broth, stirring constantly. Bring to a vigorous simmer and cook, stirring occasionally and adjusting heat as necessary to maintain a simmer, for 30 minutes.

3. Stir in vinegar. If sauce is too thick, thin with a little water to desired consistency. Stir in mustard and pepper. Season to taste with salt, if necessary. Stir in parsley (if using). Serve warm.

## Variations

This sauce encourages endless variations in the French style. Here are a couple to try.

**Mild Curry Sauce:** Omit the Dijon mustard. Add 1½ tbsp (22 mL) curry powder along with the flour.

**Horseradish Cream:** Substitute 2 tbsp (30 mL) prepared horseradish for the Dijon mustard.

# Lingonberry Cream Sauce

This sweet-and-tart sauce is really quick to prepare and tastes wonderful with Basic Pork Chops or Basic Pork Tenderloin (page 114). Lingonberries are known by many other names, including "mountain cranberries" and "partridge berries." This recipe makes enough for 3 to 4 servings.

| | | |
|---|---|---|
| **MAKES ABOUT ¼ CUP (60 ML)** | | |

## Tips

The amount of sauce can be scaled up or down as desired.

Lingonberry preserves aren't all that common in supermarkets, but gourmet and specialty stores often carry them. Believe it or not, IKEA offers a good lingonberry preserve.

*To make ahead:* Let sauce cool completely, then refrigerate in an airtight container for up to 5 days. Reheat in a saucepan over medium-low heat, stirring constantly to prevent burning.

| | | |
|---|---|---|
| 4 tbsp | heavy or whipping (35%) cream | 60 mL |
| 2 tbsp | lingonberry preserves (see Tips, at left) | 30 mL |
| ½ tsp | finely grated gingerroot | 2 mL |
| ½ tsp | finely minced shallot | 2 mL |
| ½ tsp | red wine vinegar | 2 mL |
| ⅛ tsp | kosher salt | 0.5 mL |
| Pinch | ground white pepper | Pinch |

1. In a small saucepan, combine cream, lingonberry preserves, ginger, shallot, vinegar, salt and white pepper. Bring to a boil over medium heat, stirring frequently. Boil, stirring constantly, for 1 to 2 minutes or until thickened to desired consistency. Serve warm.

# Morel Mushroom Cream Sauce

Aside from fresh truffles, morel mushrooms are the most luxurious fungi to eat. Serve this luscious sauce with Basic Pork Chops (page 114).

**MAKES ABOUT 1 CUP (250 ML)**

## Tips

This recipe makes enough for 4 servings.

This recipe can easily be halved or doubled to suit your needs.

Morels can be quite sandy, so be sure to inspect them carefully and brush them well to remove any traces of grit. Avoid washing them, as they will become waterlogged and hard to cook.

*To make ahead:* Let sauce cool completely, then refrigerate in an airtight container for up to 4 days. Reheat in a saucepan over medium-low heat, stirring constantly to prevent burning.

| | | |
|---|---|---|
| 8 oz | fresh morel mushrooms (see Tips, at left) | 225 g |
| 2 tbsp | butter | 30 mL |
| 1 tbsp | finely chopped shallot | 15 mL |
| 1 tsp | finely chopped garlic | 5 mL |
| ¼ cup | dry white wine | 60 mL |
| 1 cup | enriched beef broth (page 401) | 250 mL |
| ½ cup | heavy or whipping (35%) cream | 125 mL |
| 2 tbsp | chopped fresh parsley | 30 mL |
| 1 tsp | chopped fresh thyme | 5 mL |
| | Salt and freshly ground black pepper | |

1. Trim ends of mushroom stems. Using a soft brush, brush off any dirt or sand. Halve lengthwise, if large.

2. In a large skillet, melt butter over medium-high heat. When butter starts to foam, stir in shallot and sauté for 2 to 3 minutes. Add garlic and sauté for 1 minute. Add mushrooms and sauté for 3 minutes. Add wine and increase heat to high.

3. Add broth and cream. Boil, stirring occasionally, until liquid starts to thicken, about 8 to 10 minutes.

4. Stir in parsley and thyme. Season to taste with salt and pepper. Serve warm.

---

### Dried Morels

Dried morels are very flavorful but expensive — it takes about 1 lb (450 g) fresh morels to make 1 oz (30 g) dried. If you can't find fresh morels for this recipe, substitute 1 oz (30 g) dried morels and 8 oz (225 g) white mushrooms, quartered. In a small bowl, pour boiling water over dried morels and soak until softened. Lift out of soaking liquid without disturbing grit at bottom of bowl. Cut soaked mushrooms in half if large. Carefully add soaking liquid to broth, leaving grit in bowl. Proceed with recipe, cooking white mushrooms in Step 2 as if using fresh morels. Add soaked morels along with the broth and cream in Step 3.

# Green Peppercorn Sauce

This is a classic steak sauce that's also great with beef liver and roast venison. Other than Stroganoff, I tend not to like cream sauces with beef, so this one is lightly thickened with butter, which makes it a little less stable but gives a cleaner flavor. It's important to use a strong gelatinous broth here so the emulsion can hold. This recipe makes enough for 4 steaks.

**MAKE ¾ CUP (175 ML)**

## Tips

You can easily halve or double this recipe.

You can find green peppercorns in brine at well-stocked grocery stores.

The sauce will keep for at least 45 minutes if kept warm. If your sous vide device is available, set it to 135°F (57.2°C). Transfer saucepan contents to a stainless steel bowl, cover with a paper towel and plastic wrap, and float bowl in preheated water bath until needed. That way the sauce will hold for at least 2 hours.

This sauce will not reheat successfully. You can, however, store leftover sauce in the refrigerator for up 7 days or in the freezer for 3 months and add it to any appropriate stew that's thickened with flour or xanthan gum, such as beef bourguignon. Whisk into sauce 1 tbsp (15 mL) at a time, to taste.

| | | |
|---|---|---|
| ¾ cup | enriched beef broth (page 401) | 175 mL |
| 6 tbsp | dry red wine | 90 mL |
| 1 tbsp | finely chopped shallot | 15 mL |
| 4 tsp | drained green peppercorns in brine (see Tips, at left) | 20 mL |
| 1 tsp | brandy or cognac | 5 mL |
| ⅓ cup | butter, chilled, cut into 5 pieces | 75 mL |
| | Freshly squeezed lemon juice | |
| 1 tbsp | finely chopped fresh parsley | 15 mL |
| | Salt | |

1. In a medium saucepan, combine broth, wine and shallot; bring to a simmer over high heat. Reduce heat and boil gently until reduced to about ½ cup (125 mL), about 20 minutes. It should start to get a bit syrupy. If not, add more broth and keep reducing, if necessary.

2. Meanwhile, rinse peppercorns. Finely chop 2 tsp (10 mL) of the peppercorns.

3. Once broth mixture has reduced, reduce heat to low. Add brandy and whisk in butter, one piece at a time. The sauce should thicken slightly. Add a few drops of lemon juice, peppercorns, parsley and salt to taste.

4. Remove from heat. Cover, placing a paper towel under the lid to capture condensation, and keep warm until ready to use (see Tips, at left).

# Bordelaise Sauce

Bordelaise sauce is powerfully flavored and unctuous. It's great with steaks that are not too fatty, such as tenderloin or New York cuts. If you like the taste and texture of bone marrow, you will love this sauce. The recipe makes enough to serve 2 people generously or 4 people sparingly.

**MAKES ABOUT ⅔ CUP (150 ML)**

## Tip

This recipe can easily be doubled.

| | | |
|---|---|---|
| 1 | beef marrow bone, about 6 inches (15 cm) long, cut in half crosswise (see box, at right) | 1 |
| | Ice water | |
| 1 cup | enriched beef broth (page 401) | 250 mL |
| ⅓ cup | finely chopped shallots | 75 mL |
| 1 | sprig fresh thyme | 1 |
| ½ | bay leaf | ½ |
| ½ cup | dry red wine | 125 mL |
| | Salt and freshly ground black pepper | |
| | Freshly squeezed lemon juice | |

1. In a large bowl, immerse marrow bones in cold water. Cover and refrigerate overnight.

2. Drain marrow bones, discarding soaking water, and transfer to a microwave-safe plate. Microwave bones at Medium (50% power) for 1 minute, or blanch in a pot of boiling water for 1 minute, then drain.

3. Using a sharp, narrow knife, cut around inside edges of bones to release marrow. Then, using your thumb, push gently to extrude the marrow in one piece. Place marrow in a small bowl of ice water to chill; set aside. Discard bone or save for stock.

4. In a small saucepan, combine broth, shallots, thyme and bay leaf. Bring to a boil over high heat. Reduce heat and simmer for 5 to 10 minutes, until reduced to a syrupy, slushy consistency.

## Tip

Transfer any leftover sauce to an airtight container and refrigerate for up to 4 days. Gently reheat over low heat before serving.

5. Meanwhile, drain chilled marrow, reserving ice water. Slice marrow into thin rounds, about the thickness of a quarter. Return marrow slices and any leftover pieces to ice water.

6. Add wine to broth mixture in saucepan. Discard thyme and bay leaf. Continue simmering until almost syrupy.

7. Drain marrow pieces and add to saucepan. Simmer for 2 to 3 minutes, stirring occasionally, until sauce is slightly thickened and shiny. The marrow will render slightly, which is what you want. Season to taste with salt, pepper and a few drops of lemon juice. Serve immediately.

### Beef Marrow Bones

Beef marrow bones come from the center of the leg bones of cattle. Make sure the bones you buy are open at both ends (you should be able to see the marrow from each end). Have your butcher cut a bone in half crosswise to make extracting the marrow easier.

# Veronese Pepper and Breadcrumb Sauce

This ancient sauce, called *peará,* is one that I learned while cooking in Verona. It is typically served with boiled meats. I adore boiled beef and veal, especially in the cooler months, as long as it is prepared correctly (sous vide does an exceptional job here). If you like the taste of bone marrow, you may even want to spread this sauce on toast! *Peará* should be very peppery — remember that Venice, a neighboring city, dominated the European spice trade from the eighth century. This recipe makes enough for about 6 servings.

**MAKES 1¼ CUPS (300 ML)**

## Tips

This recipe can easily be doubled.

Store any leftovers in the refrigerator for up to 7 days or freeze for up to 3 months. Thaw overnight in the refrigerator. Reheat sauce gently over medium-low heat.

Beef marrow bones come from the center of the leg bones of cattle. Make sure your bones are open at both ends (you should be able to see the marrow at each end). Have your butcher cut a bone in half crosswise to make it easier to extract the marrow.

▶ **Fine-mesh sieve**

| | | |
|---|---|---|
| 1 | beef marrow bone, about 4 inches (10 cm) long, cut in half crosswise (see Tips, at left) | 1 |
| | Ice water | |
| 2 tbsp | butter | 30 mL |
| ⅔ cup | dry bread crumbs (see Variation, page 385) | 150 mL |
| 1 cup | ready-to-use beef broth | 250 mL |
| 2 tsp | freshly ground black pepper | 10 mL |
| | Salt | |

1. Place marrow bones in a medium bowl and immerse in cold water. Cover and refrigerate overnight.

2. Drain bones, discarding soaking water, and transfer to a microwave-safe plate. Microwave at Medium (50% power) for 1 minute, or blanch in a pot of boiling water for 1 minute, then drain.

3. Using a sharp, narrow knife, cut around inside edges of bones to release marrow. Using your thumb, gently push out marrow into a small bowl. Cover marrow with ice water and let chill for 2 to 3 hours or refrigerate overnight. Discard bones or save for stock.

4. Drain marrow through fine-mesh sieve and chop coarsely. Place in a small saucepan, add butter, and heat over medium-low heat for 4 to 5 minutes or until melted.

Antique recipes omit the butter and use pure marrow fat instead, which yields a result that's too heavy for modern tastes. If you'd like to try it, feel free to adjust the ratio of marrow to butter to suit your palate.

**5.** Stir in bread crumbs, broth and pepper; bring to a simmer. Simmer, stirring occasionally, for 30 minutes or until bread crumbs swell and sauce is thickened to the consistency of cold sour cream. If sauce is too thick, thin with a little water to desired consistency. (This sauce may separate. If it does, just stir until it comes back together, adding water a little at a time as necessary to retain its slushy consistency.) Season to taste with salt.

**6.** Pour sauce into a warm sauce boat and serve immediately.

# Onion and Black Olive Sauce

This sauce is as intense and zesty as it is versatile. I created it to go with Veal Chops (page 48), but it would be equally delicious paired with grilled lamb. This recipe makes enough to accompany about 16 servings of meat, though it freezes perfectly.

---

**MAKES 2½ CUPS (625 ML)**

## Tips

You can easily halve this recipe.

You can use this as a base for pasta sauce. Add cooked tuna or octopus and serve with long pasta such as spaghetti or linguine. The sauce also pairs beautifully with oily, meaty fish such as mackerel or swordfish and works nicely as a pizza topping. Use sparingly, as it is quite pungent.

I prefer the taste of the gluten-free Worcestershire sauce made by Lea & Perrins. It has a cleaner flavor than the regular version, which is made with malt vinegar.

A little of this sauce goes a long way. I recommend spooning it into ice-cube trays before freezing, making up convenient small portions. Once frozen, transfer the cubes to a resealable plastic freezer bag.

▶ **Preheat hot water bath to 194°F (90°C)**
▶ **Sous vide pouch**
▶ **Blender or food processor**

| | | |
|---|---|---|
| 2 cups | sliced onions | 500 mL |
| 1 cup | Moroccan black olives, pitted | 250 mL |
| 2 tbsp | extra virgin olive oil | 30 mL |
| 2 tsp | sherry vinegar | 10 mL |
| 1 tsp | grated lemon zest | 5 mL |
| 1 tsp | chopped fresh thyme | 5 mL |
| 1 tsp | Worcestershire sauce (see Tips, at left) | 5 mL |
| 1 tsp | reduced-sodium soy sauce | 5 mL |
| ½ tsp | freshly ground black pepper | 2 mL |
| 1 | clove garlic, peeled and halved | 1 |
| ½ cup | ready-to-use unsalted chicken broth | 125 mL |
| ½ cup | tomato juice | 125 mL |

1. Place onions and olives in sous vide pouch and seal. Immerse in preheated hot water bath and cook for 1½ hours. Remove pouch from bath and let stand at room temperature for 30 minutes or until cool enough to blend.

2. Open pouch and pour mixture into blender. Add oil, vinegar, lemon zest, thyme, Worcestershire sauce, soy sauce, pepper and garlic. Pulse until a fairly smooth paste forms, stopping motor between pulses and scraping down sides of jar.

3. With motor running, remove plug from hole in lid and slowly pour broth and tomato juice through opening. Blend until smooth and mixture has the consistency of a thick milkshake.

4. Use immediately or let cool for 20 to 30 minutes, pour into an airtight container and refrigerate for up to 7 days or freeze for up to 6 months.

# Cranberry Sauce

The great advantage to making cranberry sauce sous vide is that the berries stay more intact because you are cooking below the boiling point. It takes a long time to release the pectin in cranberries, which thickens the sauce. This preparation is something you can do overnight or when your stove is overloaded with making other holiday dishes. The recipe makes enough sauce for about 8 servings.

**MAKES 2 CUPS (500 ML)**

## Tips

This recipe can easily be doubled. If doubling, use a second sous vide pouch.

Because you are using the skins of the citrus, it is best to use organic fruits, if available.

Cranberry sauce can be kept for 7 days refrigerated, or frozen for up to 6 months. Defrost overnight in the refrigerator, if necessary.

▸ **Preheat hot water bath to 190°F (88°C)**
▸ **Sous vide pouch**

| | | |
|---|---|---|
| 1 | lime (see Tips, at left) | 1 |
| 1 | orange | 1 |
| 1 | bag (12 oz/340 g) frozen cranberries (3 cups/750 mL) | 1 |
| 1 oz | peeled fresh ginger, sliced (about 2 inches/5 cm) | 30 g |
| 1 cup | granulated sugar | 250 mL |
| 1 | star anise pod, optional | 1 |

1. With a vegetable peeler, remove rinds of lime and half the orange in thin strips, avoiding the white pith. Juice half of the orange, reserving the other half for another purpose.

2. Place cranberries, lime rind, orange rind, orange juice, ginger, sugar and star anise (if using) in sous vide pouch and seal. Immerse pouch in preheated water bath and cook for 5 to 9 hours. The pouch will float, so weigh it down with a heavy kitchen utensil or cutlery (see "Weigh Down Those Bags," page 317). Move the bag around from time to time to help the sugar dissolve.

3. Remove pouch from bath. Open and tip contents into a medium bowl. Remove orange and lime rind, ginger and star anise pod and discard. With a fork, stir and lightly mash cranberries to desired consistency. Cover and refrigerate until needed. Serve chilled.

# Fermented Black Bean Sauce

This is a wonderfully versatile and flavorful Asian-inspired sauce. It is served with lamb shanks in this book (page 92) but is just as good with chicken and full-flavored fish such as mackerel, striped bass or swordfish. Just make sure you use an appropriate stock for the dish you are making; for example, use fish stock for a fish dish. This recipe makes enough for 4 to 6 servings.

**MAKES ABOUT
1 CUP (250 ML)**

## Tips

You can easily double this recipe.

A regular blender works well if you don't have an immersion blender. Sprinkle the xanthan gum through the opening in the lid while blending.

Salted fermented black beans are sold damp in cellophane packages in Chinese grocery stores. They have the consistency of hard-boiled egg yolk. Since they are very salty, I recommend using unsalted stock for this recipe.

▶ **Immersion blender**
▶ **Fine-mesh sieve**

| | | |
|---|---|---|
| ½ cup | salted fermented black beans (see Tips, at left) | 125 mL |
| 1 | beefsteak tomato or 2 plum (Roma) tomatoes | 1 |
| ⅔ cup | unsalted chicken, beef, lamb or fish stock | 150 mL |
| 4 tsp | habanero-based hot sauce, such as Melinda's (see Tip, at right) | 20 mL |
| 2 tsp | unseasoned rice vinegar | 10 mL |
| 2 tsp | soy sauce | 10 mL |
| ¼ tsp | xanthan gum (see page 400) | 1 mL |
| 4 tsp | finely chopped garlic | 20 mL |
| 4 tsp | finely chopped fresh gingerroot | 20 mL |
| 2 tsp | granulated sugar | 10 mL |
| ½ tsp | toasted sesame oil | 2 mL |
| Pinch | ground white pepper | Pinch |

1. Soak black beans in cold water for 15 to 20 minutes. Drain.

2. Bring a small saucepan of water to a boil. Blanch tomato for 5 to 20 seconds, depending on ripeness. Plunge into ice water to stop cooking process, then peel. Cut in half, squeeze out seeds and discard seeds. Cut flesh into ½-inch (1 cm) dice.

Habanero hot sauce
has slightly different
nuances than a vinegar-
based hot sauce such
as Tabasco — it's hotter
and bit fruity. I like the
Melinda's brand, but
many are available, so
choose one that you like.

3. Place stock, hot sauce, vinegar and soy sauce in a tall container or similar vessel. Using immersion blender, blend for 30 seconds while carefully sprinkling in xanthan gum, stopping to scrape down sides of container as necessary.

4. Drain beans, discarding soaking water. In a small bowl, combine beans, garlic, ginger, sugar, sesame oil and white pepper. Using fine-mesh sieve, strain stock mixture over bean mixture; stir to combine.

5. Use immediately or let cool for 20 to 30 minutes, pour into an airtight container and refrigerate for up to 5 days or freeze for up to 3 months.

# Caper Sultana Relish

This relish is a unique and tangy accompaniment for rich dishes. It goes well with charcuterie and cold foie gras, and I even like it on frankfurters! This recipe makes enough for 4 to 6 servings.

**MAKES ½ CUP (125 ML)**

## Tips

This recipe can easily be doubled or tripled.

When serving this relish with warm dishes, bring it to room temperature before using.

The relish can also be made by pounding the ingredients using a mortar and pestle, if desired.

▶ **Mini food processor or mortar and pestle**

| ⅓ cup | sultana raisins | 75 mL |
|---|---|---|
| 3 tbsp | white balsamic vinegar | 45 mL |
| 1½ tbsp | drained capers | 22 mL |
| 1 tbsp | finely chopped shallot | 15 mL |
| 1 tsp | olive oil | 5 mL |
| ½ tsp | soy sauce | 2 mL |
| | Freshly ground white pepper | |

1. In a microwave-safe bowl, combine sultanas with vinegar. Microwave on High for 1 minute. Alternatively, place in a saucepan over medium-low heat and bring just to a simmer, about 3 minutes. Let cool.

2. In food processor, pulse sultana mixture, capers and shallot until a coarse paste forms. Add oil and soy sauce, and purée until almost smooth. Season to taste with pepper.

3. Serve immediately or transfer to an airtight container and refrigerate for up to 2 weeks.

# Fresh Bread Crumbs

Fresh bread crumbs are not interchangeable with the dry variety, and they are usually superior when you need bread crumbs for meatballs or stuffing. You also get the added benefit of choosing bread with the flavor that you like.

---

**MAKES ABOUT 4 CUPS (1 L)**

## Tips

Sourdough bread crumbs are good for when you want a more assertive flavor. See, for example, Spinach and Sourdough–Stuffed Lamb Shoulder (page 94).

If your sealer doesn't have a Delicate or Gentle setting, press Seal as soon as the pouch tightens around the bread crumbs.

▶ **Food processor**

| | | |
|---|---|---|
| 1 | day-old white baguette, about 10½ oz (300 g) | 1 |

1. If your baguette is baked hard, cut off any dark, crunchy portions and discard. Dice bread into approximately 1-inch (2.5 cm) cubes. Spread out cubes in one layer on a platter or baking sheet and let stand for 1 hour. Stir cubes after 30 minutes so that they dry out more evenly.

2. Using food processor fitted with the metal blade, add bread cubes in batches and process until reduced to a fine crumb.

3. Use immediately or place crumbs in an airtight container and cover. Or place in a sous vide pouch and seal, using a home sealer on the Delicate setting (see Tips, at left). Store in the freezer for up to 6 months.

---

## Variation

**Dry Bread Crumbs:** Preheat oven to 200°F (95°C). Prepare through Step 2. Spread out crumbs on a baking sheet and transfer to oven. Bake, stirring occasionally, until crispy and dry, about 6 to 7 minutes. Repeat Step 2. Strain through a fine-mesh sieve, if desired.

# 50-Hour Preserved Lemons

Preserved lemons are a staple in Moroccan kitchens and are delicious in other cuisines as well. They can be hard to find commercially and normally take about a month to prepare. However, they are a snap to make sous vide and are ready to use in about three days. For this recipe I like Meyer lemons, which are grown in northern California — they more closely resemble Moroccan lemons than the common Eureka variety. Although seasonal, they are becoming more widely available.

**MAKES
2 PRESERVED
LEMONS**

## Tips

Because you will be eating the skin, it is particularly important to use organic lemons here.

Meyer lemon juice is not acidic enough to use in this recipe. Use the common Eureka variety for the juice, if you can.

▶ **2-cup (500 mL) wide-mouth canning jar, with lid**

| | | |
|---|---|---|
| 1 cup | coarse pickling salt (see Tip, at right) | 250 mL |
| 2 | organic Meyer lemons, scrubbed and quartered (see Tips, at left) | 2 |
| ¾ cup | freshly squeezed lemon juice (approx.; see Tips, at left) | 175 mL |

1. Place ½ inch (1 cm) pickling salt in jar — about 2 to 3 tbsp (30 to 45 mL). Lay 3 lemon quarters on top and sprinkle with salt to cover. Continue alternating lemon quarters and salt until all the lemon pieces are in the jar. Add lemon juice, making sure lemons are covered with juice (add more if necessary), leaving ½ inch (1 cm) headspace to allow for expansion. Wipe rim of jar thoroughly to ensure a good seal. Add lid and screw just until snug.

2. Place jar in freezer for 24 hours, inverting it at least once.

3. Remove jar from freezer and allow to come to room temperature. Preheat hot water bath to 140°F (60°C). Check that the jar is well sealed, then immerse in water bath for 2 hours.

4. Remove from hot water bath and let cool for about 2 hours. Place in freezer for another 24 hours.

5. Remove from freezer and serve immediately or store in refrigerator until needed. Preserved lemons will keep for at least 6 months.

## Tip

Kosher salt can be substituted for the pickling salt, if desired. Because of its finer flake size, your lemons will be a little saltier. Be sure to rinse them well before use.

## Variations

**Eureka Lemons:** Substitute 2 Eureka lemons for the Meyer variety. Because they are less tender, I recommend adding an extra heating and freezing cycle by repeating Steps 3 to 5.

**Preserved Limes:** Substitute 3 to 4 limes for the lemons. Add an extra heating and freezing cycle, as for Eureka lemons. Do not substitute lime juice for the lemon juice. (Preserved limes taste very different from preserved lemons. Feel free to experiment with them. They're tasty julienned finely and scattered over fish carpaccio, along with an aromatic oil such as pine nut oil.)

# 40 Days and 40 Nights Black Garlic

Black garlic is quite popular in more forward-thinking restaurants these days. Originally used in Korea as a health food, it is very high in antioxidants. The garlic caramelizes extremely slowly, which results in a very mild but complex flavor with balsamic notes. Bonus: it doesn't leave you with garlic breath.

**MAKES 8 HEADS**

## Tips

The recipe amount can be scaled up to suit your needs. Since the process will tie up your hot water bath for over a month and the garlic will keep for 12 months, make as much as you can use.

Black garlic is sticky and hard to peel. Try to use garlic heads that have large cloves.

To reduce evaporation, a self-contained static bath, such as the Sous Vide Supreme brand, is the most practical to use here.

I view this method as curing rather than cooking, since the water temperature is only a few degrees above body temperature. Nevertheless, keep the machine out of reach of children, as you would all kitchen devices.

▶ **Preheat hot water bath to 104°F (40°C)**
▶ **Sous vide pouch**

| 8 | large heads garlic | 8 |

1. With a sharp knife, cut about ½ inch (1 cm) off stem end of each garlic head, exposing some of the flesh in the cloves.

2. Arrange garlic in 2 or 3 rows in pouch and seal. Immerse pouch in preheated water bath and close lid. Cook for 40 days. (A strong garlic odor will permeate the air during this process. I recommend placing the water bath in a well-ventilated storage room, basement or closet.) Pouch will float, so flip it and check water level in bath twice a week.

3. The exposed garlic flesh should turn dark brown to black. If garlic is still pale after 40 days, leave it in for another week.

4. Open pouch and place garlic on a rack or wire shelf. Air-dry in a well-ventilated place for 1 day, then repackage in sealed pouches and store in a cool, dark place.

### Fear Not . . .

You can use your sous vide device briefly while it's tied up making the garlic. Remove the pouch from the bath and wrap in towels. Keep in a warm place or put a heating pad on top of the towels. Return the garlic to the bath as soon as possible.

# No-Mess Perfect Steel-Cut Oatmeal

Cooking oatmeal sous vide gives you perfect results with nothing to clean up afterwards. You can take the oatmeal to work in the bag that it's cooked in and reheat it in a microwave or with boiling water from the tea kettle. I like it with plain yogurt and some agave syrup drizzled overtop.

**MAKES
1 SERVING**

Freezer Bag Friendly

## Tips

You can easily double or triple this recipe. Use more bags as required, or make each serving in its own bag if you want.

You can reheat the oatmeal from refrigerator temperature by transferring the bag contents to a bowl and microwaving it. Alternatively, preheat the water bath to 160°F (71.1°C), then immerse the bag for 10 to 15 minutes.

This recipe works well in a 2-cup (500 mL) canning jar, if desired.

▶ **Preheat hot water bath to 203°F (95°C)**
▶ **Small resealable freezer bag**

| | | |
|---|---|---|
| 1 cup | water | 250 mL |
| 1/3 cup | steel-cut oats | 75 mL |
| 1/8 tsp | kosher salt | 0.5 mL |

1. In a medium saucepan, bring water to a boil over high heat.

2. Meanwhile, combine oats and salt in freezer bag.

3. Pour boiling water into bag and seal. Immerse bag in preheated water bath and cook for 90 minutes.

4. Serve immediately by pouring oatmeal into a bowl and garnishing as desired. Or let stand to cool briefly, then refrigerate for up to 3 days.

# Yogurt

If you eat a lot of yogurt, as I do, you might be aware that plain yogurt costs two to three times more than the milk it is made from. If you start making yogurt with your sous vide device, you'll earn back the cost of the equipment relatively quickly. This recipe is perfect for beginners who have never made yogurt before. It makes about 4 servings.

---

## Tips

You can easily double this recipe. If doubling, use an additional jar.

Make sure that your starter yogurt contains live bacterial culture.

Goat's or sheep's milk also works, whether it's skim or full-fat. Skim milk will give you a yogurt that is less firm.

Yogurt can also be made in resealable freezer bags. However, agitating yogurt breaks up the coagulant and thins it, so transferring the yogurt from the bag to another container will give you a more liquid product. I recommend using jars if possible.

You can use a number of smaller jars in Step 5, if you find that more convenient.

▶ **1-quart (1 L) straight-sided canning jar, with lid**
▶ **Heavy stainless-steel or enameled cast-iron saucepan**
▶ **Instant-read thermometer**

| | | |
|---|---|---|
| 3 cups | whole cow's milk (see Tips, at left) | 750 mL |
| ⅓ cup | fresh unflavored, unsweetened yogurt, at room temperature (see Tips, at left) | 75 mL |

1. Place milk in saucepan and cover. Warm over medium heat to 176°F (80°C), stirring occasionally to avoid scorching. Remove from heat and let stand, covered, for 5 minutes.

2. Transfer milk to a large measuring cup or medium mixing bowl. Let cool to 115°F (46°C). You can set the container in a bowl of cold water to speed the cooling process. Stir occasionally.

3. Meanwhile, preheat hot water bath to 115°F (46°C).

4. Place yogurt in a small bowl. Slowly stir ⅓ cup (75 mL) warm milk into yogurt. Add yogurt mixture to saucepan and gently stir so that it is well incorporated, about 2 minutes.

5. Transfer mixture to canning jar. Wipe rim of jar thoroughly to ensure a good seal. Add lid and turn just until snug. Immerse jar in preheated water bath and cook for 5 to 10 hours (see Tips, at left).

6. Remove jar from water bath and refrigerate overnight before using.

## Tips

You can make your yogurt a bit thicker and give it more protein content by adding skim milk powder. During Step 2, stir to dissolve about 3 tbsp (45 mL) instant skim milk powder into the milk.

If you want a thicker yogurt, after Step 6 drain it in a sieve lined with cheesecloth for a few hours or overnight, keeping in mind that you will get a smaller yield. The liquid drained from the yogurt, called whey, can be used in baking.

The yogurt will keep in the refrigerator for at least 7 days.

### Cleanliness

Hygiene is critical here, since you are inhibiting some bacteria while encouraging others by providing an environment in which they can thrive. Make sure you use clean equipment and an accurate thermometer.

# Tonic Water Concentrate

Many recipes for tonic water concentrate use more ingredients than I do. However, once you get the hang of it, you can alter the recipe to suit your taste. You can also make the concentrate by simmering it in a saucepan, but cooking it in a hot water bath results in a clearer liquid.

## Tips

After grating the zest from the citrus fruits, reserve the fruit for another use. Some mixologists add citrus juice to their concentrate, but I think cooked fruit juice tastes like . . . cooked fruit juice, so I leave it out. It also clouds the concentrate and hastens spoilage.

Citric acid, also known as "sour salt," is used in some canning processes and is available in stores and online at websites that sell canning supplies. It can also be found at bulk food stores and pharmacies. It keeps indefinitely as long as it's covered. Just make sure it's labeled, because it resembles table salt!

▶ **Preheat hot water bath to 194°F (90°C)**
▶ **2-cup (500 mL) canning jar, with lid**
▶ **Cheesecloth**
▶ **Fine-mesh sieve**

| | | |
|---|---|---|
| ¼ cup | chopped cinchona bark (see box, at right) | 60 mL |
| 1 | cardamom pod | 1 |
| 3 tbsp | citric acid (see Tips, at left) | 45 mL |
| 2 | limes, zest grated | 2 |
| 2 | lemons, zest grated | 2 |
| 2 | oranges, zest grated | 2 |
| 1 | grapefruit, zest grated | 1 |
| 2 | stalks lemongrass, trimmed and finely chopped | 2 |
| 1 | whole allspice berry | 1 |
| ¼ tsp | kosher salt | 1 mL |
| 2 cups | filtered, distilled or reverse-osmosis water (approx.) | 500 mL |
| 1 cup | agave syrup | 250 mL |

1. In a sieve, rinse bark under cold water for a few minutes to remove any dust.

2. Remove cardamom seeds from pod; discard pod.

3. In jar, combine cinchona bark, cardamom seeds, lime zest, lemon zest, orange zest, grapefruit zest, lemongrass, allspice and salt. Fill with water, leaving ½ inch (1 cm) headspace. Wipe rim of jar thoroughly to ensure a good seal. Add lid and turn just until snug. Immerse jar in preheated water bath and cook for 90 minutes.

## Tips

Soft water will result in more flavorful tonic concentrate. If your water is very hard, add some distilled water or use reverse-osmosis filtered water.

There is a wide range of botanicals that you can play around with when making tonic water. Try experimenting with black peppercorns, star anise or lavender.

I prefer my tonic water on the bitter side. Add more agave syrup if you like yours a bit sweeter.

Tonic water concentrate will keep for at least 10 days refrigerated. It goes off by starting to ferment, which creates gas. Therefore you should use a corked bottle, so that if it starts to ferment, the expanding gas will pop out the cork rather than shatter the glass. For freezing, I suggest using ice-cube trays so that you have measured quantities; once frozen, they can be transferred to a resealable freezer bag.

For gin, vodka or rum and tonic, combine 2 oz (60 mL) spirit, 1½ tbsp (22 mL) concentrate and ⅓ cup (75 mL) sparkling water. Serve over ice.

4. Remove jar from water bath and let stand for up to 14 hours.

5. Place a sieve over a medium bowl. Line with a triple layer of cheesecloth that has been moistened with water and then wrung out. Strain liquid through cheesecloth. Discard solids.

6. Add agave syrup to strained liquid and stir to combine. Use immediately or transfer to a clean bottle, cover and refrigerate for up to 10 days or freeze for up to 6 months (see Tips, at left).

### Cinchona Bark

Cinchona bark comes from a South American tree and is the source of quinine, which has been used for centuries to treat malaria. The bark gives tonic water its bitterness and cannot be left out. You can find it online or at a well-stocked herbalist. It keeps indefinitely in a cool, dark place.

# Kumquat-Flavored Pisco

Pisco is a Peruvian spirit made from grapes. It has quite a neutral taste and color and can be used in many different drinks. A pisco sour, the national cocktail of Peru, is made with lemon or lime juice, egg white and a dash of angostura bitters. Try making one using this flavored pisco. This recipe uses a low temperature so that it won't evaporate any of the alcohol. Serve the cooked kumquats on toothpicks as a cool cocktail garnish. The recipe makes enough for 10 to 12 cocktails.

## MAKES ABOUT 3 CUPS (750 ML)

## Tips

You can easily halve this recipe.

The agave nectar helps bring out the latent sweetness of the kumquats. Increase or reduce the sweetness as desired.

Store the pisco in the freezer (it won't freeze because of its alcohol content). It will keep that way indefinitely. Freezing also helps extract additional aromatics from the kumquats.

Substitute vodka, rum, tequila or grappa for the pisco, as desired.

▶ **Preheat hot water bath to 131°F (55°C)**
▶ **Two 1-quart (1 L) canning jars, with lids**

| 1 lb | fresh kumquats | 450 g |
| 1 | 26 oz (750 mL) bottle pisco | 1 |
| 3 tbsp | agave nectar | 45 mL |

1. Scrub kumquats under running water with a brush or green scouring pad. Wipe dry with paper towels.

2. Divide kumquats, pisco and agave nectar equally between jars. Wipe rims of jars thoroughly to ensure a good seal. Add lids and turn just until snug. Immerse jars in preheated water bath and cook for 8 to 10 hours.

3. Remove jars and let cool to room temperature, about 3 to 4 hours.

4. Chill jars in freezer for at least 12 hours before use.

## Variations

**Jalapeño Vodka:** For spicy jalapeño-flavored vodka, use 1 well-washed and dried jalapeño pepper for each 6 oz (175 mL) vodka. Follow the method above, omitting the kumquats and agave nectar. If you find the result too spicy, dilute it with a little more vodka after it is made. It makes a great base for a Bloody Mary. Cut the jalapeños in half lengthwise and use them as garnish.

For another variation, try using tequila blanco instead of vodka.

# Curried Quinoa Salad

This salad is perfect with Shrimp Escabeche (page 270), but it goes equally well with any shellfish fresh from a hot water bath or grill. The curry flavor here is quite subtle, so feel free to increase the quantity of curry powder if you desire.

**MAKES 4 TO 6 SERVINGS**

## Tips

You can easily halve or double this recipe.

Peppermint is more commonly available than spearmint, but it has tougher leaves and a more aggressive flavor. If only peppermint is available, use ¼ cup (60 mL) and make sure it is very finely cut.

The salad will keep for up to 3 days in the refrigerator.

▶ **Fine-mesh sieve**

| | | |
|---|---|---|
| 1 cup | quinoa | 250 mL |
| | Water | |
| 1 tsp | kosher salt | 5 mL |
| ⅓ cup | vegetable oil | 75 mL |
| 2 to 3 tsp | curry powder | 10 to 15 mL |
| 1 tsp | finely chopped garlic | 5 mL |
| ⅓ cup | finely chopped red onion | 75 mL |
| 1 cup | finely diced English cucumber | 250 mL |
| ½ cup | finely diced firm mango | 125 mL |
| ⅓ cup | fine chiffonade of spearmint (see Tips, at left) | 75 mL |
| 1 tbsp | freshly squeezed lime juice | 15 mL |
| | Salt | |

1. In fine-mesh sieve over the sink, rinse quinoa under cold running water for 5 minutes. Drain.

2. In a medium saucepan over high heat, bring 2 cups (500 mL) water to a boil. Stir in salt and quinoa. Reduce heat to medium-low, cover and cook for about 10 minutes, or until most of the liquid is absorbed and quinoa is almost tender. Drain.

3. Meanwhile, in a small saucepan, combine vegetable oil, 1 tbsp (15 mL) water, curry powder and garlic. Cook over medium heat, stirring occasionally, until water evaporates, about 5 to 6 minutes. Set aside to cool.

4. In a medium bowl, combine onion, cucumber, mango, mint and lime juice. Add quinoa, then curry-garlic mixture. Add salt to taste and toss to combine.

# Cryo-clarified Pomegranate Aspic

After making Pomegranate-Poached Foie Gras (page 194), you will have quite a bit of leftover poaching liquid. It's a shame to let all that flavor go to waste, so here is a clever way to use it up. It is clarified using gelatin and takes a few days to solidify, so be sure to plan ahead accordingly. I like to use it to top jars of Chicken Liver Mousse (page 198) or Foie Gras Parfait (page 192), but it can also be chopped and used to garnish Foie Gras Roulades (page 191) or the Pomegranate-Poached Foie Gras.

## Tips

You can easily double or triple this recipe.

This recipe makes enough to cover the contents of 5 or 6 standard canning jars. If you are making it to top a full batch of Foie Gras Parfait (page 192), you will need to double it. The mixture can be refrigerated for 2 days after Step 6.

If you are not concerned about achieving an absolutely clear aspic, you may skip Step 1. Add all the pomegranate poaching liquid after boiling the wine. Chill the mixture and then proceed with Step 6.

▸ **Small freezer container**
▸ **Cheesecloth**
▸ **Instant-read thermometer**

| | | |
|---|---|---|
| 1¼ cups | pomegranate poaching liquid, at room temperature (see Tips, at left) | 310 mL |
| 1 cup | fruity red wine, such as Beaujolais | 250 mL |
| 2½ tsp | powdered gelatin (1 standard envelope), divided | 12 mL |

1. Divide pomegranate poaching liquid into 1-cup (250 mL) and ¼-cup (60 mL) portions. Pour ¼-cup (60 mL) portion into a medium bowl. Sprinkle 2 tsp (10 mL) gelatin overtop. Set aside.

2. Meanwhile, pour wine into a small saucepan and bring to a boil. Remove from heat and add remaining portion of pomegranate liquid. Add to gelatin mixture and stir. Transfer to a small, flat-bottomed freezer container, sized so that the liquid is about 1 inch (2.5 cm) deep. Transfer to freezer for 90 minutes, until just frozen.

3. Turn out frozen mixture onto a cutting board and cut into 1-inch (2.5 cm) cubes. Return to container and freeze for 8 to 12 hours.

## Tips

If you want to make this without first making Pomegranate-Poached Foie Gras, follow Step 2 of the recipe (page 194) and then proceed with this recipe.

You can substitute an ice-cube tray for the large freezer container, if you desire. This allows you to skip the chopping in Step 3. Just tip the cubes into the lined colander in Step 4 instead.

*To top jars of Foie Gras Parfait or Chicken Liver Mousse (page 198):* Prepare through Step 6. Allow liquid to cool slightly to room temperature. Scrape off oxidized portion of mousse or parfait, if desired, and pour aspic over surface. Return jars to refrigerator and chill for at least 2 hours before serving.

**4.** Rinse and squeeze dry a single layer of cheesecloth; use it to line a sieve or colander. Place sieve in a bowl that can fit in your refrigerator. Remove cubes from freezer and place in sieve. Cover loosely with plastic wrap, transfer to the warmest part of your refrigerator, and refrigerate for up to 3 days. As liquid collects in the bowl, transfer it to an airtight container or ice-cube tray, cover and refrigerate; you should do this about twice daily.

**5.** After 2 days you should have collected about ²⁄₃ cup (150 mL) of liquid. Discard cheesecloth and solids.

**6.** Measure 2 tbsp (30 mL) of refrigerated liquid and transfer to a small bowl; sprinkle with remaining ¹⁄₂ tsp (2 mL) gelatin. Place remaining liquid in a small saucepan and warm over low heat until it reaches 120°F (48.9°C), about 3 minutes. Remove from heat, add to gelatin mixture, and stir well for 1 minute.

**7.** If using as a chopped garnish, transfer aspic to a covered container and refrigerate until set, about 4 to 5 hours (it will keep for up to 5 days). Unmold and chop coarsely. Use as a garnish by placing a small pile on each plate. If using to top jars of mousse or parfait, see Tips, at left.

# Appendix

## Artichokes

It's no secret that I love artichokes, and since they figure in several recipes, I would like to share a few general tips on how to select and prepare this rather tricky vegetable.

Artichokes are the immature flowers of a thistle native to the Mediterranean. They come in various sizes, all growing simultaneously on the same plant. Their cultivation in Italy dwarfs production in any other country. California, however, produces almost all the artichokes available in North America. I prefer to use the smallest size, which are commercially referred to as "small loose." Larger artichokes range in size from 60 (the next size up from small loose) to 12 (the largest size). As they mature and grow, artichokes develop an inedible choke in the center, which is a nuisance to remove. There are two seasons for artichokes: they are most plentiful in March, April and May, with a secondary season in the fall. However, they can frequently be found all year round, but be aware that they are usually particularly expensive around Christmas.

The largest artichokes are usually singly priced. They're what you want if you're planning to serve a whole artichoke with hollandaise sauce or drawn butter. They are best boiled in salted, acidulated water until tender, so sous vide can't really help you much there.

Artichokes dry out quickly in the supermarket and at home. Select ones that look fresh, with no sign of browning. When you get your artichokes home, you'll find that a fair amount of preparation is needed, but it goes by quickly once you get a little practice. Since any cut surface will brown quickly, first set up a bowl of cold water that has been lightly acidulated with lemon juice or vinegar. The juice of 1 lemon (about $\frac{1}{4}$ cup/60 mL) is sufficient to acidulate about 12 cups (3 L) of water.

You're now ready to get to work. Using your hands, peel off about two layers of the tough, dark outer leaves, until you see the pale leaves below (discard the outer leaves). Place the artichoke in the bowl of acidulated water. Repeat with all the remaining artichokes. Then, one by one, remove an artichoke from the water. Using a sharp chef's knife, cut off about one-third of the top to remove the spiky parts of the leaves. Moving on to the stem end, cut off the little nubs that remain where you removed the leaves.

Artichoke stems are as delicious as the rest of the vegetable. Trim off the very end of the stem and then, using a paring knife, peel the stringy surface up to the base. If you are using small artichokes (about the size of chicken eggs), your preparation is finished. If the artichokes are any larger there is likely a fuzzy choke in the center that needs to be removed. Split the artichoke lengthwise and, using a melon baller or small spoon, dig out the choke and discard.

As you finish each one, return the artichokes to the acidulated water. They can be stored that way for up to 12 hours in the refrigerator. Since they float, and thus will be exposed to the air and discolor, place either a plate or a kitchen towel moistened with acidulated water over the surface of the water to cover.

When cooking artichokes, follow the instructions in the recipe. The general method that I have been using for the past 30 years is to cook them in a seasoned liquid — equal parts white wine, chicken broth and olive oil. When cooking sous vide, you can use far less liquid than you need to cook them in a pot or the oven, but you still need to bring the liquid to a boil first to cook away the alcohol.

Underdone artichokes are unpleasant, but they break if overcooked. I recommend cooking them in a resealable freezer bag so that you can start checking their doneness about 15 minutes before you think they will be ready. After cooking, the liquid can be boiled to reduce it slightly to use as a sauce for the artichokes. Alternatively, you can incorporate the cooking liquid into soups, vinaigrettes, flavored oils, mayonnaise or dips, or allow it to settle, skim off the oil and use it on its own.

Cooked artichokes can be stored in the refrigerator either in their liquid or dry. They will generally keep for 3 to 4 days. They turn black if spoiled.

## Curing Salt

Curing salt is known by the trade name Prague Powder #1, Insta Cure #1 or Readycure, depending on where you live. It is a mixture of table salt (sodium chloride) and sodium nitrite. The mixture delays spoilage and gives cooked pork a rosy color like ham. If you don't want to use a curing salt, you can omit it; replace with the same amount of table or kosher salt.

## Enriched Broth

There are three main reasons why restaurant food often tastes better than home-cooked: chefs are more generous with butter and olive oil, we salt more liberally, and there is always a good supply of concentrated stock in the kitchen. Homemade stock adds that certain extra to dishes that no prepared product can match. At my restaurants we went through hundreds of pounds of bones a week and kept gallons of stock in the refrigerator for soups, stews and sauces.

Throughout this book I have tried to advocate for DIY butchery so you can up your cooking game and take advantage of lower-priced bone-in cuts of meat. The bones and trimmings that you would otherwise discard can be used in stock — not to mention that the process of butchery connects you with your dinner in a way that makes you a better cook.

The boxed broths available at the supermarket are a good start for your kitchen. I look for low-sodium or unsalted varieties and stock(!) up on beef or chicken broth when I find them on sale. When making enriched broth (recipe on page 401), you will be reducing the boxed broth by half, so salted versions will become too salty. Here is where your butchery skills come into play. Rather than buying big bags of bones and making stock from scratch, I suggest making small quantities of enriched broth from the spoils of your butchery plus some vegetables, using boxed broth as a base.

Boxed broth comes in chicken, beef and vegetable versions. I find that the chicken has more umami, so that is what I usually use. If you are using your broth solely for beef preparations, you can, of course, use beef broth. Freshen up the broth by adding some carrots, onions and celery, plus a few parsley stems and a bay leaf. I find that a ratio of 3 parts onion, 2 parts carrot and 1 part celery (by volume) gives the right balance of flavors.

Adding as little as 4 oz (115 g) of bones and trimmings while the broth is cooking and reducing will lend richness and texture. Your bones and trimmings can be from beef, veal, pork, lamb or any poultry except quail, which I find doesn't have good flavor. Lamb bones lend a very distinctive flavor, so I don't recommend using them except for lamb preparations.

## Leeks

Leeks can be tricky to clean. To prepare, trim off any roots, leaving the leaves attached at their base. Split leeks in half lengthwise and give them a quick rinse to get rid of any visible dirt. Cut away the dark green parts (they can be reserved for use in small quantities in stocks). Chop the leeks finely, then place them in a colander set in a bowl in the sink. Pour cold running water over leeks, stirring occasionally. The idea is that the sand trapped between the leaves is more accessible after chopping. The water washes off the sand, which should fall through the sieve and into the bowl. Lift the sieve out of the bowl and drain.

## Xanthan Gum

Xanthan gum is a common food additive used in products such as ice cream, yogurt, salad dressing and gluten-free baked goods. It is produced by the fermentation of sugars and functions as a stabilizer and thickening agent, and to provide "stickiness" in place of gluten.

It is very useful in sous vide preparations as a thickening agent, because it doesn't need to be cooked (traditional thickeners must be simmered to remove their raw starch taste, something that can't be achieved in a water bath). The texture is similar to that of highly refined starches such as tapioca. It adds a slickness that somewhat resembles fat, so low-fat sauces that have been thickened with xanthan gum have a great mouthfeel.

The price of xanthan gum is high but very little goes a long way. The recipes in this book use no more than $\frac{1}{2}$ tsp (2 mL) to thicken 1 cup (250 mL) of sauce, and it is, of course, gluten-free.

Dispersal of xanthan gum in liquid can be a little tricky, as it has a tendency to clump. It is best to sprinkle it into liquid with a blender or immersion blender running. Straining the liquid afterward is an effective way to ensure that there are no lumps. You can also stir it into a small amount of oil, then whisk the oil into the liquid.

# Enriched Broth

Can Be Scaled Up

## Tips

Poultry skin adds plenty of flavor. While you don't want the trimmings to be entirely skin, it does help enhance the broth.

If you want a darker-colored broth, roast the trimmings and bones at 350°F (180°C) for 25 to 30 minutes, stirring occasionally. Proceed with Step 1.

Once the broth has thoroughly cooled, any fat rendered from the trimmings will have floated to the surface and can be removed and discarded. It's much easier to do this after chilling the broth in the refrigerator.

▶ Fine-mesh sieve

| | | |
|---|---|---|
| 4 cups | ready-to-use unsalted or low-sodium store-bought beef or chicken broth | 1 L |
| 4 oz | bones and trimmings from beef, veal, pork, lamb, chicken or duck (or more; see box, below) | 115 g |
| ½ cup | chopped onion | 125 mL |
| 6 tbsp | chopped carrot | 90 mL |
| 3 tbsp | chopped celery | 45 mL |
| 1 | bay leaf | 1 |

1. In a medium saucepan, combine broth, bones and trimmings. Bring to a simmer over medium heat. Reduce heat to medium-low and simmer for 1 hour. Remove scum from top of broth once or twice by skimming with a tablespoon or small ladle.

2. Add onion, carrot, celery and bay leaf. Continue simmering, topping up with water as necessary if trimmings protrude from broth. Simmer for another 1 to 2 hours — the longer you can simmer the better.

3. Remove from heat and let cool before straining, about 2 hours. Strain broth through fine-mesh sieve into an airtight container. Use immediately or cover and refrigerate. The broth will keep for up to 4 days in the refrigerator or up to 6 months in the freezer.

---

### Strong Broth

For a strong broth, use bones and trimmings in a ratio of 1 lb (450 g) to 4 cups (1 L) broth. The broth can also be reduced as desired for a stronger product. After straining, return the broth to a saucepan and bring to a boil. Reduce heat and simmer gently until you reach the consistency you desire. Keep in mind that although low-sodium broth usually has about half the salt of regular broth, it is still fairly salty, so reducing it by more than half may create a result that is too salty. Unsalted broth is preferable.

# Additional Reading

Many resources are available both in print and online to further your sous vide experience. All the manufacturers of sous vide equipment provide information that is useful, even if you don't have one of their specific units. Here is a short list of resources for additional reading.

- *On Food and Cooking*, by Harold McGee, is the classic reference for food science.
- *Modernist Cuisine at Home*, by Nathan Myhrvold with Maxime Bilet, is lavishly illustrated with photographs and takes readers through the steps of sous vide cooking. It focuses mainly on meat and fish.
- *Sous Vide for the Home Cook*, by Douglas E. Baldwin, is a primer on sous vide from the mathematician whom manufacturers look to for their time and temperature charts. It is heavily math-based.
- *The Food Lab*, by J. Kenji López-Alt, extensively describes the "beer cooler" method for people who don't own a sous vide device. He also has a great website, Serious Eats (www.seriouseats.com), that is very well maintained.
- *Cooking for Geeks*, by Jeff Potter, is a populist version of Harold McGee's tome that is a very interesting read for the science-inclined. If you like to fiddle with electronics, this book includes instructions on how to convert a slow cooker into a sous vide setup.
- *Under Pressure*, by Thomas Keller, is a beautifully photographed large-format book aimed at cooks who work in a restaurant environment.
- ChefSteps (www.chefsteps.com) is a great website for the enthusiastic amateur, with modestly priced online courses on various subjects, including sous vide. The team behind the site have also developed their own immersion circulator, called Joule.
- Cooking Issues (www.cookingissues.com) is the blog of Dave Arnold, director of culinary technology of the French Culinary Institute at the International Culinary Center, and several other chefs. There haven't been any new posts since 2014, but there is plenty of information on sous vide and other scientific culinary subjects, including meat glue.

# Acknowledgments

Writing a cookbook is much like opening a restaurant; you learn a lot along the way and the process takes much longer than you originally expected. You also meet many people as well. Here are a few that made the process of writing my first cookbook possible.

I would like to thank Robert Rose for coming up with the concept and their team of editors for adding clarity to my thoughts and recipes.

I am thankful to my friend, photographer Per Kristiansen for both his generosity and the quality of his work. Naomi Duguid, who coached me through the cookbook-writing process, gave me the good advice to steer clear of getting too involved in the photo shoot. Photo stylist Ian Muggridge did an admirable job making my recipes look great for Per's camera.

Sous Vide Supreme provided us with equipment. My thanks to both them and their Canadian distributor, Cedarlane Culinary.

The folks at Cumbrae's in Toronto are not only fine purveyors of quality meats but were also available to answer my specific questions about butchery.

Recipe testers Rawli Puig of San Diego, California, and Aaron Drover of Newcastle, Ontario, provided invaluable input for both the recipes and the equipment. My thanks go out to them.

George Brown College, where I was a student in the early '80s and where I have been an instructor more recently, allowed me to put up a message on their bulletin board requesting an assistant for this project. I am grateful to them, as I am to my assistant, Mandom Hui, a recent graduate. He's been fundamental to the crafting of this book. He tirelessly tested recipes, sourced products and kept me abreast of the rapidly changing world of sous vide equipment and information, as well as providing tech support through the process. This project would not have been the same without him.

Last, I would like to thank all my mentors and protégés, whom I have learned so much from over the past 35 years. You know who you are.

**Library and Archives Canada Cataloguing in Publication**

McDonald, Chris (J. Chris), author
    The complete sous vide cookbook : more than 175 recipes with tips & techniques /
Chris McDonald.

Includes index.
ISBN 978-0-7788-0523-6 (paperback)

    1. Sous-vide cooking.  2. Cookbooks.  I. Title.

TX690.7.M33 2016              641.5'87          C2016-906874-9

# Index

# W

# X

# Y